ARGOPREP
LSAT

D1192583

2019-2020
LSAT®
PREP BOOK
ARGOPREP

SATISFACTION GUARANTEED

{ **2** **PRACTICE TEST**
+ VIDEO EXPLANATIONS

HIGHER SCORE GUARANTEED

by Dr. Jill Graper Hernandez

3828722

Author: **Dr. Jill Graper Hernandez**

ArgoPrep is one of the leading providers of supplemental educational products and services. We offer affordable and effective test prep solutions to educators, parents and students. Learning should be fun and easy! For that reason, most of our workbooks come with detailed video answer explanations taught by one of our fabulous instructors. Our goal is to make your life easier, so let us know how we can help you by e-mailing us at info@argoprep.com.

Higher Score Guarantee Policy

At ArgoPrep, we know our test-taking strategies work. Our material reflects the most up-to-date content to best prepare you for your exam. If you are not satisfied with our book for any reason, you may return it for a full refund of the original purchase price (exclusive of sales tax and shipping). In order to qualify for a refund, you must return this book along with the sales receipt and provide a brief explanation for your return.

Please send to:
ArgoPrep
Attention: Customer Service Department
900 Lenox Road
Brooklyn, NY 11203

Please note, all claims for refunds must be submitted within 60 days of the date of the book purchase. Refunds are issued in four to six weeks. U.S. residents only.

OTHER BOOKS BY ARGOPREP

Here are some other test prep workbooks by ArgoPrep you may be interested in. All of our workbooks come equipped with detailed video explanations to make your learning experience a breeze! Subscribe to our mailing list at www.argobrothers.com to receive custom updates about your education.

TABLE OF CONTENTS

TABLE OF CONTENTS

TABLE OF CONTENTS

TABLE OF CONTENTS

Boost your LSAT score!

This workbook includes 2 exams (one in the book and one online). To access the second practice test, visit us at www.argoprep.com/lsat and create your free account.

Get the ArgoPrep Advantage

We provide an unmatched combination of detailed lessons, rigorous practice tests, and detailed breakdowns for every question. Our multimedia approach and high-quality content make test prep lively and engaging.

ArgoPrep is at the forefront of online test prep for two simple reasons: we have the teachers and we have the content. We've spent thousands of hours developing the most comprehensive preparation and practice materials for a variety of tests from the GRE and SHSAT to grade level Common Core exams, and we're confident our programs will boost your confidence and improve your scores.

This workbook includes a **14 day complementary access** to ArgoPrep's online LSAT resources.

Create an account on our website and unlock your workbook.

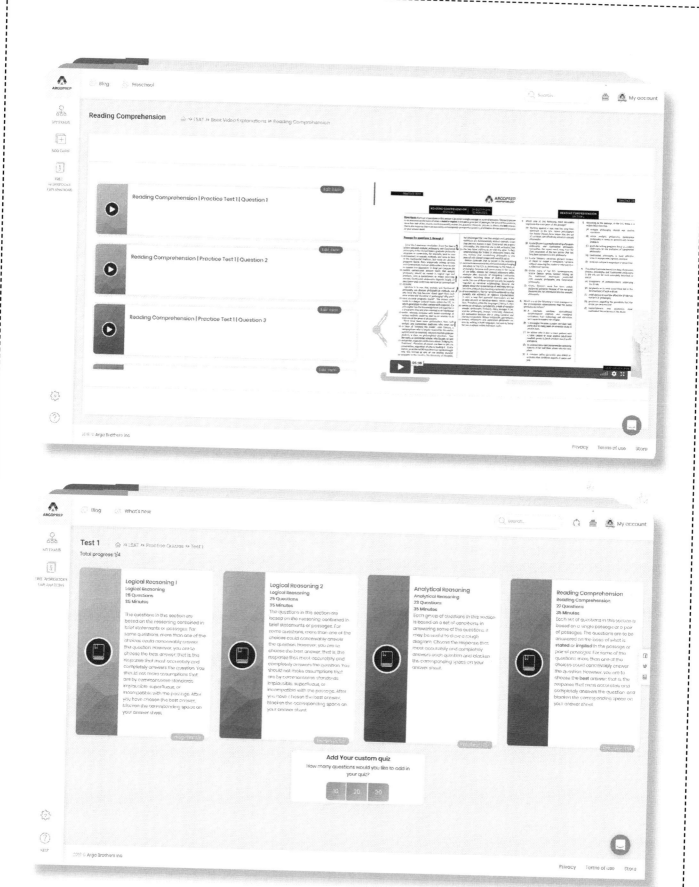

CHAPTER I | PIVOTING TOWARDS LOGIC

PIVOTING TOWARDS LOGIC
CHAPTER 1

You've reflected, prepared, and looked at your professional options, and have decided that a life in law is your next step. Although no longer required for reaccreditation, almost all law schools require the LSAT exam, and it is widely seen as a strong indicator of whether a student can be successful in law school.

Insider Info: Logic and the LSAT

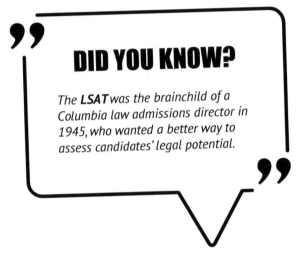

DID YOU KNOW?

*The **LSAT** was the brainchild of a Columbia law admissions director in 1945, who wanted a better way to assess candidates' legal potential.*

The LSAT isn't a test that you *beat*... it is a test you *work*. But, the only way to be able to work this test is to know what kind of test it is and to prepare for it. You *won't* be getting legal questions on this exam, and knowing about current events or political policies won't give you an advantage. You won't be quizzed on academic knowledge and the LSAT doesn't give you math questions. Instead, the LSAT is a LOGIC test.

If you've done some looking, you already know that there is some logic on the LSAT. But, what you probably don't know is that even apart from the Logical Reasoning sections, the LSAT is a logic test. The Analytical Reasoning section could be renamed "Logic Games" and the Reading Comprehension questions are chalk full of logic questions, including identifying premises and conclusions, picking out assumptions, running the implications of arguments, and evaluating the soundness of a text. So, the way you *work* the LSAT is to learn the logic you need for the exam.

That might sound daunting, especially if you are not a philosophy or a mathematics major and have not had logic training. But, fear not, this is where the ArgoPrep method comes in: you will learn how to speak the language of the LSAT, the language of arguments. By learning the language, you will do more than just take practice tests and solve puzzles (although you will do that, too!). You will train yourself to think like the writers of the LSAT.

ArgoPrep, Logic and Law School

What makes ArgoPrep different from any other test prep out there for the LSAT is our commitment to teaching you the logic required for you to do well on the test. Why is having a basic background in logic so important? Not only is the LSAT a series of logic questions, the foundational skills in logic set you up for success on the single most important component of getting into law school.

When you applied to colleges, you probably took the ACT or the SAT, and you may or may not have studied or taken practice exams for those. But, your college entrance exam was only one small piece of a range of factors that collectively helped you to get into school, and maybe earn scholarship money.

Admission into law school is different. The LSAT is a singularly important piece of your application, and for many schools (and certainly, many of the *best* schools), your LSAT score is a litmus test for review of the rest of your application materials. The result is that, regardless of your transcript, letters of recommendation, and experience, if you do not perform well on this test, those factors will not even be seen by an admissions committee at the schools to which you are applying.

So, if the LSAT is a logic test, and is the single most important criterion for having an admissions committee look at your application—what is the *logical implication?* You need to have a strong understanding of logic as a basis for success on the test, and so for admission into law school.

But, this isn't simply a logic book; or, in the language of the LSAT—this is a logic book only insofar as the LSAT is a logic test. It teaches you the framework and structure of the LSAT by teaching you the logic skills you will need in each section. Knowing the rules of computation, grammar, and vocabulary will not help you here. Instead, you are learning a new language. And...just like other languages you learn, you become a master by practicing and using your skill.

PIVOTING TOWARDS LOGIC
CHAPTER 1

Intro to the LSAT Framework

Since the LSAT is a logic test, it is framed to tax you both in time spent on it, and intellectual attention required to do well. If you don't practice marathoning on the LSAT, your time will be exhausted and you will be mentally depleted as well before you are half-way finished. You will need to condition yourself through good techniques prior to the test.

Components of All LSAT Questions

You know that the LSAT is *essentially* a logic test, you know that it is broken down into three types of sections (logical reasoning, analytical reasoning, and reading comprehension), and you know that you will have the opportunity (that you should take!) to write a non-graded essay on the exam. But, regardless of the type of section you are tackling, you will want to know the scaffolding for all of the questions...because all LSAT questions have the same four aspects:

1. The Directions. Don't miss valuable points by failing to read the directions. There are three things the directions will tell you, within each section. First, the directions will remind you that each section is timed separately, so you cannot bank any unused time that you had from previous sections onto others. You also will be reminded that you may need to take notes (and you will, whether it's drawing diagrams or eliminating answers from consideration), you will need to do so on the answer sheet itself. Finally, the directions indicate that you need to select the best answer among your choices. That *doesn't* mean that there won't be other good answers in the stack. It means that the correct answer is the best answer.

2. The Passage. Each passage is different. It might, of course, be a long passage if it is a reading comprehension text, or a single sentence. All of your passages will have a similar function: they will give you the content for you to successfully answer the question or questions associated with the passage. Sometimes the passage will be connected with conditions attached to it, and sometimes they may contain numbers, facts, or percentages from which you are meant to draw inferences. Sometimes the passage will be drawn from literature, news articles, science journals, philosophy textbooks, or political discourse. (Whether the passage is a fictional or non-fictional account will not impact your ability to work the passage to correctly find the answer.)

3. The Question. This is what you're here for! You won't be intimidated by the question when you've prepped and you're ready. It will always be true that your question will be short. Questions are very often modal in nature (what *could* or *must* be the case, or what *could not* be the case).

4. The Answer Choices. Although it was different in years past, your LSAT will only have you choose one correct answer choice among five possible.

Outcomes of Questions

It is important for prospective lawyers to be able to process large amounts of material quickly and efficiently, towards the end of making important and correct logical inferences. But we haven't covered *how* the LSAT can measure that through its questions. Like any test, the questions are designed with certain learning outcomes in mind. Here are some measurable outcomes from the various sections of the LSAT:

1. *Learning Outcome #1:* Successful test takers will be able to identify Logical Fallacies. You will be specifically asked to compare flaws in reasoning from one passage to analogous flaws in reasoning in the answer choices. ArgoPrep will help you remember the most relevant logical flaws so that you can pull those out from a text, and when matched with your ability to bring premises together to proper conclusions, you will be able to demonstrate how particular answer choices reflect the logical flaw of the passage. For example, take the following passage: "I think he can be trusted when he claims he can succeed at the brand new throat procedure. He's the best dental surgeon in the city." The subsequent question would be, "The argument is most clearly flawed for which of the following reasons?"

2. *Learning Outcome #2:* Successful test takers will be able to relate disparate concepts together. The LSAT frequently will take two interlocutors—whether fictional or real subjects—and test your ability to make inferences between the two, who typically are espousing different ideas. (In fact, you will often be asked to

suss out what two people disagree about, or to identify an answer choice that is analogous to the principle of disagreement reflected in the passage.) Typically, the sorts of questions that test this learning outcome include, "[Subject A] and [Subject B] disagree over which of the following?" and "Which of the following best describes the point at issue between [Subject A] and [Subject B]?"

3. *Learning Outcome #3:* Successful test takers will understand basic logical terms that feature in argumentation. I have already written about the modal quality of the test, and how you won't be taking a vocabulary test. Rather, your ability to navigate between "if/then" statements, to identify conditionals, to make inferences on disjunctions ("or"), necessary condition terms (such as "only" or "unless"), moral or legal necessity ("must"), and terms which indicate conclusions (including "therefore", "thus", and "given") will be crucial to your success.

4. *Learning Outcome #4:* Successful test takers will use logic to use the clock towards his/her advantage when faced with lengthy passages. If word count is considered, the Reading Comprehension section asks the most of you of any other section, but (as you will see when you study the tips for Reading Comprehension) your best chance of success does not lie in reading every passage line by line, and instead supplants careful reading with careful logic.

5. *Learning Outcome #5:* Successful test takers can perform high-order sorting and grouping operations. The Analytical Reasoning, especially, measures the extent to which you can place things in order, combine subjects, and make determinations about time and group functions within specified conditions.

6. *Learning Outcome #5:* Successful test takers can find the flaw in an argument. Recognizing flaws in reasoning is, of course, a foundation to success in the law so we are not surprised that the LSAT wants to measure whether you can recognize flaws in other people's writing. Of course, engaging in the science *of reasoning* (LOGIC) puts you ahead of the pack in recognizing flaws. When you can assess the validity and soundness of an argument, the correct answer is clarified much more easily. Given that most questions will ask you to evaluate an argument, knowing tests for validity and soundness can set you apart.

7. *Learning Outcome #6:* Successful test takers can improve an argument. Let's face it: it's pretty easy to criticize an argument. It is much more difficult to *improve* an argument. But, the LSAT assesses your ability to improve arguments by identifying fundamental disagreements between agents, inferring missing premises or required assumptions, and strengthening arguments by adding evidence or justification to premises that the passage itself excludes.

8. *Learning Outcome #7:* Successful test takers can identify a better answer among bad answers. You will rarely come across a perfect answer on the LSAT—except for on the Analytical Reasoning section, where there will always be a correct answer that shines among others that are logically incompatible with the rest of the exam. But, folks who do well on this exam know that often the answers are not great and you need to find which among them is the best of the not-great pile. The perfect is the enemy of the good in many aspects of life, including on the LSAT. You will be hard-pressed to find a perfect answer, so find the good answer.

9. *Learning Outcome #8:* Successful test takers read the question correctly. This seems simple, but is fundamental and crucial. Most LSAT questions are similar but they have key differences. If you are asked, "Which of the following is a complete and accurate list" but not, "which of the following could be a complete and accurate list," your answer will be completely different. The first question is asking you what is logically necessary and the second is asking you what is logically possible. Read correctly so that you can answer correctly.

10. *Learning Outcome #9:* Successful test takers are not thrown off with numbers but use them to draw out logical relationships. About a quarter of all logic games require the test taker to make inferences based on numbers. That *doesn't* mean that you have to "do math". But, you will have to make logical inferences that are based on numbers. If you don't love math, and are worried, you play into the LSAT writers' hands. Instead you can focus on the *relationships* between elements within the text and question to answer correctly.

Scored Sections

There are three types of scored sections on the LSAT, all of which are multiple-choice and which are 35-minutes in length: the Logical Reasoning section, Analytical Reasoning section, and Reading Comprehension. There are two Logical Reasoning sections on the LSAT, for a total of around 100 questions. You will always have an extra section thrown in, which is an unscored section and could be either Logical Reasoning, Analytical Reasoning, or Reading Comprehension. You'll never know which section is extra nor which section is unscored.

Logical Reasoning is as it sounds. Each Logical Reasoning section will have anywhere from 24-26 questions. In them, you will receive short texts (around three to six sentences in total), and will have to respond to questions about the logic of the arguments contained in the texts. The Logical Reasoning sections are crucial for you to succeed on this exam—they represent 50% of your total score! For someone who does not have training in logic, answering questions about assumptions, deductive and inductive inferences, criticisms, and logical fallacies will be difficult. But logic is the science of argumentation, so you—armed with the language of the LSAT—will be able to work through each towards success.

This book will work through all of the various types of arguments and questions you will see on the LSAT, but take the following as an example of why a basic knowledge of logic will serve you well on the exam. (This question is one of the sort that could be used in the Logical Reasoning section on the LSAT exam.)

> **FUN FACT?**
>
> Researchers from the University of California, Berkeley have discovered that intense preparation for the LSAT specifically actually changes your brain's structure. The training you do to increase your logical skills physically changes the composition of the brain!

Economist: The Bhutanese economy is stagnant, which demonstrates that the country's commitment to a Gross National Happiness rather than a Gross National Product results in excessive social welfare spending and too little job growth.

Which of the following, if true, most seriously weakens the view expressed above?

(A) Bhutan spends a lower percentage of its national income on social welfare programs than America, with higher percentages of reported domestic happiness.

(B) Most countries that invest in social welfare programs have discovered that the need for the programs exceeds their capacity to pay for them.

(C) The Bhutanese social welfare programs actually are less expensive than most of those in Western countries and meet the health, education, and welfare needs of most of their citizens.

(D) Other South American and Northern European countries who have similar social welfare nets have even more wide-ranging welfare programs than Bhutan but also have dynamic, growing economies.

(E) There are many countries, like Morocco, that have very few social welfare programs but have had stagnant economies for at least a decade.

Logic training will inform your approach to this question by helping you frame the main point of the economist's argument: Bhutan's economy reflects its government's poor priority on social well-being. (There is an implied premise here: All countries that have social welfare programs, like Bhutan, will suffer economically.) The result must be that Bhutan will suffer economically for prioritizing GNH rather than GNP. Once you supply the implied premise, the logical structure of the argument is revealed, and so is its logical weakness. Knowing this positions you to answer 'D' correctly.

PIVOTING TOWARDS LOGIC
CHAPTER 1

Analytical Reasoning sections are frequently described by blogs as "Logic Games". Typically, you will see 4 scenarios for each section, whose outcomes are determined by a set of conditions, or rules, established by the passage. Each scenario will have 5-7 questions that accompany it, so the AR contributes to roughly 25% of your total possible score. The Analytical Reasoning section tests your ability to evaluate the role that conditionals play in an argument. The conditions focus on arranging subjects in order, and in groups, and the most difficult questions ask you to do both. If you can maneuver changing conditions within a passage, you will be in a good spot to make sound inferences about what is logically necessary and merely possible for any particular question. To do well on the Analytical Reasoning section, you will need to be prepared to draw out (or, diagram) conditions within the passage for each separate question set. Being able to visualize what must be true for all of your questions within a given scenario, and what could be true for any particular question, will set you up for success. Consider the following Analytical Reasoning question:

> The American Association of Pipefitters United has decided to organize its twelve independently-held corporations into four regional cohorts: The North, the South, the East, and the West. CEO partners from each of the twelve corporations will participate in the regional cohort meetings. But, at least one of the CEOs is a partner in multiple corporations in the North, South, and East. Another one of the CEOs is a partner in multiple corporations in the North, South, and West cohorts.
>
> Which of the following must be true?
>
> (A) At least one partner of the South is a partner of the East cohort.
> (B) No partner of the East is partner of the West cohort.
> (C) The partner of the South and East cohorts is the same person.
> (D) The partner of the East cohort is a different person from that of the South and West cohorts.
> (E) The partner of the West cohort is the same person as the partner from the South cohort.

You will be able to map out conditions for those given to you within the question—and here you need two different scenarios, because the question leaves you with an ambiguity about who could be a CEO for more than one company in more than one region. The first mapping scenario gives you the conditions for two partners (A and B) who satisfy all of the conditions and the second mapping scenario gives you a scenario in which just one partner (C) satisfies the conditions:

	N	S	E	W
Scenario 1:	AB	AB	A	B
Scenario 2:	C	C	C	C

The conditions stipulated by the facts of the case provide you with 12 companies in 4 regions; some of the CEOs for companies in one region are CEOs for a company in another region. The question asks you about logical *necessity* given the conditions of this case. That helps you know that you need to focus on the regions (NSEW) and then the CEOs that could be the partner representative for a given region. The map helps you visualize what is both logically necessary and possible for any particular question. Since this question is one of logical *necessity*, "must", you can see from the map that at least one partner from the South is also a partner from the East. That option is reflected in the first answer choice, (A). You know that you are not looking further for logical necessity, no other answer choice could in fact be correct.

Whereas Logical Reasoning and Analytical Reasoning are overtly about logic, the Reading Comprehension section is frequently treated differently by test prep companies because they view this as a *reading test*. And, although it is true that if you do not read, or do not like reading, you should rethink your desire to be a lawyer, it is also true that the

PIVOTING TOWARDS LOGIC
CHAPTER 1

Reading Comprehension section is yet another way for the LSAT writers to test your logical chops. If you picked up the Reading Comprehension passages and read them top-to-bottom, left-to-right, you *might* be able to comprehend what was written. But, you also might have wasted a lot of time reading content that will not help you answer the section correctly. Here, you will learn a reading method that will decrease the amount of reading you will have to do, and increase your ability to comprehend what is written. The LSAT writers, after all, are not writing poetry like e.e. cummings or novels like Toni Morrison. You are not gently perusing the Reading Comprehension passages for aesthetic beauty or literary insight. Instead, you recognize that the purpose of these passages, and the 26-28 questions surrounding them, is to make arguments. So, you are going to read for the arguments using the method presented in this book to reduce your reading and increase your grasp. Here's an example of a question based on a lengthy Reading Comprehension passage. (Notice here that the passage has been left out although you will study passages at length later). Read it and see if you can identify why logic is crucial to be able to answer the question well.

Which of the following, if true, most strengthens the author's position on the legality of daily fantasy sports gambling leagues?

(A) Participating in daily fantasy sports gambling leagues is not a crime, even in states that outlaw other forms of gambling.

(B) Because of the increased interest in legalized gambling writ large, the emerging markets for underground daily fantasy sports leagues likely will shrink even further.

(C) The widespread participation in daily fantasy sports leagues makes regulation and taxation of such leagues an impossibility, which incentivizes states to consider them illegal.

(D) Even states that do not have a lottery are being lobbied by professional sports organizations to lift the ban on daily sports gambling leagues.

(E) Illegal gambling is a crime in all states in the US, and people who participate in underground sports leagues need to ascertain their own individual risk if they play in a league.

You don't have to know what was written in the text to see the argument you will need to build off of successfully in this question. The correct answer will be a logical implication of the argument provided in the conclusion. Since you will have read this passage for the argument, you will have been able to identify what justification was given for the conclusion and so would be able to see which answer is the best of those available.

The last section of the test is a Writing Sample section, which is another unscored section. The Writing Sample is given to all of the schools to which you apply, provides you with a writing prompt that is always about some choice an agent has to make, and you write an answer that explains the best course of action that the agent should make. You move from multiple choice questions that evaluate arguments to writing your own argument. The directions for your prompt will look like this:

Directions: The scenario presented below describes two choices, either one of which can be supported on the basis of the information given. Your essay should consider both choices and argue for one over the other, based on the two specified criteria and the facts provided. There is no "right" or "wrong" choice: a reasonable argument can be made for either.

Your writing will make an argument from among the details of the case, towards a conclusion of one of the actions possible for the main agent in the case. Although unscored, the Writing Sample can help solidify your case as a good candidate for law school admission. You should see the Writing Sample as a Great Leveler: no matter how many applicants pay as much money as they can to expert consultants to weigh in on their law school admissions essay, there are no consultants in the exam room. The applicant will demonstrate exactly whether she or he has the ability to write about arguments when they come face-to-face with the test...by themselves.

Insider Insights: Keys to LSAT Success

The benefit of the LSAT compared to other tests is that no question is weighted. You do not need to get every question right to do well and you do not need to finish every question to get an excellent score. In fact, you can miss two or three questions and still earn the highest score, 180! The result is that you should feel free to spend time mastering the easy questions and then use the remainder of your time to focus on the more difficult questions. Regardless, if you view the exam as your ability to think about arguments, you can relax about rushing through and answering every question.

1. Letter of The Day (LOTD)

You do not get docked for incorrect answers—only your correct answers are scored, so make sure that, even if you do not get to work out some of the problems, that each one has a filled-in answer choice. But, *do not choose randomly*. Select the *same letter* for any answer choice that you are not working towards the best conclusion.

2. Brake

Lots of test prep gurus will tell you to use every minute working every question, and as long as you are intellectually able to keep giving to the test, those gurus are not wrong. But, the best advice for most test takers is to "BRAKE". Stop, evaluate which questions among a set need less time and go after getting those questions correct. Since all of the test questions count the same, it makes no sense to do the questions in order and to sap your energy from the outset with the most difficult questions. (You do not get any extra credit for solving the hardest questions, so brake. Skip questions that give you a hard time initially, mark them and come back to them.) Just make sure you come back and complete all of your questions—even if you have to use LOTD.

3. Shot Clock

You will know to "BRAKE", prioritize, and attack questions that will prove easiest to start. But, you also need to be aware of the "shot clock". Just like in basketball, when each team only has a short amount of time to hit the rim of the basketball hoop with the ball—to take a shot—you only have 35 minutes in each section to complete the section, and you will not be able to return to it. Know your shot clock. Most people succumb to the shot clock by thinking about any given question for less time. (Almost all students will find that 35 minutes is too little time to reflect on each question carefully.) But, if you spend too little time on any question, you can be ill-prepared to answer it correctly. We will cover section-specific time management issues later, but the Insider Insight is to remember the shot clock even if you apply the brake.

> " **DID YOU KNOW?**
>
> The **lowest score** *you could get on the LSAT is* 120, *the* **average score** *is* 151, *and a* **perfect score** *is* 180. *You can miss a couple of questions and still land a perfect score!* "

Basic Argumentation and LSAT Prep

Logic, in its technical sense, is the science of reasoning. Reasoning is grounded in critical thinking, and so logic is the core of what is tested by the LSAT. If a good understanding of logic leads to better, clearer thinking, your prowess on the LSAT will emerge. (Hey, I just made an argument!) Logic, in a less technical sense, is the study of the form and content of arguments. The *form* of an argument refers to the way arguments are put together. Some arguments have a *deductive* form, and other arguments have an *inductive* form. The *content* of an argument refers to the "in-the-real-world" *truth* of whatever is being argued.

PIVOTING TOWARDS LOGIC
CHAPTER 1

Arguments

An *argument* is a set of *propositions* that lead to a particular *conclusion*. *Propositions* in logic are synonymous with the term *statement*, and in your LSAT prep, you can use them interchangeably. Propositions (statements, then) have a specific meaning for us. Statements are sentences that are either true or false. *Sentences* have a subject and a verb, but need not be either true or false. Both sentences and statements make use of *concepts*. (It will be important for us to identify the meaning—or, *connotation*—of concepts to understand what a proposition is saying.) Let's use an example:

concept:	philosophy
sentence:	Read ch.6 in your philosophy text for Tuesday.
statement:	You need to read ch.6 in your philosophy text for Tuesday.

In this example, the concept "philosophy" is the focus of both the sentence and the statement. If you are taking one philosophy class that has two books, you would not know the *connotation* of either the sentence or the statement. (In other words, you wouldn't know to what "philosophy text" refers. Is it the blue philosophy book, or the red one? Is it the one with cartoons, or the one with the sports page?) Critically assessing arguments—what you will do on the LSAT—requires, then, that you understand concepts and *you need to avoid mistakes about the meaning of words*.

Concepts make up sentences, as well as the special sentences we call 'statements'. A sentence, however, (like the one above) is *merely* a sentence, and so cannot tell us anything that is true or false. "Read ch.6 in your philosophy text for Tuesday" is neither a true sentence nor a false sentence. It is a simple imperative sentence with no truth value at all. *Sentences that do not have truth value do not give us information for an argument! We cannot, then, use mere sentences in arguments. Arguments must be based on statements (propositions).* Look at the difference above between our sentence and statement. The statement, "You need to read ch.6 in your philosophy text for Tuesday" can either be true or false. It is either true that you need to read ch.6 in your philosophy text for Tuesday, or it is not true that you need to read ch.6 in your philosophy text for Tuesday. If the sentence is either true or false, it is a statement (proposition), and so indeed can function in an argument. You might have a test on ch.6 on Thursday, and a necessary requirement for you to pass the test is for you to read it. And maybe the only day you can read it is Tuesday. The obvious conclusion would be: You need to read ch.6 in your philosophy text for Tuesday.

Logical Notation and LSAT Diagramming

You already know that time is going to be at a premium for your LSAT exam, so it makes sense before we cover basic argumentation rules (that will set us up for speaking the language of the LSAT) that you learn some essential abbreviations and logical "notation". This will especially help you when you diagram. Here are the essentials:

> · "and", so "Gustavo and Jill" can be abbreviated, "G·J"
>
> ⊃ "if-then", so "If I want to rock the LSAT, then I will study," translates to "A ⊃ B"
>
> v "or", so "I will study for the LSAT, or I will watch the movie," translates to "A v B"
>
> ~ "not", so "I will not watch the movie," translates to ~B
>
> ∴ "therefore", so "Thus, I will study for the LSAT", translates to "∴A"
>
> □ "necessary", or a necessary condition, so "I must study," translates to □A
>
> ◊ "possible", so "I could study," translates to ◊A

PIVOTING TOWARDS LOGIC
CHAPTER 1

Learning these notations cold will save you time and help you organize your arguments much more smoothly within the exam—saving you time but also facilitating a clearer path to a correct answer. Now that you know these logical and modal abbreviations, you can move on to connotation within propositions.

Rules for Figuring Out the Connotations of Concepts in Propositions

The section above notation made use of an example of the same term "philosophy" that may connote (refer to) two different things (a blue philosophy book, or the red one; a real philosophy text, or the Sunday paper—which may contain someone's personal "philosophy".) We need to figure out what a concept connotes. Of course, there are times when *two concepts* refer *to the same thing*. Look at the following two sentences:

1. Memphis is playing the Roadrunners tonight.

2. The Tigers are playing UTSA tonight.

In this example, the two sentences connote the exact same thing. When we say "Memphis" in the first statement, the only term that can be referred to is "the Tigers", and by the "Roadrunners" we can only infer "UTSA." A critic might say that "Memphis" could refer to the Redbirds (i.e., the AAA St. Louis baseball team housed in Memphis), and so the concept might have a different referent. But, in the context of this sentence, "Memphis" is constrained by the term "Roadrunners" in the exact same sentence, since we know that the Roadrunners will only play NCAA teams, like the Memphis Tigers. (If, however, the sentence was stated, "Memphis is playing San Antonio tonight", then there is a *lot* of ambiguity. Do the concepts refer to NBA teams? Do they stand for university teams? Lacrosse? Cheerleading? Tub-thumping?) In the context of this example, each concept only has one referent.

On the LSAT, connotation is crucial, especially for *disagreement* questions, in which your job is to discover the point of disagreement between two agents within a given short text. To know how they disagree, you have to know if they refer to the same thing in their dialogue. If you are having a hard time deciding if two sentences are equivalent, there are some rules that will help to guide you. When determining whether two sentences assert the same proposition:

1.) Try to classify and define the concepts first to identify what words the concepts designate.

2.) Ignore differences in connotation, when it simply isn't important. (Ex: sweat, perspire, and glisten have differences in connotation, but in essence mean the exact same thing.)

3.) Find a literal interpretation of all metaphors.

The Importance of an Argument's Form

We understand, then, the differences between concepts, sentences, and statements, but how do they all work in an argument? Concepts make up sentences, sentences that are either true or false are statements, and statements put together act as reasons for a particular conclusion. An *argument,* then, is a collection of propositions that give support for a conclusion. The propositions that give support for a conclusion are called *premises*. Premises are statements that give reasons for the conclusion. A *conclusion* is the statement (i.e., the true or false sentence) that the argument tries to establish as true. In a good argument, the conclusion is made true by the premises. In a good argument, then, true premises will have a true conclusion.

Watch out, though! True premises and a true conclusion do *not* guarantee that the argument is a good one. Consider the following argument—which has all true premises and a true conclusion... but is *a bad argument:*

1.) The capitol of the United States is in the United States.

2.) Washington, D.C. is in the United States.

3.) Therefore, Washington D.C. is the capitol of the United States.

PIVOTING TOWARDS LOGIC
CHAPTER 1

Although both #1 and #2 are true propositions, and #3 is a true statement, #1 and #2 together do not guarantee that #3 will be true. Consider the following *counter-example*, which shows why the argument has a flawed structure:

> **1.)** The capitol of the United States is in the United States.
> **2.)** San Antonio is in the United States.
> **3.)** Therefore, San Antonio is the capitol of the United States.

The above argument has the exact same *form* as the argument above it; however, by substituting content we can see that neither argument is a good one. In each case, the premises are not put together in a way that guarantees the conclusion. The form of the first example does not lead to a persuasive argument, because the reasons for the conclusion do not prove the conclusion to be true, and indeed the form can lead to a *false* conclusion, namely that San Antonio is the capitol of the United States.

You will notice from the above examples that arguments are set up rather peculiarly. In logic, we list arguments in a technical way, so that we can watch out for problems with an argument's form. Since premises give reasons for the conclusion, when we identify an argument, we put the premises first, followed by the conclusion.

When you identify arguments throughout the LSAT, you will be well served to use logical notation, abbreviation, and write the arguments in *logical form*:

> Premise.
>
> Premise. (etc)
>
> ∴Conclusion.

Deductive Arguments

All arguments can be divided into two types: *deductive* and *inductive*. The key word to remember for deductive arguments is *certainty*, because deductive arguments are those in which we move from the premises to the conclusion with certainty—JUST BY THE ARGUMENT'S FORM. The result is that a deductive argument's form *guarantees* the conclusion. In a good deductive argument, it is *impossible* to have a conclusion that does not "follow" (flow from) the preceding premises. If the premises are true, the conclusion must also be true. Watch out, though! A deductive argument can give us a guaranteed conclusion, but not be true in the real world. (So many things to watch out for!) Consider the following *valid*, but very false, argument:

> **1.)** All spiders have six legs.
> **2.)** All animals with six legs are arachnids.
> **3.)** Therefore, all spiders are arachnids.

Although it is factually false *both* that spiders have six legs *and* that six-legged animals are called "arachnids", the conclusion that all spiders are arachnids follows from premises #1 and #2. "Validity" ONLY refers to the proper form of a deductive argument, and so it is only one part of a good argument.

LSAT Statistics

Only 0.1% of all LSAT test takers land a perfect score, 180. Around 144,000 exams are administered each year, which means that only 144 of those exams were perfect. Guess how many people applied to law school last year? 60,401. The takeaway? **You don't have to be perfect to be competitive for admission into law school!**

PIVOTING TOWARDS LOGIC
CHAPTER 1

> ***How to find the form of an argument:***
>
> **1.)** Find the conclusion (the <u>main point</u>).
>
> **2.)** Find reasons for the conclusion. (These are the <u>premises.</u>)
>
> **3.)** Make sure the premises prove the conclusion.
>
> **4.)** In your own words, list the premises first, followed by the conclusion.
>
> **5.)** Find the *antecedent* (what sets the condition) for each premise, and then the consequent to each premise.
>
> **6.)** Assign a letter (*p, q, a, b,* etc.) to each new predicate.
>
> **7.)** Check for validity and soundness. (I'll show you how to do this in a second.)

The first step to finding an argument's form is to properly identify the conclusion of the argument, and then the reasons (premises) of the argument. Take the following passage from the sociologist Michael Harrington as an example:

> "One of the consequences of our new technology is that we have created new needs. There are more people who live longer. Therefore they need more. In short, if there is technological advance without social advance, there is, almost automatically, an increase in human misery, in impoverishment." -- from "Defining Poverty"

The word "therefore" might throw you off, because you might think it is the conclusion. But, it's not. Harrington's main point is not that people who live longer need more. His *main point* is that there is automatically more poverty in our country than there has been. THIS IS THE CONCLUSION!

> *Conclusion:* There is an increase in poverty and misery in our society.

Whenever you see any conclusion you should ask yourself, "Why?—Why is this conclusion true?" When you answer this question, you will be finding #2 above—the reasons for the conclusion, or the *premises*. Harrington offers one main reason for his conclusion, which is that technological advances without social advances lead to increased societal needs, which then leads to poverty. (And, of course, he obviously thinks we live in an age that has this result, since he contends, "we have created new needs".) So, let's identify the reasons for the conclusion as follows:

> *Reasons* (Premises):
>
> **1.)** Technological advances without social advances lead to increased societal needs (poverty and misery).
>
> **2.)** Our society has in fact suffered technological advances without social advances.

Now in order for us to fulfill step #3 above, we need to make sure that Harrington's premises set a *condition*—that is, *if* something happens, *then* something else happens. I can do this by adding an "if/then" to Harrington's first premise (which Harrington actually uses in the text), "*If* there are technological advances without social advances, *then* there will be increased societal needs (poverty)." Premise two just asserts the fact of the matter.

The only thing left is to list the argument in logical form to see if the premises do prove the conclusion:

PIVOTING TOWARDS LOGIC
CHAPTER 1

> **1.)** If there are technological advances without societal advances, then there will be increased societal needs (poverty and misery).
>
> **2.)** Our society has in fact suffered technological advances without social advances.
>
> **Conclusion:** There is an increase in poverty and misery in our society.

Intuitively, the premises do indeed seem to prove the conclusion, since if it is true that technological advances that are not coupled with societal advances lead to increased poverty and misery, and if it is also true that our society has suffered technological advances without social advances, then it MUST BE THE CASE that there is an increase in poverty and misery. (Important note: you may disagree with premise one, premise two, and the conclusion, but whether these in fact are true in the real world is a point of *soundness*, and not an issue of form or validity. Our first concern is just validity.)

Now it seems that the premises prove the conclusion, since validity is a GUARANTEE, we can be ABSOLUTELY sure whether this argument is valid. We'll check its form by performing steps 5, 6, and 7 above.

> **1.)** [*Antecedent*] If there are technological advances without societal advances, [*Consequent*] then there will be increased societal needs (poverty and misery).
>
> **2.)** Our society has in fact suffered technological advances without social advances. (This statement establishes a fact, and not a condition, so we leave it as one propositional whole.)
>
> **Conclusion:** There is an increase in poverty and misery in our society.

Now we assign arbitrary letter values to each distinct part of the argument. If a part of the argument is new (if you haven't seen it yet in the argument), assign a new value. (Note: This is where connotation is important, because you will have to determine whether two parts of the argument are equivalent.) Let's try it:

> (p)
> **1.)** [*Antecedent*] If there are technological advances without societal advances, [*Consequent*] then (q) there will be increased societal needs (poverty and misery).
>
> **2.)** (p) Our society has in fact suffered technological advances without social advances. (Since this proposition shows an instance of p, and doesn't say anything new itself, it gets p's letter.)
>
> **Conclusion:** ∴ (q) There is an increase in poverty and misery in our society. (This is a statement that there is in fact an instance of q, so it gets q's letter.)

Since we are here interested only in validity, we only need to focus on the form of Harrington's argument. We can, then, take all of the content away from the argument in order to evaluate whether the form of the argument is valid or not.

Here it is:

> **1.)** If p, then q
>
> **2.)** p.
>
> **Conclusion:** ∴ q.

On the LSAT it will be VERY EASY to determine whether an argument is valid, because any valid argument will fit one of four AUTOMATICALLY VALID forms, since the forms of these arguments automatically guarantee their conclusions. Most of the arguments you will see will fit one of these four (or will include a logical fallacy). These automatically logically valid forms follow *"rules of inference"* for their structures, which guarantees their conclusions:

PIVOTING TOWARDS LOGIC
CHAPTER 1

Modus Ponens	Modus Tollens	Hypothetical Syllogism	Disjunctive Syllogism
If $p \supset q$	If $p \supset q$	If $p \supset q$	$p \lor q$
p	$\sim q$	If $q \supset r$	$\sim p$
$\therefore q$	$\therefore \sim p$	p	$\therefore q$
		$\therefore r$	

Now, we are ready to return to Harrington's sociological argument and test its validity. Does it match one of these four? Of course, IT DOES! Harrington's argument follows *modus ponens*, and so it is a valid argument.

Watch out, though! Even though these forms are easy, there are also arguments that closely resemble these forms, but which are also automatically INVALID—their form cannot guarantee the truth of the conclusion. These are automatically logical fallacies, and can never be good arguments. Avoid these arguments!

Denying the Antecedent

If $p \supset q$

$\sim p$

$\therefore \sim q$

Affirming the Consequent

If $p \supset q$

q_____

$\therefore p$

One more word about form: the LSAT relies on standard (easy) logic. This is great news for you! You will often read modal claims that make universal statements such as, "All knowledge comes from experience." Remember that "all" and "no" statements are *really conditions*. If I say, "All philosophy students are softball players," it *must be the case* that, "If someone is a philosophy student, then she must be a softball player." "All" is another way to say, "if/then". In the same way, if I say, "No philosophy students are softball players," I am also setting a condition (or a limit), so that, "If someone is a philosophy student, then they cannot be a softball player." Whenever you see "all" or "no", then, convert it into a conditional.

> ## DID YOU KNOW?
>
> The LSAT is not scored on a curve, but the LSAC does use an equation across each year's exams so that you don't have an advantage by taking an exam in September than in February.

Soundness. Many many many scholars and lawyers make valid arguments that, under scrutiny, simply do not correspond to the evidence. They might generate true conclusions, but you will discover by setting up the arguments that the premises are not true, and so they cannot properly give reasons for their conclusions. The best kinds of deductive arguments are both valid and *sound...true in the real world.*

PIVOTING TOWARDS LOGIC
CHAPTER 1

Deductive Arguments: Let's Practice!

Directions: Read each argument, and assess whether it is valid (follows one of our valid rules) or invalid (does not follow one of our valid rules, or either denies the antecedent or affirms the consequent).

(V) Valid   (I) Invalid

(V) (I) 1. No pure water is flammable.
But, parts of the Gulf of Mexico are regularly on fire.
∴The Gulf of Mexico is not pure water.

(V) (I) 2. Everyone who is a lawyer can think critically.
Everyone who can think critically ought to take logic to become even better.
Everyone who isn't a lawyer ought to take logic.
∴Everyone ought to study logic.

(V) (I) 3. If you run a marathon when you're sick, you'll end up in the hospital.
If you don't run a marathon when you're sick, you won't give your body the exercise it needs and you'll end up in the hospital.
∴If you're sick, you'll end up in the hospital.

(V) (I) 4. Knowledge claims are either about what you think or what you feel.
If knowledge claims are about what you think, then when you say you believe something, you either have empirical or non-empirical reasons to believe it.
Nothing in the empirical realm can give you a belief.
Nothing in the non-empirical realm can give you a belief.
∴Knowledge claims are about what you feel.

(V) (I) 5. If the Raiders win, Cory will be happy.
Cory is happy after all!
∴The Raiders must have won.

(V) (I) 6. If you are Iron Man, then you are amazing.
You aren't Iron Man.
∴But you are still amazing!

(V) (I) 7. Shannon is not both in San Antonio and in New York.
She certainly is in New York.
∴Shannon cannot be in San Antonio.

(V) (I) 8. At least one of us is going to be starting in the game today.
You are going to be starting in the game today.
∴I am not going to be starting in the game today.

(V) (I) 9. If Charlize steals the car and Tom is willing, then they will free the brides, in which case the dam will be opened so everyone can have water.
Charlize was able to steal the car and convince Tom to be willing to help her.
∴The brides were free and the dam was opened.

(V) (I) 10. If Lund deals a three and cheats a little, then Robin will revolt as long as Rukes goes along with it all.
Rukes will never go along with it all.
∴Robin won't revolt and Lund won't both deal a three and cheat a little.

Answer Explanations

1. **Valid**. The first premise is saying, "All pure water is not flammable." But, the second gives evidence of some water that is flammable. Which has to mean that it is not pure water. This is a form of *modus tollens*, an automatically valid argument.

2. **Valid**. Consider the argument to answer this, "Who, based on the premises, should take logic?" The argument tells us two groups should take logic: everyone who can think critically and everyone who isn't a lawyer. Great. Now, who are the people who can think critically? Lawyers. So, that means that everyone who is a lawyer should take logic and everyone who isn't a lawyer should take logic...which means... everyone should take logic. This doesn't immediately follow one of our automatically valid forms, but the conclusion is guaranteed by the premises, so it is indeed valid!

3. **Valid**. Here, you can sketch out how you'll end up in the hospital, based on the argument. The result is a disjunction: You either end up in the hospital because you ran a marathon and you're sick or because you didn't run a marathon and you're sick. The result is that it doesn't matter whether you run or not—it logically does not count—because *if you're sick*, you'll end up in the hospital. This is another argument whose conclusion is guaranteed by the premises, and so, is valid.

4. **Valid**. This is another argument in which you can follow where the premises lead you. It starts off with a disjunction: knowledge is either from a thought or a feeling. Then it claims that if knowledge is from a thought, it is either from an empirically-grounded or non-empirically grounded belief. The argument then claims that beliefs can neither be empirically nor non-empirically grounded, so we are left with the second disjunct of the first premise—knowledge claims are about what you feel. This argument is a straightforward disjunctive syllogism.

5. **Invalid**. We hit our first invalid deductive argument! Were you able to identify this argument immediately as affirming the consequent? The first premise indicates that if the Raiders win, Cory will be happy, and the second *affirms that Cory is in fact happy*. What can logically be concluded from the fact that Cory is happy? Absolutely nothing. The fact that Cory is happy does not allow us to deduce anything validly. (He might, after all, be happy for lots of reasons).

6. **Invalid**. Rather than affirming the consequent, this argument denies the antecedent and so is automatically invalid. (Did you pick this argument out as one that denies the antecedent?) In it, the antecedent is that you are Iron Man—if that is indeed the case, something else can be said of you—you are amazing. But, alas, this argument says that you are not Iron Man. What else could be said after this news? Well...nothing at all. The fact that you are not Iron Man, given the information in the first premise, is only that you are not Iron Man. Denying that you are Iron Man does not allow us to conclude anything else. Which turns out excellently for you, because there are probably many reasons other than you being Iron Man to account for your amazingness.

7. **Valid**. Hopefully, you were able to immediately call out "disjunctive syllogism" for this argument. Remember, a disjunctive syllogism has the form, "A v B", "~A" (or, ~B), ∴B (or, ∴A). In this argument, Shannon is not both in San Antonio and New York, so when you discover she is in New York, you know she can't also be in San Antonio.

8. **Invalid**. Thankfully, this argument doesn't follow any of our automatically valid forms and its conclusion is not guaranteed by its premises, because I want to start, too! This is an excellent practice question for you on the LSAT, because you will be the recipient of many "at least" questions on the exam. For this argument, we can only know that at least one of us is going to be starting in the game today (who knows, it could be both? Whether it is both of us is indeterminate, given the premises.) We do know that you are starting, but we cannot say whether I am joining you or whether I'm going to ride the pine.

9. **Valid**. This is a multi-faceted hypothetical syllogism, involving several conjuncts. Our premise that sets the conditional up is the first one, and we can put additional brackets around each logical component to help us

figure out whether the argument is valid, (If Charlize steals the care AND Tom is willing) THEN (if they will free the brides then the dam will be opened). That is a lot of information to process without using some notation, so let's use some: $((\text{If } C \cdot T) \supset (B \supset D))$. Excellent! What do we learn in the second premise? That $(C \text{ and } T)$ occurred, or more precisely, $(C \cdot T)$. What must the result be? If the brides are free, then the dam will be opened for everyone $(B \supset D)$. You can see the hypothetical syllogism come into place if you list these in logical form:

$((\text{If } C \cdot T) \supset (B \supset D))$

$(C \cdot T)$

$\therefore (B \supset D)$

Although the terms are not singular, the argument's form is indeed a modus ponens, $(p \supset q)$, p, $\therefore q$.

10. **Valid**. Just as #9 was an involved hypothetical syllogism that ended up as a *modus ponens*, #10 is an involved hypothetical syllogism that ends up being a *modus tollens*. The argument stipulates that the conditional to "Robin revolting and Rukes going along" is that Lund will deal a three and cheat a little. We would formalize the first premise this way, $((\text{If } D \cdot C) \supset (R \supset G))$. What about the second premise? It denies the consequent of the... consequent! Rukes won't go along $(\sim G)$, and we know from an $(A \supset B)$ that if $\sim B$, the only result logically is $\sim A$. The impact on this argument is two fold: $\sim R$ and so, $\sim (D \cdot C)$. (We haven't covered this yet, but $\sim (D \cdot C)$ means "not both". It is ambiguous as to whether *either could* occur, but we know enough that they can't both occur. This argument, then, is a valid *modus tollens* argument.

Inductive Arguments

There are some types of arguments that are never valid/invalid or sound/unsound. These arguments are called *inductive arguments*, and rather than being bad arguments, they require different evaluation. *Inductive* arguments are best remembered by the term "probability," because the premises together lead to a conclusion that isn't certain, but is probable. Inductive arguments, then, do not give absolute (certain) grounds for accepting the conclusion, but instead try to show strong support for the conclusion. Inductive arguments, based on probability, can be judged as *strong* or *weak*, based on the degree of probability offered by the premises for the conclusion. Look at the following two examples. The first is an example of a strong argument, and the second is a weak argument:

> **A.** 1. The beans I have observed in this sample are grade A.
>
> 2. The observed sample is probably representative of all the beans in the barrel.
>
> 3. Therefore, the beans in the barrel are probably grade A.
>
> **B.** 1. 80% of the girls in our village look like their daddies.
>
> 2. 80% of the boys in our village look like their mommies.
>
> 3. Therefore, most girls look like their daddies and most boys look like their mommies.

My mother-in-law gave me argument B, and I had a hard time swallowing the conclusion (and perhaps even believing that 80% of the children in her village look like the parent of the opposite sex!) What was it specifically, however, that I didn't like about the argument? There are several possibilities:

-- **Comprehensiveness**. For inductive arguments, there must be a comprehensive quality about the sample that ensures an adequate representation of an entire group. Does the conclusion apply to everybody in a similar way?

-- **Sample Size**. The more instances a class of things has been observed, the more reliable is the generalization that the argument makes. Does the sample size reflect the same representative number of things made by the generalization?

-- **Randomness**. To yield the best representation, the samples should be somewhat unrelated if they are to represent a clear majority among a varied group. Is the sample group taken randomly?

PIVOTING TOWARDS LOGIC
CHAPTER 1

For inductive arguments, we use the term "probability", because the move from the premises to the conclusion is probable, but not certain. You will see probabilistic claims throughout the LSAT. Frequently you will be asked to make an inference based on inductive evidence provided by a text or by a grouping of potential conditions. Remembering how to evaluate inductive inferences can help you pick out the best from among the potential answer choices.

Deductive or Inductive: Let's Practice!

Directions: Read each argument, and identify whether they are deductive or inductive.

(D) Deductive   (I) Inductive

(D)
(I)
1. Sue isn't likely to go to Hawaii. She hates islands, hates flying, and doesn't like pineapple. To be likely to go to Hawaii, she needs to like some of those things.

(D)
(I)
2. Ethan wants to grow up to be a Chicago Bear. His main influences are Brian Urlacher and John Fox, both of whom wanted to grow up to be on the Chicago Bears. It follows that Ethan could grow up to be a Chicago Bear, since both Brian Urlacher and John Fox became Chicago Bears.

(D)
(I)
3. The best cars ever made in terms of style had wing-tip flairs near the hood. The 1957 Chevy Bel-Air had a wing-tip flair near the hood, so was one of the best cars ever made.

(D)
(I)
4. My coffee shop started selling scones with their coffee. That is confusing. Scones are from England, which favors tea.

(D)
(I)
5. Free speech is an issue that impacts all Americans. We should respect another person's right to say what they believe because that right is Constitutionally protected, and all Constitutionally-protected rights impact all Americans.

(D)
(I)
6. The sun will rise tomorrow. Every morning that has ever been a morning, the sun has risen.

(D)
(I)
7. The future will resemble the past, which is the foundation of scientific law. Science is committed to making discoveries that will prevent suffering in the future.

(D)
(I)
8. Coniferous trees are not typically found down South, because to bear fruit, they need colder weather. So, the tree you are talking about in your yard is probably not coniferous since you live in Alabama.

(D)
(I)
9. The Customs agency in Fiji is actually called the "Revenue and Customs Authority", which indicates that tourism is a main component of the Fijian economy.

(D)
(I)
10. History is written by the victors, but a main issue in political and normative theory today is the epistemic silencing that occurred during the Renaissance. If most non-white, non-male people were silenced, but can now be heard, the victors will not be the sole authors of history.

PIVOTING TOWARDS LOGIC
CHAPTER 1

Answer Explanations

1. **Deductive**. Don't be thrown off by "likely" here. Instead, ask how it functions. It functions as a condition, rather than as a way to invoke a probabilistic argument. For someone to be likely to go to Hawaii, the argument says, they will need to like either islands, to fly, or pineapple. Sue doesn't like any of those, so she is unlikely to go to Hawaii. Not only is this a deductive argument, it is valid!

2. **Inductive**. Just as you should be leery of the "likely" qualifier in the first question, you should be leery of the "it follows" indicator in this sentence. This is an inductive argument. Its main premise is that if you have two people who wanted to grow up to be Chicago Bears actually grow up to become Chicago Bears, then it could be true that someone else could do the same thing. That is a weak, but inductive, inference.

3. **Deductive**. This is an invalid but deductive argument, which affirms the consequent. The argument says that all "best cars" have wing-tips, and the 1957 Chevy Bel-Air had a wing-tip, so was one of the best cars ever made.

4. **Inductive**. This argument suggests that because scones come from England, which usually serves tea, it is confusing for a café to serve scones. The confusion is the conclusion, and is based on some implied premise such that typically we wouldn't eat foods with one drink if the geographical origin of the food didn't also serve it with the same drink. That is a probabilistic claim.

5. **Deductive**. This is a deductive argument that moves from a condition (if a right is constitutionally-protected, it impacts all Americans) to a conclusion that free-speech rights ought to be respected because they are constitutionally protected.

6. **Inductive**. Did you get this correct? 90% of students do not get this question right. You think about the most basic empirical truth- the sun rising—and you would like it to be deductively certain. But it isn't. It is inductively highly probable. Of course, you would be hard-pressed to find a stronger inductive claim.

7. **Inductive**. This is another one that trips students up. We cannot be deductively certain that the future will resemble the past, so science is built on induction (since many of its claims depend upon the future resembling the past).

8. **Deductive**. This argument uses some probabilistic language but its form is deductive: "If you're in the South, probably not coniferous. Your tree is in the South, so probably not coniferous." This is a valid *modus ponens* argument based on its logical form.

9. **Inductive**. Rather than its conclusion being rooted in its form, this argument provides a strong inference for its conclusion. If the Customs agency in Fiji is actually called the "Revenue and Customs Authority", then Fiji is not hiding the fact that the Customs part of their authority is inextricably linked to their ability to generate revenue from tourists (i.e., those who would need to use the Customs Authority).

10. **Deductive**. This is an argument that we call *reductio ad absurdum*. We'll talk more about this in the next chapter, but it is one of the best deductive ways to refute an argument. You assume the truth of your opponent's conclusion, and then show that the conclusion leads to a contradiction, which can only mean that it is absurd. Were you able to answer correctly?

Up Next

You have learned why logic is the best framework from within which to study for the LSAT. You have also familiarized yourself with the setup for the exam, and discovered some keys to approaching each section with the best logical eye. You are ready to launch into a logic-based prep tool for each section, because you have been properly introduced into basic argumentation. You know what good arguments are, you know how arguments differ in kind, you know the basic forms of always valid arguments and how to break propositions down into their logical parts. Next up, you will master translating LSAT texts into logical form, using logical notation and then you will learn the three main types of deductive arguments you will find on the LSAT and how to evaluate them.

CHAPTER II | THE LOGIC OF THE LSAT

But, Do I Really Need to Learn Some Logic?

Look, there are lots of ways to prepare for the LSAT. You've seen a lot of those products and methods. You have read this far and heard about how important it is to get targeted, directed training in basic logic and argumentation in order to be able to properly work the test. (You might have even jumped ahead and looked to see if even the Reading Comprehension exam really is a logic test.) Despite all of the evidence (and my own, *very good* arguments!) you might need just a little more convincing. Let's start with a basic pre-test in logic. Below are some very straightforward questions, let's see if you can get to the correct responses without further intervention.

Basic Pre-Test in Logic.

Directions: Read each question, and circle the answer that best fulfills the argument. There is only one correct answer per question.

1).
If you don't eat breakfast, you'll get headache.
You don't get a headache.
∴

a) You didn't eat breakfast.
b) You ate breakfast.
c) You got a headache.
d) None of these.

2).
If you don't eat breakfast, you'll get a headache.
You eat breakfast.
∴

a) You got a headache.
b) You didn't get a headache.
c) You didn't eat breakfast.
d) None of these.

3). If my partisan politician is to be believed, we are facing a crisis of democracy.
If my partisan politician is to be believed, we aren't facing a crisis of democracy.
∴

a) My partisan politician does not have knowledge about whether we are facing a crisis of democracy.
b) We are in one respect facing a crisis of democracy and in one sense not facing a crisis of democracy.
c) My partisan politician is not to be believed.
d) None of the above.

4). If Sherlock observed the Hound and the Hound was not an illusion, then the Hound killed Baskerville.
Sherlock observed the Hound.
∴

a) If the Hound was real, the Hound was not an illusion.
b) If the Hound was not an illusion, then the Hound killed Baskerville.
c) If the Hound did not kill Baskerville, the Hound was an illusion.
d) None of the above.

5). If Anne is spelled with an "e" and she loves Gilbert, then they will eventually fall in love.
She loves Gilbert.
∴

a) Either they eventually fall in love or Anne isn't spelled with an "e".
b) She spells her name with an "e".
c) She does not spell her name with an "e".
d) None of the above.

6). The only great composers were Bach, Beethoven, and Brahms.
If the only great composers were Bach, Beethoven, and Brahms, then Bach, Beethoven, or Brahms wrote the best piece ever penned.
<u>If Brahms wrote the best piece ever penned, he wanted to be the best.</u>
∴

a) Bach, Beethoven, or Brahms penned the best piece ever.
b) The composer of the best piece ever wanted to be the best.
c) Brahms was a better composer than Bach and Beethoven.
d) None of the above.

7). If time stretches back infinitely, we wouldn't get to today.
If we can't get to today, today wouldn't exist.
<u>Today exists.</u>
∴

a) Time had a beginning.
b) We cannot get to today.
c) There was not a first moment of time.
d) Today's existence depends on whether we get to today.

8). Reese's Peanut Butter cups are the best candy ever made.
If Reese's Peanut Butter cups are the best candy ever made, either Allie will collect them or Sofie will hoard them.
If Sofie hoards them, the world's supply will run out.
<u>But, it's impossible for the world's supply of Reese's to run out.</u>
∴

a) It is possible that Sofie will hoard them.
b) Allie will collect Reese's.
c) If Sofie hoards them, it is possible the world's supply will run out.
d) None of the above.

9). It's either going to be the case that we spend money to develop the technology necessary to land a human on the planet of Mars, or it isn't true that we care about NASA and the space projects this country has thus far admirably pursued.
<u>The budget came out and includes significant money to develop technology that will land a human on Mars.</u>
∴

a) We care about NASA and the space projects this country has thus far admirably pursued.
b) We either care about NASA or the space projects this country has thus far admirably pursued.
c) We either do not care about NASA or about the space projects this country has thus far admirably pursued.
d) None of the above.

10). If we do not reform our immigration system and do not improve our civil rights record, we will lose credibility with our allies and face ongoing legal battles from States.
<u>This group of elected officials will reform our immigration system and may even improve our civil rights record.</u>
∴

a) We will either lose credibility with our allies or face ongoing legal battles from States.
b) We will not lose credibility with our allies nor face ongoing legal battles from the States.
c) We will either improve our civil rights record or face ongoing legal battles from the States.
d) None of the above.

THE LOGIC OF THE LSAT
CHAPTER 2

Answer Explanations to Pre-Test

All right! Let's see how you did, unassisted by a background in logic. We'll take questions 1 and 2 together, since they are similar. (The questions and their answer options will be listed, followed by explanations.)

1).
If you don't eat breakfast, you'll get headache.
<u>You don't get a headache.</u>
∴

 a) You didn't eat breakfast.
 b) You ate breakfast.
 c) You got a headache.
 d) None of these.

2)
If you don't eat breakfast, you'll get a headache.
<u>You eat breakfast.</u>
∴

 a) You got a headache.
 b) You didn't get a headache.
 c) You didn't eat breakfast.
 d) None of these.

Did you get these right? Almost all students get the first question right (it's good to start strong!) but many erroneously choose "b" for question #2. In question one, there are only two inferences that can logically follow from premise one:

> Premise One: *If you don't eat breakfast, "then" you will get a headache.*
> Inference 1: $A, \rightarrow B$
> $\sim B \rightarrow \sim A$

Since question #1 tells you that ~B occurs (you didn't get a headache), then you can correctly infer ~A (you ate breakfast). But, question #2 tells you ~A. Guess what? There are no *logically valid inferences that can be made from these two premises together!* "If you don't eat breakfast, you'll get a headache" does not mean that if you do eat breakfast, then you won't get a headache. From these premises alone, we cannot conclude anything logically valid.

Question #1 has a logical form that you are familiar with from Chapter 1: the *modus tollens* form. *Modus tollens* arguments are always valid. Correlatively, question #2 is an example of an argument that is *always invalid* that was also mentioned in Chapter 1: denying the antecedent. Denying the antecedent means that you deny whatever sets the condition for the consequence. In the case of Question #2, we deny that you didn't have breakfast. (And, a double negation is a positive, so you had breakfast.) But, denying that you didn't have breakfast does not lead us to conclude that you didn't get a headache or that you got one, or that you didn't eat breakfast (we know, actually, that you did eat breakfast). Remember, that in a hypothetical, the only inferences that can be made are YES TO THE CONSEQUENT, if the antecedent obtains, and NO TO THE ANTECEDENT, if the consequent does not obtain.

Excellent. Now the easy questions are over and we can get a bit richer. Question 3 reads:

3). If my partisan politician is to be believed, we are facing a crisis of democracy.
<u>If my partisan politician is to be believed, we aren't facing a crisis of democracy.</u>
∴

 a) My partisan politician does not have knowledge about whether we are facing a crisis of democracy.
 b) We are in one respect facing a crisis of democracy and in one sense not facing a crisis of democracy.
 c) My partisan politician is not to be believed.
 d) None of the above.

This is a fantastic argument—a valid argument—that is a version of another modus tollens! The argument form is like this:

> If $A, \rightarrow B$
> If $A, , \rightarrow \sim B$
> ∴ $\sim A$

THE LOGIC OF THE LSAT
CHAPTER 2

My suspicion is that you answered (D). You might have been stuck on this because (B · ~B) results in a contradiction. Yes! (B · ~B) is a contradiction because it can't be the case both (B · ~B). Contradictions are *logical fallacies*, because it cannot logically hold that a term subsists and doesn't subsist in the same relation. So, the way that we write this would be ~(B · ~B). But, what does this do? It sets up a denial in the consequent...which, we remember, can only result in the negation of A (of the antecedent), which in this case is a denial that I can believe my partisan politician.

How are you doing so far? You are no doubt getting a sense of how important it is to commit to memory some basic rules of logic. Once we do this, we'll be able to apply them appropriately to LSAT questions. (And, after this test, we will practice doing that too!)

4). If Sherlock observed the Hound and the Hound was not an illusion, then the Hound killed Baskerville. <u>Sherlock observed the Hound.</u>
∴

   a) If the Hound was real, the Hound was not an illusion.
   b) If the Hound was not an illusion, then the Hound killed Baskerville.
   c) If the Hound did not kill Baskerville, the Hound was an illusion.
   d) None of the above.

Although it is true that the argument tells us that Sherlock observes the Hound, premise one lets us know that there are two conditions for the Hound to kill Baskerville: that Sherlock observed him *and* that the Hound was not an illusion. Conjunctions tie two concepts together, and in a hypothetical, ties two conditions together to produce a result. We cannot assume that the Hound Sherlock observes is an illusion (just as we can't assume the Hound is not an illusion). But, one of our answer options includes our conjunct. B.) fulfills this hypotethical syllogism. Both conjuncts occur (Sherlocks observes the Hound, as does "if the Hound was an illusion", with the proper inference that the Hound killed Baskerville).

You might think that Question #5 produces a similar result, but don't be too hasty.

5). If Anne is spelled with an "e" and she loves Gilbert, then they will eventually fall in love. <u>She loves Gilbert.</u>
∴

   a) Either they eventually fall in love or Ann isn't spelled with an "e".
   b) She spells her name with an "e".
   c) She does not spell her name with an "e".
   d) None of the above.

The reason you might think Question #5 is similar to #4 is that they both include a conjunction along with the hypothetical—and you are right about that! It's also true that the argument stipulates to one of the conjuncts being true (that "she loves Gilbert"). But, we cannot conclude that she does or does not spell her name with an "e", although we can make a valid determination based on the two premises together: (C v ~A). Since she loves Gilbert, it's either true that Ann isn't spelled with an "e" (the second disjunct) so they could not fall in love, or that it is spelled with an "e" and they do.

6). The only great composers were Bach, Beethoven, and Brahms.
If the only great composers were Bach, Beethoven, and Brahms, then Bach, Beethoven, or Brahms wrote the best piece ever penned.
<u>If Brahms wrote the best piece ever penned, he wanted to be the best.</u>
∴

   a) Bach, Beethoven, or Brahms penned the best piece ever.
   b) The composer of the best piece ever wanted to be the best.
   c) Brahms was a better composer than Bach and Beethoven.
   d) None of the above.

We can make a valid inference for this argument, but none of them are listed here. If we combine premise one and two, we can conclude that Bach, Beethoven, or Brahms wrote the best piece ever penned. We are not told enough to know whether Brahms was better, nor if he in fact wrote the best piece ever penned. Consider, too, that even if one of the three did in fact write the best piece ever penned, there is not enough in the argument to know whether a great composer wrote the best piece ever. There isn't information that can help us determine whether B is true. So, since the actual inference that could be made isn't listed here, the only correct option is D.

7). If time stretches back infinitely, we wouldn't get to today.
If we can't get to today, today wouldn't exist.
<u>Today exists.</u>
∴

a) Time had a beginning.
b) We cannot get to today.
c) There was not a first moment of time.
d) Today's existence depends on whether we get to today.

Work this one backwards—it's a *modus tollens* argument. Since today exists, it denies the consequent in premise two, which results in denying that "we can't get to today". Denying that "we can't get to today" means that we deny also the antecedent in premise one. That means it is not true that time stretches back into infinity. Of course, that just means that time had a beginning. On the LSAT, when you find an answer that is necessarily true—like here—you do not need to consider the other answer choices.

8). Reese's Peanut Butter cups are the best candy ever made.
If Reese's Peanut Butter cups are the best candy ever made, either Allie will collect them or Sofie will hoard them.
If Sofie hoards them, the world's supply will run out.
<u>But, it's impossible for the world's supply of Reese's to run out.</u>
∴

a) It is possible that Sofie will hoard them.
b) Allie will collect Reese's.
c) If Sofie hoards them, it is possible the world's supply will run out.
d) None of the above.

You know from this argument that it's either going to be true that Allie will collect Reese's or that Sofie will hoard them. But what else do you know? You know that Sofie cannot hoard them, because it can't be the case for the world's supply of Reese's to run out. Since that fact removes from possibility that Sofie hoards Reese's, the only logical conclusion is that Allie will collect Reese's. (Also, don't get tricked by the modal term "possible" in (a) and (c)). Your argument doesn't include the modal terms "necessary" or "possible", so you won't include those as terms in your conclusion.

9). It's either going to be the case that we spend money to develop the technology necessary to land a human on the planet of Mars, or it isn't true that we care about NASA and the space projects this country has thus far admirably pursued.
<u>The budget came out and includes significant money to develop technology that will land a human on Mars.</u>
∴
a) We care about NASA and the space projects this country has thus far admirably pursued.
b) We either care about NASA or the space projects this country has thus far admirably pursued.
c) We either do not care about NASA or about the space projects this country has thus far admirably pursued.
d) None of the above.

THE LOGIC OF THE LSAT
CHAPTER 2

These are tricky, because you might be tempted to infer something from the fact that you know money is going to be spent on the project. But, we aren't given a hypothetical. Instead, we are given a disjunctive syllogism: (a v (b • c)). Absent a background in logic, you might not know that for disjunctive syllogisms like the one in Question #9, if one of the disjuncts is true, we cannot infer whether the other disjunct is true or false—either one could be the case! Rather, if one disjunct is denied, then we know the other disjunct is true. In this example, the first disjunct is merely affirmed, which means that we cannot infer anything as true within the argument.

This could prove really important for you as you approach the LSAT, because you are frequently going to face disjunctive (rather than just hypothetical) syllogisms. Remember, knowing that just one of the disjuncts is true is insufficient for you to be able to validly conclude anything else from your argument. That leads us to Question #10:

10). If we do not reform our immigration system and do not improve our civil rights record, we will lose credibility with our allies and face ongoing legal battles from States.
This group of elected officials will reform our immigration system and may even improve our civil rights record.
∴

a) We will either lose credibility with our allies or face ongoing legal battles from States.
b) We will not lose credibility with our allies nor face ongoing legal battles from the States.
c) We will either improve our civil rights record or face ongoing legal battles from the States.
d) None of the above.

To get this right, you'll need to make sure you understand the "nots" and how they fit in with the argument. What it really is saying is that in order to make sure we keep credibility with our allies and avoid ongoing legal battles, we need to reform our immigration system and improve our civil rights record. From this basis, you might be tempted to answer D), since we aren't told in the argument whether we will in fact improve the civil rights record and it isn't specified that we won't lose credibility with our allies. But, we know that the first conjunct of the antecedent happens (we will reform the immigration system). What that leaves is the second conjunct of the antecedent. And we find that in C! We either will improve our civil rights record or face ongoing legal battles from the States (as well as lose credibility with our allies).

All right! How did you do on the pre-test? If you got one wrong, you're in decent shape but need some reminding about logic basics. If you got more than one wrong, that should signal to you that you're on an exciting path to have the tools to work the LSAT prep towards your advantage, and really do well.

> ## NEW CHANGE!
> The LSAC changed the LSAT testing cycle beginning with the 2018-2019 exams. There is a brand-new July exam, the September exam is just after Labor Day, and the dates in December and February have moved positions, too.

Translations

The biggest obstacle to figuring out whether arguments are valid is knowing how to translate regular, ordinary reading passages into what we call "logical form", or a formal language (like a math equation) that is needed to determine whether an argument fits into a logically valid form.

We're going to start by translating regular sentences into smaller, usable logical parts that we can later apply to LSAT passages to figure out their validity.

There are lots of ways to learn how to translate, but the most user-friendly version I have ever encountered is that of Harry Gensler's *Introduction to Logic*, and many of the translation tips I am going to pass along are those that my own logic students found invaluable from Gensler. I am not going to teach you Gensler's entire logical system, which

would be too onerous and time-consuming, but if you have time and the inclination, I strongly recommend that you spend some time tooling around on his free "LogiCola" videogame online. Since the 1990s, LogiCola has been an awesome (and addictive!) tool to teach you how to evaluate all kinds of logical arguments.

We'll start with how to take out nouns from simple sentences—and we will only start with basic *to be* verbs. (When we start translating for the LSAT, I will encourage you to translate as many of your sentences into its simplest veridical parts, with *to be* as a base, if at all possible.) We want *all nouns* to be translated into our logical form. Why? Nouns are the building blocks for logic because they signal to the scholar that a new idea is being predicated. All new ideas are new logical terms! So, for any noun, translate it by giving it some completely arbitrary letter. *For our purposes, I am going to translate nouns into their first letter to avoid confusion. I strongly recommend that you do the same!* Now, any letter can be capitalized or put into small-case, which is helpful for us. Here are two Gensler rules you need to use when you are translating nouns:

1. Translate *general ideas with lower case letters.* A general idea is any category, including: car, philosophy, shoes, dancer, apron, charger, belt, deodorant, lawyer, child, ice cream, workbook, hazard, tootsie roll, etc. *Hint:* general ideas take an *indefinite article*, "a" or "an".

2. Translate *specific ideas* with upper case letters. Specific ideas pick out a particular among the general category, including: Paris, Wollstonecraft, the birthplace of democracy, the book, this ice cream cone, her shoes, the fragrant deodorant. *Hint:* specific ideas take on the *definite article*, "the".

It might not seem significant now, but it can help when you test for validity, so it makes practical sense for you to learn how to translate these now. Here are some examples of translations for general ideas:

> ***General Ideas:***
> a softball team = S
> a simple plan = P
> a state of contentedness = C
> a belief in God = G
> an intelligent woman = W
> an automatic transmission = T

> ***Specific Ideas:***
> Jill's softball team = s
> the plan = p
> the contemplative life = c
> Mike's belief in God = m
> the most intelligent woman = w
> this car's transmission = t

Now we can put these terms to use in sentences, and translate them accordingly. You will include the terms "some", "all," "no", and "not", in the translation, and translate the main ideas with lower or upper case letters. (We'll soon add hypothetical and disjunctive syllogisms to round out our foray into validity, and then apply this to the LSAT.) So, consider the following examples:

1. Jill plays on a softball team.

    Here, Jill is a specific person, so she is translated 'j'. "Plays" can just be translated "is" for logical purposes. If this is confusing, think that "Jill is a player on a softball team." So, that leaves us to translate "a softball team", S. So, our translation would be:

> j is S

2. Billy Bob hatched a simple plan.

"Billy Bob" is a specific idea, so he gets the lower case 'b'. "Hatched" is translated "is" (for the full idea of, "Billy Bob is the person who hatched a simple plan."). And, we translate "a simple plan", P. The translation ends up as:

> b is P

3. Aristotle sought to live a contemplative life.

This might confuse you because there isn't an obvious "is", but remember, what this sentence is saying is, "Aristotle is the philosopher/dude/person who sought to live a contemplative life." Aristotle is a particular philosopher/dude/person, so we translate him "a". "Sought to live a contemplative life" is generic, so we translate that "C". The result:

> a is C

4. Mike believes in God.

This is getting easier, right? Mike is this person who has a belief in God. Translate that this way:

> m is B

5. The most intelligent woman I know drives a Honda.

Here's a little trick thrown in, but you're ready. You have a specific term, followed by a general term, still. "The most intelligent woman I know" is specific idea, so requires a small-case, and "a person who drives a Honda" is general, and so needs an upper-case. You translate this sentence properly as:

> w is H

6. Automatic transmission vehicles are not as much fun to drive as manual transmissions.

Ah! Something truly different. "Automatic transmission vehicles" are a general group (and so need an upper-case), and further points out in the text "cars that are not as much fun to drive as manual transmissions." We include the "not" here, and use the upper-case again, to translate this sentence:

> A is not F

Try practicing on your own at this point, and see if you can accurately translate these sentences.

THE LOGIC OF THE LSAT
CHAPTER 2

Translations: Let's Practice!

Directions: *Read each sentence, and translate into logical form.*

1. Texas is the best state in the Union.

    ....

2. The Cliffs of Insanity are gorgeous in real life.

    ....

3. No children of mine will eat spinach.

    ....

4. An *eudaimon* life is the best end for humanity.

    ....

5. All lawyers love morality.

    ....

6. Some judges studied philosophy.

    ....

7. People who take the LSAT are geniuses.

    ....

8. That joke isn't funny.

    ....

9. Icelanders are impervious to changes in temperature.

    ....

10. Some who break bad end up regretting it.

    ....

Answers:

1. t is b

Texas is a specific idea, and "the best state in the Union" can only refer to one, so it also receives a lower-case letter for translation.

2. c is G

"The Cliffs of Insanity" specifically refers to the Cliffs of Moher (you didn't need to know that to get this right). "Are gorgeous in real life" is a general idea since it can be predicated to anything that is gorgeous in real life. In this sentence, logically it stands for "are among the set of things that can be gorgeous".

3. No c is S

"No children of mine" is specific, though plural, and so receives the lower-case letter in translation. We keep the *"no"*, which has a separate logical function. "Are people who eat spinach" is the referent for "will eat spinach", and is general so we will capitalize.

4. e is B

"An eudaimon life" could be tricky, because it qualifies life generally with a specific term—here, *eudaimon*—but is clearly picking out a general idea, which you can see with the indefinite article. More obviously, "the best end for humanity" stipulates a specific goal for any general eudaimon life would aim towards.

5. All L is M

You will keep the "all" qualifier, and think about whether "lawyers" is specific or general...of course, in this sentence, it picks out a general category ("people who are lawyers"). "Love morality" also picks out a general category ("people who love morality"), so we translate with two capital letters.

6. Some J is P

"Some" also comes on over in the translation. "Judges" is pretty straightforward as a category, and so gets a capital letter, and "studied philosophy" just means "were among the group who studied philosophy", which is also a general idea.

7. L is G

Both groups are general—the group of folks who take the LSAT, and the group of geniuses. So both receive a capital letter. Pretty easy translation!

8. j is not F

This is a fun translation. "That joke" can only mean one, so gets a lower-case letter. We bring the "not" over, which serves an important negation function in logic. Then, "funny" refers to the general category of concepts that are not humorous.

9. I is V

"Icelanders" is a general group (similar to lawyers, judges, and folks who take the LSAT) so don't be fooled because it indicates a specific location where people are from. They receive the upper-case letter in translation. We'll use "V" for the general concept of those who are impervious to temperature changes.

10. Some B is R

"Some", remember, is carried over in translation. There are two general ideas communicated in the sentence: people who break bad and people who regret.

Insider Tip: The Same Ideas Get the Same Translation

When you take the LSAT, your job is going to be to translate and evaluate the translations for validity, so that you can make inferences required by the questions on the test. But, it can be tricky to take a paragraph and translate into logical form. Make sure that you only assign letters in translation to main ideas, and that when you assign letters, you give a new letter to a new idea. Here's the key though: if you move from a *general category* (let's say, "judges") to a *specific category* ("the best judge in Houston"), you need to assign different letters to them because they connote different ideas.

If I have a sentence such that, "Judges are concerned with human rights issues," I know that I can translate that, "J is C". But, this is different than, "Ravi is a judge who is concerned with human rights issues," to read, "r is C". We can tweak this further to indicate that "All judges should care about human rights issues," to read, "All J is C". (Note that the "should" has moral, but not different logical, force in translation.) Or, how about, "No judge should forget to care about human rights issues," which translates, "No J is F"? And, a further alteration would indicate, "Ravi is not a judge who has forgotten human rights issues," and would be translated, "r is not F".

Let's take an argument already set up in a logical structure:

Ravi is the best judge in Houston
The judge sitting in Starbucks is the best judge in Houston.

∴ Ravi is sitting in Starbucks.

And now let's attempt to translate this argument into proper logical form:

r is B
s is B
∴ r is s

Not only is this a good translation, this is a valid argument! (And, you remember from your principle of identity that if X=Y and Y=Z, X=Z.) This argument utilizes the same principle. Now that you can see how translations go in individual sentences, it's time to practice more of these within a logical structure. (*Then* we'll be able to move to LSAT paragraphs!)

Harder Translations: Let's Practice!

Directions: Translate these arguments into logical form, and weigh in as to whether you think they are valid arguments.

1. Everything that produces virtue is valuable.
   Suffering produces virtue.
   ∴ Suffering is valuable.

2. The most decorated swimmer in US history has a massive wingspan.
   Michael Phelps has a massive wingspan.
   ∴ Michael Phelps is the most decorated swimmer in US history.

3. No one who does right wants to be moral.
   No Roman statesmen does what is right.
   Cicero was a Roman statesman.
   ∴ Cicero wants to be moral

4. Dworkin is not snub-nosed.
    Snub-nosed people look like Socrates.
    ∴ Dworkin does not look like Socrates.

5. Some Broncos fans are rowdy.
    No rowdy folks are well-behaved at orchestra concerts.
    ∴ Some Broncos fans are not well-behaved at orchestra concerts

Answers:

1. All V is A
    S is V
    ∴ S is A

    This is a valid argument—though you might not think it is factually true. Do you remember the *modus ponens* argument? This has the same form.

2. d is W
    m is W
    ∴ m is d

    This argument is invalid. It is not the same as #1 in form. It is accidentally true that Michael Phelps has a massive wingspan. *You* could have a massive wingspan but it wouldn't make you the most decorated swimmer in US history.

3. No R is M
    No S is R
    c is S
    ∴ c is M

    This is an invalid argument. We could conclude from the 2nd and 3rd premises that (c is ~R) but we can't conclude anything about c's "M" status validly from this argument. Did you translate it correctly?

4. d is not N
    All N is S.
    ∴ d is not S

    You could flip this into the hypothetical syllogism to see that this commits the fallacy of *denying the antecedent*. It is saying "If N, then S", "*not* N"—that is, d is not an instance of N—therefore, not S. If an argument denies the antecedent, it is automatically invalid.

5. Some B is R
    No R is W
    ∴ Some B is not W

    This is valid! It's saying: if you are rowdy, you aren't well-behaved, some Broncos fans are rowdy, and so some Broncos fans are not well-behaved. This is a *modus ponens* argument, which is always valid!

Translations and Tip-Offs for the LSAT

So far, we've focused on clean-cut sentences for which the translation is pretty straightforward and the parts of the argument can be easily abstracted from the content. But arguments on the LSAT won't be laid out for you in premise/premise/conclusion form, and certainly they won't come pre-formalized for you. Even more, the passages will probably contain unclear wording and muddled organizational structure (especially to throw you off). Frequently, your questions will be about supplying premises or inferring assumptions from content that is missing within the passages. If your text is already opaque, it can be a real challenge to use logic to reconstruct an argument from it.

In what's been given to you thus far, the conclusion has come last. (In all of your pre-test logic questions, for example, the format premise/premise/conclusion was followed to see how your logical intuitions served you prior to starting logic.) But when we write, we throw the conclusion in whenever it suits us, and very rarely does anyone besides a philosopher put the conclusion at the end.

Take the following example, that a philosopher who liked the work of Descartes might give us (this is *not* put in logical form, to mimic everyday language use):

> **Philosopher:** If we are part of a matrix, we would have to doubt the truth of everything. But, in the least I can't doubt the fact that I am doubting. So, it can't be true that we are living in a matrix.

The conclusion (marked by the word, "So") is squarely at the end of the text, and validly infers from the first premise—here, the first thing the philosopher has said—that we can't be living in a matrix.

But, in everyday life, you might hear this argument structured in lots of different ways. (And, if you ever watched a movie that suggested that you could be living in a matrix, you might have debated using some of these very structures!)

> **Juan:** It's stupid to say we're living in a matrix! Do you doubt that you exist? Then the matrix can't trick you into believing lies about everything.

Or, how about:

> **Tyrese:** You can't doubt that you exist. So, you can't be living in a matrix, since you'd have to doubt the truth of everything.

Or, maybe even:

> **Olalu:** The matrix would fool everyone about everything. We can't be in the matrix, because we can't doubt that we're sitting here doubting about whether we can doubt our own real existence.

Tip-off words are in-sentence signposts that a logical function might be performed. In the examples above, you can see in those in which there is a "tip-off" word that a conclusion is happening. Of course, sometimes the conclusion has moved places, and very rarely do we use the same "tip-off" word—and even sometimes the passage doesn't tip you off at all. Everyday language isn't always helpful to figure out what people are really saying.

Sometimes, we do use tip-offs. Be careful, though—very few people are logicians professionally. (Very few lawyers are logicians professionally, as well.) That means that they may use a tip-off that signals the wrong thing. But, context will always point the way as to whether the tip-off is being used correctly. Consider these terms, which often indicate that *reasons for a particular conclusion* are being given. (Remember what word we use to indicate *"reasons for a particular conclusion"*? Premises.) So, the following are tip-offs that you may be running into a premise for an argument:

> **Premise Tip-Offs in the LSAT:** It's a given that, research shows, historically, evidence suggests, for, because, despite the fact that, in spite of, assuming, after all, for these reasons, since, it follows from this....

It isn't always true that these tip-offs will give you a justification for a particular conclusion, although it is frequently true that they will. Similarly, there are context-dependent clues that tip-off a conclusion in the passage:

> **Conclusion Tip-Offs in the LSAT:** thus, therefore, hence, so, it follows that, in light of this, in view of this, it must be that, it must be the case that, it cannot be that, it cannot be the case that, this demonstrates that....

The tip-offs can help. When you do not have a tip-off, you'll need to do some reflection about the passage to see what the main point is. If you can identify the main point in a short succinct phrase or sentence (using your own words), then you can ask yourself what reasons given in the passage support or reject that particular conclusion.

THE LOGIC OF THE LSAT
CHAPTER 2

Tip-Off Training: Let's Practice!

Take a moment to implement these tip-offs on the passages above. The first step is to identify whether there are any tip-offs. Then, you'll affirm whether they function properly as a tip-off for the premise or the conclusion, depending on the tip-off.

> **Juan:** It's stupid to say we're living in a matrix! Do you doubt that you exist? Then the matrix can't trick you into believing lies about everything.

Or, how about:

> **Tyrese:** You can't doubt that you exist. So, you can't be living in a matrix, since you'd have to doubt the truth of everything.

Or, maybe even:

> **Olalu:** The matrix would fool everyone about everything. We can't be in the matrix, because we can't doubt that we're sitting here doubting about whether we can doubt our own real existence.

Ok, in Juan's statement, there are no *tip-offs!* His statements are more challenging because we have to rely on inferences. We'll come back to Juan. Tyrese uses two tip-offs, one for a conclusion (**"so"**) and one for a premise (**"since"**). Tyrese is a helpful guy! It's true from his text that he is concluding that *you can't be living in a matrix*. How do you know? Well, check everything else that he says and identify whether he is giving main points or supporting main points. The "since" claim supports the conclusion as "you can't be living in a matrix" *because* (a synonym of "since", and here, which makes sense as a reason!) you'd have to doubt the truth of everything. The statement "you can't doubt that you exist" might tempt you as a conclusion, but none of the other two sentences lend support or justify it. Instead, it functions as a premise for the conclusion, "you can't be living in a matrix".

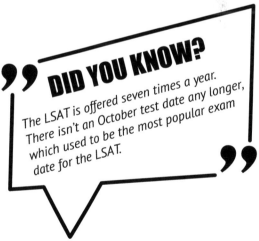

As for Olalu's text, we only have one tip-off, a premise tip-off **"because"** which functions really wonderfully here to frame *both* a premise as *well* as a conclusion. He makes a point, "We can't be in the matrix" and then directly supports it with a reason... *"because* we can't doubt that we're sitting here doubting...." The first sentence (which doesn't include tip-offs), "The matrix would fool everyone about everything" supports his claim that we can't be in the matrix, so is also a premise.

Now, back to Juan and the difficult passage that doesn't include tip-offs for our premises and conclusions. You will frequently see passages like Juan's on the LSAT, especially because the exam likes to put interlocutors together and briefly offer opposing views on topics. In Juan's case, he says three things:

1. It's stupid to say we're living in a matrix.
2. Do you doubt that you exist?
3. Then the matrix can't trick you into believing lies about everything.

You can see here that there is an *implied premise* in Juan's text. An *implied premise* is an unstated proposition, which is consistent with the premises of an argument, and required for the argument to be valid. Can you read 1-3 and

see what is missing? (You will have to do this *throughout* the LSAT, so practicing on implied premises for Juan is really helpful.) Hopefully you said something like, "4. The matrix would have to deceive you about everything." So, you have your implied premise. In what order do we put them? Ask yourself what his main point is. (At this point, we are going to take a relevant parenthetical to show why #2 cannot be the main point of Juan's argument, and then we'll come back to the other options.)

Insider Insight: *Your conclusion cannot be a question.*

Questions don't have truth value. They are neither true nor false. Only propositions that make a claim have truth value—*could* be true or false. Questions, then, are like sentence fragments and imperatives. None of them can be true. Let's take Juan's question and unpack the different ways to formulate these to see whether they are true or false or neither (for "neither", we'll write *nil*.)

Formulations of Juan's View	Type of Formulation	True/False/Nil
Do you doubt that you exist?	Question	Nil. Questions do not assert any truth about the world, and so questions cannot be true or false.
Go on—try to doubt that you exist!	Imperative	Nil. Imperatives do not have truth value because they do not assert that something happens in the world. They simply command someone to do something.
Existence... duh!	Fragment	Nil. Sentence fragments do not have truth value, because they only represent individual concepts rather than a statement about what could be happening in the world.
You don't doubt that you exist.	Statement	True or False. Statements (or propositions) function logically to report something about the world. That report could be true or it could false. (This is not to say that the person reporting *knows* *whether* the report is true or false. S/he doesn't have to commit to the statement being true or false. Instead, statements just report something that is either true or false about the world.)

So, now you can see why Juan's question, "Do you doubt that you exist?" cannot be a conclusion here. He isn't reporting whether you doubt that you exist. He is eliciting a statement from you by asking you. So, his other comments will reveal the main point, or conclusion, of his argument.

He starts off by saying, "It's stupid to say we're living in a matrix." This sounds strikingly like a conclusion. How do you know? Well, any *prescriptive* or *normative* claims frequently are conclusions. Juan is prescribing a value claim to a particular idea—he's mapping the negative value of stupidity on an idea that determines we are living in a matrix. His statement also cries out for justification, or an answer to the question, "Why?", which is characteristic of conclusions. This could very well be the conclusion. How about his last comment? "Then the matrix can't trick you into believing lies about everything." This is deceptive. The "then" seems to suggest something like a logical implication that could

serve as the conclusion. If this word is tricking us, let's remove it and see what we are left with, "the matrix can't trick you into believing lies about everything". Ah! That formulation indeed would offer support for Juan's first comment, "It's stupid to say we're living in a matrix". It *answers the question, "Why?"*. Why is it stupid to say that we're living in a matrix? The matrix can't trick you into believing lies about everything. Put our implied premise in place, *If we were living in a matrix, it would have to deceive you about everything*, and we're in solid shape. Juan's imperative to you, then, about whether you doubt your own existence falls into place as a premise.

Now that you're ready to identify the truth value of propositions, there is just one more translational piece needed before you are ready to launch into translations on potential LSAT passages. We need to cover "Murky Translations".

Insider Tip: Murky Translations

Most of the time, writers don't write in "all" or "some" language, and that can cause problems in translations. You need some practice in translating idiomatic terms that will come up, and I want to give you some rules of thumb for how these terms function logically on the LSAT!

"**All**". You know that "All" translates over into your logical form. But, how many ways are there to say "all"? It turns out...quite a few! Let's imagine that I say, "All lawyers are righteous". You can translate that without a problem into, "All L is R". But what if I said, "if you're a lawyer, then you're righteous"? Or, "Lawyers aren't lawyers unless they are righteous"? And, how about, "No one can be a lawyer unless s/he is righteous"? You will see, "If you're a lawyer, then you are righteous," as well as, "Every lawyer is righteous". How do you translate these sentences?

Guess what? They *all* translate, "All L is R"! Every one of these sentences are logically equivalent to the first sentence I started with. In logic, to say that one category is predicated with another category is just to say that all of them are that way. That is a difference than in everyday conversation, when you might mean that a lot of the members of a category fall into the other category. *You are taking the LSAT,* however, so you will be worried about the logical structures and implications of the passage, rather than what colloquial English speakers would think about a particular passage or set.

"**No**". Just like "all", "no" is a universal term—indicating that *nothing is in the set.* We will stick with righteousness and lawyers for our "no" examples. So, we are switching up the content considerably to say, "No lawyers are righteous," but the translation is still really easy, "No L is R". For these, we can say, "No one that is a lawyer is righteous." Further (have you heard this one?), "There isn't a single lawyer that is righteous", or "It's false that any lawyer (or, "some" lawyer) is righteous". The hypotheticals include, "If you're a lawyer, then you are not righteous," and, "If someone is a lawyer, s/he cannot be righteous." And, finally, "each lawyer is not righteous." Just like with our *all* translations, *all of these sentences translate to,* "No L is R". All of them! They are all logically equivalent. You will just have to commit these to memory as crucial steps to translating LSAT passages correctly. Also, don't forget that if you have "No L is R", recognize that you can translate this to "All L is not R".

"**Some**". Translating "some" need not be difficult, but understanding non-universal terms can be. If I said, "Some lawyers are righteous", you know to translate that, "Some L is R". No problem. But what about, "It isn't the case that lawyers aren't righteous"? Could you translate, "Evidence shows that there are lawyers who are righteous"? What about, "I know at least one lawyer who is righteous"? Or you could say, "At least once, a lawyer was righteous," as well as, "One or more lawyers in this firm are righteous." For these, you translate, "Some L is R".

But, it can be difficult to translate "some" terms along with a "not" or a "no". If you have the sentence, "It isn't true that all lawyers are righteous", the proper translation is not "No L is R", but, "Some L is not R". But, if "it isn't

true that some lawyers are not righteous" means you need to follow the negatives and translate this universally, "All lawyers are righteous," or our original, "L is R".

It is important to note here that you can more easily formalize "some" if you rely on some basic logical notation. This will be especially important on the LSAT when you work with numbers. We call logic that works with "some" and "all", *quantificational logic*. In quantificational logic, we use what is called an *existential quantifier*, "(∃x)" to stand in for at *least one but not all*. These English words are usually "some", "someone" or "something". If *someone* sells paletas, we would translate this, "(∃x)Px" (For some x, x sells paletas.) Now, let's say that Ron sells paletas. "x" no longer serves us logically, because we know who it is that sells paletas. So, the (∃x)Px just becomes "Pr" ("Ron sells paletas"). But, for many instances in which you will be translating, you won't know the specific someone or someones being referred to. You will just use (∃x) to stand in for "some".

To learn more logically about the "someone" being talked about in a proposition, you can use other logical functions along with your existential quantifier. If I wanted to say that there is someone who sells paletas and is handsome, I would translated this, "(∃x)(Px · Hx)" which reads in English, "for some x, x sells paletas and is handsome".

One more important qualification about quantification! "All" is also a quantificational term, which means "inclusive of a set". Instead of the existential quantifier (∃x), we use the universal quantifier (x) to mean "all/any". If I write (x)Px, then I mean "for any x, x sells paletas". Correlatively, (x)(Px · Hx) indicates that "for any x, x sells paletas and is handsome".

"Any". You might be tempted to translate "any" into "all." But that isn't necessarily a sound translation. If you have a translation that includes the word "any", see if you can rephrase the sentence to *not include the term,* and then translate the sentence. Here are some good guidelines. If you want to translate, "Not any lawyer is righteous," (that is weird, right, but you could see it), you would write, "No lawyer is righteous," and translate it, "No L is R". Frequently, it will be the case that "not any" is a universal for "none" or "no one in the group". And, sometimes "any" does stand for "all"–context will provide the clues.

"But". Any terms that we use to pivot away from a stated position, "however, nonetheless, despite, although, yet, both, etc." are not *negations* logically, in most cases. Typically, they are *conjunctions*. They join two disparate ideas. If the sentence reads, "You are a lawyer but you're righteous," two ideas are being predicated of you, *both* that you are a lawyer and that you are righteous. The sentence is not negating that you are a lawyer or the fact that you are righteous. So, the way that you translate this sentence is, "L · R". Disappointing, right? You'd expect something more exciting for a pivot point, *but*...we translate those pivots as conjunctions or predicates about the subject of the sentence.

"Assuming That...". You already probably know that a not-insignificant amount of time on the LSAT is spent navigating your way through assumptions, or figuring out what assumptions are required for an argument to follow, or obtain. For propositions, it can seem challenging to translate assumptions. Of course, if you know an assumption is required for the argument within a passage to work, you would just inject the assumption into the argument, without a problem. But, how do you translate propositions that include an assumption, or translate the injected assumption? If I say, "You are a lawyer, assuming that you're righteous," I'm really setting a condition on whether you are a lawyer. I am saying, "You are a lawyer if you are righteous." So, the sentence, "Lawyer, assuming that Righteous," translates into "If R then L", or (R ⊃ L).

It's important to note that "assuming that" is equivalent logically to some other, ordinary English phrases, such as "given that" and "provided that". Here is how you would translate a series of different English phrases using these types of conditional phrases:

1. Provided that you're a lawyer, then you're righteous.   (L ⊃ R)
2. You're righteous, if you're a lawyer.   (L ⊃ R)
3. You're righteous, given that you're a lawyer.   (L ⊃ R)

"Unless". There is a type of pivot point, however, that does not function as a pivot but as a condition. *"Unless"* serves a different logical function than the terms mentioned above as pivot points. "Unless" demonstrates

a stipulation on an event happening. If you and I are just sitting around the café, having a cup of coffee, and you lean in to tell me that I can't be a lawyer unless I'm righteous, even if I haven't studied logic, I know I might be in trouble! The "unless" there functions as a type of necessary condition on the event of my becoming a lawyer—I must be righteous. You will see "unless" frequently within your LSAT passages. They usually mean do this... *or else!* There are two ordinary English sentences in which you'll see unless:

1. You can't be a lawyer unless you're righteous. *or*

2. Unless you're righteous, you can't be a lawyer.

Translating "unless" isn't difficult, because it has the disjunctive "or else" flavor. Use your regular condition terms. Here's one way to do it, as a disjunction:

1a. Either you are righteous, or you are not a lawyer. (R v ~L) *or*

1a. Be righteous, or you cannot be a lawyer. (R v ~L)

If you're uncomfortable using the disjunctive function (although it is fun!), you can also think of "unless" statements as a type of hypothetical, in which you are saying that, "If you aren't righteous, then you can't be a lawyer." That makes the "unless" function as an "if not":

1b. If you aren't righteous, then you can't be a lawyer (If ~R ⊃ ~L) *or*

2b. If you are a lawyer, then you are righteous. (If L ⊃ R)

"Necessary/Necessary Condition". A popular question asked on the LSAT is to find a statement that is necessary for another to occur. These are called *necessary* conditions. An antecedent is a necessary condition for a consequent if the consequent can only occur if the antecedent occurs—it cannot occur if the antecedent also does not. But it can be difficult to know how to translate for these types of conditions. Let's say that the LSAT asks you to identify which of the answer choices is necessary for the conclusion to be true. We'll stick with our example and say, "Righteousness is necessary to be a lawyer." How do you go about translating that sentence to be able to be formalized into logical form? Well, to say that something is necessary for another thing just means that if it does not occur, the other thing doesn't occur either. If I say that a necessary condition for you to do well on the LSAT is for you to prepare for it, I am saying that if you do not prepare for the LSAT, you will not do well on it. So, any proposition that has the form "A is necessary for B," or "A is a necessary condition for B" will be translated, "If ~A, then ~B", which for our example means, "If ~R, then ~L" (if you're not righteous, you can't be a lawyer). *One more way* you can translate a necessary condition is "If B, then A" (since an inference from this is that if A does not occur, ~A, then B cannot occur either, ~B).

Another reminder for necessary conditions: you can have more than one of them. You will encounter several questions that require you to think about several conditions—both of which *must be true* for a consequent to occur. Imagine, in our example, that it is necessary for a person to be both righteous and communicative in order to be a lawyer. For the modified example, it isn't enough to be righteous (although it is necessary), and it isn't enough to be communicative (although it is also necessary). The statement we want to translate would look like, "Being righteous and communicative are necessary conditions to be a lawyer," which would be translated, "If (~R · ~C), then ~L".

"Sufficient/Sufficient Condition". As I just pointed out, you will *frequently* be asked to identify propositions that are logically sufficient for an argument to be complete, or to identify *sufficient conditions* for another proposition to occur. Sufficient conditions are, as their name suggests, conditions that are *enough to explain* that another thing will occur. A condition does not have to be necessary to be sufficient. Consider an example from jurisprudence. You have a client who has been convicted of armed robbery. Being convicted of armed robbery can be a sufficient condition (it is *enough*) to being judged guilty. But being convicted of armed robbery is not a necessary condition to being judged guilty. You could be judged guilty of armed robbery, for example, if you confess to armed robbery.

I'm going to step away from our hypothetical example for a second to use a real-world example to demonstrate the differences between necessary and sufficient conditions. In Texas, it is necessary that someone be at least 16

years old in order to have a driver's license. If you are younger than 16 years old, you cannot get a driver's license. But, it is not *sufficient*—not enough—for a person to be 16 to have a driver's license. (In fact, many parents in Texas lament the fact that their 17 year old...and 18 year old children do not drive.) It is necessary that they be 16 but it is not sufficient. But they also have to do other things, like pass the driving test and have proof of insurance. It is sufficient that a person in Texas who is 16 years and older pass a driving test and have proof of insurance to have a driver's license. (Each one of those is necessary, but is independently not sufficient, or enough. All three have to occur to be sufficient.)

EXPERT TIP

You have a better shot at getting into law school if you take the July or September exams and apply earlier than if you wait for December or February—especially if you only negligibly improve your score.

Translating sufficient conditions is actually really easy—you've been reading about it almost since the beginning of the prep book! If A is a sufficient condition for B to occur, we translate this simply, "If A then B". In the Texas driving example, there are three conditions that, if met, license a driver (age, exam, insurance), so we could translate this, "If (A, E and I), then N". (I am using "N" here for license so we don't get confused with lawyer!)

"Necessary and Sufficient Condition". These are the jewels of the LSAT passages, in which you find a condition that is necessary and sufficient for something to occur. These are co-dependent conditions, or conditions that require each other for either of them to occur. The way we talk about these conditions is *"A if and only if B"*. Those conditions are *definitionally true,* so if A occurs, B must and if B occurs, A must. (We also have a short-cut for abbreviating "if and only if" conditions which can save you time: either *"iff"* or "≡".) By the way, another way of saying "if and only if" in *regular English is* "Just if". If you tell me that you'll go to see the new superhero movie "just if Robert Downey, Jr is in it" you are telling me that it's true that you'll see the superhero movie with me, if and only if, Robert Downey, Jr is in the movie. We translate "just if" identically with *"iff"*, or with the "≡". Formally, we would say (S ≡ D), "superhero movie just if Downey", which is equal to (D ≡ S).

"Only if" is different logically. It might seem intuitively true that "only if" conditions are *if and only if* conditions, but they aren't! Let's imagine I now say that I'll go to the new superhero movie with you *only if* Robert Downey Jr is in it. In this case, I am actually saying that *If Robert Downey Jr is in the superhero movie, then I will see it with you.* That makes the "only if" a simple condition. The condition to see the movie is if this actor is in it. We would formalize that condition, "If D ⊃ S".

There are a number of necessary and sufficient conditions that you might have to represent formally on the LSAT to succeed. Here are some non-LSAT examples to get you started thinking about how to translate them, "It is a necessary and sufficient condition that a sister of my parent is an aunt." Now, you know this represents a necessary and sufficient condition when you get the same conclusion by flipping around the terms, "It is a necessary and sufficient condition to be an aunt that you are a sister of my parent." Both of these are logically equivalent, because it is definitionally true of "aunt" that you are a sister of my parent, and that a sister of my parent is called my "aunt". Here's another, "It is a necessary and sufficient condition of water to be comprised of H2O." That statement can be reframed, "A necessary and sufficient condition of H2O is that it is water." Water definitionally is H2O, and H2O definitionally is water, so you have water *iff* you have H2O. For translation, simply write, "W ≡ H"...and, of course, this is *logically equivalent* to writing, "H ≡ W".

Here is a quick-reference table of how to translate conditions:

THE LOGIC OF THE LSAT
CHAPTER 2

Type of Condition	Necessary Conditions	Sufficient Conditions	Necessary and Sufficient Conditions
How the Condition Appears	Being an A thing is a necessary condition for being a B thing.	Being an A thing is a sufficient condition for being a B thing.	Being an A thing is necessary and sufficient to being a B thing **and** being a B thing is necessary and sufficient to being an A thing.
What Does It Mean?	Every B thing is an A thing.	Every A thing is a B thing.	A is equivalent to B, so neither B nor A subsist without each other.
How Is it Translated?	"~A ⊃ ~B" and "B ⊃ A"	"A ⊃ B" and for multiple "(A ·B ·C) ⊃ D"	"A ≡ B" which is equivalent to "B ≡ A"

Murky Translations—Let's Practice!

Directions: This might be the single most important practice session to prep you for the LSAT. Translating so that you can evaluate arguments is central to getting the arguments right. So, read each common English sentence, and translate into logical form.

1. If he wins, then we'll never hear the end of it but will suffer through.
2. Only air marshals are licensed to carry a weapon on an aircraft.
3. Not all that glitters is gold.
4. You'll make the plane only if you are pre-screen eligible.
5. Poetry is taught at all levels.
6. He will fail the class unless he studies tirelessly.
7. None but true fans understand Totoro's magic.
8. Learning how to do laundry is a sufficient condition for you to land a partner.
9. Learning how to do laundry is a necessary condition for you to land a partner.
10. At least Robin remained true until the end.
11. She's a golden retriever just if her lineage is traced back appropriately.
12. Unless he is a mechanic, he'll never fix that truck.
13. Not all of the children were rowdy.
14. No one can accurately predict the future.
15. She neither confirmed nor denied it.
16. Only teenagers bring true happiness to the mundane.
17. Taking in oxygen is necessary and sufficient for life.
18. Every business major wants to get rich.
19. Only if you enjoy basketball will you want to see the Spurs this year.
20. Not any rich people are content.
21. We will camp, provided that we have good weather.
22. Whoever is content is willing to serve others.
23. Given your allergy to bacon, I've taken BLTs off the menu.
24. Having a moral education is a necessary condition to having a good life.
25. She'll pitch the curve or the change tonight, but not both.
26. Whoever is altruistic gives without expecting something in return.
27. I'll believe you if you cross your heart and hope to die.

Answers:

1. (W ⊃ (E · S)) * This is a pretty straightforward translation, "If he wins" is the antecedent, and gets a "W", followed by the "⊃", for "then". There are two consequences which occur if he wins—first, we'll never hear the end of it and we will suffer through. The "but" is a conjunction rather than a pivot.

2. All L is M * For this translation, we remember that "only" statements translate as "all", but need to have their letters reversed in the formula. So, "only air marshals are licensed to carry a weapon on an aircraft" means that *if you are licensed on an airplane, you are an air marshal.*

3. Some G is ~L * We translate "Not all As are Bs" into "Some As are not Bs". When applied to this sentence, the result is that at least one thing ("some") that glitters (G) is not gold (~L). *Hint: Don't use the same letter, such as "G" for two different terms because it will confuse you.*

4. (E ⊃ M) * For "only ifs", think about what sets the condition and what is the consequent of that condition. (Typically the order is switched within the logical form.) In this case, the condition for the consequent of you making the plane is that you are pre-screen eligible.

5. All L is P * Don't be fooled at the lack of hints at this ordinary sentence, or by the "all" thrown in at the end. Poetry is taught at all levels, so if the "thing" is a level, poetry will be taught.

6. (~S ⊃ F) * "Unless" statements can be disjunctive, but to make sure you compare what is said in the statement with whether there is a condition given, use the hypothetical. For this particular example, the student will fail the class if he doesn't study, so there is a strong negative condition placed logically, which makes the hypothetical the way to go.

7. All M is T * "None but" statements are really just another way of saying "All Bs are As". (Notice well: this is not the same as "All As are Bs". Rather, "none but" or "no one unless..." have the format "All Bs are As".) So, if none but true fans understand Totoro's magic, that means that all who understand Totoro's magic (M) are true fans (T).

8. (L ⊃ P) * No doubt you hit this one out of the park! Sufficient condition questions are the easiest to translate, because they take the simple hypothetical syllogism form. So, we translate the antecedent, "earning how to do laundry" with (L) and the consequent ("landing a partner") with (P).

9. (~L ⊃ ~P) *and* (P ⊃ L) * Necessary conditions switch the letters of terms before and after the "necessary condition" component of the regular English sentence. Then, they can take on two forms: you can negate that the consequent occurs, which makes the antecedent defunct, or you can indicate that the antecedent occurs, which makes the consequent also occur. In the first sense, that means that if you didn't learn to do your laundry (~L), then you didn't land a partner (~P). In the second sense, if you landed a partner (P) then you must have learned to do your laundry (L).

10. Some r is t * Did you remember on "some" questions to translate particular individuals with a lower case? If Robin at least remained true to the end, there was some person—here, Robin (r) who remained true until the end (t).

11. (G ≡ L) * "Just if" statements are *if and only if,* or iff statements that are co-dependent relations. For this statement that means that she's a golden retriever if and only if her lineage is traced back appropriately, and her lineage can be traced back appropriately if and only if she is a golden retriever.

12. (M v ~F) and (~M ⊃ ~F) * A mechanic is needed to fix this car. That is your conditional. For logical form, you are given two choices. You can either formulate this as a disjunctive: you have a mechanic, or the car will not be fixed (in the first example) or if you are not a mechanic, you will not fix the car.

13. Some C is ~R * This is the second "not all" for the practice set. As long as you recall that "not all" statements mean that "some A is not B", you'll be in great shape. Not all children are rowdy means that some are not.

14. No P is A * To say that no one can accurately predict the future is to say that there are not any who predict the future who are accurate. We would *not* translate "All P is ~A", which is ambiguous between "some P is ~A" and "no P is A". We want the latter definitively, and so will translate this "No P is A."

15. ~(C v D) * Here, you might be tempted to translate this ~(C · D), which would translate to "not confirm and deny", but that means that it couldn't be true that both C and D obtain. But, in this problem, she *neither* confirmed (C) *nor* denied (D), so we use the disjunctive, and neither disjunct is true.

16. All H is T * Another way to say "All As are Bs" is to say that "Only Bs are As". For this sentence, then, all happiness is brought to the mundane through teenagers.

17. (O ≡ L) * Oxygen is necessary and sufficient for life, from this statement. We translate "necessary *and* sufficient" conditions as *if and only if* statements, so both elements must be present for the statement to be true.

18. All B is W * If every business major wants to get rich, that means there is no exception in which a business major doesn't want to get rich. If there is no exception, then *all* business majors (B) want (W) to get rich.

19. (S ⊃ E) *and* (~E ⊃ ~S) * There are two options for this "only if" statement. If you want to see the Spurs this year, it must mean that you enjoy basketball. Correlatively, if you do not enjoy basketball, you will not want to see the Spurs this year.

20. No R is C * It's a little clunky to say, "Not any rich people", but it's important to practice clunky phrases in translation, too. "Not any _ are _" logically means that there are *no* As that are Bs. So, in this example, "No R is C".

21. (W ⊃ C) * "Provided that" clauses are in the same category as "assuming that" or "given that" qualifiers. For those, almost invariably, we swap the order of the letters, and confirm this by thinking about the condition. In this instance, we have a variation, because the condition on whether we go camping is good weather. So, *if there is good weather* (W), then we will camp (C).

22. All C is W * Statements that have the form, "whoever is A is B" is another way of saying "All As are Bs". So, whoever is content (C) is willing (W) to serve just means "All who are content are willing to serve," or "All C is W."

23. (A ⊃ M) * Here, the condition of your allergy sets up the consequent of a menu change. Given your allergy (A), or if you have an allergy (and you do), the menu (M) is altered to remove bacon from it.

24. (~M ⊃ ~G) *and* (G ⊃ M) * A necessary condition to having a good life is that you have a moral education. (This is Aristotle's view, at any rate.) That means two things, logically: if you don't have a moral education (~M), then you can't have a good life (~G), and that if you have a good life (G), it is because you had a moral education (M).

25. ~(V · C) * Here is an actual *not both* translation for you, instead of the one in #15 that almost tricked you. She will *not* pitch *both* the curve (V) *and* the change (C).

26. All A is G * Another way to write statements which have the form "Whoever is A is B" is "All A is B". In this case, all altruistic people (A) give (G) of themselves.

27. ((C · D) ⊃ B) * Think about what sets up the condition for the consequent in this proposition. The antecedent is not *if I believe you*. Rather, my belief in you is dependent on a condition—well, two conditions. So, the antecedent is that if you cross your heart (C) and hope to die (D), then I will believe you (B). Often, translations can be solved just by asking what is the condition under which the event you are thinking about must occur.

THE LOGIC OF THE LSAT
CHAPTER 2

Translations and the LSAT!

We've gone through simple translations, harder translations, and now we're ready!
Let's start with one possible passage that could be found on the LSAT:

Philosopher of Religion: Some have suggested that morality is grounded in the existence of God, since its principles are universal. I do believe that there are moral obligations. But, if I'm right, they are explainable either because of God's existence or some other explanation. It can't be the case that God's existence explains moral obligations. The only result is that moral obligations either cannot be explained or there is an explanation besides God's existence.

Start by looking for your *tip-offs* to either identify a premise or a conclusion, and see if you can build either a *hypothetical* or a *disjunctive* argument from the passage. (Use your own words for simplicity if that helps). Below, I have highlighted the logical tip-offs that are going to be crucial to translating the argument.

Philosopher of Religion: Some have suggested that morality is grounded in the existence of God, since its principles are universal. I do believe that we have moral duties to other people. But, if I'm right, those duties are explainable either because of God's existence or some other explanation. It can't be the case that God's existence explains our duties to other people. The only result is that moral duties either cannot be explained or there is an explanation besides God's existence.

You should be thinking "disjunctive syllogism" before you even engage with this argument further. You have *two* disjunctive clauses, which is great. To translate this argument, you ideally use your own words to simplify the statements into their smallest logical ideas. Let's try it. (You can do this on the exam itself as scratch paper.) Take the logical functions of the passage first.

1. If there are moral obligations, they come from God or somewhere else. (This is from "But if I'm right, they are explainable either because of God's existence or some other explanation.")
2. We do have moral duties. (This comes from the author's stated belief.)
3. It is false that our duties to other people are explainable through God's existence. (This sentence follows the one in premise #1).
4. Therefore, moral duties are unexplainable or their explanation is something other than God.

Now, you might wonder where the first two sentences of the passage went. If the LSAT was a reading test, we might be worried about it. But the LSAT is a *logic test*. We are worried about the argument in this passage, not with fluff. If the content provided does not contribute to the argument, we do not have to engage with it. Which is exciting! You get to spend less time worrying about content that will not help you answer questions correctly.

The argument has been successfully excised out of the passage. Now you need to translate the premises and conclusion into logical form so you can then engage with whatever questions are being asked of you on the LSAT about the argument. For premise #1,:

"If there are moral duties, they come from God or somewhere else."

you are not given any murky terms to translate. This is a straightforward hypothetical, if/then statement. So you can translate it:

1. If there are moral duties (M) then they come from God (G) or elsewhere (W).
$$(M \supset (G \lor W))$$
2. We have moral duties.
$$M$$
3. Moral duties didn't come from God.
$$\sim G$$
4. Therefore, moral duties are either explainable elsewhere or not explainable.
$$\therefore (M \supset (W \lor \sim E))$$

Ok, let's extract the formalized argument out of there to see what we have.

1. (M ⊃ (G v W))
2. M
3. ~G
4. ∴(M ⊃ (W v ~E))

You can see that the argument follows smoothly, except for the conclusion. The conclusion, based on premises 1-3, can only be... what? "W", that morality is explainable "elsewhere", by something other than God. We know this because the author sets up the hypothetical that *if* there are duties, *then* their origin will be either in God or another explanation. (Note here that the author does not consider that the ground of morality might be unexplainable, ~E. That is not offered as a disjunct in the first premise.) So, we have these two options: God (G) or something elsewhere (W), as long as there are moral duties. Guess what? There are moral duties (premise #2). That means that we have to have a source for those duties, if premise #1 is right. What could be the source of moral duties? The author firmly states in premise #3 that God is not the source.

The valid conclusion here is that there is another source of moral duties elsewhere ("W"). But the author instead amplifies his/her conclusion, and says that *if* there are duties, they are explainable from elsewhere (W) or not explainable (~E). To be a valid conclusion, premise #1 must be amended to read (M ⊃ (G v W v ~E)). In that case, since we know ~G, then we would be left with (M ⊃ (W v ~E)).

By going through the process, it should be easy to see how knowing how to translate straightforward, and murky, propositions will help you as you engage with passages on the LSAT. Now it's time to get down to the nitty gritty and practice translating. Once we're translating passages, we'll be able to combine that practice into answering LSAT questions.

Translations and the LSAT: Let's Practice!

Directions: Read the following passages and translate the main argument into logical form.

1. Botulism occurs when bacteria enters a food source from damage to a container that is carrying already-preserved food. Food in cans is particularly susceptible, but food in plastic containers is less so. Thus, do not eat food from cans that have been dropped and be wary of food that is in a damaged plastic container.

2. The elementary school was collecting "box tops" to raise money, and the class that collected the most box tops won a pizza party. Mrs. Hawsey's class collected more box tops than the students in any of the school's other classes. Thus, Ella was really excited to enjoy the pizza party because she raised the most box tops out of any child in the entire school.

3. A winning baseball team is characterized by successful pitching, a hard work ethic, and creative management that plays to win each game. The Texas Rangers are characterized by those three things, so the Rangers are a winning baseball team.

4. Analysts have determined that the most prominent market factor in whether a consumer buys an electric vehicle is their annual salary, rather than political party affiliation, age, or geographical location. So, our marketing team will focus on selling to the salaried group that typically buys electric vehicles.

5. Gina told me that Sue isn't a fan of brisket. That's preposterous. Sue is from the South, where brisket is king of barbeque.

6. In order to enter the concert, you have to have a barcode on your phone. Shane has a barcode on his phone and so will be able to enter the concert.

7. Emerging research universities typically are able to attract transfer students and graduate 80% of their first-generation students on time. UZ has dramatically improved their ability to attract transfer students and to graduate their first-generation college students on time. The city that houses UZ is buzzing with excitement over the growth and relative success of UZ students. Thus, we are justified in believing that UZ will emerge as a research university.

8. A recent survey measured the "happiness quotient" of various countries. 70% of citizens in the happiest countries report that having national healthcare, good education, and retirement benefits were the most important factors of being happy. This shows that countries with strong social welfare programs are the happiest.

9. Most marathon runners have low-tone muscles, which contributes to endurance over brute strength. Naomi has low-tone muscles, and since she is interested in running, there is an excellent chance that she will be a good marathon runner.

10. In initial test drives of the new Prelude, 55% indicated that the steering felt loose when they achieved speeds of 80 MPH or greater. On subsequent test drives, only 30% of drivers said that the steering felt loose at higher speeds. Hence, it's likely that most drivers will eventually not complain about the steering feeling loose.

Answer Explanations:

We'll start out by looking for tip-off words, and then rephrasing to translate.

1. *The passage with tip-off words highlighted: Botulism occurs when bacteria enters a food source from damage to a container that is carrying already-preserved food. Food in cans is particularly susceptible, but food in plastic containers is less so. Thus, do not eat food from cans that have been dropped and be wary of food that is in a damaged plastic container.* There isn't much here in the way of tip-offs. The "thus" helps us with the conclusion: Don't eat food from damaged cans and be wary of food in damaged plastic. How could we formalize that? ($\sim$C $\cdot \sim$P) As for the premises, we'll need to reframe a bit. What are the conditions? If food has been in damaged cans, it leads to botulism, and if food is in damaged plastic, it is susceptible. You can make this into two conditions, followed by the conclusion:

    (C $\supset$ B)
    (P $\supset$ S)
    ($\sim$C $\cdot \sim$P)

    Now, clearly this is missing some premises in order to be valid. (Can you tell what they would be? We would need to deny *both* B and S to get the conclusion that we have, $\sim$C and $\sim$P, so our missing premise would read something like, "You never would want to get botulism or become susceptible to it.").

2. *The elementary school was collecting "box tops" to raise money, and the class that collected the most box tops won a pizza party. Mrs. Hawsey's class collected more box tops than the student's in any of the school's other classes. Thus, Ella was really excited to enjoy the pizza party because she raised the most box tops out of any child in the entire school.* We look at the "thus" to see if it actually indicates a conclusion, and here, it does. "Ella raised the most box tops". We can translate that "∴e is m" As for the rest, we will have to do some construction work because the logical form is not obvious. The "and" as a tip-off does not function as a conjunction, but it functions as a condition. Right? What is that "and" saying? It is saying "If a class collects the most, it wins a pizza party." That the school is collecting box tops does *not matter logically* in this passage. It does not function at all in this argument. So, you can translate the first premise, "(m $\supset$ W)". The second premise is about the winning class, "h is m". That means we can put our premises together to see that this is an invalid argument (we are moving from a winning class to a student who has collected the most—who might not be in the winning class):

    (m $\supset$ W)
    h is m
    ∴e is m

    What we *should* conclude, based on the first two premises, is... that "h is W". If the class who collects the most is the winner, and Hawsey's class collects the most, then Hawsey's class is the winner. Concluding that Emma is in the class that collects the most is not included in this argument, is a new term, and so this argument is invalid.

3. *A winning baseball team is characterized by successful pitching, a hard work ethic, and creative management that plays to win each game. The Texas Rangers are characterized by those three things, so the Rangers are a winning baseball team.* This looks like an invalid argument that affirms the consequent. Let's see how. The "so" is helpful to point out the conclusion, "∴r is W". We translate the first premise, "(W ⊃ (P· E ·C))". Then the 2nd premise would be "(r is (P · E · C))". That means that the full structure of our argument is:

> (W ⊃ (P · E · C))
> r is (P · E · C)
> ∴ r is W

When the 2nd premise asserts that (P · E · C) obtains, it is *affirming the consequent* in the subject "r". The result for you is that a successful translation can make it very easy to see the logical flaws in a given argument on the LSAT.

4. *Analysts have determined that the most prominent market factor in whether a consumer buys an electric vehicle is their annual salary, rather than political party affiliation, age, or geographical location. So, our marketing team will focus on selling to the salaried group that typically buys electric vehicles.* Consistent with the first three examples, the "so" is a good marker in this argument of the conclusion, but for this one we need to translate it into its basic logical proposition. How about, "m is F" for "this marketing team is focused"? As for the premises, more translating into simple parts is needed. A conditional based on whether a consumer buys electric is helpful, such that, "If a person is from a particular salaried group, s/he is more likely to buy electric." (Then, we do not need the "rather than" at all because it would not function logically in our argument.) The translation would be, "(S ⊃ L)". That puts us at:

> (S ⊃ L)
> ∴ m is F

This is obviously invalid and needs another several premises to be valid. One obvious gap is between "L" (likely buyers) and "m" (this marketing team). We could infer, then, that if you are in the group likely to buy, then the "marketers" would be after you. That gives us (L ⊃ m). We still need to assert "S", however. We would need to say there is a salaried group that buys electric vehicles. That is a lot of inferences, but then we could build an argument such that:

> (S ⊃ L)
> S
> (L ⊃ m)
> M
> ∴ m is F

The last component would be to assert that F obtains. This is an ugly argument to salvage, but it is doable with the right translation.

5. *Gina told me that Sue isn't a fan of brisket. That's preposterous. Sue is from the South, where brisket is king of barbeque.* There aren't any good tip-offs here, so we have to build. What is the main point of this? It has to be that it is false that Sue isn't a fan of brisket, reflected in "that's preposterous". Each of the other propositions gives support for that. Can we create a syllogism for this? Let's translate the first premise, "s is ~F". Then, second, "s is H", and third, "H is k". (H gets a capital letter because it is a general area.) The argument reads:

> ASM: s is ~F
> s is H
> H is k
> ((H · k) ⊃ F) (this has to be an implied premise)
> ∴ F
> ∴ s is F

One excellent way to refute an argument is to run what is called a "Reductio" (from *reductio ad absurdum*, or "reduces to the absurd"). The idea is to assume the conclusion that you think is false. Then, run the argument, and if you hit a contradiction from that assumption, you know the assumption is false! In this argument, we know the author thinks it is ridiculous that Sue doesn't like brisket. So, assume Gina is right and Sue is not a fan of brisket. What else do we know? We know that Sue is from the South (H), and that the South (H) is the king of brisket (k). We have to infer that if you are from where brisket is king (so, both H and k), then you will be a fan (F). We know that H occurs and k occurs, so there must be an F. Since *Sue* (s) fulfills the H and the k, she must be a fan, and so Gina cannot be correct that Sue is not a fan of brisket.

6. *In order to enter the concert, you have to have a barcode on your phone. Shane has a barcode on his phone and so will be able to enter the concert.* The tip-offs do a nice job of setting us up logically for this argument, although there is a missing premise we will have to supply. The only temptation might be to read the "and" conjunctively, when really it is part of the "so" as a conclusion. Let's translate the conclusion, "∴ s is C". The first sentence provides a tip-off to a conditional, but be careful! This is not saying "if you enter the concert, then you will have a barcode..." rather, "If you have a barcode, then, you will get to enter the concert". If this is difficult, just think about what *result* or *consequent* is desired. The concert goers do not ultimately want to have a barcode; rather, they want to get into the concert. That means the concert is the result or consequent, and having the barcode is the way to do that. For translation, then, "(B ⊃ C)" (if barcode, then concert) works well. Then, our second premise is the fact that Shane has a barcode, "s is B". Let's put the argument together:

> (B ⊃ C)
> s is B
> ∴ s is C

Excellent. You are able to see, through proper translation, that when Shane meets the condition of having a barcode on his phone (premise one), he gets to go into the concert. He in fact has a bar code (premise two) and thus he gets to go to the concert (conclusion).

7. *Emerging research universities typically are able to attract transfer students and graduate 80% of their first-generation students on time. UZ has dramatically improved their ability to attract transfer students and to graduate their first-generation college students on time. The city that houses UZ is buzzing with excitement over the growth and relative success of UZ students. Thus, we are justified in believing that UZ will emerge as a research university.* There is only one obvious tip-off here, but luckily for us, it shows us our conclusion—UZ will emerge as a research university, "∴ z is E". Now, you can ask what the conditions are that establish that conclusion. It looks like the first statement is a premise that includes a condition, since it stipulates that emerging research universities ("E") are those that both attract ("A") transfer students and graduate ("G") first-gen students. Let's rewrite this condition, "If (A · G) ⊃ E". Notice here why "(A · G)" are the conditions for E. If the reverse were stipulated, a university would already have to be an emerging research university in order to produce (A · G). But, this argument is about how we could know that UZ is an emerging research university, so it is necessary for (A · G) to occur for a university to be an emerging research university (E). What about the second premise? Well, we don't have the numbers for UZ, so we wouldn't be correct to align UZ with the logical terms (A · G). We know they have *improved* their ability to attract—which is a new logical term, "I", and they improved their ability to graduate first-gen students on time—also a new term, "F". So, the second premise would be, (u is (I · F)). Here's the *invalid* argument:

> ((A · G) ⊃ E)
> (z is (I · F))
> ∴ z is E

If you were called upon, in an LSAT section, either to identify the flaw, criticize, or make something better in this argument, the fact that you could pull this argument into logical form would be hugely beneficial. You already know it is invalid and so needs a restructure in order to be valid (and so, in order to then be able to test for soundness and implication).

8. *A recent survey measured the "happiness quotient" of various countries. 70% of citizens in the happiest countries report that having national healthcare, good education, and retirement benefits were the most important factors of being happy. This shows that countries with strong social welfare programs are the happiest.* You should immediately be drawn to the conclusion, which stands out for being straightforward: Countries with strong social welfare programs are the happiest—If happy, then you have strong "∴(S ⊃ H)". Don't let the numbers throw you off when translating the numbers here. Use your "necessary conditions" translation skills! What most citizens say is that necessary conditions for being among the happiest countries (H) is that you have national healthcare (C), education (E), and retirement (R). Remember, that means that if you don't have (C), (E) and (R), you can't be among the happiest (H). So, we translate that necessary condition (~(C · E · R) ⊃ ~H). If you put that premise together with the conclusion, you'll be able to see immediately that a premise is missing:

    (~(C · E · R) ⊃ ~H)
    ∴ (H ⊃ S)

    Which terms aren't related? S and (C · E · R). The way that we get to "S" is through "H", which is excellent, because if we deny "~H", then (C · E · R) obtains. That swings in our favor because the passage suggests that (C · E · R) are social welfare programs (S). The implied premise is ((C · E · R) ⊃ S), which fulfills our need for a valid argument here:

    (~(C · E ·R) ⊃ ~H)
    ((C · E · R) ⊃ S)
    H
    ∴ (H ⊃ S)

    How would you approach that passage, without a basic knowledge of logic? It did not take much, but you needed to know how to translate passages for propositions, then break those propositions down in to logical parts, translate for necessary conditions, and then you were able to see what piece was missing to make this argument work.

9. *Most marathon runners have low-tone muscles, which contributes to endurance over brute strength. Naomi has low-tone muscles, and since she is interested in running, there is an excellent chance that she will be a good marathon runner.* This passage doesn't give you much in ways of tip-offs, but it doesn't rely upon jargon so is easy to follow. The conclusion is that Naomi will be a good marathon runner, (∴ n is M). The conditional is that if x is a good marathoner (M), x has low-tone muscles (L). (The rest of the information in that sentence does not contribute to the logical function of the argument.) The second premise asserts that Naomi is in fact a person who has low tone muscles (L) and likes running (R). Here's where we are at thus far:

    (M ⊃ L)
    n is (L · R)
    ∴ n is M

    You can see from putting this argument through its logical paces that it commits the logical fallacy of *affirming the consequent.* It says, "LOOK, THE CONSEQUENT HAPPENS! NAOMI HAS LOW-TONE MUSCLES." But, low-tone muscles are not the condition for being a marathoner—instead, this argument collects marathoners and indicates that many of them have low-tone muscles. The argument *is not saying* that if you have low-tone muscles, you are a marathoner. Rather, if you are a marathoner, then you have them. Thus, asserting that Naomi has low-tone muscles doesn't allow you to be justified in concluding that she is a marathoner—even if she likes running.

10. *In initial test drives of the new Prelude, 55% indicated that the steering felt loose when they achieved speeds of 80 MPH or greater. On subsequent test drives, only 30% of drivers said that the steering felt loose at higher speeds. Hence, it's likely that most drivers will eventually not complain about the steering feeling loose.* Here, we have an inductive argument and not a deductive argument, and we have conditions that are neither necessary nor sufficient. They are "some". Do you remember the translational tools in quantificational logic

we can use to work with "some"? One tact you could use is to use those tools, and start this argument with its premises. Some drivers felt loose steering at high speeds on first drives. We would put this in common English, "For some first drives, 70% felt loose steering at high speeds." Now we can use quantificational terms to translate this proposition in the following way, "$(\exists x)((70\%Fx \supset (Hx \cdot Lx))$" or, for 70% of first drives, there was loose steering at high speed ("high speed and loose steering"). For the next premise, we say $(\exists x)$ $(30\%Sx \supset (Hx \cdot Lx))$, or, on subsequent drives, 30% thought there was loose steering at high speeds. Can you get to the conclusion that it's likely that most drivers will not complain about loose steering? Well "complaining" is a new term, as is "eventually". This is a probabilistic claim that depends on a *statistical syllogism*. Consider this one, derived from this argument:

N% of Fx are Cx (In English, some % of drivers on first time drives complain.)
$(Cx \supset (Hx \cdot Lx))$ (In English, if they complain, it's about loose steering at high speeds.)
Fa (Al goes on a drive)
∴ It's N% probable that Al is Cx

We could do the same statistical syllogism for subsequent drives:

N% of Sx are Cx (In English, some % of drivers on first time drives complain.)
$(Cx \supset (Hx \cdot Lx))$ (In English, if they complain, it's about loose steering at high speeds.)
Sa (Al goes on a subsequent drive)
∴ It's N% probable that Al is Cx

Now, if it is true that the N% of Fx is higher than the N% of Sx, then you can accurately say that a smaller % of Sx are Cx, but you cannot say that there is, for example, a 40% less likely chance that Al is likely to Ca for Sa than Ca in Fa. This is inductive rather than deductive, and you cannot deductively know that Al himself is less likely to complain in one scenario over another just because less people do complain in one over the other.

Is your head spinning? The takeaway from #10 is that you can apply formal principles to inductive propositions but they will not follow validly. *That is ok.* Inductive arguments, remember, are never valid nor invalid. They are strong arguments or not strong arguments. Your logical ability can help you clarify the strength of an inductive argument but can't be used to do more than that.

Insider Insight: Applying Logic to the LSAT

You've come a long way in this crucial chapter. You started with no logical ability and now you have the tools necessary to be able to take any passage from any section of the LSAT and launch into it to evaluate it for validity (if it is deductive) and strength (if it is inductive). You are ready to apply your logical prowess to the LSAT test... which is one big logic test. In what follows, you will take these logic skills and learn new ones, through our work on logical flaws and fallacies. After that work, you will be able to apply your shiny new logical tools to the logical beasts waiting for you in the Reading Comprehension, Logical Reasoning, and Analytical Reasoning sections of the LSAT. You will pick up other tools that rely on logic along the way—ready for the beast!

CHAPTER III | FLAWS AND FALLACIES

FLAWS AND FALLACIES
CHAPTER 3

Throughout this book thus far, you have been learning about how to construct and evaluate arguments. You've learned the best logical tools to apply to the LSAT sections, how to read effectively and efficiently, how to extract and translate arguments to best assess them, and how to make inferences. You've also performed the range of critical assessments, including finding points of disagreements and identifying basic logical fallacies.

It's important at this point to remind ourselves of why we are here—to pick out and identify *good arguments*, and in so doing, we will have eliminated poorly inferred or wrongly deduced claims. Good arguments, if they are deductive, have a logical form which guarantees that their conclusions will obtain. If they are inductive arguments, they will provide a strong logical inference. But, we will also want arguments from both varieties to be clear, comprehensible to the average educated reader, grounded in good reasons, and germane to the topic that is contained in the passage.

We haven't yet done a deep dive into logical flaws and fallacies, and although you have prepped to be able to work through answer choices to find the best option (or, in the case of Analytic Reasoning, the *only* option possible), you still need to be familiar with the most significant and common logical fallacies, because they will make your options much clearer and can save you significant time on the LSAT questions that ask about the types of flaws within arguments.

One view of logical flaws is that they are arguments which appear to be good arguments because they are popular... but are actually bad arguments. The people who commit these flaws hold bad or false beliefs, and so they give bad or false arguments about those beliefs. Then there are logical fallacies that occur because of a flawed way of structuring an argument. You are already familiar with two of these automatically invalid arguments, those that *affirm the consequent or deny the antecedent*, and you know how to run a *reductio ad abdurdum* to show that the conclusion being posited must be false. You know, then, some *formal fallacies*, or arguments that commit a logical error in form. But, there are a plethora of logical errors that indicate fallacious patterns of thinking that are *always wrong* logically, but informally. What makes them *always wrong* is that, if you use the same thought pattern—only with different examples—you end up with problematic (or sometimes, even, nonsensical) results. Good reasoning of the sort measured by the LSAT follows a solid logical structure that guarantees the truth of any argument that has an identical form. Faulty reasoning ends up with faulty conclusions. In what follows, I provide examples of types of reasoning that are commonly found on the LSAT, and are *always fallacious*. We will start with quickly differentiating between formal fallacies and informal ones, and begin with the types of arguments that are most commonly found on the LSAT.

Formal Fallacies vs. Informal Fallacies

You have already worked quite a bit with formal fallacies, even if you didn't know they were fallacies. Denying the antecedent and affirming the consequent are two examples of formal fallacies. Any time you show an argument's conclusion does not validly follow from its premises, you have identified a formal fallacy within the argument. Many formal fallacies are just those errors in which the premises do not guarantee that the conclusion will obtain, and almost all informal fallacies are formally invalid if you run the proof tests on them. But there are some fallacies that you will find on the LSAT that are more formally fallacious than others. We'll talk about formal fallacies of hasty generalization and errors with false disjunction before turning to look at the three kinds of informal fallacies you will find on the LSAT (causal fallacies, distraction fallacies, and crowd fallacies).

FLAWS AND FALLACIES
CHAPTER 3

Causal Fallacies

Fallacies that fall under the "causal" umbrella all erroneously make a conclusion on the basis of some flawed reasoning about causes. The most common LSAT causal fallacy is the hasty generalization, and you will also see correlation/causation fallacies, false disjunction fallacies (sometimes called *false dilemma*), and quantificational cause fallacies. You may see these within passages, or they may be contained within the answer choices themselves. Be on the lookout!

Hasty Generalizations and the LSAT

Aristotle was the first to point out that people frequently make inferences based on insufficient sample sizes. This logical fallacy has come to be known as "hasty generalization". Here is a list of hasty generalizations that you no doubt have come across, even if you didn't know they were committing a logical fallacy:

1. *Joaquin fell smack on his backside, in front of his friends, on his first attempt at roller-skating, so he is swearing it off altogether.*
2. *Your mom almost got sideswiped by a New York City taxi. That's because City taxi drivers don't know how to drive.*
3. *You teach philosophy? I had a philosophy class in college. The guy who taught it was crazy. You must be at least a little crazy too to study that stuff.*
4. *Xunwu's four guy friends all wear Theatetus shoes. They are all in their 50s. My guess is that Theaetetus shoes must be really popular with guys in their 50s.*

Each of these examples are different, but they all make hasty generalizations. Their inferences are broad and sweeping, and they build their conclusions about a broad audience based on a minute number of exemplars. Arguments that rely on hasty generalizations rush to a wide, sweeping conclusion about a group (in our examples, roller-skating, NYC cabbies, philosophy, and males in their 50s). But, their experiences are so limited that they cannot make a strong conclusion.

Hasty generalizations occur in inductive arguments in which an inadequate sample size serves as the basis for a conclusion to be drawn. Not enough experiences are had to make the inductive inference (or not enough people are asked, etc.). Here's one:

> *Have you ever tried to drive in Chicago? I drove through there this summer on my way to Milwaukee, and there was construction, accidents, and torturous toll roads. I will never drive in Chicago again.*

This hasty generalization is a tough one to assess, because the author does indeed make a generalization, "I will never drive in Chicago again," but does so on the basis of some solid evidence—construction, accidents, and torturous toll roads would make anyone want to turn around. But, the problem is that this driver is explaining, on the basis of one day, why s/he will never drive in Chicago again. For anyone who is driven in a big city, you'll know that one day can't serve as the basis for explaining a life-long future ban on driving in the city. More observation is needed. It could be that the driver hit Chicago on a particularly bad day, or during rush hour, or during a time in which construction had been advertised on a toll road that also experienced an accident. Bad luck could explain all three bad instances. But, the argument gets better if there is a larger sample size. Consider this modification:

> *I am throwing in the towel and selling my car. After having to commute through Chicago for the past three years between home and family, I have never had a commute that wasn't interrupted by construction, accidents, and torturous toll road conditions. I feel like my life has been sucked away on the Dan Ryan Parkway.*

The inference—"I am throwing in the towel and selling my car"—has the same force as the conclusion in the first example, but the grounding is much more substantial. This particular author draws the inference after years of experience of driving through Chicago, and even makes the existential claim of angst following trauma on a particular Chicago parkway. This argument is much stronger inductively than the first example.

The second example proves the point that the strongest inductive reasoning will draw from as big a sample as possible. Let's take our initial hasty generalization examples and make them stronger, better arguments:

1. *Joaquin fell smack on his backside, in front of his friends, on his first attempt at roller-skating. He was so embarrassed, he was tempted to swear it off altogether, but instead he decided to practice at home before going out to skate in a group next time.* Rather than swearing off roller-skating altogether, in this example Joaquin provides a reason why he is tempted to swear it off (he was embarrassed), but combats a too-hasty generalization with the commitment to practice more first.

2. *Your mom almost got sideswiped by a New York City taxi. That cabbie must have been distracted.* This reasoning is stronger. Your mom might think all cabbies are bad drivers, but the only conclusion that we can make from this one instance she experienced is that this particular taxi driver made a bad decision.

3. *You teach philosophy? I had a philosophy class in college. The guy who taught it was crazy. Philosophy makes you raise surprising questions you never thought you would raise.* In this revision, philosophers in general aren't being disparaged, and the author moves from an empirical claim about this one particular professor (who might indeed been a little crazy) to a solidly-inferred statement about the rigors of philosophical inquiry.

4. *Xunwu's four guy friends are all in their 50s and wear Theatetus shoes.* We can't make a conclusion about men in their 50s based on Xunwu's four friends who wear a certain type of shoe. Sometimes, the brute observation is as far as you can take a claim within an argument. For the LSAT, it is perfectly appropriate to pare down to what can be testable.

Hasty generalizations indicate flawed logical inferences. If you need to identify a flaw within an argument on the exam, and you see a hasty generalization, zero in on it as a strong answer choice.

False Disjunctive Inferences, False Disjunctions, and the LSAT

You remember from our basic logic introduction that the disjunctive syllogism can contain ambiguities if you are not careful. To say that either A or B is going to occur is ambiguous. Let's use and example, "Today Carrie is either going to see the next RDJ flick, or she will mope around in her pajamas." (Both of these disjuncts seem like reasonable things to do, after all!) This sentence could indicate three things, logically, if no sharper designations are made:

> Carrie sees the RDJ flick, but does not mope around in her pajamas.
> Carrie mopes around in her pajamas, but does not see the RDJ flick.
> Carrie sees the RDJ flick and mopes around in her pajamas.

"Or" need not be exclusive. If both disjuncts occur, the "or" functions to indicate that "some" of these events will occur—and, you remember—"some" logically simply means "at least one".

It isn't difficult to see, then, that it is quite easy to make a mistake on the LSAT when dealing with disjunctive syllogisms. *It is almost always true* that disjunctive syllogisms are not inclusive on the LSAT. *Almost always* it will be the case that you will see a disjunct and *one of the disjuncts does not occur,* which will make the other disjunct *necessary* in order for the consequent to occur. But... not always. Almost always, but not always. This means that the biggest logical flaw that surrounds disjunctive syllogisms on the LSAT occurs *in the mind of the test-taker,* and not within the passage. Although you will frequently encounter disjuncts and disjunctive syllogisms on the exam, it is infrequently the case that logical flaws result within the disjunctive syllogism. Instead, "user error"—you—sometimes get in the way of the valid argument. Instead, clear reading, translation, and logical assessment will save the day.

Insider Insight: User Error Flaws in Disjunctive Syllogisms

The easiest way to ensure that user error flaws do not occur on disjunctive syllogisms on the LSAT is to make sure that you translate the syllogisms correctly. Most of the user errors occur at the point of when a disjunct does *not* occur, or when it is unclear whether a disjunct occurs.

FLAWS AND FALLACIES
CHAPTER 3

Imagine that you have a passage which includes the following, "Carrie will either see the RDJ flick or she will mope around in her pajamas". The way that you want the syllogism to go (which means that it is the easiest to prove valid) is to show either that Carrie does not go see the RDJ flick or that she did not mope in her pajamas. We would translate this argument's potential arguments in the following ways:

1. (R v M), Carrie will either RDJ or mope.
~ R, Carrie did not RDJ
∴ M, Carrie moped.

2. (R v M), Carrie will either RDJ or mope.
~ M, Carrie did not mope
∴ R, Carrie RDJ'd.

Both of these are simple, and valid. Depending on what the passage tells you about the fact of whether ~R or ~M obtained, you will validly conclude either of M or R. But, what if the passage tells you "Carrie neither saw the RDJ flick or moped in her pajamas"? In such a case, you negate *that the disjunction was true:* ~(R v M).

The user error tends to be to want either R or M to occur, to show that the other disjunct could not occur. But, denying that the disjunct is true means that *neither disjunct is true*. The result is that when you have a proposition, ~(R v M), you then conclude: ((~R) · (~M)). In everyday English, ~(R v M) means, it is true *both* that Carrie didn't see the RDJ flick *and that* she did not mope in her pajamas.

The insider insight take-away is that if you negate an *entire disjunctive proposition,* you end up with a *conjunction.* To say that Carrie will neither see the flick nor mope is to say that Carrie will not see the flick *and* she will not mope.

There are other fallacies that occur on the LSAT, however, than mistranslations that result from disjunctives. It is always a logical fallacy to break down options into only two disjuncts when there are other options available (and so, it is a fallacy not to introduce a new translational term in a proposition when it is available to you). Fallacies of this sort are called *false disjunctions.* False disjunctions are propositions with an either/or that fail to identify other logically possible disjuncts. If I tell you that tonight before bed, you can only read *Grapes of Wrath* or the *latest Iron Man* comic, and you don't own either one of them...guess what? It's evidentially false that you can only read the book or the comic, because you can't do either. If you own all of the Steinbeck books, the entire *Iron Man* series (lucky you!), as well as Lewis, Vonnegut, Evanovich, and Cooper, then it would be false to say that you could only read those two particular items.

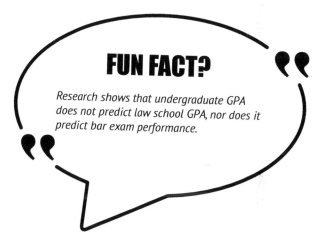

FUN FACT?

Research shows that undergraduate GPA does not predict law school GPA, nor does it predict bar exam performance.

Consider the following passage:

If there is objective truth, and morality is objective, then moral knowledge should be possible. If we have moral knowledge, then either moral truths are provable, or they are self-evidentially true. There is objective truth, and morality is objectively true. We do have moral knowledge, but moral truths are not provable, and there aren't self-evident moral truths.

Now, let's imagine an LSAT question that corresponds to this passage that looks like this:

Which one of the following most accurately describes a flaw in the argument above?

A. The argument assumes, without providing justification, that even if there is moral knowledge, moral truth is not provable.

B. The argument assumes, without providing justification, that morality is objectively true just because there is objective truth.

C. The argument collapses the correlation of moral truth with causation of objective truth.

D. The argument overlooks the fact that if moral knowledge is objective, it could be intuited without the need for self-evident or empirical provability.

E. The argument overlooks the fact that moral knowledge does not require objectivity as long as truth can be subjectively experienced or felt.

This passage is an excellent example, because it has the features of a Logical Reasoning or Reading Comprehension passage that could slow the typical exam-taker down. But, not you. You can appreciate the logical systematicity of the argument. Let's put this argument down into logical form so we can actually find a logical flaw that might be present:

> If there is objective truth, and morality is objective, then moral knowledge should be possible. (If (T · M) ⊃ K). If we have moral knowledge, then either moral truths are provable, or they are self-evidentially true. (K ⊃ (V v E)). There is objective truth (T), and morality is objectively true (M). We do have moral knowledge (K), but moral truths are not provable (~V), and there aren't self-evident moral truths (~E).

By now, you might be able to extract why this argument is invalid without even listing these premises in order. But, let's go through the exercise:

> ((T · M) ⊃ K)
> (K ⊃ (V v E))
> T
> M
> K
> ~V
> ~E
> ∴ nil

All of our antecedents obtain (T and M), which leads to K, our antecedent in premise 2 (and which is confirmed in the fifth premise). The result is that the following disjunction must occur: (V v E). But, neither V or E obtain, which means ~K, which means ~T and ~M. Those are contradictions, so this is invalid! But, running through the translation and logical form helps us identify where the problem resides with the argument: *in the disjunction*. We have a false disjunction. If there is one more disjunct that could obtain as the result of "K", or moral knowledge, then we could have a valid argument. So, what is the author suggesting is the disjunct? If you have moral knowledge, moral knowledge will either be provable or self-evident. But, that is not a true disjunct. You could have moral knowledge that is self-inferentially justified—that is neither empirically justified nor self-evidently true, but needs to "seem right" to people. Moral intuitions seem to be something like this (although many people could contend that moral intuitions are self-evident, and don't need any other justification). At any rate, regardless of where you fall in the debate, there *is another disjunct* that is possible: the subjectively felt moral intuition. We'll call this "S", and then we can modify the argument:

> ((T · M) ⊃ K)
> (K ⊃ (V v E v S))
> T
> M
> K
> ~V
> ~E
> ∴ S

Excellent. We have added a logically possible result of "K", having moral knowledge, which is the subjectively-felt intuition, and validly concluded that S results from K, since neither V nor E obtain. We have made the argument valid, but are there answer choices that identify the flaw that the original argument made, which needed to be fixed? The answer cannot be (A), because the argument asserts that moral knowledge is not provable—it does not assume it. (It *is* true, however, that the argument asserts the truth of the premises without providing justification but that is not a potential flaw identified by the answer choices, and at least is not the structural flaw made by the argument.) Answer (B), similarly, cannot be correct, because the argument states, but does not assume, that morality is objective. (C) could be eliminated out of hand. You might get excited to see a correlation/causation answer choice, but even a glance at the passage shows that the text is not about causation. That leaves you with (D) and (E). You might be tricked by (E) because it mentions "subjectively experienced" so ask yourself what the difference

is between (D) and (E). (D) has the antecedent, "if moral knowledge is objective"; answer (E) has it, "if truth can be subjectively experienced". Although these are very similar in content, answer (D) is what makes the argument valid! The proposition needed isn't about whether truth is subjective but whether if moral knowledge is objective, what other disjunct could be possible? The other disjunct is whether moral knowledge could be intuited. So (D) is the closest option to avoid the false disjunctive claim that makes this argument invalid.

Why are false disjunctions always wrong? Because they set up an 'either/or' scenario that *isn't* either/or—there are more options than what is given by it. Your chances for seeing false disjunctions are pretty good. Careful reading will make sure that you keep your eye out for including options that aren't already included.

Quantificational Fallacies and the LSAT

You already know that the LSAT is not a math test, but that it can use quantificational methods to assess your logical abilities. But, quantification—here, when we are talking about *numbers* and not about "all", "none", or "some" *quantifiers*-- is just another "X" in the logical structure of your argument, so don't be daunted! Just as you will see some numbers on the LSAT, you also are likely to run into fallacies that are grounded in quantificational causal errors. The most common fallacy that you will see is an equivocation between a *percentage* of a set and the *corresponding quantity* of a set. If I tell you that I spend 50% of my paycheck on soda, that might be astounding. If you find out that I am 16 years old, and my first paycheck is for my training session and is $20, then you might not be so astounded. Here's an example of a passage you might find on the Logical Reasoning section that challenges you to be aware of causal fallacies within quantificational scenarios on the LSAT.

> In the discipline of academic physics, only 2% of tenure track faculty are women. To address the issues, major research universities joined together to share financial resources to recruit and retain "underserved" populations in physics positions at the universities. So far, 90% of the positions created under the program have been filled by male applicants who are members of other underserved groups. Thus, tenure-track jobs at universities fail to attract female physicists, even with sweetened financial incentives.

This author contends that female physicists are not attracted by tenure-track jobs at universities but the data reflect only an effort to incentivize recruitment of underserved populations and does not explain why *departments are not hiring women*. Women could be attracted to the hiring departments that are utilizing the incentive program, and if sexism (for example) remains prevalent in those departments, the job could go to another participant in the program who is not male. To get at the quantificational truth of this passage, we need to know how many female PhD candidates are participating in the incentive program, and then how many are landing interviews. Inferring a conclusion from these percentages is attractive in part because the percentages are shocking—2% women, and 90% of the initiative positions are going to men. But, such an inference is flawed because the inference from percentages to a raw quantificational assessment is unjustified.

Although you will infrequently run into numbers on the LSAT, being able to pick out inferential flaws within quantified sets can help you ensure that you are on your way to choosing correctly among answer choices.

Informal Fallacies and the LSAT

Informal fallacies are extremely common on the LSAT, but are substantively different than other formal fallacies, or fallacies that exhibit a structural logical problem (such as deductive problems of invalidity or inductive problems of inference). It is important to point out that many informal fallacies *also* are invalid, but we typically think it is useful to categorize informal fallacies differently—in part because we don't want to have to run logical proofs to show that an argument is invalid and in part because informal fallacies are so common, it makes sense to recognize them for what they are... logically fallacious! For our purposes—domination of the LSAT!-- there are three main categories of informal fallacies that you need to be familiar with :); *Causal Fallacies* (correlation, post hoc ergo propter hoc, division/composition, and circular arguments—which are a type of causal fallacy in which the conclusion is asserted as true

by way of itself); *Crowd Fallacies* (the conclusion is not related at all to the premises except some feature of a group compels you to conclude in that way; appeal to authority, appeal to ignorance, appeal to force, appeal to emotion); and *Fallacies of Distraction* (the conclusion is not related at all, but the testifier is suspect; ad hominem, red herring and straw man).

FUN FACT

*For **first-time takers** of the bar exam, performance on the LSAT has been shown to significantly predict bar exam performance.*

Causal Fallacies

Causal fallacies share, at their core, a broken relationship between an event that happens and an event that subsequently occurs. These are fallacious for similar reasons, but make distinct mistakes. The most common "fallacy" question you will see on the LSAT is the causal fallacy that mistakes correlation with causation. It is worthwhile, because of the popularity of that particular flaw with the LSAT writers, to go in-depth into that fallacy.

Confusing Correlations with Causation

David Hume famously contended that the best we could ever do in science was to observe "constant conjunction", a series of events preceding a subsequent series of events, but without an observation of actual cause. The difference between correlation and causation has been drawn in science and logic since that time, at least. A correlation is Humean constant conjunction, A preceding B and followed by C. You will frequently be called upon to disentangle mere correlation with causation on the LSAT, in various types of questions. Confusing correlation with causation is indeed a logical error, not just one of evidence.

There are observational trends that can make disentangling the two challenging. We tend to equivocate cause with any two things that have a strong relationship. Consider the following example:

> College students frequently are youthful.
> College matriculation is correlated with youth.
> Going to college makes you more youthful.

The reasoning thread for this example takes events that are connected—being a college student and youth—and infers that if you participate in one, the consequent will emerge. You can think the first premise is justified without thinking that the consequent is also justified.

The logical fallacy in that example is obvious, but the consequences are logical only. You might find yourself observing a City Council meeting some day and hear a council member confuse correlation and cause, which will lead to more prudential consequences. Here's one such example:

> Drivers tend to slow down if there is a red-light camera at an intersection.
> We can reduce accidents by putting in more red-light cameras across the city.

This is a logically fallacious argument because it infers a causal relationship between the first premise and the second premise when there is only correlation between them—and correlation that would require more justification in order to be proven to be true. To demonstrate the difficulty with correlation, consider the below alteration to the argument:

> Drivers tend to slow down if there is a red-light camera at an intersection.
> We will increase accidents by putting in more red-light cameras across the city.

Do you see the logical difficulty? The logical framework of the argument yields completely opposing, yet equally justified, conclusions. Given that the argument does not show why driver behavior at red-light cameras produces certain results, we are unable to logically conclude anything else beyond the asserted fact that drivers tend to slow down when red-light cameras are present. (But, as we know from experience, their presence can create the conditions under which accidents occur as well.)

There are correlations which more strongly associate an antecedent event with a consequent. Think about this (commonly held) view:

> The #MeToo movement has demonstrated that we need to do a better job modeling healthy relationships between men and women, and implementing training from the earliest ages about how to respect others. Children are surrounded by images that commodify women.
> If children are surrounded by images that commodify women, they are less likely to view women with equal respect, and may believe as they become adults that women are objects.
> Children need to be less inculcated with images that commodify women.

This example is interesting for several reasons logically. It doesn't make the leap to a causal claim, but makes an evidential claim based on correlation: "If children are surrounded by images that commodify women, they are less likely to view women with equal respect, and may believe as they become adults that women are objects." The problem is that the author does not provide evidence for this claim, so relies on some further inductive inference. The conclusion that "children need to be less inculcated with images that commodify women" is a valid inference given the premises that go before it, but to show that children are less likely to view women with equal respect if they are surrounded by images that commodify women, the author needs more justification.

Insider Insight: Types of Correlation/Causation LSAT Questions

There are so many instances in which you could be called upon to identify flaws between correlations and causes on the LSAT that we can actually thematize the types of questions you could be asked. If you see questions of these particular forms, you can be confident that the correct answer will always relate to the issue of correlation.

Flaw Questions: "Flaw" questions require you to pick out the logical flaw that undergirds a particular argument. You will probably see quite a few of these. Since 2007, questions that asked the test-taker to "identify the flaw in the reasoning" have comprised no less than 10% of all Logical Reasoning test questions—and have comprised up to 20% of them. You will want to be able to pick out logical flaws in arguments, and to be able to know the difference between correlation and cause, because most of the correct answers in flawed-reasoning questions will represent the difficulty of associating correlation and cause. Answer choices which indicate that the argument, "infers a cause from a mere correlation" will be the correct answer for arguments that are based on reasoning that depends on correlation.

Assumption Questions: You'll see "assumptions" in two places on the LSAT: as a question, and as an answer choice. Answer choices will tell you that the argument, "assumes that a correlation between two ideas is evidence that one is the cause of the other." This just is the logical problem of correlations! So, if you know that the passage that you are working with sets up the problem of correlation, this will be your correct response. But, the most common place you will find assumptions on the exam is in the questions on the Logical Reasoning sections. They typically have the form, "The [interlocutor's] conclusion follows logically if which [answer choice] is assumed?" When you are asked this question of passages which rely upon correlation/causation reasoning, your correct response typically will present some substitute cause to the association provided by the text.

Strengthen Questions: For questions that confuse correlation and causation, a simple way to correct the logical error is to strengthen or improve the evidential link between the antecedent and the consequent. You can think of strengthening questions as ways to help the author prove his or her point. You can provide better justification, bring in more data, or address a potential criticism of the view espoused in the test. As with assumption questions, eliminating an alternative cause is a way to strengthen a correlation and causation argument. Another possible correct answer involves other examples that corroborate the causal relationship.

Weaken Questions: One way to weaken a correlation/causation question should be obvious: you show that the author confuses cause with correlation. And, you will be given this option frequently on the LSAT. The correct answer choice will provide you with an opportunity to evaluate the passage, rather than describe the passage. To weaken a correlation and causation argument, you want to show that you should look to do the opposite of what you would do in the strengthen context. So, you should look to establish, as opposed to eliminate, an alternative cause, or show that in another similar situation the correlation in the argument didn't hold up.

Correlation and Causation: Let's Practice!

Directions: Read the passages, and choose the answer choices that best answer the questions.

Questions 1-2

> **Sociologist:** The introduction of e-cigarettes has led to a precipitous increase in teen smoking. Recent surveys indicate that an estimated 16% of high school students vaped this school year, compared to 7% of high school students who smoked cigarettes. That adds up to 2.39 million teens. By comparison, just 1.37 million high school kids smoked cigarettes. What's more, vaping seems to encourage smoking, and possibly other drug use. This is true even for teens who weren't rebellious or risk-takers who would have seemed the least likely to start smoking.

1. Which of the following, if true, most strengthens the conclusion made by this passage?
   - A. Studies have shown that vaping in teens drastically reduces their ability to focus in school.
   - B. Whether a person ends up smoking cigarettes or using illicit drugs depends upon a series of factors, including whether a student has vaped.
   - C. Recent studies of those who have continued to vape in their 20s show they largely prefer vaping to tobacco cigarettes.
   - D. Teens who began vaping before high school have been shown to be dramatically more at risk to overdose on illicit drugs than those who vape later.
   - E. Teens whose friends do not vape are less likely to begin smoking or using illicit drugs.

2. The sociologist's argument is most vulnerable to which one of the following criticisms?
   - A. The argument relies on the testimony of experts who do not have sufficient experience to justify their view.
   - B. The argument confuses the cause of a future problem with an effective solution to that problem today.
   - C. The argument assumes that a correlation between two events is evidence that one event causes the other.
   - D. The argument infers that a behavior evidenced in one group of people will be a behavior that other groups will demonstrate.
   - E. The argument broadly infers a conclusion about a group based on data that does not accurately represent that group.

Questions 3-4

> There are strong reasons to want to get rid of the tenure system in higher education. Every time a university grants tenure to a professor, the university assumes some risk that the faculty member will abscond on his or her research, lose interest in being a vested teacher, and will refuse to take on committee assignments that all departments need in order to thrive. A main difficulty for universities is that there is no method to assess risk for any given professor—or indeed, for the professorate on the whole. The professional history of faculty is maintained and reported annually on each member's annual report, but there are no disincentives (apart from the paltry annual merit that some faculty might receive) to underperforming on these. The result is that universities risk a great unknown in tenuring their faculty, and in a landscape in which care for the student should be overriding, this is too great a risk to ignore.

3. Which one of the following uses flawed reasoning that most closely resembles the flawed reasoning used in the argument above?

   A. All athletes at the college level are superlative at their sport. But some athletes who are not at the college level are also superlative at their sport. Melanie sometimes demonstrates that she is a superlative athlete. Thus, Melanie sometimes is an athlete at the college level.

   B. All berries are antioxidants. All plums are not antioxidants. Ken has genetically engineered a "plumerry", a hybrid plum and berry. It has moderate antioxidant properties.

   C. All tables from Market World are solidly built. All tables from Souk Planet are aesthetically pleasing. The Sandovals purchased a table from Market World for the kitchen and a table from Souk Planet for the dining room. Hence, all of the Sandoval's furniture is solidly built and aesthetically pleasing.

   D. All logicians know modal logic. All ethicists know how to run trolley problems. Menzel is a modal logician who does ethics. So, Menzel knows modal logic and how to run trolley problems.

   E. All of Taylor's confections are made with chocolate. All of Brantley's confections are not made with chocolate. The truffles in this box are made with chocolate, and so half of them came from Taylor and half of them came from Brantley.

4. The author's conclusion follows logically if which one of the following is assumed?

   A. Tenure is risky and shouldn't be awarded because faculty do not care if they perform well after tenure.

   B. Tenure is risky and shouldn't be given out by universities as long as universities do not have a way of protecting themselves if faculty choose to become lazy.

   C. Universities should consider eliminating tenure if they feel at risk of professors who might take advantage of them and cannot protect themselves.

   D. Universities can lessen their risk of being taken advantage of by professors after tenure by incentivizing merit-based performance measures after tenure.

   E. Universities are not at risk for professors becoming lazy after tenure as long as they only award tenure to faculty who have strong performance in research, teaching, and service.

Notes:

Answer Explanations

1. The answer that you choose will be consistent with the conclusion, and provide further justification for it. To answer correctly, then, you will need to identify the conclusion. You do not have a tip-off, but it has to be "vaping seems to encourage smoking, and possibly other drug use". (The view the author presents, that this is true for teens who typically aren't rebellious or risk-takers, qualifies the author's conclusion.) The author's conclusion associates the rate of teen vaping with teen experimentation with cigarettes and drugs. High school students who vape seem to start smoking cigarettes (and perhaps use other drugs). The strength of the argument is in part an emotional appeal that the correlation brings—if it seems like students are encouraged to smoke and use drugs, then we don't want to encourage that trend. But, the author has not proven a causal link between the two.

The author doesn't have to prove a causal link between vaping and smoking and/or drug use, though, to succeed. S/he could strengthen the argument by strengthening the correlation between the antecedent and the consequent. Which answer option does this best?

Option (A), even if true, might provide you another reason not to like vaping (we want kids to do well in school, after all) but it doesn't strengthen the association between vaping and increased rates of smoking cigarettes or using drugs. It does not further justify the author's main point. (B) might be tempting—it does, after all, indicate that one of the reasons someone might end up smoking or using drugs is whether they vaped. But, it doesn't further justify why they would, or provide more evidence that the association between vaping and smoking and/or drug use is a strong one. It simply reiterates that there is a relationship between the antecedent and the consequent. For correlation passages in which you are asked by the question to make the answer stronger, make sure to ask yourself whether the answer option you are looking at moves the argument further along. If you are at the same place after the answer than before it, you haven't strengthened the argument!

Option (C) does not undermine the conclusion exactly. (If those in their 20s prefer to vape, the implication is that they have tried smoking but choose vaping over smoking for matters of preference.) But, the option certainly does not strengthen the conclusion made by the passage, either. In contrast, (D) is an excellent alternative. It strengthens the association between vaping and drug use by demonstrating that those who start vaping at the earliest moments have a documented higher rate of overdosing. (And, of course, to overdose, they need to use drugs.) Is it a perfect option? No. (D) is certainly defeasible. It could be the case, for example, that the reason children who vape are at greater risk of overdosing isn't that children who vape use drugs less than children who do not vape at all, but that they have higher rates overall of high-risk behavior, which includes taking an amount of drugs that could lead to overdose. But, we do not need a perfect answer option—we need a correct one. Thus far, given our answer options, (D) does strengthen the correlation the author makes. Let's look at (E). (E) provides a good reason for teens to have friends who make healthy choices, but does not strengthen the author's main conclusion that there is a relationship between vaping in high school and graduating to cigarettes or drugs later. (D), then, is our best option.

2. For this argument, you are identifying a weakness in the sociologist's argument. This is not the same thing as finding a flaw in the argument. If you find a flaw, you demonstrate how the sociologist's reasoning fails logically. But, with a weakness question, you want to undermine the sociologist's position by introducing some new aspect to the text. When the question asks you to identify which criticism the sociologist's argument is most vulnerable to, you are going to both raise an objection to the argument and show that there are reasons that the author has not considered that, when introduced, undermine the author's position.

Let's try that here. (A), that the argument relies on the testimony of experts who do not have sufficient experience to justify their view, cannot be supported by the text. A sociologist (who is already an expert on data) is giving us data about children who vape and smoke, and we do not have any evidence to suggest that the data that we are reading about comes from some measure of insufficient experience. So, eliminate (A). Option (B) has rhetorical force. But that is true in any instance in which someone says that an effective solution today might be a cause of a problem tomorrow. This is, essentially, an indefeasible claim because we cannot ever have enough knowledge to know whether it could be true. Answer choice (C) is salaciously tempting! You know that we are talking about logical problems with confusing correlations with causes, and certainly in this argument, the sociologist is indicating

that there is an association between early vaping and later cigarette and/or drug use in high school students. Let's hang onto this response and see if it is as strong as the two remaining answers. (D) seems also to be an excellent selection. The sociologist is contending that the risk-taking behaviors of children who vape end up eliciting risk-taking behaviors in high school students and adults. The ending up piece of this logically is important for us, because it reflects why we need (C) over (D). (C) is about the association of an antecedent to a consequent, whereas (D) would only work if there was that strong association. That makes (C) a better answer choice for us than (D). To confirm (C) as our answer, we compare it with (E), which does not relate to this passage at all, since the data about the children who end up smoking cigarettes is based on the same children who previously vaped. (C), then, is the criticism that this particular argument is most vulnerable to.

3.   For some unknown reason, LSAT students spend a disproportionate amount of time on the Logical Reasoning section on a single type of question: flaws over the correlation/causation issue. And this passage does indeed conflate a correlation with a cause. It argues that if you give a professor tenure, she or he will no longer be dedicated to, and effective in, research, teaching, and service. The cause of the terrible performance in faculty is that they received tenure. So, to correctly approach the logical reasoning in Question #3, you have an interesting job ahead of you—you don't just find the flaw, but you need to find another flawed argument in the answer choices whose flaw is the same kind of flaw as the one presented in the passage in Question #3! That means you need to really know the flaw in the reasoning presented to you in the passage. You know already that this argument irregularly draws a causal relationship between awarding someone tenure at a university, and that person refusing to do more work later. Given that you are not just identifying the flaw, you need to look at the framework the flaw operates under. Think about the passage in this way: there is a collection of faculty members who earn tenure and then do nothing. Since the university cannot perform general or specific risk assessments to predict which faculty might be at risk to be lazy after tenure, the whole tenured pot is poisoned, and we need to get rid of tenure altogether. Ok. Now that you have that framework in place, you can approach your answer choices to identify a correlative flaw.

Answer (A) is not an analogously-flawed argument. The argument in Question #3 takes the behavior of some and applies it uniformly to all within the relevant set (here, of tenured professors). In (A), the logical flaw is that it infers from a character trait that is sometimes evident in a single person, because when the trait occurs it matches the behavior of other people, that she sometimes *is* other people. That is a different kind of flaw of composition than this particular argument exhibits. How about (B)? Its reasoning is fallacious in a similar way to (A), because it takes two objects, summarizes that one separate entity is comprised of traits from both objects, and so concludes it also must be both objects. That reasoning does not follow. (Imagine that I take generic shampoo and put it in my empty name-brand travel shampoo container. It would not be logically valid to say that the shampoo in the bottle is both name-brand and generic, or even that it is a little-generic and a little name-brand.) Differently, the argument in (C) might be competitive as a correct answer, at least at first glance. It says that an entire set of objects has one property, an entire set of objects has a different property, and infers that a person who has one individual from each set will not just have individuals with properties from each particular set, but all of that person's objects will have characteristics from each particular set. (The Sandovals could have furniture from Trader Jane's, for example, which might neither be solidly built nor aesthetically pleasing.) So, the flaw in C is that it applies properties to objects that are not within the relevant set. (This is distinct from the flaw in the passage, which misapplies properties to members within a set.) (D) is different from all of these answers—it is actually valid! So you can't pick (D) as a correct answer, because it does not contain a logical flaw. (E), however, is where we find the appropriate, relevant match. It takes a single box of candy—a single set—and infers that because there are members of the set that share qualities with each of the two exemplars, all of this box contains individuals from those exemplars. But, we cannot make any attribution at all about what kinds of individuals are in this box. (It could have been made by Alenia, for all we know, and neither from Taylor nor Brantley). Similarly, the passage takes individuals and because they have properties (like, "being a tenured professor"), it infers membership in another set ("being lazy", for example) which is a misapplication. (E) is the correct response because it has the same form of logical flaw in the argument's reasoning.

4.   For questions that evidence faulty correlation-to-causation reasoning, you are very likely to see a question that either asks you to: 1) fix the argument by inserting an assumption; 2) identify an assumption that is made by the

author; 3) more generally, identify an assumption that the argument depends upon; or 4) more specifically, identify an assumption upon which the argument fails if it does not include. These questions require that you think about the argument fully as a logical device. There is something wildly wrong with the argument, and a piece of what is wrong is that its form does not work. To bolster its form, another premise would have to be included within the passage. You have to identify the gap in the logical reasoning, and your correct answer choice will fill in that logical reasoning gap.

It may be true, as we saw in Question #3, that there are other flaws within the reasoning. (This is especially true if the author makes an egregious logical leap between correlation and causation.) But it is also true that you are going to see these sorts of questions frequently, in every single section of the LSAT. To succeed, have a myopic focus on the logical structure of the argument given, and remember that you might not be able to make the argument's premises obtain. In Question #4, for example, your job cannot be to fix the argument in full. You can't fix the association problem between those who are tenured and lazy and other (non-lazy) members of the group. What you can do—and, indeed, what this question asks you to do—is to fix the logical structure of the argument.

The most efficient way to fix the logical structure (so, to make the argument valid), is to sketch the logical form of the argument and then find the answer choice that has the identical form that is required by the argument. Regardless of anything else that might be tempting you... do not read the answer choices until you find the argument! Let's try it. Step One is to identify the tip-offs:

There are strong reasons to want to get rid of the tenure system in higher education. Every time a university grants tenure to a professor, the university assumes some risk that the faculty member will abscond on his or her research, lose interest in being a vested teacher, and will refuse to take on committee assignments that all departments need in order to thrive. A main difficulty for universities is that there is no method to assess risk for any given professor—or indeed, for the professorate on the whole. The professional history of faculty is maintained and reported annually on each member's annual report, but there are no disincentives (apart from the paltry annual merit that some faculty might receive) to underperforming on these. The result is that universities risk a great unknown in tenuring their faculty, and in a landscape in which care for the student should be overriding, this is too great a risk to ignore.

Identifying tip-offs helps in this passage to identify the conclusion—it is actually in two different locations, the beginning and the end. The conclusion is that we should eliminate the tenure system in higher education. Now, we need to use our tip-offs to identify reasons the author gives for the conclusion. Here they are: All tenure awards run significant risks. No university can be protected from those risks. All professors are motivated to exploit those risks. So, we should eliminate tenure. We can formalize the argument as it currently stands this way:

    All As are Rs. (All awards are risky.)
    All Us are ~P. (All universities are not protected.)
    All S are M. (All professors are motivated.)
    ∴ ~A (Therefore, no awards.)

What is missing, logically? Right now, there is no connection between R and ~A (the risk of the award and the denial of the award.) We have a connection between R and A in premise #1. Think about conditionals that can tie these premises together. What is the author saying? The author is saying that if awards are risky and universities are not protected against risk, we should not award. The conditional is the assumption—it is what is required to make the argument valid. Consider this argument, with the conditional:

    If tenure awards are risky, and universities cannot inoculate themselves against the risk, tenure awards should not be given.
    Tenure awards are always risky because professors are motivated to exploit the system.
    Universities cannot protect themselves generally against the risk of professors exploiting the system.
    Therefore, we cannot award tenure.

Here, the conditional frames the premises that are explicit in the passage, but makes the argument valid:

(If (R • ~I), then ~A)
R
~I
∴ ~A

Excellent. With the inclusion of a conditional, the argument is valid. Now we need an answer choice that reflects the conditional. Which of the 5 have the proper form? Well, (A) doesn't provide you with the proper conditional (it essentially says "All A is R", just like the passage, and expands to "If R ⊃ ~A", which is insufficient, because our conditional needs the "R • ~I" conjunction to be valid.) (B) is perfect. As long as the syllogism is an "if" conditional: If universities can't protect themselves, ~I, and tenure is risky, R, then we shouldn't award, ~A, or (If (~I •R) ⊃ ~A). Bingo. Now, given that we are dealing with logical validity, rather than weighing other flaws of inference, you do not have to continue to evaluate answer choices. Unlike "find the best answer", whenever you are evaluating the form of an argument, you can only find one correct answer, and it is correct not because it is the best, but because it is the only answer that has the proper form. You should not spend time evaluating the other answer choices.

When we are practicing, however, it makes sense to at least practice breaking premises down so you can extract their logical form. And, in doing so, you will see that they also are invalid options for this particular passage. (Again, you should not waste time on the actual LSAT once you find the assumption that makes the argument valid. But, practicing here is not a waste of time when you are learning to apply logical form to an argument.) What does (C) look like, then? Pick out the conditional, "If risk, R, and can't protect, ~I, then...." Then, what? (C) looks almost identical to (B), and might be attractive on the facile level because it puts the "R" first. (Remember, though, in a conjunction it does not matter which conjunct comes first because they both have to occur in order for the consequent to happen.) Well, "considering eliminating tenure" is not the same as "eliminating tenure", logically. The former does not have an actional component to it—it is the equivalent of saying "think about it!". But, the passage, at both "bookend" positions, contends that tenure is something that should be eliminated, so (C) does not adequately, logically, reflect the conclusion of the passage, and so is not a valid option. (D) and (E) might have you look twice because they take on the fact of whether universities are at risk. (They both engage with whether "R" is true.) If you had not extracted the argument first, prior to looking at the answer choices, you might get drawn into the content, rather than the form of the argument, and believe that one of these options could be an assumption of the argument. (D) would logically be represented: (If M, ⊃ <R), or "if merit, then less risk". But, both M and <R are new logical terms within the argument and so cannot validly be included within it. Similarly, (E) has new terms represented, with the conditional as long as helping our translation "(If (A • P) ⊃ ~R)". (Here, the performance piece is the new logical term. We translate the "who have strong performance" as a conjunction, because they award on the basis of the performance.) Introducing new terms in the argument yields an invalid argument.

This exercise should only help you on your quest to effectively, efficiently work the flaw answers on the LSAT. Once you know you hit the logically *perfect* answer, you do not need to spend time continuing to work through those responses. Of course, practice gets you to perfect, so practicing here will help you identify those assumptions which fit perfectly with the originally invalid argument.

FLAWS AND FALLACIES
CHAPTER 3

Circular Arguments and the LSAT

It might be odd to think of "circular arguments" within the family of causal arguments, but there is a good reason to include them: they use the truth of the conclusion to cause an assertion of the truth of the conclusion! It can be difficult to adequately capture why circular arguments are incompatible with strong logic, if for no other reason than most people think they know what a "circular argument" means, but they cannot identify one on an exam. A circular argument uses the main point of something to prove the main point. For someone who is making a circular argument, they start with their main point, and end up supporting their main point with their main point.

The logical problem with circular reasoning, is that if you use it, you are trying to assert something that you are supposed to be proving is true. Let's imagine that you are having a theological conversation with your roommate. He says, "God has to be omnibenevolent because God is love." This line of reasoning might be emotionally convincing. Your roommate could even sweeten the pot by saying, "What other love is there but perfect love? And wherever there is perfect love, there is God." This is not an uncommon discussion to have, whether you are in college or have been out for years. But, the reasoning is fallacious. It grounds the conclusion that God is love on an attribute that God exhibits—whether perfect love or omnibenevolence. (Omnibenevolence is "all goodness", so that if a perfect being exists, it would contain all perfection. If love is a perfection, God must contain it. Note well, this argument for divine perfection is not circular; it's given to explain omnibenevolence in this example.)

One common example of circular reasoning that you might discover on the LSAT is using synonyms for words to create similar meaning. Take the following as an example of a popular argument about the soul's immortality (here, adapted from an argument Andrew Bailey provides):

Everything is either in a state of Being or in a state of Becoming.
Everything that is in a state of Being is immortal.
Socrates' soul is not in a state of Becoming.
Therefore, Socrates' soul is in a state of Being.
Therefore, Socrates' soul is immortal.

This argument is valid—so, no formal fallacy has been committed. But, as Bailey argues, premise 3 needs further reasons to be demonstrable. What reasons might Socrates give for not being in a state of Becoming? Well, he would give attributes for his characteristics that could only come from someone in a state of Being. But, Being in premise #2 has already been identified as immortal, so this argument is using Socrates's immortality to prove that he has an immortal soul. Now, before you try to rescue the argument by saying things like, "Well, to support the claim that the soul is immortal, we have to show that it cannot die" or, "the soul doesn't die", "the soul lives forever", "reincarnation is true", and "immaterial substance cannot be destroyed"...consider: all of these claims are just another way of saying that the soul is immortal. None of them can demonstrate *why* the soul could be immortal.

To sum up, circular arguments are *always wrong,* because you can't prove the truth of something by restating what you're trying to prove is true. On the LSAT, you are going to be on the lookout for evidence that is dressed up to look a little different than the idea that is being stated. It just might be a circular argument!

FLAWS AND FALLACIES
CHAPTER 3

Post hoc ergo propter hoc and the LSAT

Another logical fallacy that falls under the "causal fallacy" family for popular LSAT fallacies is *post hoc ergo propter hoc*, which literally means, "after this, therefore because of this". These are causal fallacies because they base the justification of the conclusion from the fact that the event in the conclusion happened after the fact that the antecedent occurred in the premise. That an event follows another in time leads to the conclusion that the first event caused the second, "B was caused by A *because* B occurred after A." For example,

> The high school's drop-out rate decreased this year because two years ago the school removed the requirement that students take foreign languages in order to graduate.

The dip in the school's drop-out rate occurred after the event in which the high school removed the requirement for students to take foreign languages. But, there may have been a plethora of other decisions that explain the decrease in the high school's drop-out rate. It might not be the case that whether students were required to take a foreign language relates to the drop-out rate *at all*. We simply do not have enough information to be able to make a sound inference from the evidence given.

Post hoc ergo propter hoc is not a logical fallacy in the same way as circular arguments and correlations are. They demonstrate that the author has not properly explored the association between two events. The difficulty might be a problem of epistemic laziness—someone just couldn't be bothered to explore the association closely enough. Or, they may not explain carefully the features of a case. But, you can pick out a post hoc ergo propter hoc because the justification for the conclusion is that one event *temporally* follows another. If it temporally follows, it is caused by the antecedent event... which is fallacious reasoning.

Division/composition Fallacies and the LSAT

The final causation fallacy that you will need to familiarize yourself with because it is common on the LSAT is the fallacy of division/composition. There are two forms of the fallacy, both forms of which are causal fallacies because they assert a causal relationship between the conclusion and the premises based on *the unity of the whole*. If something can be predicated of the whole, it can be predicated to the part because the part is... a part of the whole. Here are the two forms:

This is an instance of A.

∴ Every part of this is A.

Every part of this is A.

∴ This is an instance of A.

In the first form of the argument, the inference divides the whole into parts. This is fallacious because it might be the case that there are parts of A that are not an instance of A. A car is a fantastic example. Let's say you look at my car and say, "That's an amazing Rav4!" To which, I look at you approvingly, until you say, "Every part of that thing is an amazing Rav4!" Not every part of my Rav4 is a Rav4. In fact, only the Rav4 collectively is a Rav4. It is a collection of parts, not all of which are even Toyota parts but generic car parts. So, knowing that a particular instance of a vehicle is called a Rav4 does not make the parts of the car an instance of a Rav4.

In the second inference, a fallacy of composition, moves from the parts to the whole erroneously. The conclusion of the second form of the argument would not obtain if the parts individually did not work cooperatively to form an instance of an A. To use the Rav4 example, I can have a collection of genuine, Toyota Rav4 parts that are not assembled properly—imagine the wheels on top of the hood, the sunroof where the muffler goes, the seats attached to the engine block—in which case it would be improper to call the collection of parts "a Rav4".

For division/composition fallacies, the important thing to remember is that something could be predicated of parts of a thing without being predicated of the thing. (My eyesight could give out but that doesn't mean that my body has, even though my eyes are a part of the body.) Similarly, something could be predicated of a unity or whole of a thing without being predicated of the parts. To stick with the body example, my body could actually decease without individual organs perishing, which contributes to the efficacy of arguments for being an organ donor.

Division/composition fallacies on the LSAT questions can usually be identified by the following structures: "The

author assumes that if something is true of the whole, it is also true of each of the parts of the whole;" "The passage improperly infers that every instance of an entity possesses a trait, on the basis that many instances of an entity possess that trait;" or, "The text assumes, without providing justification, that what can be predicated of a whole must also be predicated on the parts that constitute the whole."

Consider the following prospective example, which you might find on the Logical Reasoning section:

> **Sports Journalist:** Critics who say minor league farm systems in baseball cannot grow talent—that talent is something players have when they are brought into the farm—would be ashamed of themselves, if they paid any attention at all to the way the Astros farm system works. Farm systems like that of the Astros cause regular players to become superstars. The major league club reflects the values of their minor league farm systems.

Which one of the following principles, if true, would most help to justify the sports journalist's argument?

A. If individual major league players reflect the values of the farm systems, their teams will succeed.
B. A major league team's relationship with their farm team is the best way to measure what the owners value.
C. The recent success of the Astros farm system ran counter to the predictions most sports analysts had for it.
D. Major league baseball teams with strong farm teams win more regular season games than major league teams that trade for good players.
E. The characteristics of a unit determine the properties of the things that constitute it.

Analysis: The sports journalist makes a claim that should not be unfamiliar to you, because it is prevalent with talking heads today: If you want to know what the final result will be with one group, look at the constituencies of that group and see to what extent they are succeeding. In this particular example, the conclusion is that the individuals in the minor leagues become superstars because of the structure of the major league team as a unit. Characteristics of the whole are reflected in the constitutive parts. The part/whole relationship is not evident in (A) or in (B). (C) is completely irrelevant. (D) does not as obviously employ a parts/whole relationship (although it does in the sense that D relates the numbers of wins to whether the unit has strong parts.) (E) has part/whole relationships, and matches the flawed reasoning of the sports journalist, whereas (D) does not utilize the same flaw.

Distraction Fallacies

Now that we've looked at the most common fallacies of causation on the LSAT, we are ready to tackle *Distraction Fallacies*. These occur when the conclusion is not related at all to the premises, and the testifier to the claims in the argument is suspect for some reason—so they distract the reader from the arguments by building something extra in that could be attacked. (As a parenthetical, if you've ever debated, you might be well-versed in distraction fallacies. If you can get your opponent to latch on to a "squirrel plank"—or, a completely disposable part of your argument that is salacious and provocative—you can enjoy watching him or her waste their time attacking a plank that you will happily give up to have the main premises of your argument sail unscathed through the debate.) As fallacies, we call the two main types of distraction fallacies ad hominem arguments and "red herring", or "straw man" arguments.

Ad Hominem "Against the Man" Arguments and the LSAT

The clearest way to think about ad hominem "against the man" arguments (those that attack the speaker or testifier) is to think of them as character assassinations. Instead of providing evidence that an argument is wrong, ad hominems attack the person who is giving the argument, or attacks the authority that the person who is giving the argument draws upon.

Especially in today's society, where ad hominem arguments are an everyday occurrence in politics, it can be easy to rely on ad hominems when developing our arguments, or—even worse for the person taking the LSAT—overlook them for what they are...logical fallacies. Consider the following recent exchange between two competing Senate candidates. Pay attention to the parting shot of one Senate candidate, when asked to compliment his opponent, (who complimented him), at the end of a televised debate:

Question: What do you admire about your opponent?

Opponent 1: I admire his sacrifice and love of country.

Opponent 2: I think he is absolutely sincere, like another politician, he sincerely believes in expanding government and higher taxes.

There is no doubt about the rhetorical force of an ad hominem. The idea is that the opponent presents you with the truth of a claim, but you believe the person giving it is an idiot, or immoral, and so could never be believed. The truth of what is being said then *relied upon a personal attack*, rather than on evidential claims provided by the author.

Ad hominems may appear to be attractive on the exam, as well. After all, if you can show that whomever provided the argument is biased, should be mistrusted, or is wrong in the beliefs that they hold, you might go far in convincing another person not to believe them. But, the source of the claim doesn't necessarily mean that the claim is wrong. (If you've heard the cliché "a broken clock is right twice a day", you'll know what I mean—sometimes even our opponents are right, and certainly, just because they espouse a position that is different does not make the position unjustified.) This is especially true on the Logical Reasoning of the LSAT, in which you will have to mediate between two interlocutors on "disagreement" questions, and suss out when logical fallacies like ad hominems are being employed.

EXPERT TIP

*The American Bar Association no longer requires schools to report the average LSAT score—now, schools just report the highest score. In *most* cases, you are at an advantage to take the exam **more than once** if you think you can improve your score by doing so!*

Why are ad hominem arguments *frequently wrong?* Because whether a statement is *true* does not depend on the person who is saying it—just like whether something is true doesn't come from whether *you* say it. Rather, whether something is *justified*—or, has good reason to support it—*does* frequently depend on who is reporting about it. Whether something is true comes from whether what's in the world matches what someone is saying. This just means that you need to exercise caution when you are identifying ad hominems, because it is true that we generally count people who have significant experience in an area as epistemic authorities, and we generally discount the view of someone who is not an expert—or who has proven he or she is untrustworthy in some domain. So, like most of our reasoning on the LSAT, we'll use context clues to ascertain whether a particular instance commits an ad hominem fallacy, or rather is a justification for believing someone's testimony. Who an agent is, and whether she or he is reliable, can be important considerations when you are making that determination. Imagine that you have the following passage on the LSAT:

> *Lucy contends that I should invest in an in-ground swimming pool in my house in Rapid City, SD, even though it sometimes snows 10 months out of the year. She owns the pool company and lives in Phoenix, so I shouldn't build the pool.*

In relationship to whether I should spend the money ("invest") to build a pool in Rapid City, there are some contextually-dependent reasons I need to consider. The first, of course, is that it sometimes snows 10 months out of

FLAWS AND FALLACIES
CHAPTER 3

the year in Rapid City. (So, presumably, I wouldn't be able to use the pool as often as I would probably like to, and there may be additional maintenance costs associated with an in-ground pool being built in a wintry location.) But, another feature of this case is whether I can trust Lucy. Here, the case is not so clear. Lucy owns the pool company (and so, has a fiduciary interest in whether I spend the money to build the pool), but the case casts some shade onto whether Lucy can be trusted as *an epistemic source. Why not?* She lives in Phoenix. Now, the case doesn't tell us whether she spends time in Rapid City or grew up there or whether she knows what it would be like to have an in-ground pool in an area that experiences lots of winter. It tells us instead that I shouldn't build the pool because she seems to not be a good epistemic source.

That distrust is grounded on an attack against Lucy, but we don't know enough to know whether it is an unjustified attack. Certainly, the conclusion "I shouldn't build the pool" seems unjustified because of the attack against Lucy—at least, it does not seem strongly justified. If the question you get from the LSAT is:

1. If true, which one of the following statements most seriously weakens the author's conclusion?

you would want to make sure you hone in on an answer that dissuades the author from using ad hominem-like reasons (or, that evidentially shows Rapid City to be an amazing place to build an in-ground swimming pool, which would also cast doubt on the truth of Lucy's testimony). Correlatively, if you have a question on this passage such that:

2. If true, which one of the following statements most clearly strengthens the author's conclusion?

then you can focus on answer choices that further show that Lucy is not a good source of information about why I should buy the pool.

There is one more tool—a logical tool, actually—that you can employ to discover whether the argument you are reading employs a fallacious ad hominem. Arguments which use emotional content about the expert, or other non-rational features, to conclude that an argument must be rejected should be suspect. But, arguments which could be inductively strong would have the following form:

Premise:	Person A believes X.
Premise:	But, to believe X, A would have to rely on incomplete, inaccurate, and/or biased information.
Conclusion:	It is improper for A to believe X.

Let's apply this format to the following argument:

Claire believes that unwed mothers that come through her medical clinic are promiscuous and she gives them medical information about STDs that she does not provide to wed mothers. Claire's belief about unwed mothers is unduly biased, because it assumes without evidence that unwed mothers are promiscuous and that wed mothers are not. Therefore, Claire shouldn't believe that unwed mothers are promiscuous.

This argument is properly formatted because it faults Claire for a belief that she has that is not justified because it is unduly biased. She believes that unwed mothers are promiscuous, but she shouldn't because there isn't evidence for her belief.

Red Herring & Straw Man Arguments and the LSAT

Red herrings are beautiful, attention grabbing, and hard to look away from, in everyday life. In everyday English conversation, red herrings are ridiculous claims that people make to distract you from the main idea. What makes the red herring fish beautiful, attention grabbing, and hard to look away from in everyday life is the *exact* thing that makes red herrings beautiful, attention grabbing, and hard to look away from in conversation and arguments. The red herring is so distracting, you feel compelled to focus on it.

You have no doubt met folks who are masters at the distracting fallacy of the red herring. Hopefully you don't have a roommate that tries the red herring to get out of paying the rent, but we can imagine such a case. When you ask him if he's paid the rent, he might blurt out, as a response, "What does it matter if I did or not? Nothing I ever do makes you happy!" Now...apart from needing a new roommate... you should be thinking:

"RED HERRING!" What your roommate is trying to do is to distract you with something completely irrelevant so that you will focus on the ridiculous at the expense of the meaningful. The main point of your question is, of course, to figure out whether you're going to get evicted, and whether it's in fact true that nothing he ever does makes you happy, that point is completely irrelevant—it is a distraction—from the issue as to whether you are going to have difficulties with the landlord this month.

Red herrings are distracting, but what makes them logical fallacies? Red herrings never focus on the reasoning, evidence, or truth of the passages that you will be engaging with on the LSAT. A key to solving the riddle of red herrings is to remember that the red herring fallacy is fundamentally *not* about whether the conclusion is tied importantly to the premises (it won't be, because it is an informal fallacy) but instead the uniqueness of this fallacy is that it makes the conclusion completely irrelevant to the premises. It will not even matter if the conclusion is true—its content is disconnected from the content of the premises.

Straw Man Arguments: A form of the red herring arguments is the "straw man" argument, whose success as a convincing argument depends upon it being a very attractive, flashy distraction from the substance of the issue being discussed. Whereas red herring arguments in general can be criticized for being weak inferences, straw mans specifically sound like good arguments, and they can even convince people of their truth. Here's an example of a red herring, followed by a straw man variety:

Topic: Should the US start a trade war with China?

Red Herring
Politician: People love me! I'm a great businessman, so if I tinker with the trade policies, it's because I know business. People love me because I love business. People love our tax cuts, businesses love our tax cuts, because they love keeping their paychecks.

Straw Man
Politician: China is the leading depreciator of US currency in the world. Our pro-import policies with China are hurting our domestic enterprises. We need to evaluate our trade policies from top-to-bottom.

Not surprisingly (since we are talking about logical fallacies, after all), both of these arguments are bad arguments. And, they are related in their badness in that they both seek to distract the interlocutor from the main issue at hand, which is whether the US should start a trade war with China. In neither instance do we receive an answer to the topic's question. But, there are differences between the two. The red herring's complete content is off-topic, and the conclusion is about the popularity of the politician rather than relating to the question. (The words "trade war" and "China" are absent completely in the red herring case.) It may or may not be persuasive as a response to the topic, but if it is persuasive, it is because the person being persuaded does not require the content of a claim to be tied to the topic at hand. The straw man variety of the red herring, on the other hand, may be compelling because it invokes the issue raised by the question, and relies on jargon—but the purpose is to distract from answering the question. The straw man politician does not address whether we should have a trade war. Instead, the politician provides three statements, each of which are disconnected logically from the other. (Whether China is a leading depreciator of US currency is completely disentangled from whether our import policies hurt American businesses, and neither of those

independently or corporately lead to the conclusion that our trade policies should be evaluated.) And, of course, the conclusion about reevaluating trade policies does not relate to the issue of a trade war at all.

The straw man succeeds by distracting the reader or listener by distorting the issue at hand, whereas the red herring distracts by being irrelevant. It is more difficult to critique a straw man on the LSAT because the text that includes the argument may appropriate technical terms or a pseudo-logical structure to make it difficult to refute the argument.

I mentioned the "squirrel plank" tactic in debate at the beginning of the chapter. A version of a straw man that is similar to the squirrel plank occurs when there are at least two positions being presented, and one version of the argument is misrepresented. The fallacy creates a fake plank (the misrepresented view) to attack in order to create the perception that the argument has been successfully defeated—though what has been defeated is the "scarecrow" or "squirrel plank" of the argument. The straw man is a false representation of what the argument is so that the argument seems weaker than it actually is.

We see this type of straw man argument throughout political rhetoric today. Consider the two opposing views on proposed gun control regulations:

> Politician A: We should place restrictions on access to military-grade assault rifles on individuals who are former felons or have certain documented mental health problems.

> Politician B: Politician A wants to take away your 2nd Amendment rights and have you live in an America where the only people who have access to self-protection offered by guns are gang-bangers and potential rapists.

The first politician raises the possibility that most voting citizens are in favor of in the form of some narrow restrictions on who can have access to a certain kind of weapon. The second politician misrepresents the first politician's view by suggesting that A wants to eliminate 2nd Amendment rights. Rather than engaging with the content of A's suggestion, B creates another (straw) argument and beats up on that instead.

Red herrings and straw man fallacies are distraction fallacies that will appear consistently throughout the LSAT. When you run into them (either as correct or incorrect answer options), they frequently will have the following form: "the argument depicts the views of opponents as more extreme than they actually are"; "Interlocutor #2 rephrases the opposing viewpoint to make it more vulnerable to criticism"; "Agent B distorts the argument presented by advocates of the position"; and "Debater #2 misrepresents Debater #1's position so that she can refute it more easily".

Consider the following example, which is suitable for an appearance on the Logical Reasoning section:

> **Lobbyist for the National Endowment for the Humanities:** I'm asking you to help encourage Congress to pass the funding bill which sustains 1% growth at the NEH for P-20 initiatives in schools at all levels across the entire country.
>
> **Opponent:** How can the NEH ask for federal funds? To fund the NEH is to take away money from grant opportunities in the sciences and engineering, not to mention the military, and those are the cornerstone of our future economy, national security, and research innovation. Have you ever tried to eat a poem? Have you ever tried to breathe a cross-cultural analysis of women superheroes? Funding the NEH is akin to telling our children to eat poetry and breath stories.

Question: The Opponent's reasoning is flawed because it:
  A. misrepresents the Lobbyist's position in order to make it easier to refute.
  B. presupposes a slippery slope of consequences that may not occur if the Lobbyist receives what s/he is looking for
  C. confuses evidence for an argument with emotional content
  D. relies on emotion for the success of the argument
  E. fails to consider that the Lobbyist's argument is aimed to benefit research development

Analysis: This is an strong set of potential answers, and the LSAT likes to provide the verbal stems as a framework to rest answer choices upon. Don't let the framework distract you from finding the correct answer! Here, we are looking for a flaw in the opponent's reasoning. Before reading the answer choices, you should be able to peg this as a straw man argument. The Opponent does not correctly represent the Lobbyist's argument, and instead takes it in an irrelevant direction (and uses fear tactics to make you think that the Lobbyist's position would lead to a world where ideas were breath and food, which is clearly a hyperbolic deception to distract away from the Lobbyist's main point). So, you are looking for an answer choice that reflects that deception. (A) clearly fits the bill. (B) could be tempting, if the main flaw for the Opponent was that s/he was concluding that we would have to eat fiction if the NEH had its way. (Of course, that is subterfuge to the bigger purpose of distracting.) And, although the Opponent uses emotion, neither (C) nor (D) are specific enough to be the correct flaw. (E) is not incorrect as a factual statement. A justificatory function of the Lobbyist's argument is that it will increase research, but (E) does not reflect the logical flaw made by the Opponent. (A) is the best answer choice.

Now that you have a good exposure to *Distraction Fallacies*, you are ready to dive into the last sort of fallacies found on the LSAT, *crowd fallacies*. Crowd fallacies are those in which the conclusion is not related to the premises, except in virtue of some relationship to the views of the crowd—whether a group looks at the conclusion in a particular way, an authority expresses an opinion on the conclusion, there is ignorance of the conclusion, there is fear of what would happen if the conclusion was true, or if emotion was used to engage with the conclusion.

Crowd Fallacies

Appeals to Emotion Fallacies and the LSAT

Appeals to emotion work in a similar way as ad hominem and, sometimes, red herrings. They are persuasive because they have an attractiveness that is not rooted in logic. Attacking an argument from a position of emotion distracts similarly so that the reader does not engage with the logical content of an argument. Appeals to emotion require that the *evaluative content*—what makes the argument a good argument—of an argument depends upon the interlocutor's ability to play on another person's emotions. But, logic indicates that a proposition's ability to make us feel a certain way doesn't produce a justified reason to believe the proposition is true.

Since the LSAT's correct answers will be based in evidence, rather than on emotion, you can be sure that the writers of the exam will throw some non-evidenced-based answers your way in the form of arguments from emotion! Arguments from emotion usually come in three steps:

STEP ONE:	This thing is true! (a declaration of fact)
STEP TWO:	Because this thing is true, you should feel a certain way about it! (a call to your emotions)
STEP THREE:	Do what you can to make sure #1 happens or doesn't happen (a call to action, depending on whether the emotion is positive or negative)

Let's try out an example:

STEP ONE:	The city should ban plastic bags! (a declaration of fact)
STEP TWO:	Plastic bags that aren't recycled are ugly and are a horrific blight on our city. Imagine what tourists must think when they come to town and see plastic bags in ditches or in a tree!
STEP THREE:	Make sure to call your City Council rep and demand that we ban plastic bags!

This argument seems persuasive—plastic bags that aren't recycled are ugly if they are littered. But, *the reason the argument uses to persuade* is emotion: "imagine"... just use your imagination at the disgust tourists must feel when they see a plastic bag littered in the city! (The "horrific blight" usage is entirely an appeal to the emotion of disgust.) The argument doesn't show why banning plastic bags would mean people wouldn't litter. Rather, it relies on emotional language to compel you to call your City Council rep to "demand" an end to plastic bags.

The reason arguments from emotion tend to work is that we have strong negative emotions about things that cause harm, and usually powerful positive emotions about things that benefit us. You will see arguments from emotion on the LSAT, and in the passages of the LR and RC sections, you will find them shrouded in emotional content, especially when they hide in answer choices that use *value words*, like: unbelievable, very, really, awesome, horrible, fantastic, horrific, bad, interesting, or fun. The answer choices will typically help you identify those errors by using the following frameworks: "the argument is flawed because it relies on an appeal to emotion rather than on evidence or reason;" or "the author attempts to persuade by appealing to emotion, rather than to logic and fact".

Don't forget, when you evaluate arguments that make the emotional appeal fallacy: it is insufficient to fault a passage for making an appeal to emotion just in virtue of whether the author discusses or expresses emotions within the passage. The logical fallacy is when the author's conclusion is justified on the basis of emotion instead of evidence, facts, data, or reason. Make sure to take caution when you see the answer option that allows you to pick out an emotional appeal that the conclusion is grounded in a fallacious appeal to emotion.

EXPERT TIP

Most test prep companies say that the Reading Comprehension section is the most difficult to improve upon. **(That's because they don't view the RC as a logic test!)**

Appeals to Authority Fallacies and the LSAT

In arguments from authority, the claim's truth or falsity is directly based on the source of the testifier—where the claim originates determines whether the claim is true. If we value the source of the idea, we'll be more likely to think the idea is true. If we don't think the source of the idea is good, we'll think it is false.

Here's an example:

"Brazil's most famous soccer coach visited our team to talk about soccer in the future. He explained that, although there might be a risk of concussion in playing soccer, such a small number of concussions occur when compared to the rate of touches players come in contact with the ball, that changes to the game itself are not necessary to reduce head injury. We only need to change how we coach players who go up for headers. So, I make sure to encourage my team to be smart with their heads, and use a header only when it is most important in the game."

The difficult aspect about appeals to authority is that one test for whether an argument is sound is whether it comes from a reliable epistemic source—and authorities tend to be reliable sources! There are, then, many proper appeals to authority, and it can be confusing to differentiate between proper and improper appeals, but the LSAT will frequently require you to do so. *Proper* appeals to authority are those in which the entirety of the justification for a claim is grounded in something *additional* to the authority of the testifier. The testifier will be an expert (specifically on the topic at hand), but other evidence can be given, such as data sets, experiential evidence, agreement with other experts in that field, or first-hand testimony. **The logical difficulty with improper appeals to authority is that the sole justificatory force of the argument—the reason you believe it is true—is that it comes from an authority, and it is not always true that authorities are right on their subjects, or that they can speak authoritatively to a given subject.**

In the above example, the world-famous soccer coach is not an expert on concussions, yet he is speaking with authority on the subject of head injuries based on his own experiences coaching soccer. He doesn't provide data to support his claims (even though he brings up an item that *looks like* a data point, that the ratio between

concussions to ball-touches is low). Although his ancillary view, that we can coach differently, can be seen as authoritative when the topic at hand is soccer coaching, his main conclusion is that we do not need to change the game of soccer to reduce the rate of head injuries. Unfortunately, his authority as a soccer coach just won't be enough to justify that conclusion.

Thankfully—the LSAT is a logic test, and you can actually use logic to help you assess whether appeals to authority are proper! Consider the following example:

> Ron has been working on cars for 40 years, and served in the Air Force as an auto and airplane mechanic. He also happens to be an honest guy. When he told me my transmission was going out on my car before it hit 100,000 miles, I was a little surprised, but I also knew a common complaint with my brand of car was that the transmissions tended to be a little weak. I'm taking it to Ron to be fixed.

The conclusion this author makes, that s/he will take the car to Ron for a transmission fix, is based on Ron's testimony as an expert mechanic. But, it is bolstered by other testimony (here, that the buyer knew that this particular brand of car was susceptible to the problem that this car is actually having). We can use a logical test to see if the appeal to authority is proper:

Premise:	Expert A says X about topic Y.
Premise:	Expert A is an expert about topic Y.
Premise:	There is additional support for A's view about X.
Conclusion:	There is evidence that X is true.

In the mechanic example, the author's argument is *properly justified*—the conclusion that the car needs a new transmission is rooted not just in the fact that Ron is an expert about cars. Rather, there is additional support for his claims, both that he is honest and that this problem plagued cars of this type. Of course, the more evidence you have for your argument, the more strongly justified your claim is, despite the fact that the conclusion of experts is never indefeasible. (We might discover centuries from now that those authorities were wrong, but as an inductive claim, the stronger the pool of experts, the stronger the inductive force of the argument.) Correlatively, if the third premise, here, is *mixed* (so that there is some evidence to support the conclusion and other evidence to reject A's view on X) the inductive claim is weakened and doubt about the conclusion might be cast altogether, depending on the type of evidence and the source of disagreement.

Slippery Slope

Slippery slopes are in the "crowd" category in part because they are frequently used by appealing to the sentiments of a group for their efficacy. The term "slippery slope" is a common one. The slippery slope is a fallacy because it argues that one event, which on its own seems pretty innocuous, will generate a series of consequences, the end of which is far worse than the first event could produce on its own. If we don't want those terrible consequences, we should not allow the initial event or action. Here's an example:

> If we allow children to stay seated for the pledge of allegiance, we communicate the message that loyalty and respect for our country are not important. We have already seen the deleterious impact of criminals in our community who do not have loyalty or respect for others. There is a pervasive moral decline in our country, and its initial cause is a lack of respect for God, country, and others that starts in school, and then leads to an increase in hate and crime outside when they become adults. This lack of respect eats away at the social fabric that binds us together, and before we know it, we will not have shared values. We need to require students to stand for the pledge of allegiance before that happens.

This example does not provide evidence that allowing children to stay seated for the pledge actually leads to the erosion of shared values in the US. Rather, it suggests a "slope" that we will slide down if we allow the initial act.

FLAWS AND FALLACIES
CHAPTER 3

Slippery slopes turn one event, whose consequences could be minimal or even, debatable, and translates them into a significant event without providing justification for the significance of the event. In passages, you can identify when you are hitting a slippery slope within the argument if you can connect events within the passage with the colloquial English phrase, "the next thing you know…". (In our example, you could say, "Let children sit for the pledge today—the next thing you know, our social fabric will be eaten away and we won't have shared values!")

The persuasiveness of the slippery slope is that it appeals to some *sensus communis,* or common sense, that is appealing. "Just think about it!" is a common finale to a slippery slope argument. If you just think about it, the suggestion is, the slope will make sense. The fallacy of slippery slopes is not that there is a correlation between one event and another. (We know that from our correlations discussions.) Instead, what makes the slippery slope sound right is that the consequences from the first event seem plausible. If the author can convince you that an aggregate of consequences could ensue if the first event happens, you are likely to be convinced that the first event should not occur. Inquiring into effects isn't a logical mistake, of course, but relying without evidence on an untested series of consequences indicates faulty logical reasoning.

Where We Go from Here

You are now fully ready to apply the logical skills that we have honed, specific to LSAT success, to LSAT sections. You have learned forms of validity, tests for soundness and strength of arguments, and evaluated the varieties of logical flaws that you are likely to see on the LSAT. You are able to distinguish between formal fallacies and informal flaws, and are ready to criticize, improve upon, or invalidate arguments that may appear on your LSAT exam. To do this well, we will practice well. The next three chapters, then, will help you apply these specific logical tools to the three sections on the LSAT. Enjoy!

CHAPTER IV | READING COMPREHENSION SECTION

READING COMPREHENSION SECTION
CHAPTER 4

You've gotten through your high school and college career and are thinking about a life dedicated to the law... which means you are not only good at reading, but you enjoy it. (If neither one of these things are true, you should reflect on whether a life dedicated to the law really is your calling, given that a large percentage of practicing law is reading through large amounts of tedious documents, and writing your own briefs to reflect your knowledge of what you have read.)

Despite your desire and acuity at reading, you may believe that the LSAT Reading Comprehension section should be approached like any other long passage—read all the words very carefully and then reread sections that you might not have grasped fully the first time for clarity and understanding.

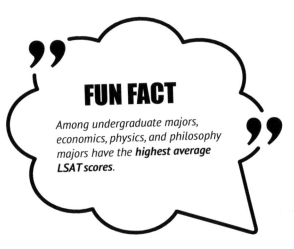

FUN FACT

*Among undergraduate majors, economics, physics, and philosophy majors have the **highest average LSAT scores**.*

WRONG! The LSAT is not a Cooper novel, or a cummings poem, to be lingered over and digested carefully. *Careful* reading is not even required to do well on the Reading Comprehension section! Rather, *attentive reading* is the standard. In what follows, I am going to give you a *new way to read.*

You have already learned that the LSAT is a logic test, rather than anything else. The same holds true for the Reading Comprehension section. The LSAC writers know that you know how to read. So, the RC section is not a section that tests your grade-level reading ability.

If the RC is testing logic and not reading ability, you might wonder why the passages are so long. Think about it this way—if the RC is really a logic section, and you know that logic fundamentally deals with the structure of arguments, then the writers of the LSAT do not need to care about the content of the passages. They care about hooking you into the idea that you have to read for content (for information) in order to understand what they have written. The RC texts all do this to some degree or another by way of the sort of technical subjects from which they borrow. (All of the RC passages will involve jargon-laden writing from across the sciences, business, social science, engineering, and—occasionally- humanities.) The questions themselves will revolve either around key words, the function of the passage (why is it that the author wrote this, apart from torturing you?), numerical values, arguments from authority, Latin or Greek words, or competing viewpoints. They may feature two interlocutors that are having a debate. They may quote from a discipline-specific text that will try to discourage you with words of art that you will not be familiar with. They may instead be a historical narrative of some culture, traditions, people, or even, a specific person. Or, they could delineate some breakthrough that has occurred at some point, which may either create new avenues for exploration or new ethical dilemmas to be solved by the LSAT test taker. Since all of the passages include some of these features, the LSAT writers know that they can get you to take a long time to read.

There are between 4500 and 8000 words in an RC section total. College students on average read 400 words per minute, and these passages are technical. So if you are the average student, you are going to need a minimum of 20 minutes just to read the section, which leaves 15 minutes to answer the questions. The LSAT isn't a math test, but... do the math! The LSAT folks are happy to see you try to read all of these passages, but it makes sense instead to use a technique that helps translate the RC section from a long trek through rich paragraphs which you will barely finish—if you're lucky—to a logic test that is easily digestible.

Insider Info: The Reading Comprehension Section is a Logic Test

So.... What? Why does it make a difference that the RC is a logic, rather than a reading, test? The differences are many: a logic test will ask you questions about logical premises, conclusions, assumptions, inferences, and criticisms, and a reading test will ask you about the meaning of a passage. A logic test will require you to only know

what the logical form of a passage represents and connotes, so that you can determine the scope of inferences that could be made by that argument—a reading test will ask you to think about the content of the reading. A logic test will not bother with whether the point of view of the writer is a physician, a lawyer, a novelist, or a scholar, but a reading test would find those points of view to be valuable. Finally, a logic test *will not require you to read the entire passage*, because it requires attentive reading, whereas a reading test mandates that you read and reread passages for comprehension.

There is that word again—*comprehension*—which may make you think that you indeed do have to read and reread pages-long LSAT passages. But, you don't. Whereas Cooper and cummings must be mulled over to be appreciated and understood, since you are interacting with a logic test, rather than a piece of literature, your point of departure is to *read for argumentation*. You are not reading even to understand everything that is being said. You *do not need to know* everything that is being said in the passage to ace the RC section. You *only need to know the answers to the questions*. What type of questions do you end up with on the RC section? Logic questions! Since logic questions are always about the validity, soundness, and implications of arguments, you need to change what you think you know about reading and *read for argumentation*.

As an important aside, the technique that I am going to teach you to *read for argumentation* is applicable in any discipline in which you are reading for arguments rather than literary content. It may seem counterintuitive that you will not be reading in the same way—top to bottom, left to right—as you have read for your entire life. But, my method does two things: 1) it decreases the amount of time you have to spend reading and 2) it *increases* your comprehension. This isn't to say that my method is a lightning-in-a-bottle approach. Rather, like all good skills (you know, like logic and acing LSAT exams), you get better at it with practice. You should see results pretty quickly. So, try this method on any non-literary sort of writing and see how you do.

Insider Insights: RAG *(Reading for ArGumentation)* Technique

I'm going to list the RAG technique for reading on the LSAT and then will break down each component for you to digest.

> ### RAG for LSAT
> **Pre-screen: read each RC question (but not their answers)**
> 1. Read the first and last sentence of the first paragraph.
> 2. Summarize in your own words (write down key phrase).
> 3. Read the first and last sentence of the final paragraph.
> 4. Summarize in your own words (write down key phrase).
> 5. Read the first sentence of every paragraph in-between the first and last paragraphs.
> 6. Summarize in your own words (write down key phrase).
> 7. Read the passage, if necessary.

These are the 6 essential steps (step 7 is to be employed only if necessary). Know them, live them, love them! They will save you time and help you hone in on the correct answer quickly.

Now, for an explanation of the method. Your "pre-screen" is something that *is unique to the RC section of the LSAT!* In other sections, you will not read the questions prior to looking at a corresponding passage. But, the RC is different. It is designed to get you to spend a ton of time reading content that you will never need to successfully complete the section! So, your job is to outwork the LSAC writers by doing less, more focused work. In the RC section, that means getting to know what questions are being asked of you prior to reading the passage. To illustrate this (and the other steps), I'm going to present a reading passage from the ArgoPrep first practice exam, along with correlative questions for the RC section, and you will see what I mean:

READING COMPREHENSION SECTION
CHAPTER 4

Passage for questions 21 through 27

The following passage is modified from a recent academic article on the habitat selection of wintering lemmings.

Some small mammal populations are famous for their phenomenal cyclic fluctuations in abundance. Small mammal species with a wide geographic distribution tend to exhibit more pronounced population cycles at northern latitudes where seasonality is strongest. During the cold and dark Arctic winter, small mammals may spend up to 9 months of the year under the snow. Winter remains the least known period of their annual cycle, yet this period may play a key role in their population dynamics. At northern latitudes, snow cover dramatically changes the structure and functioning of ecosystems in winter. Temperature gradients within the snow result in the formation of a stratum of fragile and loosely arranged snow crystals near the ground, which creates a subnivean space, the primary wintering habitat of small mammals.

Their survival is dependent upon accessibility to food and the protection against harsh temperatures and predators offered by this particular environment. Freeze–thaw cycles induced by warm winter temperature disturb the subnivean space and may lead to the formation of ice at ground level, which prevents rodents from feeding on the vegetation. Small mammals require a high rate of food intake because of their low digestive efficiency and high metabolic rate increased by cold. Therefore, limited accessibility or depletion of winter food may induce a deterioration of their physiological condition and increase mortality. Winter reproduction under the snow occurs in some species of small mammals and is especially common in lemmings. In fact, successful reproduction under the snow is often considered a necessary condition for the occurrence of a peak in abundance in cyclic lemming populations. The early onset of a thick and dry snow cover combined with the absence of freezing rain and days with above zero temperatures should favor survival and reproduction.

Recent evidence suggests that population cycles of small mammals of the tundra may be fading out in some areas, especially in Fennoscandia. Increased frequencies of freeze–thaw cycles during the winter due to climate warming and their influence on snow conditions have been invoked as a possible cause for the dampening of these. Alterations in snow cover may also affect winter predator–prey interactions. Even if subnivean specialist predators, such as stoats and weasels, should continue to be efficient predators during winter, thick snow cover may reduce the success of other predators of small mammals, such as arctic foxes or snowy owls. There is increasing evidence that the winter dynamics of these populations may be dominated by the effect of stochastic climatic events on snow conditions.

Previous studies suggested that freezing rain and frost/thaw events should reduce small mammal winter survival both directly and indirectly. Directly, such climatic events reduce the thermal protection offered by snow cover, fragment the subnivean space through the formation of an ice crust, and can induce water flooding. These phenomena may greatly reduce the probability of individuals surviving the entire winter by increasing thermal stress and reducing food availability, and possibly by the drowning of animals during floods. Indirectly, mild weather during the winter may reduce the protection offered by snow cover against some generalist predators, such as arctic foxes and increase the competition among predators for lemmings during the winter. Therefore, alterations of winter climatic conditions brought by the current global warming could reduce small mammal winter survival and destabilize their cyclic population dynamics, which would affect the whole tundra ecosystem.

21. The primary purpose of the passage is to

A. explain how the lemming reproduces given the conditions of a changing tundra ecosystem

B. present some recent scientific research on why the population of Fennoscandian mammals is falling

C. present the author's scientific contributions to research about the relationship of climate change to the population patterns of lemmings

D. assess the value of previous studies on the relationship between cold weather events and small mammal winter populations

E. describe two different views on subnivean space and predator/prey populations

22. Which one of the following statements best expresses the main idea of the passage?

A. Subnivean specialists have established that predator populations are unaffected by the depth of snow cover, but the populations of the lemmings are.

B. Subnivean specialists have established that thermal protection offered by deep snow drifts will lead lemmings to leave relatively flat, wet tundra.

C. Subnivean scientists have established that snow depth is fairly important in explaining the winter habitat selection of brown lemmings particularly.

D. Subnivean scientists have concluded that climate change is the leading direct and indirect factor on small mammal winter populations in Arctic ecosystems.

E. Subniviean scientists have concluded that the predation of lemmings is directly correlated to overwinter ground temperature.

23. Which of the following statements, if added to the passage, would bolster the author's claim that snow cover dramatically impacts the structure and functioning of ecosystems in winter?

A. During the cold and dark Arctic winter, small mammals may spend up to 9 months of the year under the snow.

B. Temperature gradients within the snow result in a subnivean space by forming a stratum of fragile and loosely arranged snow crystals near the ground.

C. Small mammal species with a wide geographic distribution tend to exhibit more pronounced population cycles at northern latitudes where seasonality is strongest.

D. The cold, wet Arctic habitat is characterized by polygon tundra, that forms wet meadows, fens, and a mesic habitat.

E. The probability of encountering lemming nests increases with increasing heterogeneity of the microtopography, slope of the terrain, and non-linear landscape level.

24. Which of the following strategies is most similar to the author's research strategy as it is described in the passage?

A. to determine the mating habits of lemmings, a biologist enters the ecosystem of the mammal to test temperature settings each day of winter

B. to determine whether certain mammals reproduce under certain weather conditions, a biologist measures the weather conditions

C. to determine whether the populations of predators and prey depend on ecosystem climate conditions, biologists manipulate the climate conditions and measure the mammal populations

D. to determine the relationship between climate change and reproduction behavior of mammals, biologists sampled winter nesting sites and measured temperature and precipitation variability on those sites

E. to determine the probability of encountering lemming nests in snow-covered areas, biologists identified subnivean spaces by a relatively low abundance of lichen cover

25. It can be inferred from the passage that Arctic stochastic climatic events of the sort that would impact lemming populations would include which of the following?
    A. Arctic drought, which limits the formation of subnivean spaces for lemmings to nest
    B. periods of heavy rain, which can flood subnivean spaces and reduce species diversity
    C. aboveground biomass erosion, which causes species-specific reproductive loss for mammals that nest in the Arctic tundra
    D. Arctic warming, which can fluctuate the freeze-thaw cycle of the Arctic biomes, and interrupt the ability of mammals to nest
    E. a subduction zone shift in the Atlantic Ocean, which causes the rare event of rising ocean levels in the Arctic and the destabilization of mammal subnivean habitats

26. Which one of the following best describes the organization of the passage?
    A. A hypothesis is presented and defended with supporting examples.
    B. A conclusion is presented and the information supporting it is provided.
    C. A thesis is presented and defended with an argument.
    D. Opposing views are presented, discussed, and then reconciled.
    E. A theory is proposed, considered, and then amended on the basis of evidence.

27. Based on the passage, identify why successful reproduction under the snow is not a sufficient condition for a peak in cyclic lemming populations.
    A. the early onset of a thick and dry snow cover combined with the absence of freezing rain and days with above zero temperatures favors survival and reproduction
    B. at the landscape scale, the selection of the winter nest sites is generally affected by the same variables in both predators and prey
    C. stochastic climate events demonstrate that unpredictable causal chains can interfere with typical scientific predictions about lemming reproduction
    D. mean snow depth over subnivean sites does not differ between random sites and sites where lemming nests were depredated by predators
    E. elevation and slope aspect do not affect nest site selection, and plant variables have a relatively weak influence on nest site selection

Notes:

_____

_____

_____

_____

_____

_____

_____

_____

_____

READING COMPREHENSION SECTION
CHAPTER 4

You are on the pre-screen part of this passage, so you are going to *read the questions* (but not the answers first). What are you looking for when you do this? **Two things:** 1) you want to know what sort of logic problems are being asked of you and 2) you want to get a heads up when you actually RAG the passage for what part of the content will be relevant for you to home in on. Take a look at this passage and see what questions are being asked:

i. You are asked a *purpose* question (21). Purpose questions are *justificatory*, so they will provide a *reason* why the author is writing this. Sometimes purpose questions are main point questions, but at root, they are *motivational*. They answer the question "why"? So, your job is to hunt down the *why* of this particular passage. When you apply the RAG technique, it will be easy for you to focus in on the why.

ii. You are asked a *main point* question (22). Well, now you know that the main point (in 22) is a different question than (21), the *purpose* question! Prior to even reading the thing, you know you are looking to answer the question "why" in (21) and to identify the thesis of the author in (22). You can be on the lookout for the thesis when you perform the RAG technique on this passage.

iii. You have a "bolster the claim" question (23). These are great! Bolstering the claim is simply adding further justification to a statement the author makes in the passage. These are *non-evaluative*—you aren't asked to weigh whether an answer choice is implied or justified. Rather, you are already given what needs bolstering—here, the author's claim that snow cover dramatically impacts the structure and functioning of ecosystems in winter—and your correct answer will be consistent with the author's claim about snow cover and will provide an additional reason for it. *It will not be in the text, so you don't need to spend time hunting for it in the passage.* See the benefit of the pre-screen? You know for (23) what the content of the question is, and will know after RAG what answer best fits.

iv. (24) asks you to compare the *research strategy* of the passage with the answer choices. This is excellent information prior to reading, because it tells you both that this passage is a research text and that you will need to look for a strategy—a method—of research belied in the passage.

v. (25) is not straightforward. Part of its complexity is in the way it is written, but...look... still a logic question: "It can be inferred from the passage that Arctic stochastic climatic events of the sort that would impact lemming populations would include which of the following?" (25) is asking you to draw an inference, and it is even being kind to you by providing the main content point in the passage...the passage you have not yet read, "Arctic stochastic climate events that would impact lemming populations...". Inferences, as you know, are logical devices that allow you to explore the implications of a given claim, so here you already know to home in on stochastic climate change components of the passage as well as textual indicators of lemming populations.

vi. (26) is about organization—which you are going to pick up by looking at the thesis, conclusion, and main points in between.

vii. Finally (27) is a *sufficient condition* question. You already know that necessary and sufficient conditions are logical functions. So, this question is asking you to identify a logical function within the passage.

So, all of the logical abilities that you have honed as preparation for the LSAT so far remain intact, and you are largely being asked logic questions. Of course, the reason you are performing a pre-screen and looking at the questions first is not just to confirm that you are being asked logic questions, but those questions provide you the basis with which you can approach the test and use the RAG method. Now that you have those questions in mind and the pre-screen is in place, you are ready to apply RAG!

Step 1: Read the first and last sentence of the first paragraph.

Step 2: Summarize in your own words (write down key phrase).

You are Reading for ArGumentation, so you know you aren't going to look at the LSAT passage like a passive observer who has to suffer through a lecture on the reproductive behavior of lemmings. Instead, you are going to attack this passage to find its argument! To do that, you are going to think about one or two phrases of main points that emerge from the first and last sentence of the first paragraph. Here those sentences are in full below, along with some ways to summarize them for main points:

Some small mammal populations are famous for their phenomenal cyclic fluctuations in abundance.	Small animals reproduce in flux.
Temperature gradients within the snow result in the formation of a stratum of fragile and loosely arranged snow crystals near the ground, which creates a subnivean space, the primary wintering habitat of small mammals.	Mammals burrow under spaces in loose snow.

Step 1 and 2 Focus: Ok, you've summarized the main points of the first paragraph in your own words. You know this passage is about the reproduction of small mammals who burrow in subnivean (and cold) spaces, which depend on external temperature. Now you can go to step three.

Step 3: Read the first and last sentence of the final paragraph.

Step 4: Summarize in your own words (write down key phrase).

Previous studies suggested that freezing rain and frost/thaw events should reduce small mammal winter survival both directly and indirectly.	Cold/warm cycles were thought to impact mammal survival.
Therefore, alterations of winter climatic conditions brought by the current global warming could reduce small mammal winter survival and destabilize their cyclic population dynamics, which would affect the whole tundra ecosystem.	Changes in winter conditions shrink mammal populations/threatens tundra.

Step 3 & 4 Focus: These steps give us the conclusion of this argument: changes in winter conditions shrink mammal populations and threaten the entire tundra. Remember, we're thinking about this from an ArGumentation standpoint, so we can put 3 & 4 in relation to 1 & 2. Small mammals need constant subnivean spaces to guarantee successful reproduction, and climate change through rain/thaw cycles threatens that and so destabilizes the whole tundra. Do you see the process? You have read a total of four sentences, but already know what this long passage is about as well as some structure of its argumentation. You can proceed with steps 5 & 6.

Step 5: Read the first sentence of every paragraph in-between the first and last paragraphs.

Step 6: Summarize in your own words (write down key phrase).

Their survival is dependent upon accessibility to food and the protection against harsh temperatures and predators offered by this particular environment.	Small mammals need food and safe shelter to survive.
Recent evidence suggests that population cycles of small mammals of the tundra may be fading out in some areas, especially in Fennoscandia.	Small mammals are not reproducing as necessary for survival in the tundra.

Step 5 & 6 focus: Great! We're getting a clear picture. Stability in a subnivean (under snow) space is required for proper reproduction cycles of certain small mammals. Climate change, however, has been interfering with that reproduction, and so with the survival of small mammals. One question that remains is whether the rain/thaw/freeze cycle that is being interrupted is impacting the nesting locations for these mammals, since we know from our first step that they burrow under the snow to reproduce. That might be an implication of this text.

The next question you will need to determine for yourself is whether you need to read this entire passage on its own (Step 7). Step 7 is always "if necessary". If you believe that there is information that you just don't yet have that you need right away, then definitely read the entire passage. When you do, however, *make sure to keep the ArGumentation focus!* You are reading for an argument even if you read the entire passage. And don't worry—if you get to Step 7 and believe you need to read the whole passage, you have *not wasted time* by following the RAG steps. Instead, you will have ensured that when you do read the whole passage, you will be looking for support for the conclusion and premises, most of which you have already identified.

Insider Insights: RAG Practice!

It might sound obvious, but RAG is a technique. As a technique, it is neither intuitive nor basic. Intuition says—do what you have done since kindergarten! Read top-to-bottom, left-to-right until you have read the entire passage and are then so gassed you don't have energy for the questions! A basic technique is one that doesn't require practice, like opening a pickle jar. The LSAT isn't quite like the pickle jar. It is workable when you have the right techniques for the task. In this case, RAG is an intentional tool that, with practice, helps you 1) identify the argument quickly; 2) reduces the amount of time you have to read; and 3) increases your reading comprehension. You can practice the RAG technique on almost any kind of writing (except e.e. cummings—make sure to read him en toto!). That means that you can practice the technique even when you are not sitting down to study for the LSAT.

Let's try a couple of the questions out (you already have the answer explanations, but this will help you apply the technique to quickly identify on the correct questions). How about (21)?

21. The primary purpose of the passage is to
   A. explain how the lemming reproduces given the conditions of a changing tundra ecosystem
   B. present some recent scientific research on why the population of Fennoscandian mammals is falling
   C. present the author's scientific contributions to research about the relationship of climate change to the population patterns of lemmings
   D. assess the value of previous studies on the relationship between cold weather events and small mammal winter populations
   E. describe two different views on subnivean space and predator/prey populations

Now, you may have read the entirety of the passage as Step 7, or you might not have. I'm going to approach this question as though you haven't *because you don't need to in order to successfully answer the question.* Question (21) is a *primary purpose question.* The primary purpose could be the main point, but you know in this passage it is going to be different, because you know that (22) is the main point. The correct answer will be the response that best captures the reason the author presents the reading selection, so even choices that are factually true or strongly implied by the text may not be the best answer. So, think about what you take to be the purpose of the passage—start with the action verbs of the answer choices and move from there: *explain, present, present, assess,* and *describe.* None of these can be eliminated out of hand, so we need to read the rest of their answers. (A) is not obviously wrong, since we know from our RAG technique that this passage is about the changing reproductive patterns of small mammals based on climate change. But, recognize a *crucial* word here—"HOW". From our technique, can we say that this passage is about HOW lemmings produce, given changing climates? No—we haven't read anything about the mechanics of the reproduction. So, (A) is not a good answer. You might find (B) attractive, especially because it uses a particular

term that you did read when you used the RAG technique, *Fennoscandia*. Don't be fooled by the glitzy. Instead, think about what (B) says as a whole. If you do that, you'll see that it too general, because it commits you to saying that the purpose is to present some general research on a too-specific topic. We need a better purpose statement. (C) could be it! Of course, the point is to provide this author's research on how climate change impacts the spaces in which small mammals (like nesting lemmings) reproduce. Notice, that you can get this *without slogging through the entire science writing!* For optimum results, of course, you want to compare (C) to the remaining choices to make sure there isn't a better one (although we can't imagine a better choice). Although we know from steps 3 and 4 that there is a statement about past research, we also know the author pivots from that research towards what s/he has discovered about climate change, so its primary purpose cannot be (D). Finally, (E) is most straightforwardly not the correct answer; in none of our reading have we seen contrasting views. If nothing else, this author's research is deepening the claims posited by former research.

Look at that! You have used RAG and been able to identify the correct answer as (C) without wasting time bogged in the details that are unnecessary to this argument. Reading for ArGuments helps you focus on the structural components of the passage which yield the conclusion and premises. Excellent. Let's try one more.

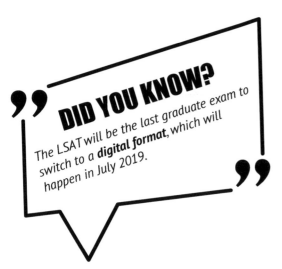

To show you the strength of the technique for more substantive, less formal questions, I'll pick a question that is the least tied to logic and more to content. (26) is perfect to use for demonstration. The question asks, "Which one of the following best describes the organization of the passage?" This question is solely about how the evidence structurally relates to the thesis of the passage. That means that we can approach the answer choices in the same way as we did above, but instead of looking for an action verb (these answer choices don't begin with verbs, after all), let's look for the descriptive noun presented. Our options are: *a hypothesis, a conclusion, a thesis, opposing views,* and *a theory.* Well—look at that! Just on the basis of those descriptions, we can begin eliminating. We know we can keep "hypothesis", "conclusion", "thesis," and "theory" because our RAG technique illuminated each of these. Which *didn't* it illuminate? (D). And as we read it entirely, we see we are right: there aren't opposing views presented, discussed, and reconciled in this paper. You've just eliminated an answer and increased your chances of success by 20%! (Without even reading an entire answer choice to begin! Pretty great.)

Now we have four to navigate through, and just keep in mind that we are looking for structure, since this question is about organization. You can look at your "key phrases" to remind yourself that the reading starts off with some facts about the reproductive patterns of small mammals, and it establishes a thesis: "increased frequencies of freeze-thaw cycles during the winter due to climate warming and their influence on snow conditions have... dampen[ed] these." Now, you can go back to where you found this in the text and see clearly that this thesis is contrasted with what the author first thought, that the early onset of thick, dry snow, combined with the absence of freezing rain and days with above zero temperatures should favor survival and reproduction. S/he found an inference that turned out not to be true. That means that you have honed in on the organization of this passage by reading a single additional sentence. The passage proposes a theory, considers it, and modifies it (to include research about climate change). Now compare this organization to those suggested in your answer choices. (A) and (B) are insufficient. Without doing the early work of identifying the organizational structure based on RAG, you would be tempted to include (C) as a possibility, but you have seen how the third paragraph's first sentence pivots the passage, and you identified the author's conclusion, "therefore" at the end of the text. That makes sense, though, since you know that (E) represents exactly the kind of structure given to you in the passage and revealed by the RAG technique.

So, even for questions that do not ask you to make a logical inference, to find a cause, to unearth a logical fallacy or to identify a conclusion, Reading Comprehension questions still fundamentally are logic questions and you can use logic, and logic-based techniques like RAG, to successfully answer them.

READING COMPREHENSION SECTION
CHAPTER 4

The Insider Insight for Reading Comprehension here is *very different* than other test preparation materials. Most leading test prep authors will tell you that the only thing you can really do on the RC section is to read carefully and try hard to understand what is being written. Sure, that makes sense if the RC section was merely a test of your ability to read. But, it's not. It's a test to determine how you can maneuver through lengthy passages of technical writing to address the logical structure and implications of the passage. The goal is to bog you down in the morass of technical terms and data structures to suck time away from you. The technique I have provided here is unique, proven, and will help you read only what you need in order to make the logical moves necessary to work the test successfully.

There are, of course, other techniques that will help you prepare for the RC, including some exam know-how skills and being able to figure out what sorts of questions mean in the section.

Exam Know-How

There are some dyed-in-the wool techniques that, when paired with RAG, will help you work the RC section to your fullest.

Know How #1: Order of Passages.

After doing a glance at all of the passages offered to you, you should work through the passages that you think are easiest first, and save the most difficult for last. Each scholar may have different standards for what constitutes the "easiest", but for many, those that are in fields furthest away from a student's major might be the most difficult. If you are a history major, you might put the STEM passage as the last in the queue. There is a general assumption on the LSAT that scholars will have a more difficult time assessing subject matter for fields of study outside their area or in subject matter they dislike. (RAG as a technique is actually built to mitigate this worry for you—since RAG is a system to approach passages, it is mostly disconnected from the content of a text and is excellent for saving you from weighing whether Passage 1 or 3 is a topic you dislike more!) Of course, most scholars will also look at the length of a passage as an indication as to whether it is difficult—which is OK, but I find that the number of questions is more indicative of difficulty than simply length of passage.

Certainly, once you have identified your first passage to attack, you are working the Pre-step and looking at the questions for that passage. Just as you would do in other sections, you will gravitate towards the questions that are seemingly easier to approach, such as main idea questions.

Know How #2: Most Passages are Badly Written.

The structure of the LSAT RC will throw you off, because line numbers are included to help you—you might think, "Excellent, they are helping me out by giving me line numbers!" The line numbers are hash marks for every 5 lines of the passage, and sometimes the questions will refer to the content of the RC specifically by line (which, actually, is a help). But more often or not, even if a question refers to a line, the correct answer will be an inference of something marked in or near that line. The passages themselves, after all, are not solidly written. They are intended to drag you down by their use of jargon, their length, and the lack of structure in and between paragraphs. The passages themselves can run more than 600 words, and include a significant amount of material that you will never use. (Which is why the RAG technique is so important- you will never have to engage with sections of text you won't need for correct responses.) The LSAT writers are counting on the fact that they can throw you off by not using headings, by condensing several paragraphs worth of material into one, or by including material that reflects competing viewpoints. Also, most of the passages are written as an editorial (even if they are science-based). Rather than reporting facts and data, the passages are often rife with opinion that is not strongly justified. (This helps the writers test your inference ability.) But, so much opinion-content can be off-putting.

Know-How #3: Most Passages Make You Feel Unprepared for Their Vocabulary.

The writers of the LSAT know you have 35 minutes for this section, and the more time they can get you sucked into stumbling over unfamiliar words, the less time you will devote to reading the questions and solving the puzzles they present to you. If you use the RAG method of approaching, you are far better off than a student who has a better vocabulary but spends inordinate amounts of time reading every word of the exam. That isn't to say that vocabulary

isn't important. Instead, you can place the proper value on vocabulary. It is a tool. If you have it as a tool and use it properly it can benefit you. If you do not have it, it cannot benefit you. However, if you use it improperly, it will hurt you. But, if you use the correct tool, you can work the LSAT to your advantage.

Know-How #4: RC Passages Differ from Logical Reasoning Texts.

Of course, you are well-versed in how the LSAT is a logic test, across its sections. But, the RC section is different in the form and content of the passages than the LR sections. The LR texts tend to be succinct and they can be vague, because they do not offer much in the way of detail. They are the same in that they present arguments. But, the RC will typically ask two types of questions: description questions and expansion questions. Description questions will direct you to identify the answer that best describes the principles, examples, or conditions that the passage stipulates. These are fairly easy questions because they usually direct you to the passage line (the lines are numbered) in which the ideas or concepts they are asking you about are found. You can relate description questions to key words within the passage. Here's an example of a description question:

1. The passage indicates that "Republicans" initially referred to:

   A. Precursors to today's Democratic party
   B. Eighteenth-century economists
   C. Loyalists committed to King George's ideals
   D. Freedom fighters who fought without pay for the Revolution
   E. Resistance to the Federalists

What makes description questions excellent is that, by employing RAG, you will have discovered an easy question *before* getting bogged down with the details of a long passage. The direct connection between the descriptive element of the text and the question should immediately be obvious to you. (The result should be that you work to identify the descriptive questions within all of your passages as your first steps in RAG, and then work the harder, expansion questions later.) For this question, that means that you will be able to target "Republicans" in the text as a key word search to discover where the passage discusses the early Republican party. Description questions usually ask a series of questions that relate to the text's meaning itself, and so you will not have to expend a lot of time and energy interpreting the information upon which the description questions draw.

Expansion questions are more difficult, and have a different function than description questions. Expansion questions focus on what *could*, what *must*, and what *cannot* satisfy certain conditions – so they expand logically from what is given in the passage. Here's an example of an expansion question:

1. The passage implies that which of the following could occur if the federal government tightens control over which news agencies receive direct access to press briefings in the White House?

   A. Radio media would experience a resurgence in audience numbers and impact.
   B. The citizenry would more fully trust news outlets to deliver fair, accurate depictions of major news events.
   C. Individual rights to free speech would be better respected.
   D. The right to free speech would be hampered.
   E. News outlets would become more conservative.

This expansion question demands that the reader go beyond the main point of the text and infer a further proposition from what is given in the text. If you had employed the RAG technique to the passage that corresponded to this question, you would have pulled out the main premises and conclusion and would be able to see which of these RC answers is best suited as an inference that is tightly tied to the content of the passage but appropriately predictive based on that content. Expansion questions test your ability to make logical inferences, and your ability to do this is enhanced if you have enough time to think clearly about your options. Employing RAG will give you time and comprehension advantages over others who are taking the LSAT.

Know-How #5: Wrong Answers are Disguised in the RC Sections.

Make sure you don't focus on picking out the right answers on the RC section to the exclusion of identifying the wrong answers. When you have knowledge about patterns the LSAT writers employ for wrong-answers, you can quickly eliminate many wrong answers and increase your chances of doing well on any particular question. The best answer choice will satisfy the conditions placed by the question within the context of the passage given to you. There are some patterns of wrong answers that you should know and be on the look-out for when you are completing the RC section. First, wrong answers often repeat the content of the passage. Exam-takers get lulled into the comfort of similarity, and yet very infrequently is it true that a correct answer mimics the content exactly of the RC passage. Second, wrong answers *misinterpret the conclusion* of the argument within the passage. They might use obscure language and seem authoritative but actually misrepresent the conclusion. Third, *overgeneralization* invariably indicates a wrong answer choice. The correct response will be specific enough to relate to the main argument within the passage. The main argument will never be general, so the correct response will never overgeneralize! Finally, wrong answers are often disguised in true content that does not meet the conditions placed by the argument or the question itself. (You will see this *frequently*). These wrong answers are attractive because the truth is attractive! But, if the conditions of the argument are not met, the answer cannot be correct even if it asserts a proposition that is in fact true.

> ## EXPERT TIP
>
> *Proper prep beats lengthy prep hands-down. Proper prep means **learning the LSAT logic** you are going to need, applying that to test questions, and figuring out where you went wrong when you get an answer wrong. **Don't spend a lot of time practicing the wrong way.** Spend better time prepping the right way.*

Insider Insight: A Constellation of Tessellations

It is frequently true in the Reading Comprehension section that LSAT writers use obfuscation to intentionally put errors among the answer choices that really look tempting. Your Know-How #5 introduces you to this, but it is so prevalent that it can be helpful to know what kinds of patterns there are for "Errors within the Answers" (or, EWA). Knowing what patters of EWA can occur can help you identify wrong-answers from among those that you have remaining as viable options for any question. By using EWA to eliminate erroneous options, you will more efficiently identify—and be confident in—the correct answer. Know How #5 picks out some attractive, but wrong tessellations. Let's review them and some more before we practice identifying them within a passage. Watch out for them!

Tessellation #1: Repeating Repeaters. You will be attracted to answer choices that quote the passage directly.

Tessellation #2: Obscurity Attracts. When you are on the receiving end of obscure, technical language and you see obscure, technical language within an answer choice, rather than working the logical form of the argument given, it can be much easier just to give into the obscurity and choose the technical answer.

Tessellation #3: Condition Flipping. You've already worked a good amount of these arguments, and so you are already familiar with how easy it can be to "flip" a condition, so that you create a valid argument out of an invalid argument by setting up an antecedent that really is a consequent, or vice versa. That leads to a conclusion that can't be guaranteed.

Tessellation #4: Hyped Conclusions. Writers on the LSAT will include answer choices that overgeneralize and overstate, or underdetermine and understate part of the conclusion and so can't meet the conditions which are provided to you in the passage.

Tessellation #5: Truthiness. That's right—included in your answer choices will be those that are true but aren't true enough. They have a "truthiness" about them that is attractive, they are compelling because they make good sense, but even true answers that do not fulfill all of the conditions from the passage are not correct. Don't be fooled by this pretty tessellation!

Tessellation #6: Fake News. Unfortunately, there will be some answer choices that use very similar language as the passage (like in Tessellation #1), but get a condition or a modal term wrong, or they might misconstrue or wrongly illustrate part of the passage. They seem like news, it rings true to your ears, but ultimately, they are wrong.

Picking Out Errors within Answers (EWA): Let's Practice!

Given that there is a constellation of tessellations that can impede your ability to identify Errors within Answers (EWA), it's important for us to practice. We'll start off more easily, by practicing picking out *Tessellation #1: Repeating Repeaters*. Remember, that this tessellation uses the content of the passage—even quoting from it at times—to reach an incorrect conclusion as an answer option. The question may even include an answer choice that contradicts the passage, but it seems attractive because it employs the language of the passage to do so. Watch out for those, as well as answer choices that use even technical jargon from the selection to move beyond the logical implications of the text, which can serve to misconstrue the argument. For this text, here's what you are going to do: you're going to pre-screen the passage, perform the RAG technique on the passage, and then you will practice identifying the tessellations in the answer choices so that you can more efficiently hone in on correct answers. Good luck!

Although numerous studies detail rates of online social media use among youth and adult populations, and although the correlations between such activities and a range of political activities have been explored, scholars are still working to clarify whether and when particular forms of online activity with social media foster political engagement. A meta-analysis of early studies of the relationship between exposure to politics through Internet use and offline political participation found that although most of those studies identified a positive association between the two, that association was typically not very strong. As scholarship has advanced and new media have continued to evolve, more recent research has focused more specifically on the relationship between exposure to political topics through social media and political participation. Meta-analysis of this research found that most of the studies examined reported a positive association between social media use and political engagement. However, because the vast majority of those studies relied on cross-sectional survey data, they were severely restricted in their ability to test hypotheses about the causal relationships between the variables; the few studies to employ panel data were much less likely to report a positive, statistically significant relationship between social media use and political participation than were those using cross-sectional data. Central to the political communication is the discussion of whether news media have the potential to strengthen democracy by encouraging citizens' engagement in politics, or whether the news media only attract those citizens who are already politically interested and active. Stimulating or reinforcing political interest in teens includes using panel data to examine reciprocal effects between news media and political interest. At the heart of this discussion lies the Virtuous Circle Thesis (VCT), which is the idea that the "most politically knowledgeable, trusting, and participatory are most likely to tune in to public-affairs coverage. And those most attentive to coverage of public affairs become more engaged in civic life". Through a reinforcing spiral, a divide between politically engaged and non-engaged teenagers emerges. Despite the widely recognized and applied assumptions, the VCT rests on assumptions that are seldom tested empirically due to lack of longitudinal data.

1. It can be inferred from the passage that the author would be most likely to believe which one of the following?

   A. Teenagers actively engage in politics in this society.
   B. The research that has been done thus far on the relationship between teens' online news habits and their political engagement support the VCT.
   C. Researchers can weigh patterns of exposure to the news by observing teens' online behavior.
   D. The associations between internet use and offline political exposure are not fully understood.
   E. Democracy should be strengthened by utilizing better tools to understand the relationship between teens' social media use and their political participation.

All right. We're practicing identifying the first Tessellation: *Repeating Repeaters*, and we have a lot of examples in the wrong answers here, for question #1! Answer choice (A) falls prey to repeating the text's own language to make too general claims that cannot yet be supported by the text, even though the question asks you to go beyond the passage and make an inference based upon it. Option (B) might be attractive to you. It seems the author is going to hypothesize that there is a relationship between how teens interact with the news (whether online, off line, or with exemplars) and their realization of the VCT. So, we'll hang onto this as a potential right answer. Choice (C) repeats the voice of the passage, but yields a too-general conclusion that really isn't an inference as much as a repeat of what the author would like to see happen. For (D), the writers lift some of the passage, "the associations between internet use and offline political exposure", so repeats...and also uses some *Tessellation #6:* Fake News to come to a different conclusion than the author does, since the author is not saying that we don't understand the association but that the positive associations couldn't adequately be expressed because of the methods that were used to assess the data. Answer (E) is indeed excellent. Although the text's primary focus is the research on teens, the broader scope for the research is to strengthen democracy by accurately measuring, assessing, and highlighting teen participation in politics. How does (E) compare to (B)? Well, it must be stronger than (B). (B) is about research generally, and (E) makes a claim specific to the purpose and point of the research and so is a more complete, correct answer...which is the sort of answer we want to come to through the Reading Comprehension questions on the LSAT.

Now that we've specifically practiced the first Tessellation, let's practice one of the other more popular patterns you will see on the LSAT, *Tessellation #6: Hyped Conclusions*. The Hyped Conclusion Tessellation leads you to error, not by repeating the text's content, but either by over-estimating or under-estimating the conclusion of the argument or the relationship of the premises to the conclusion. We'll use the same passage to work through this Tessellation for the following question:

2. Based on this passage, the author would most likely want to discuss the answer to which one of the following questions regarding exposure to politics via social media?

   A. Can exposure to politics via social media be comprehensively measured?
   B. Must exposure to politics via social media be measured in teens of all societies?
   C. Will contemporary research fill the significant gap in knowledge about teenage involvement in politics through exposure to it?
   D. Who is responsible to explain both teenage and adult political behavior through the research being done on exposure to politics through social media?
   E. Can exposure to politics via social media help dissolve the spiral between teens who participate in politics and teens who don't?

The question helps you a bit in that it focuses you to the question of "exposure to politics via social media" and directs you to pick out which answer choice the author would most readily want to discuss (and so, inferentially, would be tied to this particular passage). Each of the answer choices are tied in some important way to the passage, but all of the answer choices save one engage in the 4ᵗʰ Tessellation. Where you able to find the one that didn't? Answer (E) is the best selection. It is an answer choice that ties into the main point of the research the author reports upon, and also moves outward to the implication of the research. More importantly for our practice session here, it does not over-generalize or under-emphasize the point of the passage. We can see that the other answer

choices do so. (A) contradicts the main point of the passage, which is to show that previous studies "were severely restricted in their ability to test hypotheses about the causal relationships between the variables" and so, we need a more comprehensive analysis. Choice (B) is too general, since the author surely would not suggest that the teens in this particular society could serve as models (whether positively or negatively) for the measurement of political engagement in any other society. Answer (C) might seem viable, since the passage is about contemporary research, there is a gap in knowledge because of the limitations of method. But the main point of the passage is not about whether exposure to information about the use of social media will fill a knowledge gap, but about what we can say about the participation rates in politics for teens—so (C) is too-general as well and needs more specificity. Option (D), in comparison, over-reaches, because the passage is not a morality play about who should be held responsible—and certainly does not extrapolate as to who could be responsible for adult political behavior. So, Answers A-D all either are over-general, over-broad, or under-emphasize the main points made in the passage, and so cannot be correct.

3. Which of the following best states the conclusion to which the author's statements lead?

   A. Statistically significant relationships between social media use and political participation in teens is worth studying.
   B. Confidence in the observations of the variables that are weighed by those who are virtuously involved in political engagement will reinforce participation in politics by teenagers.
   C. Understanding teenagers' exposure to online and offline political exposure is imperative to understanding how citizens in general engage virtuously in politics.
   D. Many researchers have reached too-hasty conclusions about the relationship between exposure to news online and the engagement of teens to politics.
   E. Engaged political citizenship ultimately reflects the fact that virtuous engagement requires active participation with online news sources.

All right—you pre-screened the question, broke down the passage into usable parts so that you could employ the RAG technique, and you are ready to avoid EWA to answer this question correctly. Wrong answers here will not satisfy the conditions set out in the passage, and the right answer will not be the conclusion itself, but will be the next inferential step past the author's conclusion. Now let's assess each option.

Answer (A) is an excellent choice, even if a bit general. The generality here is tied directly to the text.-- we're set up for (A) by the last sentence in the passage, which requires us to study the empirical findings more because they are so important. Certainly, though, its generality is sufficient for you to analyze all of the other answer choices. This is Reading Comp, after all and not Analytic Reasoning, so the correct answer will be the best option, not the perfect one. Answer (B) looks like our *Tessellation #1: Repeating Repeaters* as well as *Tessellation #2: Obscurity Attracts.* (B) repeats "virtue", "political engagement" and "participation" but the way in which it is listed, "confidence in the observations of the variables" and "weighed by those who are virtuously involved in political engagement will reinforce participation" are pretty obscure phrases, especially since the text is straightforward. Despite the fact that almost every word of (B) is lifted from the passage, and so is attractive, the passage isn't about confidence but about what we need to do to strengthen our knowledge of the relationship between teenager political engagement and their absorption of news from online sources.

Similarly, choice (C) obfuscates through *Tessellation #4: Hyped Conclusion* and *Tessellation #6: Fake News.* On one hand, (C) overgeneralizes by saying if we understand teens, we understand citizens, but on the other it takes aspects of the passage itself to twist it incorrectly. It is true that the passage pushes us to explore teens' exposure to online and offline political exposure, and that the goal is to tie this into the Virtuous Circle Thesis, but not to the citizenry, generally. Option (D), on the other hand, relies on *Tessellation #5: Truthiness,* because it is true that the author wants researchers to do more; it just isn't true that researchers have used hasty generalizations in their conclusions. Finally, (E) uses the 1st Tessellation (*Repeating Repeaters*) by employing the same verbage as the passage as well as #6: *Fake News,* because it isn't true that research has shown this for teenage participation. In fact, the conclusion is indeed (A), that we need to do more research so that we can know the link between engagement with online news sources and active, virtuous teen participation in politics.

Insider Information: What Are My Chances?

The biggest challenge of the Reading Comprehension section is time management. This is why in every LSAT test prep book, you will have entire chapters dedicated to time management. There aren't techniques to solving RC questions—but pages upon pages of how to save time while engaging in careful reading of content that will not help you answer the questions. I have yet to find a reading technique on an LSAT test prep. But, that is *time wasted*, time that could be spent on learning about how to work the LSAT RC section, just like you learn how to do logic games on the AR section or learn how to assess disagreements in the LR sections. As has been mentioned, the LSAT is not a reading test, even when it is asking you to do copious amounts of reading. It is a *logic test*, so it is throwing lots of logic at you. It only makes sense to spend a lot of time learning how to manage your time if you need help in managing time on the RC to evaluate arguments. But you *don't*.

The ArgoPrep method is the only LSAT test prep that saves you time by saving you from learning time management techniques in favor of learning logic techniques that turn your attention back to the test and away from your watch. Not only will you save time, you will need to read less and *you will comprehend more*. In addition to the amazing, copyrighted *Reading for ArGumentation (RAG)* technique that will help you ace the Reading Comprehension section, it gives you tools to avoid EWA.

So, with those techniques, what are your chances on the RC section? As with most exams, it depends on if you've practiced the techniques and can apply them to the test. Only 40-60% of LSAT test-takers select the correct answer on medium-level questions on the RC section. That answer drops precipitously for harder questions, which is odd because the harder questions just are the logical implication questions that we would expect students who have prepped for logic to be able to do. Unfortunately, that is because most students haven't been trained in logic. Rather, they learn expensive techniques that only work for a small percentage of questions and aren't translatable to other sections of the LSAT.

You are in a different position. You have the logical basis to do well on every single section of the exam, and will practice in each section so that you will be ready to face whatever question comes at you on the exam. One final reminder, as you get ready to launch from RC into Analytical and Logical Reasoning. It won't be the case in any section that the questions that come later on in the sections are more difficult, or that the last questions on the exam are harder than the first. It might seem that way after you are exhausted. But, you won't be exhausted. When you see the entire exam as a logic puzzle, you won't exert effort to read things you won't need to and focus on questions that won't help you land an excellent score. Keep focused on what you can control—your logical assessment of each question, and you will own the LSAT and the shot clock!

CHAPTER V

ANALYTICAL REASONING SECTION

Analytical Reasoning sections are frequently called "Logic Games" by writers, bloggers, and test-takers, and the moniker is not entirely wrong. Of course, by pursuing your success through ArgoPrep, you are already thinking about the entire exam as a logic puzzle, and so, the questions in the AR section will fit in well. Generally, the AR section assesses your ability to organize, apply conditional reasoning, use modal reasoning, and test the validity of arguments using strong deductive and inductive logic skills.

> ## EXPERT TIP
>
> **Don't score yourself** on a practice test, unless your practice test is taken with the exact same time constraints as the real exam. This means that you need to practice with five sections of the LSAT, since the real LSAT will have a non-scored experimental section as well.

More particularly, the AR section gives you a series of conditions that order the relationships between subjects in the passage. Logical organization will be a primary resource for you to draw upon, because the question sets will demand that you put subjects in order and sequence events to draw valid conclusions about the passages. There are two facets of the AR question sets that are differentiated from other sections, and which are most daunting: 1) numbers or abbreviations are often used as formalized substitutes for full ideas and 2) the answers require you to draw from relationships between the subjects provided within the question's conditions. Compared to other sections on the LSAT, most students waste the most time in the Reading Comprehension section, and have the most difficult time with the Analytical Reasoning section. The AR's daunting facets are frequently unfamiliar to students. One reason the task seems daunting is that students approach the AR section as a *different sort of section*. But—it is not fundamentally different from the LR and RC sections. It is simply more overtly a logic section. When you apply the strategies for effective Shot Clock management, and the rules of logic, to the AR question sets, you are going to find that you are prepared to take on the task. You will have fun with the AR section!

Problematic Relationships

The AR section is fundamentally and essentially about evaluating the relationships between subjects based on certain conditions given to you by the passage. So far, not daunting, right? Our individual relationships work like that too: maybe you will give Dan a ride to the doctor on Friday as long as Alicia is unable to take him. That is a relationship, based on a condition! The question sets on the AR are built with the same sort of conditions in mind, but there generally will be more conditions and more subjects.

Many test prep companies suggest that you should spend a great deal of time learning systems of diagramming, blocking, trees, and clusters to approach the AR section because it is the most "abstract". Nothing could be further from the truth! The games in AR are logic games, so they require deductive ability much more frequently than inductive ability. Deductive ability, as you know, is about logical structure and form—which are not abstractions. They are concrete, workable problems. A benefit to the AR section that usually goes unmentioned is that, to succeed, you will solely rely on logic and not on definitions, facts, or formulas. You won't even have to rely on the experiences you have had on other tests (except for our Insider Insights into beating the test in Chapter 7). You won't schlep flashcards around while you drive to test your ability to remember techniques, even. You only need to rely on your logical abilities—which you have learned here. LSAC has even sweetened the deal for you on this test—they are printing the LSAT's Analytical Reasoning sections on more pages to give you additional space to map out your logic problems.

What logic problems? They are *relationship problems*. The AR is solely about problematic relationships between subjects (i.e., whomever the question sets are about). The reason they are problematic relationships is because their subjects within the passages are *disorganized* and *ungrouped*. Your job is to use your logical abilities to organize and group appropriately.

You will typically have *four or five question sets* in the AR section, in which you are given a scenario about a group of subjects that have to be organized according to a series of conditions. You will see around 4-7 questions for each question set. Differently than the Reading Comprehension and Logical Reasoning sections, the AR questions are all fundamentally the same. They will ask you to use conditions that relate to all of the questions within a question set to see what the "relationship status" is for each of the subjects that are conditioned by the passage. When the question introduces a new condition, the relationship status of the subjects change.

Approaching the Questions - Set-Up

The directions on the AR aren't super illuminating—but they are different from the other sections. The AR directions will let you know that each question set is based on a set of conditions, and that there is only one answer that meets the conditions accurately and completely. That means that the answer choices that are correct won't compete for excellence with other answer options and require a significant amount of time for you to see which inference is stronger. There is only one correct answer—not answers that are "best" in the AR section. If there is only one correct answer, then you should not equivocate about whether an answer is correct. You will *know* that it is by following the conditions of the scenario to their logical conclusion.

A result of the set-up for the AR is that, while you are prepping, you should not time yourself on the AR questions. Instead, your focus should be on getting them stone-cold correct.

What the directions do not tell you for AR is actually the most important aspect of what you should know about the AR: the conditions that are provided in the passage apply to all questions, but if a new condition appears in a question, it applies to that question only. It can be difficult to keep in mind when you are working the questions, but you will not apply conditions that are found within questions to other questions within that answer set.

The questions almost always will ask you about *modal logic:* based on the conditions listed, the question will ask you for an answer which *could* be true, *could* not be true, or *must* be true. You will, then, be asked about what is *logically possible* and what is *logically necessary*. Although you will frequently find more *must* and *could* questions on the AR than questions than are about what could not be the case, you will get some variation as to how the questions are presented. You could see the following variation, for example:

"Any of the following could be in the 1st and 2nd positions, respectively, of an acceptable series, EXCEPT:"

Here, the question is asking you about logical necessity, "given the conditions, it cannot be the case that is correct could have its subjects in the 1st and 2nd positions, respectively".

Insider Insight: Modal Terms

It is really quite easy to identify when the exam is asking you to choose logical possibility and when it is saying a consequence is logically required, or necessary.

Here are some terms you could frequently see to tip-off logical possibility:

> *some, might, could, perhaps, can, may, possibly, possibly will, only if*

Here are some terms that indicate logical necessity:

> *all, no, must, cannot, needs, obliged, should, require/required, necessary and sufficient*

All of the questions on the AR section of the LSAT will test your ability to differentiate between necessary and sufficient conditions, between necessity and possibility, and between what is certain and what is only contingently known.

Many prep companies have you spend time memorizing "question stems", by which they mean the types of modal terms you find within a question. You have been using these modal terms since the beginning of your prep, so there is no reason to have to memorize question *stems*. All you need to do to succeed in figuring out what the question is

asking you on the AR section is use your modal logic *tip-offs*. The tip-offs function as your heads-up that a logical notation is happening in the statement.

Questions and Organization

As mentioned above, logical organization is key to setting up the relationships correctly. The Analytical Reasoning section requires you to organize subjects into groups. The names of the subjects will not matter—in fact, you will want to only use the first letter of each subject's name for simplicity on the LSAT. (So, use "J" for "Jill" and "L" for "Logician".) Roughly half of the relationship problems on the AR section will require you to organize subjects into groups—and a small number of those will require you to sub-divide into further groups based on conditions placed on the subjects by the passage. The conditions contain information about the order or grouping of subjects. It can be really helpful to map out the logical conditions (using logical notation, which you have already used) in a spatial drawing, to help you clearly visualize the content within the passage and use that information for every question in the question set. Don't worry—this *isn't* about drawing. It is about helping you visualize a significant amount of information readily, so that you can apply that information to all question sets. The bulk of the time crunch in the Analytical Reasoning section is being able to model all of the information within a passage so that you can work it into its basic logical parts. Rather than learn a system of diagramming that will compete with the logical notation you need for the entire exam, it makes good sense instead to use the same logical notation that will keep you succeeding at the LSAT questions.

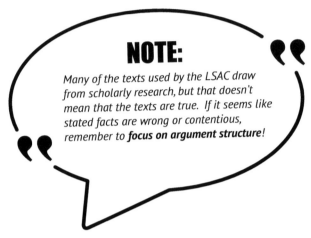

NOTE:

*Many of the texts used by the LSAC draw from scholarly research, but that doesn't mean that the texts are true. If it seems like stated facts are wrong or contentious, remember to **focus on argument structure**!*

AR Pre-Test

Let's see where you are at with your comfort level on AR games, and how you feel applying logical notation to an actual passage.

Directions: Each group of questions in this section is based on a set of conditions. To help you answer the questions, it may be useful to map out the conditions from the passage. Choose the response that most accurately and completely answers each question.

Questions 1-5

The youth bowling league is setting up match play for the season. There are seven teams this year: Manuel Prep, Navasota Academy, Omicron Excel, Penny School, Queen High, Richland Magnet, and Sunnyvale Study. Each of the teams will roll, one at a time, on any given night. The teams will roll according to the following guidelines:

Queen High will roll either first or seventh.
Omicron Excel rolls some time after Manuel Prep.
Sunnyvale Study rolls some time after Navasota Academy.
Exactly one team rolls between Manuel Prep and Penny School, whether or not Manuel Prep rolls before Penny School.
Exactly one team rolls between Navasota Academy and Queen High, whether or not Navasota Academy rolls before Queen High.

ANALYTICAL REASONING
CHAPTER 5

1. Which one of the following is an order in which the youth team could roll, from first to seventh?

   A. Manuel, Omicron, Richland, Penny, Navasota, Sunnyvale, Queen
   B. Queen, Sunnyvale, Richland, Navasota, Manuel, Penny, Omicron
   C. Navasota, Sunnyvale, Queen, Richland, Manuel, Omicron, Penny
   D. Queen, Omicron, Navasota, Richland, Penny, Sunnyvale, Manuel
   E. Penny, Richland, Manuel, Omicron, Navasota, Sunnyvale, Queen

2. Which of the following could be true?

   A. Richland rolls seventh.
   B. Sunnyvale rolls second.
   C. Sunnyvale rolls first.
   D. Omicron rolls first.
   E. Navasota rolls fourth.

3. If Omicron rolls fourth, which one of the following could be true?

   A. Manuel rolls first.
   B. Manuel rolls second.
   C. Richland rolls first.
   D. Navasota rolls third.
   E. Penny rolls fifth.

4. If Sunnyvale rolls fourth, which team must roll seventh?

   A. Queen
   B. Manuel
   C. Omicron
   D. Penny
   E. Richland

5. If Navasota rolls after Penny, the team to roll fifth could be any of the following EXCEPT:

   A. Manuel
   B. Navasota
   C. Omicron
   D. Richland
   E. Sunnyvale

Notes:

ANALYTICAL REASONING
CHAPTER 5

AR Pre-Test: Draw Your Conditions.

It is almost universally true on the AR section of the LSAT that you will be asked to identify a logically possible order in which your subjects could act. If you set up your conditions correctly—and a visual set up of them based on the passage can help—you will be prepared to understand what is logically possible for a certain group of subjects, what is necessary, and what cannot occur. Remember that in AR questions, there is *one answer that must be true*. This is good news for you! All of the answer choices *except for one* will violate some logical rule. If you find the answer choice that does not violate the rule—you have the right answer! Also, remember that you will use our Insider Insights to select the *easiest questions first*. Almost invariably, the *hypothetical syllogisms are the easiest*. You remember how easy it was to run *modus ponens* and *modus tollens* arguments, right? Well, when you are looking to identify the easiest question within an answer set, hone in on the questions that have the first premise of the MP and MT, "If x is a condition, then... [it must be true] y". The easiest questions will always be the ones that are about *logical necessity—what must be the case*. When these are tied into a hypothetical structure, you are golden. Start there. (Logical possibility is a little more time consuming because so many options are likely possible given the conditions for any answer set.)

Once you have identified which answers you are going to go after first, draw your conditions, and then remove any answers that are not logically possible, given the conditions that you have drawn. *You will use these conditions for all of the questions within the set, so make sure you draw them clearly.*

For this particular question, let's remind ourselves of the conditions:

> Queen High will roll either first or seventh.
> Omicron Excel rolls after Manuel Prep.
> Sunnyvale Study rolls after Navasota Academy.
> Exactly one team rolls between Manuel Prep and Penny School, whether or not Manuel Prep rolls before Penny School.
> Exactly one team rolls between Navasota Academy and Queen High, whether or not Navasota Academy rolls before Queen High.

The first condition tells us there will be one of two options: One in which Queen High rolls first or seventh. There isn't another option for them. (You can scan your answer options and eliminate answer choices that have Queen in any position other than first or seventh. Do you see any? *You should eliminate Question #1, Answer C,* because it has Queen in the 3rd place.) Here are your two options, delineated by # for the first option and $ for the second to avoid confusion with positions, questions, and options:

```
#.     Q    __    __    __    __    __    __

$.     __    __    __    __    __    __    Q
```

The second condition can just be written **MO**. *This helps you remember that Omicron must come after Manuel.* The same function holds true for our third condition, **NS**, in which Navasota rolls before Sunnyvale.

For the fourth condition, we can list, **"M_P"/ "P_M"** *to indicate there will always be exactly one team to roll in between Manuel and Penny.* Similarly, for the fifth condition, we will write, **"N_Q"/ "Q_N"**. Ooooh! Look, this is helpful! We already know that Q can only be in one of two locations for our bowling map. That means that *N* can only be on two locations on the map. Let's put them in for our 2 options:

```
#.     Q    __    N    __    __    __    __

$.     __    __    __    __    N    __    Q
```

Now that we have walked through all of our conditions, we can put the entire map together:

ANALYTICAL REASONING
CHAPTER 5

#.	Q	_	N	_	_	_	_	M_P/P_M
$.	_	_	_	_	N	_	Q	MO NS

This map is going to help us figure out each question, and from it, we will be able to add conditions that each question offers us. Let's look at Question #1. (As a note, you will be choosing easier questions first on the LSAT. But, here I need to teach you the method so will work through the answer options top to bottom. Question #1 isn't the easiest question, but we have already eliminated an answer choice from it!):

1. Which one of the following is an order in which the youth team could roll, from first to seventh?

   A. Manuel, Omicron, Richland, Penny, Navasota, Sunnyvale, Queen
   B. Queen, Sunnyvale, Richland, Navasota, Manuel, Penny, Omicron
   C. ~~Navasota, Sunnyvale, Queen, Richland, Manuel, Omicron, Penny~~ (has Queen 3rd)
   D. Queen, Omicron, Navasota, Richland, Penny, Sunnyvale, Manuel
   E. Penny, Richland, Manuel, Omicron, Navasota, Sunnyvale, Queen

Don't run through these A-E, testing every one. Use your conditions first to eliminate answers. We have already used the first condition to strike out C, which is a helpful move. Let's make sure each answer choice is consistent with the 2nd condition, "MO". Are there any answer choices in which Omicron comes *before* Manuel? Sure- D! So, we will strike it from consideration:

   A. Manuel, Omicron, Richland, Penny, Navasota, Sunnyvale, Queen
   B. Queen, Sunnyvale, Richland, Navasota, Manuel, Penny, Omicron
   C. ~~Navasota, Sunnyvale, Queen, Richland, Manuel, Omicron, Penny~~ (has Queen 3rd)
   D. ~~Queen, Omicron, Navasota, Richland, Penny, Sunnyvale, Manuel~~ (has Omi. before Man.)
   E. Penny, Richland, Manuel, Omicron, Navasota, Sunnyvale, Queen

How about our 3rd condition—are there any answers that have Sunnyvale before Navasota? Sure! (B) does that, and so is in violation. Look at that! We have eliminated three answer choices before our last two conditions. We already have a 50% chance of getting this answer correct!

   A. Manuel, Omicron, Richland, Penny, Navasota, Sunnyvale, Queen
   B. ~~Queen, Sunnyvale, Richland, Navasota, Manuel, Penny, Omicron~~ (has Sun. before Nav.)
   C. ~~Navasota, Sunnyvale, Queen, Richland, Manuel, Omicron, Penny~~ (has Queen 3rd)
   D. ~~Queen, Omicron, Navasota, Richland, Penny, Sunnyvale, Manuel~~ (has Omi. before Man.)
   E. Penny, Richland, Manuel, Omicron, Navasota, Sunnyvale, Queen

Now, just by glancing at (A) and (E), we see that they both have exactly one bowling team between Navasota and Queen, so that fulfills the last condition. But, we also require exactly one team between Penny and Manuel, regardless of who rolls first. (E) has one team (Richland) between them, but (A) has both Omicron and Richland—two teams—between (M · P). That means (E) is the correct answer!

For Question #2, we are asked about *logical possibility*—not necessity. How do you know? We are asked what *could be true*. Similar to Question #1, this sort of question could be so open-ended, it sucks your time away. Don't be suckered into giving up your precious 35 minutes on logical possibility! Use the conditions for the question and answer options:

2. Which of the following could be true?

   A. Richland rolls seventh.
   B. Sunnyvale rolls second.
   C. Sunnyvale rolls first.
   D. Omicron rolls first.
   E. Navasota rolls fourth.

The exact same conditions—the same map—is going to be used for Question #2. And, this particular question does not give you any additional conditions to add to the map:

#. Q	_	N	_	_	_	_	M_P/P_M
$. _	_	_	_	N	_	Q	MO NS

Ask yourself if there are any answers that could be immediately eliminated based on a visualization of the map and the answer options. There are two that should immediately stand out! Omicron cannot roll first because Manuel has to go before it, and Navasota cannot roll fourth, since it needs to roll either in the 3rd or the 5th spot. So, we eliminate (D) and (E):

- A. Richland rolls seventh.
- B. Sunnyvale rolls second.
- C. Sunnyvale rolls first.
- D. ~~Omicron rolls first.~~ (Omicron rolls after Manuel).
- E. ~~Navasota rolls fourth.~~ (Navasota rolls in 3rd or 5th).

Of course, that leads us to good 'ole Sunnyvale. Sunnyvale must follow Navasota. That means that (C) is incorrect. But, if Sunnyvale must follow Navasota, the earliest Sunnyvale can roll is 4th, because the earliest Navasota can roll is 3rd—which means that we have to eliminate (B) as well.

- A. Richland rolls seventh.
- B. ~~Sunnyvale rolls second.~~ (Sunnyvale rolls after Navasota, which rolls earliest at 3rd).
- C. ~~Sunnyvale rolls first.~~ (Sunnyvale rolls after Navasota).
- D. ~~Omicron rolls first.~~ (Omicron rolls after Manuel).
- E. ~~Navasota rolls fourth.~~ (Navasota rolls in 3rd or 5th).

And, just like that, we have solved Question #2. Of course, we know there is only one correct answer and in the Analytical Reasoning section, it is the *perfect* answer, not just the best answer, but we always could test our view, here, that (A) is correct by showing the following:

Queen, Manuel, Navasota, Penny, Omicron, Sunnyvale, Richland

as the proper order. All of our conditions are filled—Queen is first, with exactly one spot between it and Navasota. Manuel rolls before Omicron and has exactly one spot between them and Penny, and Navasota rolls before Sunnyvale.

You are likely getting the hang of this particular question set! We'll use our standard condition map to address Question #3, If Omicron rolls fourth, which one of the following could be true?

- A. Manuel rolls first.
- B. Manuel rolls second.
- C. Richland rolls first.
- D. Navasota rolls third.
- E. Penny rolls fifth.

#. Q	_	N	_	_	_	_	M_P/P_M
$. _	_	_	_	N	_	Q	MO NS

ANALYTICAL REASONING
CHAPTER 5

Insider Insight: New Conditions in Questions

For Question #3, we are given a *new condition*, which will help us. We'll put Omicron fourth on our map—but only for this question! It's incredibly important to remember that conditions that are introduced in the questions do not carry over into other questions. They are *question specific conditions*. You will use them to help flesh out your condition map and solve that single question, and then you will forget it as a condition for your passage. So, let's add this condition:

#.	Q	_	N	O	_	_	_	M_P/P_M	
$.	_	_	_	O	N	_	Q	MO	NS

For Question #3 we are not looking for what *must* be true, but what *could* be true. This is helpful, because if we find answers that *could not* be true, we strike them out as logically possible. Finding logically impossible answers is excellent for us! Are there any answers which stand out as logically possible—given our conditions and the new location of Omicron? The first answer to jump out as logically impossible is (B). If Manuel rolls second, and requires exactly one space between it and Penny, then neither # is an option—because there are two filled spaces between it and the next open spot. For $, there is one open spot (good for Manuel) but the next open spot (required for Penny) is filled by Omicron. So, we eliminate (B).

- **A.** Manuel rolls first.
- **B.** ~~Manuel rolls second.~~
- **C.** Richland rolls first.
- **D.** Navasota rolls third.
- **E.** Penny rolls fifth.

The next condition which is going to give us some traction is MO, coupled with {M_P}/{P_M}. There has to be exactly one team rolling between (M · P), and M must come before O, which we know already is in the 4ᵗʰ spot. *These conditions together eliminate # as a possible order!* # has more than one space between M and P if M comes before O:

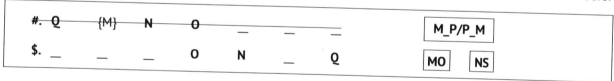

So, $ is going to carry the day for us. We now know where P and M are going to go—either in the first or the third spots, and we know where S is going to be (after N):

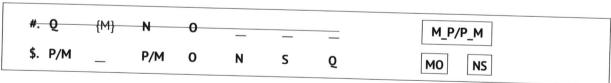

This is a great time to look at our answer choices:

- **A.** Manuel rolls first.
- **B.** ~~Manuel rolls second.~~
- **C.** Richland rolls first.
- **D.** Navasota rolls third.
- **E.** Penny rolls fifth.

Look at that! We know it *is* possible for Manuel to bowl first, which puts Penny in the third spot, and the other conditions are fulfilled. Answer (A) is correct! I won't take time here to show you the frustration of trying to see if the other options are logically possible (because they aren't!), but it involves a lot of trying and failing to fit pieces together. We have our correct answer, and we're ready to look at Question #4:

4. If Sunnyvale rolls fourth, which team must roll seventh?

   A. Queen
   B. Manuel
   C. Omicron
   D. Penny
   E. Richland

Great! This gives us a new condition, and it should be pretty straightforward, since we know that Queen either rolls first or seventh in all cases. Let's use our conditions, and this time add the condition (for this question only!) that Sunnyvale bowls in the fourth position:

#.	Q	_	N	S	_	_	_	M_P/P_M
$.	_	_	_	S	N	_	Q	MO NS

Just based on our new condition, we can see that $ is eliminated from logical possibility. Navasota must roll before Sunnyvale, and there can only be exactly one team between Queen and Navasota, which means that Navasota is either in the third spot (when Queen is in the first spot), or in the sixth spot. But in $, Sunnyvale comes in the fourth spot, before Navasota, so we are going to remove it as logically possible on our map:

#.	Q	_	N	S	_	_	_	M_P/P_M
$.	~~_~~	~~_~~	~~_~~	~~S~~	~~N~~	~~_~~	~~Q~~	MO NS

Now that we are focused on #, what answer choices can be eliminated as possible from rolling seventh? Obviously, none of the teams we already have assigned can be filled by the seventh spot, so if Queen, Navasota, or Sunnyvale are potential answers, we eliminate those. There, of course, is Queen sitting at (A), so we remove that.

   A. ~~Queen~~ (must roll 1st)
   B. Manuel
   C. Omicron
   D. Penny
   E. Richland

Of course, we know that Manuel cannot go in the seventh spot, because Omicron must roll after it.

   A. ~~Queen~~ (must roll 1st)
   B. ~~Manuel~~ (must precede Omicron)
   C. Omicron
   D. Penny
   E. Richland

But, in what order could Manuel go, given our conditions? Manuel *cannot* roll second, because there would not be space for Penny to accompany close by. We know Manuel could not go in the sixth spot as well, because there would not be room for a team to squeeze between them and Penny. Since Omicron comes after Manuel, and we need exactly one team to bowl in between, them and Penny, the order looks like this:

#.	Q	_	N	S	M	O	P

The result is the Penny will roll seventh (Richland will roll second, if we are completing the picture.) Now, we are ready for the final question:

5. If Navasota rolls after Penny, the team to roll fifth could be any of the following EXCEPT:

A. Manuel
B. Navasota
C. Omicron
D. Richland
E. Sunnyvale

We have another opportunity to add a condition here to help us approach the answer choices, which is excellent—the more conditions we have, the more efficiently we will find the correct answer choices. Navasota must roll after Penny, so let's see where they could be able to fit under each scenario, and let's add in the other conditions we know to be true:

#.	Q	P	N	M	_	_	_	M_P/P_M
$.	{P/M}	{M}	{P/M}	{P}	N	S	Q	MO NS

Let's walk through our filled-out map. We know in our # example, Queen and Navasota are first and third. With our new condition from Question #5, Navasota (which is already in the third position) must follow Penny, but there is only one position before Navasota open, the second spot. We remember that there is exactly one team between Penny and Manuel, so Manuel must roll fourth in Scenario #. This leaves the fifth, sixth, and seventh spots open—and any order for Richland, Sunnyvale, or Omicron could fill those spots—which means that (C), (D), and (E) are incorrect—all three could be in the fifth spot with now logical ramifications.

For Scenario $, Navasota is in the fifth spot (which removes option (B) as being correct), and Queen is in the seventh position. This leaves us with one answer choice remaining (A)! If we want to run our options—we *will not do this on the actual LSAT exam!*—we could. We know that Sunnyvale must roll after Navasota, so Sunnyvale rolls sixth in $. That leaves us with the important condition of {M_P}/ {P_M}. Penny could roll first, followed by Richland, then Manuel and Omicron, which means (C) is not correct.

If Navasota rolls after Penny, the team to roll fifth could be any of the following EXCEPT:

A. Manuel
B. ~~Navasota~~ (in $ is in fifth position)
C. ~~Omicron~~ (in 5th, if Penny is first).
D. Richland
E. Sunnyvale

That leaves us with (D) and (E), both of which just by giving a visual glance could indeed sit on the fifth spot without logical implication. (A) indeed is our correct response!

Insider Insight: Complex, Complex Scenarios

You know, it's fascinating. Regardless of the book you pick up or the video you watch, you will have a tough time finding insight into how to beat the Analytical Reasoning section. You will get a multiplicity of ideas about how to draw a picture for the conditions—and that, to some degree, is important because you need to be able to visualize the conditions that apply to entire question sets in order to answer efficiently and correctly. But, at the end of the day, success on the AR comes down to one thing: working problems. Then, working more problems.

So, we are going to work a lot of problems here so that you can see how an expert uses logic to succeed at the logic games in AR. You already know that there are two sorts of activities you will have to do: organize and group, and three sorts of modal terms you will be asked to evaluate in the answers: must, could, and could not. *Most* of the questions will focus around those actions and terms. There are some answer sets that are a bit more complex, because they will ask you to break down groups into smaller groups and set additional conditions on the members of the smaller set. (We can call these "Complex, Complex Scenarios".) The strongest piece of advice is to be consistent with your notation so that you don't find yourself lost in your own notes, in the middle of a question.

There is a way to practice *better*, though, instead of just running headlong into practicing complex exercise sets for Analytical Reasoning. Try to identify what sort of complex scenarios you are being given for any exercise set. One type of complex scenario that is additionally complex is whether there are other conditions that are placed on a certain smaller set of subjects within the group. This is a different complex, complex scenario than the kind that places additional conditions on the order of sub-groups within the question set. Of course, the Ultimate Complex, Complex Scenario will combine the features of each type, and place additional conditions on a smaller set of subjects as well as conditions on the ordering of the groups.

Let's Practice: Complex, Complex Scenarios!

Given that practice really is key for (especially) complex, complex questions on the Analytical Reasoning section, we're going to tackle some of each. But, first we are going to identify which kind of complex, complex scenario we are looking at. Then, we'll know where the conditions will need to apply.

Scenario A: Three baristas have invited one friend each to come in for taste testing of the café's new coffee roast. The baristas, Alicia, Cami, and Dev will taste test alongside their guests, Frank, Goyo, and Hugo. Only one person can try a coffee at a time, and the order they will taste will be guided by the following:

> A guest must take the first taste test.
> A guest will take a taste directly before and after Cami tastes.
> Either Dev or Alicia will take the last test.

1. Which of the following is a complete list of the order in which Cami could taste test the coffee?

   A. first, second, third, fourth, fifth, sixth
   B. second, third, fourth, fifth
   C. third, fourth, fifth
   D. second, third, fourth
   E. fourth, fifth, sixth

Scenario B: An archeologist has discovered that an ancient civilization used pottery for two different functions: cooking and decoration. She finds six pieces of different pottery in one dig location which she identifies as: a pot, a cup, a plate, a skewer, a serving bowl, and a vase. She wants to divide the six pieces into three groups, and each group would have been able to cook or to decorate. She groups them according to the following rules:

> The cup and vase will be in the same group.
> The plate and vase will have the same function.
> The pot will not be used to cook.

2. If the plate is used for cooking and the skewer cannot be in the same unit as the pot, how many pieces can we identify as being in the decoration group?

   A. zero
   B. one
   C. two
   D. three
   E. four

Scenario C: SugarBear is a cereal company that is looking to expand its line of cold cereal. It will release five new brands to stores this week (one at a time), in order: AlphaSugar, BetaMarshmallow, CryptonBits, DulceCrunch, and EatThis. Each new cereal features a different key ingredient to set it apart from its other brands: malitol, nutrisweet, oats, pumpkin, and rice. The release of the brands will follow these guidelines:

BetaMarshmallow does not contain pumpkin.
EatThis will be released prior to BetaMarshmallow, and will contain malitol.
Whichever brand contains pumpkin will release before EatThis.
The second cereal to release will contain nutrisweet.

3. If CryptonBits contains oats and releases third, which is a full list of the cereals which could release first?

   A. AlphaSugar, BetaMarshmallow
   B. AlphaSugar, DulceCrunch, EatThis
   C. DulceCrunch, EatThis
   D. AlphaSugar, BetaMarshmallow, DulceCrunch, Eat This
   E. AlphaSugar, Dulce Crunch

Scenario D: The alumni for the 5-on-5 softball tournament starting lineup was announced to the crowd, one at a time, and in exact order in which they will bat. The rookies were ready to take on the alumni, Hone, Loni, Meredith, Rukes, and Shooter. Each of them were either lefties or righties, and each of them were known either for their defensive or offensive prowess. The voice talent announced them according to the following rules:

The lead-off hitter for the alumni is either Rukes, who is a leftie, or Shooter, who is also a leftie.
Loni will be announced immediately after Hone.
Loni is not a leftie and she isn't known for her defense.
Whoever is batting third is a leftie and known as an offensive powerhouse.

4. If Meredith bats last, what is a list of the players who could bat second?

   A. Rukes, Shooter
   B. Loni, Hone, Rukes, Shooter
   C. Hone, Shooter
   D. Loni, Shooter
   E. Hone, Rukes, Shooter

Notes:

Answer Explanations

1. **D**

   A nice feature of this question is that it allows you to immediately pick out that this complex, complex question is divided into two, smaller sets of subjects. You might get tripped up on the idea that the baristas invite a guest, and try to figure out if knowing who invited whom is important. That is a time suck, so don't fall into that trap. Stick to what matters for the question—which is asking you about the order of a given person. What is singularly important to the order is, instead, the subgroups the question forms between baristas and invitees. From this information, you can divide the groups into two lines, the conditions that we know, and the six spots in which the subjects will taste test the coffee:

Baristas	Guests	1st: (G) →	(G) _ _ _ _ _
Alicia	Hugo	(G)C(G)	
Cami	Isela	6th: (D v A)→	(G) _ _ _ _(D/A) This is our final known setup.
Dev	Justine		

   We will keep in mind the second condition, (G)C(G), as we approach our question. This question asks the *complete list* of the order in which Cami could participate in the taste test. Cami is a barista, not a guest. That means that she cannot go first. We also know either Dev or Alicia have to go last. So, any answer choice which includes the first position or the last position must be removed from consideration because those spots are taken by the condition we are given elsewhere in the passage. That is helpful to us, because we can eliminate (A) and (E) without any effort! We also know that Cami will be flanked by guests. That means she could taste second (as long as a guest followed her). So, if an answer choice does not include "second" among the possible positions, we remove it as a correct choice. That helps us remove (C), and just like that we have a 50% chance of getting this question correct, even if we guessed. But, we aren't going to have to guess. Dev and Alicia, either of whom are in the last position, are baristas, not guests. So, they cannot flank Cami. That means Cami cannot be in the fifth position, which excludes (B) from being logically possible. (D), then, is our correct choice! And, we are glad that it is, because Cami could logically be either in 2nd, 3rd, or 4th position to taste test, and still be flanked on both sides by guests:

   Scenario 1: G C G G B (D/A)
   Scenario 2: G G C G B (D/A)
   Scenario 3: G B G C G (D/A)

2. **C**

   You can start off by identifying this complex, complex scenario as one that requires you to have three different units of pottery that are divided by their two functions (pottery that cooks, C, and pottery that decorates, D). Use abbreviations for your subjects (I'm going to use P for pot, U for cup, L for plate, S for skewer, B for bowl, and V for vase). Set up the two functions first, and then put in the conditions prior to approaching the question:

   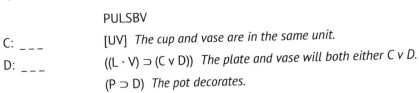

   PULSBV

   C: _ _ _   [UV] *The cup and vase are in the same unit.*

   D: _ _ _   ((L · V) ⊃ (C v D)) *The plate and vase will both either C v D.*

   (P ⊃ D) *The pot decorates.*

Given the 3rd condition, we know that:

C: _ _ _   Unit 1: UV

D: P/ _ _   Unit 2:

                  Unit 3:

Now, the question gives us two new conditions: the plate functions to cook and the skewer is not in the same unit as the pot. Let's add those conditions.

C: L V   Unit 1: UV

D: P   Unit 2: P

                  Unit 3: S

This is helpful as a visualization technique. We can see that UV are teamed together, that L and B will be with either P or S but not together. But, what about the question? How many can we determine will function to decorate? We know the pot will decorate, and we know that the skewer is not in the same units as U, V, and P. U must have an opposite function than V, with which it is paired, so U must decorate, (D: P U). We know that S will be paired either with L or B, though we do not know the function of S. If S cooks, then S will be paired with B, which will cook. But, if S decorates, S will be paired with L, which must cook in any scenario. Based on these facts, we can determine with finality only *two* of the three positions in the decorating group, P and U, and so the correct answer is (C).

3. **E**

This complex, complex question requires you to group two different types of subjects but does not give you further conditions to help you align them across all question sets. Now, the question itself provides two additional conditions (CryptonBits contains oats and releases third) and from our total conditions we can start mapping the question. In complex, complex questions like these, it makes good sense just to put units together that can help you determine some groupings.

Brands: ABCDE

Ingredients: MNOPR

(B ⊃ ~P) *B does not contain P*

[(E• M)B] *E contains M, before B*

[PE] *brand with pumpkin before E*

_N *2nd cereal contains nutrisweet*

(C · O) *C has oats*

_C *C is 3rd*

Let's start with the ordering that is easiest: the cereal with the nutrisweet is 2nd, and 3rd is CO:

[] [/N] [CO] [] [] []

[EM] is one of the units, but we aren't yet sure where it goes, except that it must come after the brand with pumpkin, and before BetaMarshmallow. Since BetaMarshmallow does not contain pumpkin, that means it will contain either nutrisweet or rice. *But*, BetaMarshmallow cannot contain nutrisweet, because nutrisweet is in a brand that comes second, and we know BetaMarshmallow cannot come second because it must come after [EM], and [EM] cannot go first. That means that BetaMarshmallow contains rice [BR], leaving either (A v D) to contain pumpkin. Here are the two scenarios which are logically possible:

[AP] [DN] [CO] [EM] [BR] *EM is before B, Pumpkin before E, CO.*

[DP] [AN] [CO] [EM] [BR] *EM is before B, Pumpkin before E, CO*

Although, definitely a "complex, complex scenario", we have a definitive answer of the brands that could release first: AlphaBits and DulceCrunch, which is found in (E).

4. **A**

We've reached a most complex, complex scenario! In this one, we have a logic game that includes three different sorts of groups—the players, their ability to hit from the left or right, and whether stronger in defense or offense. There are a lot of moving parts, and clear organization can save the day for you to come to a logical conclusion here. We start with the list of players, the known batting order, and whether they are leftie (I'm using "F" since "L" is used for Loni) or rightie (I'm using "T" because "R" will be used for Rukes) and known for offense (O) or defense (D):

LMHSR   _ _ _ _ _

[RF v SF] _ _ _ _   *1st position is either Rukes or Shooter, both lefties.*
[HL] *Hone then Loni*
[(L ⊃ (T · O))] *Loni is not a leftie and she isn't known for her defense.*
(3 ⊃ (F · O)) *Whoever is batting third is a leftie and offensive.*

Mapping these conditions, along with our question's condition that Meredith bats last, onto our batting order allows us to fill it out a bit:

1st: [RF v SF]

2nd:

3rd: ~L (Loni can't bat third because she is not a leftie.)

4th:

5th: M

This is a great time to talk about the second condition. Hone must go immediately before Loni. Since Loni cannot bat third, the only place Loni can bat is 4th (because we know that Hone does not bat 1st). That means Hone bats third, to fulfill the second condition:

1st: [RF v SF]

2nd:

3rd: H

4th: L

5th: M

We have the complex, complex scenario almost completely filled out—but certainly, filled out enough to correctly answer the question. There are two possible people who could hit in the 2nd spot: Rukes or Shooter—the same people who could hit in the 1st spot. (A) indicates the full list of people who could hit 2nd if Meredith bats last.

You should have a really good idea about how to 1) identify complex, complex scenarios and then, 2) how to map them so that you are capturing the conditions properly, not confusing yourself, and then 3) working whatever conditions are given to you to correctly apply the conditions so that you can derive the correct answer, even if the conditions are insufficient to give you a complete list of the groups possible in the problem. We are ready to do some shorter passage sets, with some straight-forward questions as well as some complex, complex scenarios!

Let's Practice! Shorter Analytical Reasoning Games.

Scenario 1

During a family reunion, nine siblings (Rowdy, Stan, Tilly, Uma, Vince, Walt, Xav, Yuriel, and Zena) want to play cards but there are too many of them for a good game. They decide to split into three groups to make the game more fun. They split the teams accordingly:

Xav and Uma cannot play in the same group.
Vince and Walt will play together, either with Zena or Yuriel.
Tilly will play in a group if and only if Rowdy is in the group.

1. The groups could contain the following trios EXCEPT:

   A. Xav, Tilly, Rowdy
   B. Uma, Tilly, Rowdy
   C. Yuriel, Xav, Stan
   D. Yuriel, Tilly, Rowdy
   E. Zena, Uma, Stan

2. Which of the following conditions, if true, would help you establish all three groups?

   A. Yuriel is grouped with Vince
   B. Tilly is grouped with Xav
   C. Stan is grouped with Xav
   D. Rowdy is grouped with Uma
   E. Zena is grouped with Uma

Scenario 2

Gustavo is cooking for a prime-time television show, and wants to show off his six pasta dishes, which are cooked three different ways. The dishes (Fettuccini, Lasagna, Manicotti, Pomodoro, Ravioli, and Ziti) can be broiled, grilled, and fried. Gustavo will cook the dishes according to the following recipe rules:

Pomodoro will not be broiled.
If the Fettuccini is fried, the Manicotti will be grilled.
Lasagna and Ravioli will be prepared with the same method.
Two times as many pasta dishes will be fried as are broiled.

1. If the Fettuccini is not broiled, which of the following must be false?

   A. Lasagna is broiled.
   B. Fettuccini is grilled.
   C. Ravioli is grilled.
   D. Ziti is grilled.
   E. Pomodoro is fried.

2. Which of the following conditions, if true, would determine how each dish is prepared?

   A. Ziti is broiled.
   B. Pomodoro is grilled.
   C. Manicotti is grilled.
   D. Fettuccini is fried.
   E. Lasagna is fried.

Scenario 3

The mad scientist generated seven new chemical elements, all of which he believed would send him back to the future. To successfully go back to the future, the scientist needed to place each element (Arboretetich, Boggledoch, Centaush, Dillydallysh, Effusiumch, Gargantish, and Hermitsh) into a petri dish, one at a time, from left to right across the dish, in the following way:

Effusiumch will be placed fourth.
Either Centaush or Boggledoch is placed first.
There are exactly three elements between Gargantish and Dillydallysh.
There is one element placed between Centaush and Dillydallysh.

1. If Centaush is not placed first, which of the places could Arboretetich occupy?

    A. 2
    B. 2, 3, 5
    C. 2, 5, 6
    D. 2, 6
    E. 6

2. Which of the following could be true?

    A. Centaush is placed second.
    B. Gargantish is placed second.
    C. Dillydallysh is placed second.
    D. Boggledoch is placed second.
    E. Boggledoch is placed seventh.

Scenario 4

It's time for parent/teacher conferences, which can always be a nightmare to schedule. Ms. Carden has the parents of six children (Jax, Kai, Leo, Mia, Nia, and Obi) left to accommodate in the last six schedule spots, and she has to fit them in according to the following constraints:

Neither Jax's nor Mia's parents will be in the last spot.
Mia's parents must be scheduled in a spot after Nia's.
Either Leo's or Nia's parents will be scheduled in the third spot.
Leo's parents will be scheduled for the spot before Jax's or after Mia's parents, but not both.

1. If Nia's parents are scheduled for the first spot, each of the following could be true EXCEPT:

    A. Mia's parents are scheduled in the second spot.
    B. Jax's parents are scheduled in the second spot.
    C. Kai's parents are scheduled in the fourth spot.
    D. Mia's parents are scheduled in the fifth spot.
    E. Obi's parents are scheduled in the sixth spot.

2. Which one of the following must be false:

    A. Kai's parents are scheduled in the first spot.
    B. Leo's parents are scheduled in the second spot.
    C. Nia's parents are scheduled in the in the fourth spot.
    D. Kai's parents are scheduled in the fifth spot.
    E. Leo's parents are scheduled in the last spot.

Answer Explanations: Shorter Scenarios

Scenario 1

1. C

To set up this scenario, we want to set up our potential groups of play, according the conditions that we have. The great thing about this scenario is that the first two conditions tell us a significant amount about how the teams will be constituted:

RSTUVWXYZ

Group: X _ _   ~[XU]
Group: U _ _ $((V \cdot W) \supset (Z \lor Y))$ *V and W are together, with either Z v Y*
Group: VW[ZvY] $(T \equiv R)$

Ok, this is what we know: Xav and Uma are in different groups, so we separate them immediately into different groups on the map. The second condition tells us that Vince and Walt will be in the same group. You might worry that they could be paired either with Xav or with Uma—but remember that as long as Vince and Walt are together, they need to be in the same group either with Zena or Yuriel. The result is that Zena or Yuriel will be the third member of the group with Vince and Walt, and so can't play together with Xav or Uma. So, one group is known completely. Keep in mind that Tilly and Rowdy must play in a group together, so they together will go either with Zena or Yuriel.

Now that we have our map set up, let's look at the first question, in which we are asked to identify the group that could not be together. Rather than spend time writing down each possibility, we know that this question is asking us to identify an answer choice *that is not logically possible*. That should be really easy to identify! You know that Tilly and Rowdy are going to go together (always), and that Vince, Walt and either Zena or Yuriel are possible. So, eliminate (A), (B), and (E) right away. That leaves (C) and (D), but you don't have to do much to see that (C) is logically possible—if in the first group, we have Xav, then Yuriel will be in the first group (leaving Zena in the 3rd group), and Stan has no conditions so can go with the other two. (D) is not logically possible. Tilly and Rowdy are together, sure, but that means the only people they logically could be paired with are Xena or Uma.

2. E

We use the same map set-up for the second question:

RSTUVWXYZ

Group: X _ _   ~[XU]
Group: U _ _ $((V \cdot W) \supset (Z \lor Y))$ *V and W are together, with either Z v Y*
Group: VW[ZvY] $(T \equiv R)$

Unfortunately, we aren't given more conditions with this question to plug-in. Instead, this question's *answers* are a set of conditions, and our job is to identify which of them, if true, could help us figure out the constitution of all three groups. The huge temptation for this kind of question is to waste too much time on the wrong answers. *As soon as you hit an uncertainty in a group, move to the next answer choice.* The questions that ask you to identify a condition that sets up the correct set-up for all other groups indicate that there cannot be indeterminacy with an answer. So, as soon as you find indeterminacy, move on to the next answer choice!

For (A), if Yuriel is with Vince, she is also with Walter and we have one group determined. But we won't know if Zena is with Xena or Uma, so (A) is incorrect. (B) is similarly indeterminate, since if Tilly is with Xav, we still won't know if either Zena or Yuriel is with Vince and Walt. (C) does not help. If Stan is with Xav—do we know whether Zena or Yuriel are paired with Vince and Walt? (D) cannot lead to determinacy in all three groups, for the exact same reason—we don't know if Zena or Yuriel will be joining Zena. (E), however, does determine every single group:

Group: X T R   ~[XU]
Group: U Z S   ((V · W) ⊃ (Z v Y)) *V and W are together, with either Z v Y*
Group: V W Y   (T ≡ R)

Scenario 2

1. **A**

Don't be daunted by mathematical conditions—mathematical conditions are logical conditions, and we are working this LSAT for what it is—a logic test. So, we welcome conditions like the fourth condition of this passage, which determines a very basic disjunction for the dishes: since it is true that two times as many dishes will be fried as broiled, the *only two results are* that there will be either two dishes broiled and four dishes fried, or there will be one dish that is broiled and two dishes that are fried. We set up our map with those two logical possibilities as the foundation for our deliberations on these questions:

FLMPRZ

Possibility A.   Broiled: _ _   Possibility B.   Broiled: _
                 Grilled: nil   Grilled: _ _ _
                 Fried: _ _ _ _   Fried: _ _

[LR]
((F is D) ⊃ (M is G)) *if Fettuccini is fried (D), then Manicotti is grilled.*
(P is ~B)

Now, let's plug in our pasta dishes onto the map, starting with Possibility A and using the conditions of Gustavo's recipes, along with the first question's condition that Fettuccini is not broiled:

FLMPRZ

Possibility A.   Broiled: _ _   Possibility B.   Broiled: _
                 Grilled: nil   Grilled: _ _ _
                 Fried: P _ _   Fried: _ _

[LR]
((F is D) ⊃ (M is G)) *if Fettuccini is fried (D), then Manicotti is grilled.*
(P is ~B)
Question 1: (F is ~B)

We immediately run into a problem with Possibility A, if Fettuccini is not broiled. If it isn't broiled, it must either be grilled or fried. We know, in the first possibility, that no dish is grilled. So, Fettuccini in Possibility A must be fried. But, the second condition tells us that if Fettuccini is fried, then Manicotti must be grilled. That leads to a contradiction, because there are no grilled dishes on Possibility A. So, *for this question*, under this new condition, we have to run with Possibility B. Let's fill it in.

FLMPRZ

~~Possibility A.~~   ~~Broiled: _ _~~   Possibility B.   Broiled: [Z v M]
                     ~~Grilled: nil~~   Grilled: _ _ _
                     ~~Fried: P _ _~~   Fried: _ _

[LR]
((F is D) ⊃ (M is G)) *if Fettuccini is fried (D), then Manicotti is grilled.*
(P is ~B)
Question 1: (F is ~B)

Possibility B gives us far fewer determinates. We do know that neither Pomodoro or Fettuccini are broiled, and we know that Lasagna and Ravioli have to be prepared the same way. But, if Lasagna and Ravioli are prepared the same way, they have to be either grilled or fried—they cannot be broiled because in Possibility B there is only one dish that is broiled. There aren't other logical implications if Lasagna and Ravioli are either grilled or fried—they both are logically possible. (If they are fried, both Pomodoro and Fettuccini must be grilled. If they are grilled, both Pomodoro and Fettuccini are fried. Of course, if Fettuccini is fried, Manicotti is grilled—which would make it determinate that Ziti is broiled. But, we can't know if Fettuccini is fried or grilled.)

So, we aren't left with many determinations in Possibility B—*except that either Ziti or Manicotti is broiled.* Based on this knowledge, let's approach our answer choices to determine which of them must be false. It should be clear! Lasagna can't be broiled (A), because the only determinant we actually have for this particular possibility is that either Ziti or Manicotti (but no other dish) is broiled. There isn't a need to evaluate other answer options—we have found our logical impossibility in answer (A)!

2. D

The second scenario gives us the same question (and so, a similar approach) as the second question of the first scenario. Just as we did there, here we are not given more conditions to help but are asked to identify which additional condition, if true, could lead to a logical determination of how each dish is prepared. A difference with this question is that we have to run the conditions for two different logically possible scenarios. *As soon as you hit an uncertainty in a group, move to the next answer choice.* The questions that ask you to identify a condition that sets up the correct set-up for all other groups indicate that there cannot be indeterminacy with an answer. So, as soon as you find indeterminacy, you are rolling on to the next choice. Our set-up will be the same (without the added condition placed by Question #1, because that only applies to the answer choices for Question #1).

FLMPRZ

Possibility A. Broiled: _ _
Grilled: nil
Fried: P _ _

Possibility B. Broiled: _
Grilled: _ _ _ [LR]/P
Fried: _ _   [LR]/P

[LR]
((F is D) ⊃ (M is G)) *if Fettuccini is fried (D), then Manicotti is grilled.*
(P is ~B)

Prior to evaluating each answer option for the logical determinacy of the entirety of the dishes, prior to even looking at the answer choices, evaluate the conditions and the placement that is determined on the Possibility Maps. Ask yourself which condition, if known, could really be beneficial. There seem to be some obvious helps, right? If we knew how any one of Lasagna, Ravioli, or Fettuccini were prepared, we would be in at least a better position to know. Comparatively, it does not look like knowing how Ziti, Pomodoro, or Manicotti are prepared will help us. ("Manicotti!" you might say, "If I knew Manicotti was grilled, I could know that Fettuccini was fried!" Stop, and evaluate that logical fallacy. If you know that Manicotti is grilled, what can you deduce about Fettuccini? Absolutely nothing. That is an example of the "affirming the consequent" logical fallacy. If, however, a condition indicated "Manicotti is not grilled", *then* you can validly deduce a fact about Fettuccini—that it is not fried.)

Now that you have in mind that you are looking for conditions that help you know the placement of Lasagna, Ravioli, or Fettuccini, you can take a glance at the answer choices and see if any of them can help you determine the preparation of *more* of the dishes. This is an important step instead of diving right into a top-to-bottom assessment of each answer choice, especially in complex, complex scenarios like this one, in which there are two logical possibilities that must be run. Chances are good that if you pick out one or two that look promising, you actually can get to a correct answer in a much more expedient time, since there *is only one answer* that will

provide a condition that will determine the mode of cooking for every other dish. Which answer choices should you be paying particular attention?

A. Ziti is broiled.
B. Pomodoro is grilled.
C. Manicotti is grilled.
D. Fettuccini is fried.
E. Lasagna is fried.

Just by honing in on the conditions that make a difference to figuring out the most conditions, we have whittled away the answers we should focus on to two, (D) and (E). You can run both of these, or start with your favorite and see if it leads to a determination of placement of other objects. Let's start with (D), the condition that Fettuccini is fried.

FLMPRZ

Possibility A.
Broiled: L R
Grilled: nil
Fried: P F M Z

Possibility B.
Broiled: Z
Grilled: L R M
Fried: F P

[LR]
$((F \text{ is D}) \supset (M \text{ is G}))$ *if Fettuccini is fried (D), then Manicotti is grilled.*
$(P \text{ is } \sim B)$
$(F \text{ is D})$

Look at that! By *only knowing that Fettuccini is fried*, we can determine the preparation for every single one of Gustavo's pasta dishes. Here's how we did it: for both Possibilities, place F in the "fried" spot. For Possibility A, Pomodoro must be fried (because there are no grilled options), so Fettuccini's placement there makes Lasagna and Ravioli (the pair) move to broiled, and Ziti take the remaining spot in the fried category. In Possibility B, Fettuccini is the first of the fried dishes, but we know that Lasagna and Ravioli either have to be grilled or fried in this Possibility, because there is only one dish that is broiled. Given that there is only one fried spot left after Fettuccini is fried, Lasagna and Ravioli must be grilled. We know that Pomodoro cannot be broiled, so it moves to the last fried spot. So, which of Ziti or Manicotti are broiled? Well, the second condition tells us that if Fettuccini is fried, it must make Manicotti grilled, so Manicotti takes the last grilled spot and leaves the final preparation spot for Ziti in the "broiled" category!

There isn't a need to run (E), but if you wanted to for posterity, you could. (This will be a good exercise in giving up on an answer for this particular question type when it leads to indeterminacy.) Let's run the Possibility Maps, with our conditions along with the new (E) condition that Lasagna is fried, and see how far we get:

FLMPRZ

Possibility A.
Broiled: F _
Grilled: nil
Fried: P L R _

Possibility B.
Broiled: _
Grilled: P _ _
Fried: L R

[LR]
$((F \text{ is D}) \supset (M \text{ is G}))$ *if Fettuccini is fried (D), then Manicotti is grilled.*
$(P \text{ is } \sim B)$
$(L \text{ is D})$

This is all we can determine from knowing that Lasagna is fried (L is D). We can complete more on the Possibility A map—we know Pomodoro there must be fried, and if L is fried, Ravioli also is. So those three spots are filled up, leaving one more fried spot available. We know that results in Fettuccini being broiled, because if it took the last fried spot, Manicotti would be grilled, which is a logical impossibility. We can't, however, determine whether Ziti

or Manicotti are broiled or grilled based on the condition that Lasagna is fried. On the Possibility B map, we know even less. If Lasagna and Ravioli (which must accompany Lasagna) are fried, they take the only fried spots, which moves Pomodoro to the grilled prep, because Pomodoro cannot be broiled. But, we cannot determine whether Fettuccini is broiled or grilled, and cannot know the preparation method of Manicotti or Ziti, either.

Hopefully, you can see how much time you save on these questions by, first, asking yourself (without looking at the answers) what the conditions tell you about which subjects could provide you with a lot of information if you knew about them and, second, by eliminating answer choices that do not relate to those conditions.

Scenario 3

In Scenario 2, you were required logically to have two different Possibility Maps, but there are instances in which you will find yourself with a map that, after you have factored in all of the conditions, reveals that you really need another Map. Scenario 3 could be that case for you. The Scenario essentially gives us 3 logically possible ways to organize Dillydallysh, Centaush, and Gargantish. When you are able to determine, from the condition that Centuash or Boggledoch are placed first, so much of the other positions fall into place. For the possibility in which Centaush is placed first, a logical necessity occurs for the organization of Centaush, Dillydallysh, and Gargantish, which allows you to determine the placement of most of the other elements. In the logical possibility that Boggledoch is placed first, the result is a disjunction: either you will have a placement of [Gargantish_Centaush_Dillydallysh] *or* [Dillydallysh_Centaush_Gargantish]. Additionally, the seven elements and the other conditions mean that either the [GCD] or [DCG] placement will be in the 3rd, 5th, and 7th spots, respectively. For that Possibility Map, only Arboretetich and Hermitsch need to be placed.

ABCDEGH (L-R)
Effusiumch will be placed fourth.
Either Centaush or Boggledoch is placed first.
There are exactly three elements between Gargantish and Dillydallysh.
There is one element placed between Centaush and Dillydallysh.
(I'm using "Xs" here to designate open spaces because of the number of subjects)

XXXEXXX
[C v B] X X E X X X
[3_G/D/D/G]
[1_C/D/D/C]

1. D

Now we're ready to approach the first question—we don't have a lot determined, because we are not told whether Gargantish comes before Dillydallysh (or vice versa), or if Centaush comes before Dillydallysh (or vice versa). So, the first question gives us some determinacy, when coupled with the second condition:

ABCDEGH (L-R)
B X X E X X X
[3_G/D/D/G]
[1_C/D/D/C]

On a question like this, I always run the numbers on our answer choices:
- **A.** 2
- **B.** 2, 3, 5
- **C.** 2, 5, 6
- **D.** 2, 6
- **E.** 6

All of the answer choices *except for (E)* include the second spot. I am going to take it as a logical possibility that Arboretetich could be placed second, so I am going to ignore (E), unless it turns out that this is a weird, unmathematically-grounded inference, in which case, I still have (E) to evaluate. But, I'm saving myself some time. I also am going to assume that Arboretetich could be in more than one spot, since we know there are three spaces between Gargantish and Dillydallysh and we can't determine most of the positions on the board. So, I am going to ignore (A), which suggests a level of indeterminacy I just don't have with this massive, complex question set. If I look at (B), (C), and (D) as my remaining answers, I look for commonalities and differences. The key difference is whether Arboretetich could be in 3, 5, or 6. For now, I am going to ignore (D), because it doesn't include 3 or 5. If it turns out that I don't need 3 or 5—guess what? (D) is going to be correct. For (B) or (C), the difference is the 3 and the 6. Since (D) includes the 6, I am going to first assess the answer that includes the 6 (answer C). If it turns out that Arboretetich cannot be placed 6th, I will have determined that answer (B) is correct without having to actually plug in the possibilities for (B). If it turns out that Arboretetich can be placed in the 6th spot, I eliminate (B), and check to see if Arboretetich can be placed 5th. If it can't then answer (D) is my answer! So, let's look at whether Arboretich can be placed in the 6th spot:

    ABCDEGH (L-R)
    B X X E X A X
    [3_G/D/D/G]
    [1_C/D/D/C]

The easiest next step is to put in our "G_ C_ D" possibility in the 3/5/7th spot to see if it fits (this would include one element between C and D, and we remember that we could swap out their positions without facing any negative logical implications):

    ABCDEGH (L-R)
    B H G E C A D
    [3_G/D/D/G]
    [1_C/D/D/C]

Having "A" placed 6th is logically possible. It allows us to fulfill the conditions that there are three elements between Gargantish and Dillydallsh, and one element between Centaush and Dillydallsh (and, this question's condition that Centaush not be placed first). So, since the 6th position is logically possible for Arboretetich, we know that (B) cannot be true (and it allows us to fulfill our predication that (A) cannot be true):

   A. ~~2~~
   B. ~~2, 3, 5~~
   C. 2, 5, 6
   D. 2, 6
   E. ~~6 (ignoring)~~

Given that the difference between (C) and (D) is whether Arboretetich can be placed 5th, that is what we are next going to test, remembering here that Centausch cannot be placed first for this question:

    ABCDEGH (L-R)
    B X X E A X X
    [3_G/D/D/G]
    [1_C/D/D/C]

The sticky point is that we need three placements between Gargantish and Dillydallysh, regardless of which element is placed first. We could place G second, let's try it:

    B G X E A D X

We do need to place C and D in the remaining Xs, but that leaves a problem...the third condition stipulates that only one element can separate C and D. So, (G v D) cannot go in the second spot. We could try putting it in the third spot, but just take a look at the problem *for any spot that remains if A is in the fifth position:*

B X X E A X X

There simply are no spots that allow for exactly one element to be placed between C and D. What is the logical implication? Arboretetich cannot be placed in the 5th position, so (C) is incorrect:

- A. ~~2~~
- B. ~~2, 3, 5~~
- C. ~~2, 5, 6~~
- D. 2, 6
- E. ~~6 (ignoring)~~

We initially ignored (E) as an option, because the other four answers contained the possibility for Arboretetich to be in the second spot. We don't need to do a huge analysis to show that it is logically possible for Arboretetich to be in the second spot, and so for (D) to be correct:

B A D E C H G

Here, Arboretetich is placed second, there are exactly three elements between D and G, and exactly one element between D and C. Perfect! (D) is the correct answer.

2. D

We will start with the same set-up as Question #1, but will not include the determination that Boggledoch will go first (so either (CvB) will go first for this question).

ABCDEGH (L-R)
[C v B] X X E X X X
[3_G/D/D/G]
[1_C/D/D/C]

Your question feels wide-open, but it isn't, actually, when you apply your logic lens. Look at your answer choices, and you will see (just as in Question #1), there is one answer choice that simply doesn't belong, (E). (E) would be quite extraordinary as a single answer choice that does not look at the second position, so ignore it for now. Three of remaining answer choices are logically impossible. ~◊. So, you just need to find the one that is possible, ◊. You know (A) is ~◊, because E is in the fourth spot, which eliminates the possibility of one element being between C and D. *For the exact same reason*, you can eliminate (C).

- A. ~~Centaush is placed second.~~
- B. Gargantish is placed second.
- C. ~~Dillydallysh is placed second.~~
- D. Boggledoch is placed second.
- E. ~~Boggledoch is placed seventh.~~

We are left with (B) and (D), terrific odds to do well here. Let's try (D) first, because we know if D is true, C must be placed first:

C B D E G [A/H]

This works! Centaush is first (so fulfills the second condition), Boggledoch is second, there is exactly one element between Centaush and Dillydallysh, and exactly three elements between Centaush and Gargantish. *We do not have to know whether Arboretetich or Hermitsch are placed sixth or seventh*, as long as the other conditions are fulfilled

without the positions of (A v H) impacting them. They don't—so (D) is the correct answer! Once you find the statement that could be true, there is no need whatsoever to evaluate the statement in (E) which you have been ignoring, because only one of the statements will be logically possible, and you (without equivocation) found it!

Scenario 4

Scenario four gives us a fairly straightforward scheduling scenario, in which the subjects for scheduling spots have to be ordered according to a series of conditions. The driving consideration is the last one, and you might not feel prepared for the odd logical structure of the condition, but we've seen this before: ~(before X · after Y). These are the "not both and" categories which we talked about in Chapter 2. What logically follows from "not both ands" includes (X ⊃ ~Y) and (Y ⊃ ~X). In this particular case, we aren't told whether X or Y obtains, so we will have to rely on other conditions to see if we can make determinations about how the other parents are scheduled.

1. B

In question one, we are given an additional condition, that Nia's parents are in the first spot, and we have to identify which of the options among the five could not be a logical possibility. Let's build our schedule, with that and other conditions:

> JKLMNO
> Last = ~(J v M) *neither Jax nor Mia in last spot*
> [NM] *Nia followed by Mia*
> Third: (L v N) *Leo or Nia in 3rd*
> (L ⊃ ((before J v after M) · ~ (before J · after M))) *Leo will be before Jax and after Mia but not both before Jax or after Mia*
> Question #1, First = N
>
> N X(L)XXX ~(J v M)

Excellent. The condition in the first question allows us to determine the conference schedule for at least some of the spots. Let's run two scenarios—one in which Leo's parents are scheduled before Jax's, and one in which they are scheduled after Mia:

> Possibility A: N M L X J X ~(J v M)
> Possibility B: N X L J M X

Ok, we have some more deductions, which put us in good shape to approach the question. Nia's parents must go first, which means Leo's are in the third spot. Our two scenarios reflect the two logical possibilities that are reflected in the last condition, either Leo's parents immediately follow Mia's, or they immediately precede Jax's. In Possibility A, if Leo's parents are immediately preceded by Mia's parents, we know Jax's cannot be in the fourth position, immediately behind Leo's—but they also cannot go last, according to our conditions, so they must go in the fifth position. Now, we don't have enough information to know whether Obi's parents or Kai's parents go in fourth or sixth in Possibility A, but we'll keep that in mind when we approach the answer choices. In Possibility B, we have Jax's parents immediately following Leo's, which means that Mia's parents cannot go second. They also cannot go last, so the only position they could be scheduled for is the fifth position. In Possibility B, we still won't know whether Obi's or Kai's parents fill in the second or sixth spots.

What then, of the question, in which we are asked to identify which of the answer choices could be? Logically, "could be true" is the crucial phrase. There are four logical possibilities in this question—four answers that *could* be possible under either one of our Possibility Maps. There is one answer that is impossible regardless of the Map. So, we are looking for the statement that cannot obtain regardless of the Possibility Map, on the basis of the conditions provided by this case.

Here is our schedule as it currently stands, given the condition in the first question, for both Possibility Maps:

Possibility A: N M L X J X ~(J v M)
Possibility B: N X L J M X

Look first at the answer choices and eliminate any of the options that contradict what we know to be true (the positions of NML and J in both possibilities), and the two possible positions of (K and O) in each.

- **A.** Mia's parents are scheduled in the second spot.
- **B.** Jax's parents are scheduled in the second spot.
- **C.** Kai's parents are scheduled in the fourth spot.
- **D.** Mia's parents are scheduled in the fifth spot.
- **E.** Obi's parents are scheduled in the sixth spot.

Clearly, (A) must not be false, since they are scheduled in the second spot in Possibility A. Kai's parents could be scheduled in the fourth spot (C) in Possibility A, so we have to remove (C) from consideration. Similarly, (D) cannot be correct, because Mia's parents are scheduled in the fifth spot for Possibility B. We further determined that either Obi's or Kai's parents could be scheduled for the sixth spot. But, (B) can't be true—it must be false, because Leo's parents have to be scheduled third if Nia's are scheduled first, and Leo's parents must either be preceded immediately by Mia's parents (in which case, Jax's parents cannot be scheduled second), or followed immediately by Jax's parents... in which case, they cannot also be scheduled second. Answer (B) is the correct answer, then!

2. B

Interestingly, the second question in this Scenario also asks us to identify a false claim, just in a more direct manner, with which one must be false. We aren't given any more conditions, and we have to remove the condition we were given with the first question, so that we no longer know who is going first. Here is what we have:

JKLMNO
Last = ~(J v M) *neither Jax nor Mia in last spot*
[NM] *Nia followed by Mia*
Third: (L v N) *Leo or Nia in 3rd*
(L ⊃ ((before J v after M) · ~ (before J · after M))) *Leo will be before Jax and after Mia but not both before Jax or after Mia*

X X(L v N)XXX ~(J v M)

Let's run our two logically possible options—this time either with Leo's parents in the third position or with Nia's parents in the third position:

Possibility A: X X L XXX ~(J v M)
Possibility B: X X N XXX ~(J v M)

Several sub-scenarios happen from this Question's Possibility A, for Leo. Let's run at least the obvious iterations of them:

Possibility A1: N M L XXX ~(J)
Possibility A2: X X L J M X
Possibility A3: X J L N M X

Several sub-scenarios also happen from this Question's Possibility B, for Nia. We know that Mia's parents have to follow Nia's. So, they are either in the fourth or fifth position (they cannot go sixth). But, we also know that Leo either must come directly after Mia, or directly before Jax. Let's run the most obvious scenarios:

Possibility B1: X X N M X X ~(J)
    Possibility B1a: L J N M X X
    Possibility B1b: L J N X M X
Possibility B2: X X N M L X
Possibility B3: X X N X M L

In Possibility A1, Leo's parents must come directly after Mia's, but Mia's parents must still come after Nia's, so Nia must be first. Jax's parents then would either be in positions 4 or 5, but we aren't sure. In Possibility A2, we know the same, but end up with different results. Jax's parents must follow Leo's, and since Mia's parents cannot go last, Jax's parents must follow Nia's parents—but, in this possibility, not precede Leo's parents, and so Mia's parents must go fifth. We do not know the composition of the others, except that either the first or second position must be filled by Nia's parents.

In Possibilities B1 and B2, we look at the difference between Nia's parents going third and having Leo's parents immediately follow Mia's or precede Jax's parents. We know the least amount in the latter instance.

OK, we have several logical possibilities based on the disjunction that either Leo's or Nia's parents will take the third position. Now, we compare those possibilities to the answer choices and see which answer choice is incompatible with our Possibility Maps:

    A. Kai's parents are scheduled in the first spot.
    B. Leo's parents are scheduled in the second spot.
    C. Nia's parents are scheduled in the in the fourth spot.
    D. Kai's parents are scheduled in the fifth spot.
    E. Leo's parents are scheduled in the last spot.

(A), of course, is not false because in A2, Kai's parents could be scheduled first, followed by Nia's, and then Obi's would be last. (B) cannot be true! If Leo's parents are in the second spot, then Nia's parents must be in the third position and Leo's parents must be immediately preceded by Mia's parents (since Jax's parents cannot immediately follow him). But, Mia's parents must follow Nia's parents, and so cannot precede Leo's parents here. Now, just for due diligence's sake, we'll continue to eliminate our choices. (C) is found in Possibility A3, so cannot be the correct answer. Kai's parents could be in the fifth spot (D) under Possibility B1a, and Leo's parents could be in the last spot as long as Mia's parents directly precede them and come after Nia's parents, as we see in Possibility B3. So, (B) is confirmed as not logically possible—false—for this question.

Notes:

Scenario Review before Longer Sets

We are rolling in our ability to take passages, and focus on the logic of the conditions used to map and visualize our scenarios—even complex, complex scenarios—correctly. It's important to take a breather here and review what the Analytical Reasoning section primarily asks you to do, so that we can attack *longer scenarios and question sets*. The logic games in AR are primarily about grouping subjects according to certain traits, and then organizing them according to rules. The rules are conditions that govern how to think about the subjects in general, or according to specific qualities. As we have seen, the most straightforward of these provides you with some conditions that allow you to determine at least some of the qualities or ordering of subjects. The most challenging provides you with little guidance and may have you *both* order and qualify subjects—and do this for smaller groups within a passage, as well. But, you have the logical tools needed to approach even the most difficult AR logic games. You are adept at logical notation, and structuring conditions *logically* to reduce confusion and to ensure the proper application of a condition to a passage. I've also given you some strategies for eliminating answer choices out of hand so that you can focus on the few that logically could carry the day for you.

> ## FUN FACT
>
> *Research shows that law school applicants tend to apply only to schools they believe they have a decent shot at getting admitted to, and the top schools receive very few applicants who had middle-and-lower LSAT scores.*

Now that we've taken a moment to catch our breath, let's dive into some question sets that are a bit longer. Longer sets can challenge your ability to stay focused, to not import question-specific conditions to other questions, and to use time wisely. Feel free when you practice these to employ the Insider Insights on these questions—choose the easiest questions first, look for questions that add a condition, and look for questions that raise a hypothetical syllogism. Attacking these questions first will allow you to quickly set up conditions for entire question sets, but then easily dispense with questions that you might otherwise get bogged-down on.

Let's Practice—Longer Scenarios!

Questions 1-4

The State Charitable drive every October frequently turns into a vicious competition among businesses. Goddell's Gas Station this year challenged Pierre's Popsicles to a fundraising campaign. Goddell's staff (Coco, Ellie, Megan, Sue) bet a year's worth of barbeque that Pierre's staff (Brandi, Ann, and Lori) would not be able to raise more money (even though Pierre's was a more popular business). The competition went this way:

Ann raises the fifth most.
Sue raises just more than Lori, or Lori raises just more than Sue.
Exactly one staff member from Pierre's lands in the top three for fundraising.
Brandi raises more than Coco but less than Ellie.

ANALYTICAL REASONING
CHAPTER 5

1. If Brandi raises the sixth most of the staff, what is the last possible position Lori could land in comparison with the group?

    A. first
    B. second
    C. third
    D. fourth
    E. seventh

2. If Brandi raises the third most of the staff, in how many different orders could the staff place?

    A. 1
    B. 2
    C. 4
    D. 5
    E. 6

3. Which of the following conditions, if true, determines the placement of all of the fundraisers?

    A. Brandi raises just less than Ellie and just more than Ann
    B. Brandi raises just less than Megan and just more than Coco
    C. Ann raises just less than Megan and just more than Brandi
    D. Ann raises just less than Coco and just more than Lori
    E. Ann raises just less than Megan and just more than Lori

4. What is the minimum number of fundraisers who raised between the amounts of Brandi and Lori?

    A. 0
    B. 1
    C. 2
    D. 3
    E. 4

Notes:

ANALYTICAL REASONING
CHAPTER 5

Questions 5-11

> The Rare Book Librarian's assistant failed to archive eight new artifacts, into the science or humanities collection, so the Librarian has to do it. The artifacts, from researchers Boon, Contreras, Dega, Euribe, Qui, Rho, Picasso, and Tuto, have to be carefully evaluated to end up in the right collection. Here's what she knows:
>
> Boone is a humanist.
> If Contreras is a humanist, Dega is a scientist.
> If Euribe is a scientist, both Rho and Picasso are humanists.
> The work from Dega and Tuto will not be classified in the same collection.
> The work from Rho and Tuto will be classified in the same collection.

5. Which of the following could be a complete list of the newly archived materials in the sciences?

   A. Contreras, Qui, Rho, Tuto
   B. Contreras, Qui, Rho, Picasso
   C. Contreras, Qui, Rho, Euribe, Tuto
   D. Contreras, Euribe, Tuto, Boon
   E. Qui, Rho, Picasso, Tuto

6. Which of the following conditions, if true, would determine the Librarian's classification of all of the new archive material?

   A. Contreras, Euribe, and Tuto all are scientists
   B. Contreras, Euribe, and Picasso are all scientists
   C. Qui, Euribe and Picasso are all scientists
   D. Contreras, Dega, and Qui are all scientists
   E. Contreras, Dega, and Euribe are all scientists

7. The work of which two researchers cannot be classified in the same collection?

   A. Dega and Rho
   B. Contreras and Dega
   C. Euribe and Rho
   D. Euribe and Picasso
   E. Qui and Picasso

8. If Dega's work can be classified as science, which of the following is a complete list of the researchers whose artifacts could be classified along with Dega?

   A. Contreras, Euribe
   B. Contreras, Euribe, Qui
   C. Contreras, Euribe, Qui, Picasso
   D. Contreras, Euribe, Qui, Picasso, Boone
   E. Contreras, Euribe, Qui, Picasso, Boone, Rho

9. What is the maximum number of researchers whose work could be classified under the humanities?

   A. 3
   B. 4
   C. 5
   D. 6
   E. 7

10. Which of the following conditions, if substituting for the condition that Dega and Tuto must be classified differently, would have the same effect on the classification of the other research?

    A. If Rho is classified as science, Dega is in the humanities.
    B. If Rho is classified in the humanities, Dega will be in science.
    C. Rho will be classified in science if and only if Dega is in the humanities.
    D. If Tuto is classified in science, Contreras will be also.
    E. Tuto will be classified in science if and only if Contreras is classified in science.

11. If the condition that Tuto and Rho will be classified in the same category is replaced by a condition in which Tuto and Rho must be classified differently, which of the following is a complete list of researchers whose work is classified in science?

    A. Dega, Rho, Euribe, Qui, Picasso
    B. Contreras, Euribe, Picasso, Tuto
    C. Contreras, Dega, Qui, Picasso
    D. Contreras, Qui, Tuto
    E. Contreras, Euribe, Tuto, Dega

Notes:

ANALYTICAL REASONING
CHAPTER 5

Questions 12-17

Narciso is adding to his herd of cows and is pitching to his customers that he has six different breeds, all of which are massive and hail from around the world: Anjou, Brahman, Chianina, Glan, Normande, Voerderwald. In his brochure, Narciso writes:

Voerderwald weighs more than Chianina.
Chianina weighs more than Anjou.
Brahman weighs less than Glan.
Chianina weighs more than Normande.
Normande weighs more than Glan.

12. Which of the following statements must be true?

 A. Chianina is heavier than Glan.
 B. Chianina is lighter than Glan.
 C. Anjou is lighter than Brahman.
 D. Chianina is lighter than Normande.
 E. Normande is heavier than Anjou.

13. Which of the following cannot be true?

 A. Glan is heavier than Chianina.
 B. Glan is lighter than Chianina.
 C. Anjou is lighter than Brahman.
 D. Chianina is heavier than Normande.
 E. Normande is heavier than Anjou.

14. How many breeds must be lighter than Normande?

 A. 0
 B. 1
 C. 2
 D. 3
 E. 4

15. How many breeds must be heavier than Glan?

 A. 1
 B. 2
 C. 3
 D. 4
 E. 5

16. If Narciso adds an additional breed to his herd, a Pinzgauer, which is lighter than three of the original six breed sizes, which of the following must be true?

A. Normande is heavier than Pinzgauer.
B. Chianina is heavier than Pinzgauer.
C. Glan is heavier than Pinzgauer.
D. Anjou is lighter than Pinzgauer.
E. Anjou is heavier than Pinzgauer.

17. If Narciso adds a new breed to his herd, a Holstein, and it is heavier than three of the original six breeds, which of the following CANNOT be true?

A. Holsteins are heavier than Anjous.
B. Holsteins are heavier than Glans.
C. Holsteins are heavier than Normandes.
D. Holsteins are lighter than Chianinas.
E. Holsteins are lighter than Glans.

Notes:

ANALYTICAL REASONING
CHAPTER 5

Questions 18-23

A department chair is assigning twelve courses to three faculty members, Griff, Irwin, and Shady, to their four equal course timeslots during the week. Griff's classroom is adjacent to Irwin's, and Irwin's classroom is adjacent to Shady's. Each course is taught exactly once, and three of the courses are taught simultaneously. The courses are Aesthetics, Boulean proofs, Culpability, Deontology, Existentialism, Frege, God, Happiness, Inferences, Justification, Kantianism, and Liberty. The chair scheduled the courses by using the following guidelines:

Only Irwin teaches Justification, Kantianism, and Liberty.
Boulean proofs and Happiness must be taught by Shady.
Culpability, Existentialism, and Frege cannot be taught by Shady.
Aesthetics, Deontology, and Happiness are taught at the same time.
The following courses cannot be taught in adjacent rooms at the same time: Boulean proofs, Deontology, Existentialism, Frege, Happiness, and Inferences.

18. Which of the following must be true:

   A. Courses (B, D, E, F, H, and I) will not be taught by Griff.
   B. Courses (B, D, E, F, H, and I) will not be taught by Irwin.
   C. The complete list of the courses taught by Shady is (B, D, E, F, H, and I).
   D. The complete list of the courses taught by Irwin is (B, D, E, F, H, and I).
   E. All three professors teach the courses (B, D, E, F, H, and I).

19. Which three courses CANNOT be the first courses for Griff, Irwin, and Shady, respectively?

   A. Existentialism, Justification, Boulean proofs
   B. Frege, Kantianism, Inferences
   C. Deontology, Aesthetics, Happiness
   D. Culpability, Liberty, God
   E. Existentialism, Kantianism, God

20. If Happiness is taught in the first class, which of the following must be true?

   A. Culpability is the third course.
   B. Existentialism is the second course.
   C. Liberty is the fourth course.
   D. Frege is the first course.
   E. Boulean proofs is the third course.

21. If Justification is the second course, which of the following could be true?

   A. Existentialism is the second course.
   B. Happiness is the third course.
   C. Culpability is the fourth course.
   D. Liberty is the third course.
   E. Aesthetics is the last course.

22. If Aesthetics is the first course, which of the following cannot be true?

   A. Existentialism is the second course.
   B. Frege is the second course.
   C. Inferences is the second course.
   D. God is the second course.
   E. Kantianism is the second course.

23. If Culpability and Deontology are the second and fourth courses, respectively, which of the following could be true?

   A. Kantianism is the first course.
   B. Frege is the third course.
   C. Liberty is the second course.
   D. Aesthetics is the first course.
   E. Existentialism is the fourth course.

Notes:

ANALYTICAL REASONING
CHAPTER 5

Answer Explanations: Longer Scenarios!

For this first passage, we set up our conditions that apply to the entire question set. We have seven fundraisers, and we are trying to gauge the order in which they raised money, from most to least.

Goddell: Coco, Ellie, Megan, Sue; Pierre: Brandi, Ann, Lori

ABCELMS
(A is 5th) Ann raises the fifth most.
((SL) v (LS)) Sue raises just more than Lori, or Lori raises just more than Sue.
Pierre: (=1 in top 3) Exactly one staff member from Pierre's lands in the top three for fundraising.
(E > B > C) Brandi raises more than Coco but less than Ellie.

1. C

Question 1 provides us with a new condition, that Brandi finishes sixth, and then asks us something specific, based on that condition, about Lori's performance. We are supposed to evaluate the lowest rank in which Lori could have completed the fundraiser. If Brandi finished sixth, that means that Coco finishes seventh, and that Ellie must finish in one of the first four spots. Let's take a look at how our Map will look:

XXXX A B C
[E]

Because both Brandi and Ann are outside of the top three spots, that means that Lori must have finished in the top three for Pierre:

XXXX A B C

[L] [E]

Despite not being able to determine with precision the first four fundraisers (given these conditions), this question is asking about how Lori finished. Now we know! She could not have ranked lower than 3rd among the fundraisers! Looking at our answers below, (C) is the correct choice.

    A. first
    B. second
    C. third
    D. fourth
    E. seventh

2. C

This question positions Brandi quite differently. The new condition has her placed third, in which case Sue and Lori must finish in sixth or seventh (regardless of order). We'll use our conditions and Map to visualize:

ABCELMS
(A is 5th) Ann raises the fifth most.
((SL) v (LS)) Sue raises just more than Lori, or Lori raises just more than Sue.
Pierre: (=1 in top 3) Exactly one staff member from Pierre's lands in the top three for fundraising.
(E > B > C) Brandi raises more than Coco but less than Ellie.

X X B X A [S/L]

ANALYTICAL REASONING
CHAPTER 5

We know that both that Sue and Lori are going to follow each other, which originally would put them either in the first/second spot, or the sixth/seventh spot. However, Brandi, from Pierre's team, is already in the top three, which disqualifies Lori from being either in the first or second spot. So, Sue and Lori will anchor the list at six and seven. That means that Coco has to raise the 4th most, because the conditions indicate she raises less than Brandi, who is in third (and there are no more spots open!). There are, then, two alternate possibilities for the first and second highest, and two different options for the sixth and seventh spot—which means there are four different ways in which the fundraisers could have finished. Looking at our answer choices:

- **A.** 1
- **B.** 2
- **C.** 4
- **D.** 5
- **E.** 6

we'll see that (C) is the correct response.

3. E

We are going to need to start with our conditions and Map prior to wrangling with this complex question.

ABCELMS
(A is 5th) Ann raises the fifth most.
((SL) v (LS)) Sue raises just more than Lori, or Lori raises just more than Sue.
Pierre: (=1 in top 3) Exactly one staff member from Pierre's lands in the top three for fundraising.
(E > B > C) Brandi raises more than Coco but less than Ellie.

X X X X A [S/L]

Let's apply the Texas Two Step, since this is a question that asks us which condition provides determinacy for the group. Step One is to, once you face one of these questions, ask yourself (without looking at the answers) what the conditions of the passage already tell you about the subjects within the passage that could provide you with a lot of information as long as you knew about them. I think if we know more about Brandi's position or Ann's position, in comparison to the other fundraisers, we'll be in better shape to figure out the correct answer. We're now ready for Step Two.

Step Two is also easy: eliminate any answer choice that does not include a condition about the subjects you identified in Step One as those that would provide significant information if you had a condition about them. Shoot! In this case, all of the answers follow either Brandi or Ann, so this is one time the Two Step doesn't help us save time. It does provide us with useful information, however. Megan is mentioned the most (3 times), followed by Coco and Lori (twice). Let's start with (A) and move down:

- **A.** Brandi raises just less than Ellie and just more than Ann
- **B.** Brandi raises just less than Megan and just more than Coco
- **C.** Ann raises just less than Megan and just more than Brandi
- **D.** Ann raises just less than Coco and just more than Lori
- **E.** Ann raises just less than Megan and just more than Lori

Option (A) lets us know that [Ellie/Brandi/Ann] place in that order, which means that they are in 3rd/4th/and 5th positions, but we don't know enough to know who is in 1st, 2nd, 6th, or 7th. So, (A) leaves us still unclear about who ends up in the sixth and seventh places, and well as the first two places. Answer (B) gives us [Megan, Brandi, Coco], which (because of the last condition) helps us know where they sit next to Ann, but we still don't know who finishes sixth or seventh. Further, (C) leaves us with the first three positions unclear, since if the known placement is [Megan/Ann/Brandi], they will finish 4th, 5th, 6th, leaving 1-3 open. (D) is similarly problematic,

because knowing that [Coco/Ann/Lori] finish together means they either are in 1st, 2nd, 3rd or 2nd, 3rd, or 4th. That leaves us with (E), in which [Megan/Ann/Lori] will finish 4th, 5th, 6th. That helps us know that Sue must be in 7th place (next to Lori). That leaves the top three spots open—but guess which staff haven't been mentioned yet? Brandi, Coco, and Ellie. They will need to finish: 1st (Ellie), 2nd (Brandi) and 3rd (Coco), according to our conditions. (E), of course, reflects this perfectly: EBCMALS.

4. A

This kind of question is fairly unique, because it asks you to play around with the participants to see the smallest logically possible distance between two particular fundraisers in their final fundraising efforts. We know that we can place Brandi second (we did that in Question #2, after all), which would put Lori sixth in fundraising: EBCMALS. That is the furthest to the top Brandi can go, but can we shorten the gap for Lori? We can do this if we can move the [Lori/Sue] grouping up to rearrange the EBCMALS end piece. Can we get the number of fundraisers between Brandi and Lori to zero? We need to keep Sue and Lori together, and Ellie needs to earn more than Brandi and Coco.

We can't have Ellie come after Sue and Lori, because it wouldn't allow for zero spaces. But we can have Ellie go first, followed by Sue:

ESL x A XX

We have exactly one Pierre staff member in the top three, and we don't have any more conditions which govern our placement, except for the placement of Brandi. This placement helps us out tremendously, however, because we can put her 4th, directly next to Lori:

ESLBA{M/C} We can't confirm the last two orderings exactly, but we have successfully placed Brandi and Lori in relationship so that there are no fundraisers between them—ZERO! So, (A) is our correct response.

- **A.** 0
- **B.** 1
- **C.** 2
- **D.** 3
- **E.** 4

We are now going to attempt our longest question set yet—are you up for it?

Questions 5-11

This passage has a lot of subjects, but only two groups you will put them in, which makes the ordering really important (not surprisingly) but for the most part, really straightforward. As we'll see, the questions are going to be more interesting (read: NEW CHALLENGES!) than we have yet seen. Let's list our subjects, and then the conditions for the passage:

BCDEQPRT
Science:
Humanities: B

(B is H) Boone is a humanist.
((C is H) ⊃ (D is S) If Contreras is a humanist, Dega is a scientist.
((If E is S) ⊃ (R · P is H)) If Euribe is a scientist, both Rho and Picasso are humanists.
~(D · T) The work from Dega and Tuto will not be classified in the same collection.
(R · T) The work from Rho and Tuto will be classified in the same collection.

Great, we have a significant list of hypothetical conditions that, if filled in with conditions from questions, can go far to help us. Without equivocation, however, we know that Boone is in the Humanities, so we can scan for answer choices that list him as a scientist, and remove it from a possible answer choice.

5. A

Ok, now we are ready to see which could be a complete list of the newly archived materials in the sciences:

    A. Contreras, Qui, Rho, Tuto
    B. Contreras, Qui, Rho, Picasso
    C. Contreras, Qui, Rho, Euribe, Tuto
    D. Contreras, Euribe, Tuto, Boon
    E. Qui, Rho, Picasso, Tuto

We are going to follow our Insider Insight, and ignore (E), which is the only option that doesn't include Contreras. It's clear we are going to have Tuto (he's on all five lists, actually). Bingo! That helps us eliminate (D) immediately, because we know that Rho and Tuto are in the same category. The difference between the remaining is Picasso and Euribe. Euribe is interesting, because of the condition that says ((If E is S) ⊃ (R · P is H)). If (C) is correct, then, Rho would have to be a *humanist,* according to this condition. But, (C) includes both Euribe and Rho on the science list, so it cannot be correct. Here's where we stand so far:

    A. Contreras, Qui, Rho, Tuto
    B. Contreras, Qui, Rho, Picasso
    C. ~~Contreras, Qui, Rho, Euribe, Tuto~~
    D. ~~Contreras, Euribe, Tuto, Boon~~
    E. ~~Qui, Rho, Picasso, Tuto~~ (ignore)

So, is it Picasso or Rho who make the list? Are there conditions that can help us? Well, you should remember immediately that whatever list Tuto is on, Rho has to be on as well, and vice versa. That means that (A) is the correct answer, because (B) has Rho without Tuto.

6. C

This is one of the exciting questions, where we apply the Texas Two Step to see if we can eliminate any answer choices prior and make the path more efficient towards a correct answer. The question is asking which conditions, if true, would determine the Librarian's classification of all of the new archive material, so, first, without addressing the answers, we'll look at our Possibility Map and see which subjects would give us the most information if they fulfilled certain conditions. Here are the universal conditions for this passage:

BCDEQPRT
Science:
Humanities: B

(B is H)
((C is H) ⊃ (D is S))
((If E is S) ⊃ (R · P is H))
~(D ·T)
(R ·T)

From a glance at our conditions, if we learn that Contreras is a humanist, or any information about Euribe, Rho, or Tuto, we will be on better footing to know something determinant about the grouping of the subjects. I'm going to ignore (D), which does not include Contreras as a humanist, Euribe, Rho, or Tuto:

    A. Contreras, Euribe, and Tuto all are scientists
    B. Contreras, Euribe, and Picasso are all scientists
    C. Qui, Rho and Picasso are all scientists
    D. ~~Contreras, Dega, and Qui are all scientists~~
    E. Contreras, Dega, and Euribe are all scientists

At this point, we can just quickly run through each, and see if there is indeterminacy. This is, remember, the key end point of the Texas Two Step: If indeterminacy arises, *move on to the next answer choice,* because it will not be a correct answer. The correct answer determines the position of every subject. (A) leaves indeterminacy. We could conclude that Rho is a scientist, but we would not know in what category either Picasso or Qui would be classified. (B) gets us close, since if Euribe is a scientist, Rho and Picasso are humanists—and so would Tuto, who follows Rho. But, we still don't know where to classify Qui. (We really need determinacy on Qui as well as Euribe, which is an important piece to uncovering the humanists in the group.) (C) gives some of that to us-- Qui, Rho, and Picasso are scientists, which makes Tuto a scientist.

Now, we need logic to keep the inferences going. What are the two deductions we can make from this condition: ((If E is S) ⊃ (R · P is H))? We can deduce 2 things, both through *modus ponens,* that if E is S, then R and S is H. *But,* we can also use *modus tollens* to deduce that ~(R and S is H) then, ~(E is S). Guess what? In (C), we get ~(R• P is H). (R · P) instead are *scientists,* so in this case, ~H but S. The result is that we have to reject (E is S). That means, E is ~S, so H. Here's our list so far:

BCDEQPRT
Science: QRPT
Humanities: BE

What to do about C and D? Well, we have to invoke a condition that hasn't been needed so far: ~(D · T), or any list will not have both Dega and Tuto on it. We *do* have Tuto already on the Science list, so that means Dega will be a Humanist.

BCDEQPRT
Science: QRPT
Humanities: BED

Now that we have determined that Dega is a humanist, we can use *modus tollens* once again. (See why logic is *so important* to working this test?) We haven't yet used this condition, but it turns out that *modus tollens* will save the day to help us find the correct answer by applying it there: ((C is H) ⊃ (D is S)). Just like with the Dega component, here we *deny the consequent.* It is false that (D is S), because instead (D is H). If we deny the consequent, we have to validly conclude that ~(C is H), which in this case means that ~H = S. Contreras is a scientist, officially, and we can know that indubitably by applying our laws of logic. The final list, then, reads:

BCDEQPRT
Science: QRPTC
Humanities: BED

Answer choice (C) allowed us to determine the categorization for every artifact on the list. We're ready to move on to question #7.

7. A

This type of question tries to distract you by running through the logically possible pairs of eight researchers to find the two that can't be placed together—*don't do it!* Instead, look at the conditions first and identify individuals that you know have to be classified together, eliminate those from the list and quickly move on. First, look at your answer choices:

    A. Dega and Rho
    B. Contreras and Dega
    C. Euribe and Rho
    D. Euribe and Picasso
    E. Qui and Picasso

Then, look back at your Possibility Map:

BCDEQPRT
Science:
Humanities: B

(B is H)
((C is H) ⊃ (D is S))
((If E is S) ⊃ (R · P is H))
~(D · T)
(R · T)

The Archivist must group Tuto and Rho together, and she can't place Tuto and Dega together (the last two conditions tell us these things), so we can easily pick out that Rho and Dega cannot be together. Answer (A) is correct! It doesn't get better than that on the LSAT.

8. C

The question helps us by giving us a new condition, *that Dega's work is classified as science.* (Here, you should immediately be thinking that Rho and Tuto are humanists, joining Boone, since they cannot be classified together with Dega.) The remaining researchers to be classified are Contreras, Euribe, Qui, and Picasso. As we glance at our conditions, there is nothing within them that prevents any one of them from being classified along with Dega—so they all should be included in a complete list of researchers whose artifacts could be classified along with Dega. The answer that provides that:

    A. Contreras, Euribe
    B. Contreras, Euribe, Qui
    C. Contreras, Euribe, Qui, Picasso
    D. Contreras, Euribe, Qui, Picasso, Boone
    E. Contreras, Euribe, Qui, Picasso, Boone, Rho

9. D

Although you never want to make the mistake of importing new conditions from old questions into the question you are working on, it isn't actually true that the work that you do in other AR questions does not help inform your work in subsequent questions. This is especially true when you are dealing with "minimum/maximum" questions. If you get a question that asks you "What is the maximum number of subjects that can be classified into Category X" and you worked on a previous question within the question set that had more subjects in Category X than in other questions, you should start with the set up for the question that yielded the maximum (or, minimum, depending on the question) number of subjects.

Question #9 is a great example, because you are asked to identify the maximum number of researchers who could be classified in the humanities, and you already worked on one type of classification for that in Question #7, so start with that classification and then you can see if you can move members:

BCDEQPRT
Science: QRPTC
Humanities: BED

Now your answer choices:

    A. 3
    B. 4
    C. 5
    D. 6
    E. 7

Start at three folks, but we want to try to maximize that number by relying on our conditions.

(B is H)
((C is H) ⊃ (D is S))
((If E is S) ⊃ (R · P is H))
~(D · T)
(R · T)

Under our current setup, Euribe is a Humanist, but you can see that we will be able to bring over Rho, Picasso, and Tuto (because of Rho) in to the Humanist camp if Euribe is a scientist. There is no other condition that limits Euribe's participation, so let's make that move:

BCDEQPRT

Science: EQC
Humanities: BDRPT

(You will see a quick change that must be made with that alteration. Dega cannot be with Tuto, so we need to move him to the Science category.):

BCDEQPRT

Science: EQCD
Humanities: BRPT

We need, now, to ask whether there are any limitations from the conditions on whether Qui or Contreras must be in the Sciences. You may remember (or, know from a quick glance), that Qui is not encumbered either way, so we need to move her to the Humanities:

BCDEQPRT

Science: ECD
Humanities: BRPTQ

Contreras, however, is encumbered by a condition, but we will like this condition to maximize participants in Humanities: ((C is H) ⊃ (D is S)). If Contreras is a humanist, Dega is a scientist. That works perfectly because we already knew that Dega could not be in with this group of humanists. So, we are ready to complete our list with that final move:

BCDEQPRT

Science: ED
Humanities: BRPTQC

As a refresher, we can't have any more than these six as humanists, because Dega can't be with Tuto and we moved Euribe to science to get Rho and Picasso (and, consequently, Tuto) into the humanities. There it is! Six researchers can ultimately, maximally be humanists, which, looking back at our list, was answer (D).

10. C

This question provides us with the chance to make a complex scenario a little less complex with the addition of an excellent condition.... Oh, if only that was the case! This question is the first you have seen here. It asks you *to substitute* a condition. You won't see many of these on the LSAT, but when you do see them, you don't want to be thrown for a loop. The question asks that you take out the condition that Dega and Tuto can't be classified together. (That condition has played significant roles in every question we've seen so far.) Then, the *correct answer choice* will have the same effect on how other research is classified.

What hasn't changed is the relationship between Tuto and Rho—they are still going to be classified together,

regardless of how they are classified. If you are told that Dega and Rho are classified differently, since Rho must be together with Tuto, that condition would have the exact same effect as the original condition, of denying that Dega and Tuto could be classified together. The result is that, when we look at the answer choices, we are going to look for a condition that rejects the ability of Dega and Rho to be on the same list. Let's look at our answer choices:

- **A.** If Rho is classified as science, Dega is in the humanities
- **B.** If Rho is classified in the humanities, Dega will be in science.
- **C.** Rho will be classified in science if and only if Dega is in the humanities.
- **D.** If Tuto is classified in science, Contreras will be also.
- **E.** Tuto will be classified in science if and only if Contreras is classified in science.

There are two that should stand out to you, (A) and (C). How are they different? Well, (A) could not determine that Tuto and Dega would be on opposite lists if Dega was in the humanities! They could all end up on the humanities list. Logic is so crucial here! The "if and only if (iff) in (C) ensures that they are on separate lists. It tells us that Rho and Dega cannot be on the same list. (C) is the correct answer.

11. C

If you enjoyed the condition-swapping game, you're in luck because Question #11 takes a similar tack by asking you to reconsider the relationship between Rho and Tuto this time. If Rho and Tuto were on different lists, our conditions do change. Here are the two possible options you have:

Possibility A
Science: Contreras, Tuto
Humanities: Boone, Dega, Rho
Unknown: Euribe, Picasso, Qui

Possibility B
Science: Dega, Rho
Humanities: Euribe, Boone, Tuto
Unknown: Contreras, Picasso, Qui

So, if we are looking to see, based on the condition that Tuto and Rho are now classified differently, and we want a complete list of researchers whose work is classified in science, we compare the Possibility Maps to our conditions:

(B is H)
((C is H) ⊃ (D is S))
((If E is S) ⊃ (R · P is H))
~(D · T)
~(R · T)

For Possibility A, we can move both Qui and Euribe from "unknown" to "science", which moves Picasso to humanities:

Science: Contreras, Tuto, Euribe, Qui
Humanities: Boone, Dega, Rho, Picasso
Unknown: nil

If we are trying to maximize our scientists, there is another *modus tollens* move we can make. If we deny (R• P is H), we deny (E is S). That makes us move Euribe back down to humanities, and move Rho and Picasso up to science. Of course, Tuto cannot be with Rho or Dega in the new scenario, so we will move Tuto down to humanites, and Dega up to science. Let's look:

ANALYTICAL REASONING
CHAPTER 5

Science: Contreras, Qui, Dega, Rho, Picasso
Humanities: Boone, Tuto, Euribe,
Unknown: nil

When we compare this list to our revamped conditions, they work: Contreras and Qui are unconditioned, Tuto cannot be with Rho or Dega, and the only other conditional that holds with this current set-up is that Boone is in the humanities. So, we have the most complete list possible, and we compare that to our answer choices:

A. Dega, Rho, Euribe, Qui, Picasso
B. Contreras, Euribe, Qui, Tuto
C. Contreras, Dega, Qui, Picasso, Rho
D. Contreras, Qui, Tuto,
E. Contreras, Euribe, Tuto, Dega

And, (C) is the correct answer.

Questions #12-17

Our new passage focuses on relationships between subjects, rather than their organization. About 25% of your Analytical Reasoning questions will be relationship-based. In relationships, context can be important so you can be significantly helped by using the Insider Insight about how to handle passages of reading, and starting with the easiest question first. You get no more points—no kudos—for answering the most difficult questions than you do from answering the easiest ones correctly. Start with the easy questions and move to the most difficult across question sets. In almost all instances, the question sets will not appear on the exam in the order in which you are most well-off to answer them. You can remember that, even when you do your test prep. Although the questions are laid out in a particular manner, you are not obligated to answer them in that way. Let's start with some easier relationships, and we'll round out our Analytical Reasoning chapter with a mind-blowingingly difficult logic game!

This passage gives you an accessible relationship pattern. Narciso is buying six different kinds of big cows, and he is trying to communicate with his buyers how big they are in relationship to each other. That's it! Let's map out the conditions:

Voerderwald weighs more than Chianina.   [V > C]
Chianina weighs more than Anjou.   [C > A]
Brahman weighs less than Glan.   [B < G]
Chianina weighs more than Normande.   [C > N]
Normande weighs more than Glan.   [N > G]

Now that we have each condition, prior to approaching the questions, let's put them in some sort of order, from **lightest** to **heaviest**

A C V *This one is transitive:* If V > C, and C > A, ∴ V > A.
G N C *Another transitive:* If C > N, and N > G, ∴ C > G
[B G] B is lighter than G.

Ok, now that we have the relationships fairly well mapped, we are ready to take the questions, and any conditions that they have, and see what we can do with them.

12. A

This question does not provide a new condition, but just asks the simple question of logical necessity—given the conditions that Narciso delineated, what cannot *not* be true? We can start with (A), and when we find an answer that must be true, there isn't a need to continue. If Glan weighs less than Normande, and Normande weighs

less than Chianina, the result is that Chianina is heavier than Glan. Guess what? That is option (A)! Our answer choices are:

A. Chianina is heavier than Glan.
B. Chianina is lighter than Glan.
C. Anjou is lighter than Brahman.
D. Chianina is lighter than Normande.
E. Normande is heavier than Anjou.

For questions of logical necessity, there are no other viable options, so since we know it is necessarily true that Chianina bulls are heavier than Glan bulls, we fill in the question sheet and move on to question #13!

13. A

Similar to Question #12, Question #13 is a type of logical necessity relationship question. It asks, of the available answer options, which one cannot logically occur. We use the same conditions as our first question on the passage to visualize:

Voerderwald weighs more than Chianina.	[V > C]
Chianina weighs more than Anjou.	[C > A]
Brahman weighs less than Glan.	[B < G]
Chianina weighs more than Normande.	[C > N]
Normande weighs more than Glan.	[N > G]

Now that we have each condition, prior to approaching the questions, let's put them in some sort of order, from **lightest** to **heaviest**

A C V *This one is transitive: If V > C, and C > A, ∴ V > A.*
G N C *Another transitive: If C > N, and N > G, ∴ C > G*
[B G] B is lighter than G.

The Map helps us to see that Glan bulls weigh less than Normande bulls (as in the previous question), and Normande bulls weigh less than Chianini. The result is that the Glan bulls can never weigh more than Chianina bulls. So, if we evaluate our answer options to satisfy our conditions, we can see *of course*, that it cannot be true that Glan bulls are heavier than Chianina. In fact, we had determined for the previous question that it was necessary logically that Chianina bulls weighed more than Glan bulls. The result from our answer choices:

A. Glan is heavier than Chianina.
B. Glan is lighter than Chianina.
C. Anjou is lighter than Brahman.
D. Chianina is heavier than Normande.
E. Normande is heavier than Anjou.

is that (A) is the only option that is false, given our conditions.

14. C

From here, the relationship questions do not focus on the Glan/Normande/Chianina relationship and they run a little deeper into the comparison of weights we have in our Possibility Map:

Voerderwald weighs more than Chianina.	[V > C]
Chianina weighs more than Anjou.	[C > A]
Brahman weighs less than Glan.	[B < G]
Chianina weighs more than Normande.	[C > N]
Normande weighs more than Glan.	[N > G]

Now that we have each condition, prior to approaching the questions, let's put them in some sort of order, from

lightest to **heaviest**

> A C V *This one is transitive: If V > C, and C > A, ∴ V > A.*
> G N C *Another transitive: If C > N, and N > G, ∴ C > G*
> [B G] *B is lighter than G.*

This question specifically asks us to use the Map to discover how many breeds must be lighter than Normande. That means that the wrong answers are those that either could or could not weigh less than Normande bulls. Our Possibility Map tells us that Glan is lighter than Normande, and Brahman bulls are lighter than Glan bulls, too. (We don't know if Normande bulls are heavier than Brahman bulls.) We can also observe that, because both Chianini and Voerderwald bulls weigh more than Normande, those bulls can't weigh less than Normande bulls. Subsequently, we see from the Map that Anjou bulls *could* weigh less than Normande bulls (but whether they must is indeterminate.) The result is that three breeds of bulls either could or could not be lighter than Normande bulls, and two must be lighter. Comparing this to our answer choices reveals:

> **A.** 0
> **B.** 1
> **C.** 2
> **D.** 3
> **E.** 4

(C) is the correct answer.

15 C

Whereas the relationship question in #14 was interested in the logical necessity of relationships compared to bulls that weigh less than Normande, this question reinforces the logical necessity of the relationships but asks about those that must be heavier than Glan bulls. We look at our relationship Possibility Map:

> Voerderwald weighs more than Chianina.   [V > C]
> Chianina weighs more than Anjou.   [C > A]
> Brahman weighs less than Glan.   [B < G]
> Chianina weighs more than Normande.   [C > N]
> Normande weighs more than Glan.   [N > G]

Now that we have each condition, prior to approaching the questions, let's put them in some sort of order, from **lightest** to **heaviest**

> A C V *This one is transitive: If V > C, and C > A, ∴ V > A.*
> G N C *Another transitive: If C > N, and N > G, ∴ C > G*
> [B G] *B is lighter than G.*

We remember that since we are identifying the number of breeds that *must* be heavier than Glan bulls, wrong answers include those that either could or could not be weigh more than Glan. If we look at the Map, we see that Glan weighs more than Brahman bulls, so those cannot be heavier. We also see that Glan bulls could weigh less than Anjou bulls, so Anjou bulls could be heavier, but need not be. So, two breeds of bulls could or could not weigh less than Glan bulls, which leave three bulls that must be heavier than Glan. Our answer options include:

> **A.** 1
> **B.** 2
> **C.** 3
> **D.** 4
> **E.** 5

The result is that (C) is the correct answer choice for question #15.

16. B

Here, we are adding a new condition—not only a new condition, a new breed of bull into the mix, which means that we can import the old conditions only as long as they still relate to the new set-up Narciso has for his bulls. Let's take a look at what is being altered. There are a couple of pieces of new information: the new cow is a Pinzgauer; the Pinzgauer is lighter than three of the original six breeds.

So, given that new information, we are asked a "must" question—which of the following must be true. Wrong answers aren't logically necessary, just possible, or those that cannot be true. We need to add our new pieces to our Map:

Voerderwald weighs more than Chianina.	[V > C]
Chianina weighs more than Anjou.	[C > A]
Brahman weighs less than Glan.	[B < G]
Chianina weighs more than Normande.	[C > N]
Normande weighs more than Glan.	[N > G]

Now that we have each condition, prior to approaching the questions, let's put them in some sort of order, from **lightest** to **heaviest**

A C V *This one is transitive: If V > C, and C > A, ∴ V > A.*
G N C *Another transitive: If C > N, and N > G, ∴ C > G*
[B G] *B is lighter than G.*

Heaviest: Voerderwald, Chianina, [Anjou]
Lightest: [Normande], Glan, Brahman

We will need to add the Pinzgauer between the heaviest and the lightest, with the understanding that we are not sure what the relationship is between Anjou bulls and Normande bulls:

Heaviest: Voerderwald, Chianina, [Anjou]
New: Pinzgauer
Lightest: [Normande], Glan, Brahman

Now we can use the revised Map to determine that Voerderwald and Chianina are the two heaviest breeds, but it is indeterminate whether Anjou or Normande are the next heaviest bull. This indeterminacy makes this question more difficult. Answer (A) directly picks up the uncertainty:

   A. Normande is heavier than Pinzgauer.
   B. Chianina is heavier than Pinzgauer.
   C. Glan is heavier than Pinzgauer.
   D. Anjou is lighter than Pinzgauer.
   E. Anjou is heavier than Pinzaguaer.

(A) reflects the indeterminacy of the conditions here, since Normande could be heavier than Pinzgauer bulls, option (A) is wrong. Given that Chianina bulls weigh more than all other breeds besides Voerderwald, it must be the case that Chianina is heavier than Pinzgauer bulls. Success! That answer is reflected in option (B). We know for logical necessity questions that only one answer can satisfy all of the conditions, and (B) does satisfy all of the conditions provided by the new information, so we do not need to move to evaluate the other answer options.

17. E

This is a fun supplementary condition to the original passage. We learn that this time, Narciso is adding Holsteins to the herd, which are *heavier* than three of the original breeds. We'll use the same possibilities that came out of the bigger Probability Map in Question #16—we know that we have two breeds that are determinately largest (V and C), we have two breeds that are determinately lightest (Glan and Brahman), and we have two that are indeterminate as to how they compare in the herd (Anjou and Normande bulls).

Heaviest: Voerderwald, Chianina, [Anjou]
New: Holstein
Lightest: [Normande], Glan, Brahman

With the added condition, this question asks us which of the following logically cannot occur:

- **A.** Holsteins are heavier than Anjous.
- **B.** Holsteins are heavier than Glans.
- **C.** Holsteins are heavier than Normandes.
- **D.** Holsteins are lighter than Chianinas.
- **E.** Holsteins are lighter than Glans.

The visualization possibilities help us see a bit about how the answer should go. We still are uncertain about where the Holstein will fit compared to the Anjou and Normande breed. We have no information in the conditions that can give us more detailed help. So, our answer will reflect the indeterminacy at the middle weight of the breeds. Answer choices (A) and (C) both demonstrate that uncertainty—we simply do not know if Holsteins are heavier than Anjou (A) or Normande (C). It could be that Holsteins are heavier than Anjous and Normandes, which means that neither answer is correct. Because Glan weighs less than all sizes other than Brahman, it might be lighter than the Holsteins, which would make (B) true, and so a logical possibility. And because Chianina bulls weigh more than all breeds except Voerderwalds, it must be heavier than the Holstein, which makes (D) false. That leaves (E), which is an excellent answer. It is logically impossible for Holsteins to be lighter than Glan bulls when they must be lighter than three of the original bull breeds, and Glan is one of the two lightest bulls.

Notes:

ANALYTICAL REASONING
CHAPTER 5

A Note on the Last Longer Scenario

This question set is more difficult than any that you are likely to see on the LSAT, not only because it has three subjects who juggle twelve duties (in particular order), but they are also in separate, but related, rooms. The relationships, then, are extremely rich, knotty, and hard to disentangle. I'm including it here to challenge you, especially if you're up for the challenge. It can open your eyes to the possibilities in Analytical Reasoning, and be a "worst case" for you, certainly. If you were to open up your AR section and see this in-depth of a logic puzzle, my strong recommendation is that you save it for absolute last, and then have fun with it! See what you can do! To that end, I've saved this for last here, so that you can have fun with it.

The scenario is worth repeating:

A department chair is assigning twelve courses to three faculty members, Griff, Irwin, and Shady, to their four equal course timeslots during the week. Griff's classroom is adjacent to Irwin's, and Irwin's classroom is adjacent to Shady's. Each course is taught exactly once, and three of the courses are taught simultaneously. The courses are Aesthetics, Boulean proofs, Culpability, Deontology, Existentialism, Frege, God, Happiness, Inferences, Justification, Kantianism, and Liberty. The chair scheduled the courses by using the following guidelines:

> Only Irwin teaches Justification, Kantianism, and Liberty.
> Boulean proofs and Happiness must be taught by Shady.
> Culpability, Existentialism, and Frege cannot be taught by Shady.
> Aesthetics, Deontology, and Happiness are taught at the same time.
> The following courses cannot be taught in adjacent rooms at the same time: Boulean proofs, Deontology, Existentialism, Frege, Happiness, and Inferences.

These conditions confirm how rich the problem is: we have twelve courses, three agents (in adjacent locations), and four time slots. We can abbreviate the coursework ABCDEFGHIJKL. The intersection of time and place for the agents will determine how we set up the visualization, and I recommend that we have this in a 3x4 table.

Griff	Irwin	Shady

The first condition tells us that Justification, Kantianism, and Liberty will be taught by Irwin

The second condition tells us that Shady will teach Happiness and Boulean proofs.

Since condition three tells us that some courses can't be taught by Shady, rule four demonstrates that Deontology, Aesthetics, and Happiness will be taught at the same time—and the second condition explains that Happiness is taught by Shady. It follows, then, that Deontology will be taught by Griff, and Aesthetics will be taught by Irwin. We know, then, the four courses that Irwin will teach:

162

Griff	Irwin	Shady
	Aesthetics	
	Justification	
	Kantianism	
	Liberty	

The second condition also shows that Shady cannot teach Culpability, Existentialism, and Frege, and since Irwin has all of her courses, Griff must teach them, along with the Deontology course we just stipulated:

Griff	Irwin	Shady
Deontology	Aesthetics	
Culpability	Justification	
Existentialism	Kantianism	
Frege	Liberty	

This visualization lets us know the courses Shady can teach!

Griff	Irwin	Shady
Deontology	Aesthetics	Happiness
Culpability	Justification	God
Existentialism	Kantianism	Boolean proofs
Frege	Liberty	Inference

Do you see how important a careful map can be? Now we are ready to attack the questions!

18. B

This question asks about logical necessity—given the schedule we have above, which of the following answers must be true:

    A. Courses (B, D, E, F, H, and I) will not be taught by Griff.
    B. Courses (B, D, E, F, H, and I) will not be taught by Irwin.
    C. The complete list of the courses taught by Shady is (B, D, E, F, H, and I).
    D. The complete list of the courses taught by Irwin is (B, D, E, F, H, and I).
    E. All three professors teach the courses (B, D, E, F, H, and I).

This should be fairly accessible if our Possibility Map is set. Option A cannot be true, because we can see that Griff does teach D, E, and F. (B), however, meets the conditions. Irwin does not teach any of those courses, and so we do not have to continue with our list. (B) provides a statement that must be true.

19. D

This question adds an organizational aspect, which is a new element to this already-difficult question to set up. It requires us to think about which courses CANNOT be the first courses for Griff, Irwin, and Shady. We look at the map:

Griff	Irwin	Shady
Deontology	Aesthetics	Happiness
Culpability	Justification	God
Existentialism	Kantianism	Boolean proofs
Frege	Liberty	Inference

We'll keep this open and compare it to our answer choices:

- **A.** Existentialism, Justification, Boulean proofs
- **B.** Frege, Kantianism, Inferences
- **C.** Deontology, Aesthetics, Happiness
- **D.** Culpability, Liberty, God
- **E.** Existentialism, Kantianism, God

to see that Existentialism will be taught by Griff, Justification by Irwin, and Boolean proofs by Shady, but without time constraints. There is no other information to suggest that it could not be true, so it could be the case (A), so we remove it from possibility. With option (B), we look at the map to see that Frege is taught by Griff, Kantianism by Irwin, and Inference by Shady, and none of them are time-constrained; since (as with (A)), these all *could* be taught first by their respective professors (there are no limiting conditions on it), we will reject (B) as a correct response. Answer (C) is also the same, since Deontology is Griff's class, Aesthetics is Irwin's, and Happiness is Shady's. Option (D) gives us a different result, however. Culpability is indeed in Griff's section of courses, but must be taught between Irwin's Liberty and Justification courses, so Culpability and Liberty cannot be taught at the same time, which means that (D) cannot be true in fact, and so is the correct answer.

20. A

There is another sequence question offered here by this question, in which we are given a new condition, that Happiness is taught as a first class, and then asked which must be true given that constraint. Happiness is one of Shady's courses, which will then impact the Deontology and Aesthetics courses as the first courses offered by (respectively) Griff and Irwin. That line-up of courses in the first spot results in a disjunct, such that either (Justification or Liberty) must be taught by Irwin in the second time slot, because the Culpability course must be taught between Justification and Liberty. The result is that, given the condition offered here, Culpability must be among the third set of courses taught:

Griff	Irwin	Shady
Deontology	Aesthetics	Happiness
Existentialism	Justification	God
Culpability	Kantianism	Boolean proofs
Frege	Liberty	Inference

We can collate this information with our answer options:

- **A.** Culpability is the third course.
- **B.** Existentialism is the second course.
- **C.** Liberty is the fourth course.
- **D.** Frege is the first course.
- **E.** Boolean proofs are the third course.

Option (A) satisfies the conditions of the question specifically and the passage, generally, so we do not need to move to evaluate more answer choices.

21. A

This question provides us with a new condition to consider, that Justification is taught in the second time spot, and then asks what is logically *possible* on the basis of that new condition. Logical possibility is a could question, so we won't accept as true anything that could not logically be possible. From the new condition that Justification is taught in the second time slot, and the universal requirement that a course be presented between it and the Liberty course, the logical result is that Liberty must be the fourth class taught. We know that Culpability must be taught between Justification and Liberty, so it must be taught third. It is given to us in the conditions that, across professors, Deontology, Aesthetics, and Happiness must be taught at the same time, and the only available time slot is first, as seen in our Map:

Griff	Irwin	Shady
Deontology	Aesthetics	Happiness
Existentialism	Justification	God
Culpability	Kantianism	Boolean proofs
Frege	Liberty	Inference

Our answer choices for Question #21 include:

- **A.** Existentialism is the second course.
- **B.** Happiness is the third course.
- **C.** Culpability is the fourth course.
- **D.** Liberty is the third course.
- **E.** Aesthetics is the last course.

When evaluating our answer options, for this question of logical possibility, as soon as we determine that there is no reason that the answer could not be true, we have hit upon the correct answer. Option (A) indicates, for example, that Existentialism is taught second, which directly is listed on the table above. We could go through the rest of our choices, however, since we have not had too many questions about sheer logical possibility. The rest of the answers will not be logically possible. (B) cannot be true because Happiness must be Shady's first course. Culpability cannot be fourth, because it must be taught between the Justification and Liberty course taught by Irwin, so (C) is eliminated from possibility. Liberty cannot be the third course, for a similar reason given for (C), that our conditions indicate that Culpability is taught between Justification and Liberty, and Aesthetics is rooted in at the first spot for Irwin. And, since Aesthetics is so rooted for Irwin, it is logically impossible that (E) could be the correct answer because Aesthetics cannot be removed from the first teaching spot.

22. E

We are back to logical necessity, with a question that provides a condition that is familiar, given the other conditions together—that Aesthetics is the first course taught for Irwin. Which of the following cannot be true, if Irwin teaches Aesthetics first? Our answer choices are:

- **A.** Frege is the second course.
- **B.** Inferences is the second course.
- **C.** God is the second course.
- **D.** Existentialism is the second course.
- **E.** Kantianism is the second course.

This question asks what cannot be the case, and the condition fleshes out what we have discussed thoroughly in this passage, that Deontology, Aesthetics, and Happiness are the first sequence of courses taught by the three professors in their respective time spots. We know that this leads to the disjunction of either Liberty or Justification being taught second by Irwin (we need Culpability to be taught between them in the third spot by Griff). From this, we know that Kantianism must be the third course taught, at the same time as Culpability. We'll pull up the map to correspond to our answers:

Griff	Irwin	Shady
Deontology	Aesthetics	Happiness
Existentialism	Justification	God
Culpability	Kantianism	Boolean proofs
Frege	Liberty	Inference

Frege could be the second course (A), and just swap places with Existentialism, without logical implication. Since (A) is possible, it isn't the correct answer. This insight is helpful for the rest of the answer choices, all of which are about the *second course* possible. We know there is only one second course that is governed by a condition, and it's either that Justification or Liberty is in the second, with the other in the fourth spot. Inferences (B) and God (C) are taught by Shady and so can be moved since they are not the Happiness course. Existentialism (D), like Frege (A) is taught by Griff and so can be moved. But, Kantianism is one of two courses (the other is Aesthetics) that cannot be taught by Irwin in the second position. (E) is not logical possible, so is the correct answer.

Finally, we have reached the end of our mock on long, complex scenarios for the Analytical Reasoning section. There are some take-aways from the journey that can help you as you transition over to the Logical Reasoning section, and work the exam properly.

Take-Aways.

We've discovered the ways in which the AR section is similar to, and different from, other sections on the LSAT. It is, at root, an overt test of your logical ability, and throughout this chapter we have applied all of the logical tools we have learned thus far to understand, distinguish, and evaluate correct answers from among incorrect answers. Rather than spending an enormous amount of time learning tricks that you then have to pair with other new concepts, or richly-layered diagramming that requires a significant piece of the 35-minutes we have during this section, you learned how to use your logic skills to diagram AR passages and conditions, and create a simple Possibilities Map that shows the logical implications of those possibilities for you to use throughout question sets. The result is an AR section that you can work confidently and completely, armed with a few Insider Insights (like Texas Two-Step!) to help you only

focus on answer choices that logically relate to your particular question. There is no more being daunted by the AR section. You've learned the difference between conditions that relate to organization and conditions that relate to subject grouping. You've seen complex, complex scenarios in both short and longer passages, and you are able to move in and through those question sets accurately and efficiently. You've demonstrated that when you apply the strategies for effective Shot Clock management, and the rules of logic, to the AR question sets, you are going to find that you are prepared to take on the task.

CHAPTER VI | LOGICAL REASONING SECTION

LOGICAL REASONING
CHAPTER 6

Despite the time and attention that are required to learn how to apply logical principles towards success on both the Reading Comprehension and Analytical Reasoning section of the LSAT, the single most important section on the LSAT is the Logical Reasoning section—or, sections, as it stands. There are actually two scored Logical Reasoning sections on the LSAT, which means that an entire 50% of your exam and score comes from your ability to apply logical principles to shorter passages and to find assumptions, areas of disagreement, logical necessity, logical possibility, and logical implications from short texts.

How will this be packaged for you? As mentioned, you have two LR sections. Each one will have 25-26 questions. Each passage in the LR section is significantly shorter than we encounter in the Reading Comprehension section (usually around three to six sentences), and they all will contain an argument (whether a full argument or a partial argument), typically drawn from headline news, historical documents, research articles in various fields, or (even) comedy sketches. A short passage might apply to 2 or more questions, but you will be prepared for one-off questions as well. A key difference from the AR section, actually, is that the LR section does not typically provide long question sets that relate to one particular passage. The LR's goal, rather, is to see how many distinct arguments and different logical tools you can use within a section to be able to answer correctly as often as possible.

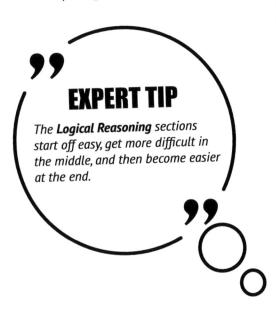

EXPERT TIP

The **Logical Reasoning** sections start off easy, get more difficult in the middle, and then become easier at the end.

The Logical Reasoning section used to be called, simply, Arguments. Arguments really involve a position, often which may not be clearly articulated and is almost never neutral on a topic. The narrator is giving you his/her opinion. There are good reasons to think about the Logical Reasoning section as a section on the LSAT devoted to the evaluation of arguments. The content of the passages is selected because it provides evidence that is used to either support, reach, or reject a conclusion through a framework of argumentation. The passage usually contains a statement that supports a viewpoint or several viewpoints, but very briefly. (The "brief" part is intentional because the lack of content often leads to an opaque argument for which your logical talents are sorely needed to decipher.) Part of evaluating those arguments well is your ability to assess whether the framework itself is functional (which is why the chapter on Logical Flaws is so important). You may receive passages in which you need to supply a conclusion that validly follows, or in which you need to provide a missing premise or assumption. You may have to weigh different pieces of evidence that are given for justification to see which is sound and makes an argument better. You will frequently have to identify pieces of evidence that weaken or critique an argument that is provided in the passages.

Although the passages, texts, and arguments might not be readily accessible to you, the questions that are asked during the LR should be straightforward and clear. Questions typically will require you to be able to apply logic in different ways. You might be asked to restate the main conclusion of an argument, or simply to identify which answer choice contains the main point of the narrator. You frequently will be asked to pick out the underlying assumption that the given argument relies upon to succeed, and just as frequently you will be asked to draw out the logical inferences of a particular view. Sometimes you will be asked to pick out a pattern within a specific line of reasoning, and you will also be asked to measure evidence within interlocutors' debates.

At root, you will be using logic to assess the deductive argument's internal structure (validity) and content (soundness) or the strength of logical inference. Your ability to problem-solve on the LSAT depends on your ability to be organized *and to apply organized (logical) rules* to problems on the section. From what we know about problem-solving on the LSAT, the most successful exam-takers are those who can efficiently comprehend and remember information from passages so that they can generate relationships between passages and answers without having to reread. We also know that **simply practicing this skill** is highly effective to translate into higher scores on the LSAT.

LOGICAL REASONING
CHAPTER 6

Insider Insight: How the LSAT Writers Trip You Up

The LSAT writers love the LSAT and believe in its efficacy as a tool to measure your ability to apply logic in a myriad of ways. They want to deceive you, get you to waste your time, entrap you into small mistakes, and lead you to the wrong answer. The best way for the LSAT writers to do so on the LR sections is to get you to believe that the wrong answer is the correct answer. Sometimes that takes more work on their part than on others, sure. But, any time the LSAT writers convince you that a wrong answer is a right one is too many. There are some Insider Insights you can use to be on the look-out for overt (and sometimes subtle) tricks the LSAT writers rely upon to get you to buy into the wrong answer. First, the LSAT writers know that almost all of the test-takers are students who have not been trained in the logic they need to take the LSAT, and so they rely on patterns that obfuscate improper logical inferences. A common way they do this is to confuse you with modal terms of logical possibility and necessity. You know that if something *could* be the case, then answer choices that *cannot* occur are eliminated. If something must occur, answer choices are eliminated that could not occur, but also that could occur, since "could" connotes logical possibility rather than logical necessity, similar to "must".

The result is that students who are equipped for the Logical Reasoning sections will take significant care to prepare for the obfuscation techniques on the LR section. "Obfuscation" on the LSAT is the intentional techniques used in the Logical Reasoning arguments to couch bad arguments in terms that make them look like good arguments. Obfuscation has been a part of the LSAT since 1948 when the first exam was administered, and even expert exam takers must learn to deal with obfuscation. Interestingly, there is significant academic research that has been done to classify the types of obfuscation that LSAT writers use on the Logical Reasoning section, and experts agree that there are four main tactics (Maeder, 1997) on the LR section specifically: (a) providing an answer response that is true, but irrelevant, (b) repeating the same language used in the argument, (c) couching a false claim in authoritative language, and (d) overstating or understating the point in the argument. Multiple-choice problem solving requires an awareness of distractor answers intended to sidetrack the test taker. Another way they sucker the unsuspecting student to choose wrongly is by mirroring language in the answer choices with language in the passage. (This happens in the Reading Comprehension section, too, and we discussed an example in the RC of when this can be pernicious.) They can provide hyperbolic answers that seem outlandishly ("wildly wrong") attractive because they are not nuanced. Yet, very rarely are outlandish answers correct. They will also provide you with a false disjunction (also discussed in our chapter on Logical Flaws), where they create a disjunct that isn't related to the argument at hand so that you don't actually focus on the argument at hand.

Let's use an example of a case in which the writers make it difficult for the test-taker to use basic reasoning (along with practiced logic) to answer correctly. In this example, you will be asked to answer a question about a barbeque pit-master (and your inability to equal his skill in the pit!). See if you can identify the ways the writers could complicate your task.

Example

Aaron is a world-renowned pitmaster and is dedicated to his craft of smoking the best brisket in the state. Part of his secret is his tools. He has four pits for brisket. Each pit burns a unique wood for a unique taste and has a letter stamped on the inside to correspond to the type of wood, and each pit is stamped with a different local college's mascot on the front and the number of a local sports hero's jersey. The pitmaster says that if a pit has a letter stamped inside that is a consonant, it will have an odd jersey number on the outside, as an interesting curiosity. The pitmaster brings you into the pits, where you see some of the stamps, including the letters E, D, 11, and 12, respectively.

Question:

Of the following, which identifying features of the pits do we have to see in order to determine whether the pitmaster has told the truth?

- **A.** The pit stamps showing E and D.
- **B.** The pit stamps showing E and 11.
- **C.** The pit stamps showing E and 12.
- **D.** The pit stamps showing E, D, and 11.
- **E.** All of the pit stamps.

You can list the pit stamps available to you just in list form: E D 11 12. You remember that each letter stamp has a corresponding jersey stamp on the top of the pit, and every jersey stamp has a corresponding letter stamp on the inside of the pit. The goal for you is to find a stamp that has a consonant with an odd number on the front of the pit. You know you can't use outside information to solve the puzzle (as with any Logical Reasoning question). You haven't asked (and despite the presence of (E) on the answer sheet), you probably don't need to see all of the possible pit stamps, whether letters or jersey numbers. The question you are being asked is what you can to do establish whether the pitmaster is telling you the truth.

Your first stamp is the E on the inside of the pit. You know that E is a vowel, so if you were able to see the outside of that particular pit, you would be able to see an even number corresponding to it. You know that if you see the outside of that pit and see an even number, you will have simply duplicated the information that the pitmaster has given to you. If, however, there was an *odd number* on the outside of the E pit, you will have established that the pitmaster is lying to you. So, you have to look at the inside of the E pit. (Which...let's face it... is good news since every answer choice has you doing that!)

The second pit has the D stamped inside of it. That's a consonant—exactly what the pitmaster said you would find. This is not helpful to you, because it does not help you exclude as true either the pitmaster's honesty (from one case) or his duplicity (since this evidence was consistent). The third pit is stamped with an 11, which is an odd number and so should correspond to a consonant inside of the pit. If you look inside the pit and you see a consonant, you still won't gain any evidence about the epistemic status of the pitmaster. But, if you peek inside and see a vowel, you will know that the pitmaster is a liar. So, you need to look inside that pit. The fourth pit has a 12. If you look inside the pit and find a vowel, you will not gain (or lose) confidence in the pitmaster. But, if you peek inside and find a consonant, you still are no closer on the fourth look to knowing about the pitmaster's integrity than you were when you peeked for the third pit. So, you do not have a good reason to peek at the fourth pit.

That means that, after reflection, the best answer choice is B. It involves the relevant logical considerations that can help you know about the pitmaster without also involving unnecessary or redundant actions to do so.

Most students struggle with this question, however. It is designed to trick you into believing that you need more opportunities to look inside the pits than are necessary to make a strong inference. Here, you were encouraged to believe that odd numbers could not be stamped on a pit with a vowel. You further were pushed to assume that the task at hand was to prove the pitmaster was right rather than to demonstrate that he wasn't telling the truth. You will be prepared to gird yourself against these deceptions and to hone in on the best answer.

LR and Deductive or Inductive Arguments

As you know from our LSAT logic training, there are key differences between deductive and inductive arguments, and you are prepared to evaluate both kinds on the exam. The most relevant difference between the two types of arguments, for you on the Logical Reasoning section, is that problems that draw valid conclusions frequently require that you rely on formal, deductive reasoning skills that can be governed by the rules of logic from Chapters 1 and 2. The LR problems that require you to engage with questions in which there are unwarranted, broken, or weak inferences typically require inductive reasoning skills. When you aren't taking the LSAT, it's frequently the case that you can be persuaded by inductive arguments and can find deductive arguments unpersuasive, for a host of reasons. The LR section of the LSAT, however, is mostly myopically focused on generating conclusions that are

validly deduced by given premises within an argument. (In those questions, you will be asked to find the answer that supports the conclusion or that picks out the right-making feature of an argument.)

Almost invariantly, the LSAT LR section will use inductive arguments for when you are required to find bad reasoning within a passage, or to extract an informal fallacy that the author is trying to use to ground the provided argument. So, whereas the deductive components of the LR section frequently have you reaffirm the strength of the arguments, the inductive components are used to undermine the argument or to pick out some wrong-making feature of the argument.

Knowing the distinct function of inductive and deductive arguments on the LSAT can give you a leg up when it is time to engage with the answer choices. In one sense, it allows you to constrain the logical tools you need to have available on any given question. Rather than a paralysis of action because of a plurality of tools, you can achieve more success by focusing deductive skills on questions that direct you to good logical reasoning, and inductive tools on questions that require you to find a flaw or critique an argument. Consider the following:

Example:

All people who are good at math are recruited to join the Honors society. Some activists, anarchists, hippies, and other people with less-than-reputable characters are good at math.

If the statements above are true, which of the following must also be true?

- **A.** All who are recruited to join Honors Society are good at math.
- **B.** All who are recruited to join Honors Society are people who have less-than-reputable characters.
- **C.** Some who are recruited to join Honors Society do not have less-than-reputable characters.
- **D.** Some hippies are recruited to join Honors Society.
- **E.** Some hippies are not recruited to join Honors Society.

This is a deductive inference, that is made stronger by the addition of a true statement by the correct answer (which is (D)). We know that whether an argument is valid logically is completely independent of whether the premises and conclusion obtain in the real world. Validity is a formal operation, only. The validity of a sentence or proposition in an argument is best understood through the concept of "if the premise obtained", rather than that the premise actually does obtain in the world in which we are living. The result for this particular example is that (D) is directly implicated by the two statements in the passage: all people (the universal!) who are good at math are recruited to join the Honors Society, some hippies and people who have less-than-reputable moral characters, as it turns out, are good at math; therefore, some hippies are recruited to join the Honors Society. This deductive argument is valid from the principle of transitivity: all As are Bs, some Cs are As; therefore, some Cs are Bs.

Another example can show us what an inductive argument could look like on the LR section of the LSAT. In this case you will be asked to use an analogy to logically evaluate the strength of the argument:

Example:

Top 40 Song: Anyone who is anyone knows that romantic love makes every part of you better. Your body is better, your mind is better, your emotions are better, your spiritual life is better and all you need is love to improve in all of those ways. Love love love. Better better better. Love me, and I will make you better. When you love me, you will make me better.

The Top 40 Song employs which one of the following argumentative strategies?

- **A.** It persuades by showing that a romantic relationship with the singer will have desirable, full-person consequences.
- **B.** It mocks people who are not in love by suggesting that they do not believe that romantic love has full-person benefits.
- **C.** It explains the process by which romantic love results in full-person positive consequences.
- **D.** It supports its recommendation by carefully analyzing the relationship between love and making someone better.
- **E.** It implies that the emotions, spiritual life, mind, and body share characteristics that would be improved by romantic love.

The Top 40 Song draws an analogy between parts of a person that are not normally brought into an analogy. If romantic love improves all aspects of a person's life, the inductive generalization in correct response (E) is that there must be some shared characteristic between those disparate parts of the self that are improvable by romantic love. Certainly, the passage relates us to a *song*, which is not meant to be structurally strong, but in this case, the song does provide us with some sense of a general inference to be evaluated.

> ## FUN FACT
>
> *Studies show that the 3 biggest factors that show you will apply to a law school are your **desire** to go to a particular school, your **willingness** to bear risk of being denied admission, and your **belief** that you could be admitted.*

A real logical benefit of inductive arguments is that they are not so closely tied to proper form. Logical reasoning problems that use inductive inferences can rely on more than just an understanding of an argument's structure to show that they are good arguments. That might mean that a Top 40 Song provides us with an inductive inference. But, the more adept you are at moving with ease between the structure of deductive arguments to the inferences which follow directly from the argument's content, the more you will develop as an excellent exam taker for the LSAT. Such a skill will help you develop a keen sense of how to classify various logical components within arguments as well as become adept at figuring out the nature of a question's task. Being "adept" and having a "keen sense" really just mean being able to generate alternate possibilities for arguments that are consistent with the argument's premises, to create counterexamples to potential conclusions, and to map out inference schemes (like our Possibility Maps in the Analytical Reasoning section) to navigate differing strands of arguments. Inductive reasoning arguments, even compelling ones, can contain premises that lead to competing results. Consider the following example, in which your ability to generate alternative possibilities can help you determine the flaw of the argument:

A survey of newly hired computer engineers produced surprising results. When asked to indicate their most significant worry about their new job, they noted they were worried they would not have enough free caffeine on-hand to stay up the late nights that would be required for their work, despite the fact that the engineers were told they could always ask for free caffeine. Which one of the following most helps account for the apparent tension above?

A. A disproportionately high number of new hires responded to the survey.
B. Few, if any, respondents were mistaken about how much caffeine they needed to stay awake.
C. Not all the new hires who had worries besides caffeine responded to the survey.
D. Almost all of the new hires were told they should respond to the survey.
E. The new hires believed asking for free caffeine, rather than having it provided without asking, would be stressful.

For any inductive inference that depends upon a survey, the strength of the inference made is closely tied to sample size and representativeness of the sample, as we discussed in Chapter 1. Answer (A) does not explain the disparity between what the new hires were told and their worry. Option (B) does not help account for the tension, and if anything, just strengthens the paradox by providing another reason we should believe the engineers are worried about their access to free caffeine. (C) could resolve the tension if the numbers were sufficient enough to change the results, but we are not given any indication that would be the case. (D) neither helps nor hinders us, but it can't be the correct response because it does not relate to the tension between the views in the passage. Rather, (E) is the correct answer. It justifies why the new hires would indeed worry about requesting free caffeine—it would be stressful to do so, especially given the alternative, which would simply be to have the caffeine available without having to ask for it. The argument requires strong inductive inferences for a flawed original argument, but after careful reflection, inductive reasoning can also provide an accessible route to the correct answer.

LOGICAL REASONING
CHAPTER 6

One More Logical Tool: the Venn Diagram

Although you have been given a solid set of tools in Chapter 1 and Chapter 2 to deal with most arguments, there is one more tool that I want to introduce, only because it can save you time on certain arguments. My strong suspicion is that you know what Venn diagrams are and have maybe even used them in math or in the sciences. The reason why Venn Diagrams can be used in the LR section is that the Diagrams can visually represent the relationships of group members who have shared (but different) characteristics. Consider the following example (Lander, 2018):

No monsters party on Halloween. (No M is P)

All Sandmen are monsters. (All S is M)

No Sandmen party on Halloween. (No S is P)

The Venn Diagram is set up to represent each of the subjects in the argument. *Here's the rule: if it is a main (distinct) idea, it gets its own circle.* So, in the diagram below, we have the circle "M" which indicates all monsters. The "P" circle represents anyone who parties on Halloween. The "S" circle models the Sandmen. We shade out groups that are not represented. So, "All Sandmen are monsters," means that the entirety of the "S" circle is shaded out except for where it overlaps with the "Monsters" circle because the entirety of the Sandmen group are monsters. Similarly, no monsters party on Halloween, so anywhere in which the two "M" and "P" circles intersect will be shaded out to indicate an empty set. The *intersection* of the Diagram is where the subjects intersect. Note, in the diagram below, how the area in common between S and P has been completely shaded out indicating that "No S is P." The conclusion has been reached from diagramming only the two premises.

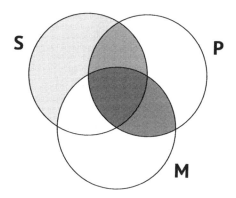

Insider Insight: Recognizing Questions and Answers

"Question-recognition skills" refer to the necessary determination by the problem-solver of the exact nature of the task at hand. Those who are successful on the LSAT can often figure out what the question is asking by rephrasing it. For example, the question, "In order to act in accordance with the position above, it would be necessary to rely on each of the following EXCEPT:" can be rephrased to "Which one of the following is not necessary to support the argument?" Similarly, question types that contain phrases such as "all of the following must be false EXCEPT:" can be translated into the clear question, "which one can be true?" The ability to redefine the question helps you be able to restructure what work is in front of you to be able to answer correctly. If you can more simply and clearly represent the problem to yourself, the question becomes much more accessible to solve.

Question-recognition also refers to understanding keywords that are found throughout the LSAT so that you can process them quickly and (hopefully, with enough practice) without effort. For example, LSAT logical reasoning problems that ask for an inference typically require some sort of inductive reasoning, to help you generalize information based on what is either explicit or suggested from the passage's premises. On the other hand, as mentioned above,

LSAT logical reasoning problems that ask for a conclusion typically require excellent deductive reasoning skills. Generalization is not needed when you are primarily focused on the logical structure of an argument. Instead, your effort is on tying the conclusion together with two or more of the argument's premises more coherently. As a result, those who do well on the LSAT are typically able to correctly differentiate between deductive and inductive reasoning—and be able to tell when each reasoning type is required of them on the exam through "tip-off" words we looked at in Chapter 2.

That isn't to take away from the fact that a number of LR questions demand a more thorough examination of the answer choices, whether through more in-depth logical analysis, a comparison exercise about the connotation of particular words being used in an argument, modal concepts, or gradational words (like, "most", "least", "some" or "ideal"). Examples include, "Which of the following arguments is most parallel in structure to the argument above?", "Which of the following statements, if true, least undermines the argument above?", and "Which of the following best summarizes the passage above?" Those who excel on the LR sections will be adept at fulfilling the requirements to assess the answer choices efficiently (both adequately and in a timely manner) in order to select the answer that, logically, is strongest and has the best chance of being correct. As mentioned with Brake! and Shot Clock, many exam-goers find that they do not have enough time to review all of the responses for all of the problems, but those who excel are able to recognize question "tip-offs," logical keywords, and apply logical notation to make their deliberations as seamless as possible, and always consistent with the laws of logic.

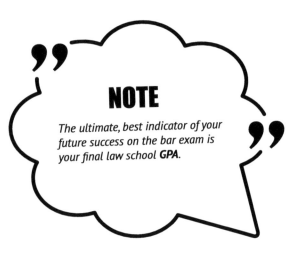

NOTE

*The ultimate, best indicator of your future success on the bar exam is your final law school **GPA**.*

Whereas "question-recognition skills" relates to your ability to know what a question is asking of you, rephrase it so that you can better perform the task, and relate it more effectively to the deductive or inductive reasoning needed to solve the questions, "answer-search skills" is a term that refers to six different strategies available to increase efficiency for finding the desired response among answer choices on the LSAT: direct, semi-direct, semi-elimination, elimination, exhaustion, and guessing. These strategies are arranged in a continuum according to your ability to exert logical skill over the problem (so that the direct method represents the greatest amount of control and guessing represents the least). Evaluate each of these to see which are preferable for you. You don't have to limit yourself to one kind of approach, but read each to see if you can learn a new approach to LR questions!

Direct. On the LSAT, the direct method of answer-searching is used when the student taking the LSAT has determined what answer she believes is correct before she has read any of the responses. The direct method is not only the most efficient in terms of time and effort, but it also emphasizes that you, as the person taking the exam, have the most control over the problem-solving process. When you control the time, the pace, and your engagement with questions, you are more likely to do well with a direct method... on some question types. (You can't directly infer the answer to an "EXCEPT" question, for example.) The direct method has the additional benefit that you are encouraged to answer questions on the LSAT solely to find the answer you have envisioned and not to check the remaining options. In problems where a direct solution can be constructed by the solver, this time-saving strategy is a sound one.

Semi-direct. As the name suggests, the semi-direct method of approaching the multiple-choice questions on the LSAT involves the student who is taking the exam to identify who, or what, she believes the solution *involves* rather than positing the solution itself. The semi-direct method thus allows the test-taker to narrow the number of possible responses down to two or three. (A great example of a "semi-direct" method that we have talked about in ArgoPrep is the Texas Two-Step method of reducing answer choices for additional condition questions. For more, see the chapter on Insider Insights.) In the LSAT logical reasoning section, some problems are constructed so that the solution must

clearly involve one or two components of the argument. In these cases, the student taking the LSAT knows where to start looking and can find the desired response without having to examine all of the others.

Semi-elimination. Similarly, in the semi-elimination method, the student taking the LSAT knows aspects (the "who or what") that are not logically implicated by the passage, and can quickly eliminate answer choices that are not related to the logical reasoning evidenced in the text. The goal is a more efficient method of choosing the correct answer. Similar to the semi-direct method, semi-elimination helps test-takers focus their attention and regulate their search for a solution. This is particularly true for questions on the LR exam in which there are strong deductive frameworks that are required for valid conclusions which must be measured against inferior reasoning, or for instances in the LR in which the problem may have many solutions and the goal is simply to find the one in the answer options that suffices.

Elimination. Students can also use the elimination method in cases in which the student taking the LSAT cannot determine beforehand who or what the solution is about but will be able to recognize the desired response when reviewing the choices. The student taking the LSAT eliminates responses one by one until the correct answer is found and then the test-taker does not need to read any further. Although it is tempting to review the remaining responses to verify one's choice, the compressed time in which you have to take the LSAT limits your ability to review answer choices that, deductively, you *know cannot be correct!* You need to sluff off the feeling that you need to evaluate every answer. For deductive argument questions, as soon as you find the answer that, logically, must be true, do yourself a favor—save yourself precious time—and move ahead. (This is a skill that you can practice, by the way, as you prepare for the LSAT. Just as you need to practice LR problems, practice using the elimination method to analyze answers on the LR. Be honest about your performance on each practice test and watch how much you improve by using the elimination method.)

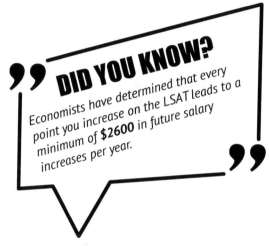

DID YOU KNOW?

Economists have determined that every point you increase on the LSAT leads to a minimum of $2600 in future salary increases per year.

Exhaustion. The exhaustion method requires that you, as the test-taker, examine all of the possible answer choices. The exhaustion method is less desirable because of the time required to rank the answer choices, but in some question types, the exhaustion method is necessary. Imagine that you have a "tip-off" word such as "most," "some," "ideal," or "least," etc., and you have to make a comparison between the subject that is qualified with the tip-off word and the answer choices. In those cases, you have to exhaust all of your options, so you have to read them all. This is especially true given that the LSAC frequently constructs the LSAT to distract you away from the efficient, correct answer. In the instances in which tip-off words (like those just mentioned) are used, students sometimes fail to adequately consider all of the answer options and instead simply pick the first response that seems appropriate, and so, may unknowingly miss the correct solution. The result is that those who choose the exhaustion method might need to do additional practice to hone their ability to recognize questions, along with their answer-search skills.

Guessing. The final method of answer-search skills is the one most to be avoided, even if it is the most intuitive. Guessing should only be used when no other method is feasible and, as in the case of the LSAT, there is no scoring penalty for incorrect choices. HOWEVER, you will be armed with Letter of the Day (LOTD, remember? If not, visit the Insider Insights into Letter of the Day to maximize your chances of success). So, you only guess when you are able to eliminate some answers and get the answer options to a competitive level. You can, of course, use LOTD as your "guess" option to complete any answer choices that you have not had time to finish for the rest of the section, if you are just about out of time. It is appropriate, as you use Brake! and Shot Clock to effectively manage your time, to use LOTD to guess on a few questions that are either too difficult or take up too much time, especially if you find that you have answered a threshold number of questions effectively to put you in range of the LSAT score you want.

Overall, the trade-off among these answer-search solution strategies is that problems that allow for the direct method probably require some solution time prior to reviewing the answer choices (either during the original set-up phase of the problem set or when processing the specific problem's additional information). The exhaustion method

requires time to solve the question after you have exhausted the answer choices. In between resides the penumbra of other choices, all of which can be used together to make the best use of time for the exam. What one gains with the direct method in time saved and control of the solution process, one may lose in terms of reassurance when compared to the exhaustion method. The key to remember, regardless of the strategy or strategies you choose, is that problem solving on the LSAT is not the result of luck. Instead, there are cues in the passage, in the question, and in the answer choices that can prompt you to the correct answer choice, and save you from the distractions LSAC would love for you to fall prey to.

Types of Logical Skills Tested by the LR

There are at least four logical skills that you will need to succeed on the LR, that are tested to a broader and lesser degree by specific question types on the LR. Below, I explain what the logical skills mean, and then I give you an example of each kind that is found on the LR sections.

INTERPRETATION means "to comprehend and express the meaning or significance of a wide variety of experiences, situations, data, events, judgments, conventions, beliefs, rules, procedures, or criteria." Within the LSAT, however, there are many ways in which your ability to interpret will be evaluated. Whether you can categorize appropriately, draw parallels, decode significance, or explain the meaning of an argument all relates to whether you can interpret well.

Here's an example of an *interpretation question:*

Heidegger believed in an "alethic" conception of truth for aesthetics—that art reveals true being. The Student Government president is using Heidegger's view to argue that the University mascot should attend final exams to motivate students to perform well, in keeping with their identity as students of this university.

This passage raises which of the following questions?

- **A.** Can a student accurately apply Heidegger's aesthetics?
- **B.** What truth about student life does a mascot at final exams represent?
- **C.** Would Heidegger have presaged a student movement to use aesthetics to self-identify with a university brand?
- **D.** To what extent are mascots representative of an identity relation?
- **E.** What aspect of true being does a mascot represent for students?

You may wonder that the question is not "interpretative" at all. You aren't trying, for example, to interpret a conception of alethic truth here. But, that sense of "interpretative" is different than what is meant here. On the LSAT, the connotation of "interpretative" means that you are able to *express the meaning* of a term or statement. The reason this LR question is an example of interpretation is that the question requires that you, first, understand the passage (which is technically difficult) and then express the meaning of the passage through a main question that could be raised.

Answer Explanation

When you work the answer choices, you can see more clearly why the question really is an interpretative one. The correct question will be relevant to the main point (the relationship between theory—that art reveals true being—and the concrete, the mascot and exams). This allows you to eliminate (A), since the issue that the passage is raising isn't whether students can apply Heidegger, and (D), given that the question is not about identity relations. (B) is a possibility, except for the qualifier "student life"; alethic conceptions reveal true being, so the correct answer will relate to that. (C) is too far afield of the main point, and tangentiality to it. The best answer is (E), which raises the question relevant to establishing the mascot as aesthetic for this context, in Heideggerian terms.

ANALYSIS is your ability, from a question, "to identify the intended and actual inferential relationships among statements, questions, concepts, descriptions, or other forms of representation intended to express belief, judgment, experiences, reasons, information, or opinions." Of course, analysis questions are a centerpiece of the AR and LR sections, because it is through those sections that we apply logic to weigh competing ideas, detect arguments, and analyze logical reasoning. The core tool in analysis is the ability to think critically, which involves *communicating a clear statement of the issue, identifying assumptions, determining the strength of an argument, and judging whether the question has been appropriately solved.* There are many examples that I could provide from the LR on analysis, but I'll include one that we haven't yet seen: an actual "situation/analysis" question!

Analysis Example:

Situation: When we meet cannibalistic hunters in zombie comics, there are two laws in conflict: "Preserve one's own life," and "Don't kill innocent people."

Analysis: Cannibals always face competing obligations, since the only way to preserve their own life is through killing innocent people so they can eat them.

The analysis provided for the situation above would be most appropriate in which one of the following situations?

A. Doctors without Borders requires American physicians in private practice who travel with them to contribute to the cost of their medical trips abroad, which suggests American medical practices get rich off of sick people's suffering.

B. Some defense attorneys switch to prosecution because they do not feel comfortable defending clients who admit to them that they committed heinous crimes.

C. Conscientious objectors believe the oath of military service could contradict itself if the oath of allegiance to defend the Constitution conflicts with the oath to obey the orders of the President of the United States.

D. Some who believe the sanctity of life is the fundamental legal and ethical principle also believe that capital punishment is an appropriate punishment for guilty people responsible for the worst sorts of crimes.

E. Friends who discover their friends are cheating typically feel compelled to tell their partners about the adultery even when they promise not to disclose the infidelity.

Answer Explanation

For situation/analysis questions, apply the analysis in the text to a new situation listed in the answer choices that is similarly logically framed. The *principle* the analysis uses is that individuals can face competing moral obligations that seemingly contradict. (A) does not act on the same principle, but shows a potential irony for American doctors who work with this group. (B) does not show a competing obligation, given that defense attorneys are able to get out of a difficult moral situation by joining the prosecution. (D) observes a seeming contradiction for those who believe in the sanctity of life *and* are proponents of the death penalty, but the contradiction is observed, instead of felt by the individuals who hold those beliefs. (E) is a potential choice, if friends have promised not to reveal a confidence but feel compelled (obligated) to tell their partner, but (C) is the best choice, because it reveals a competing obligation for the individual to uphold the Constitution but also to obey orders that might not uphold the Constitution.

INFERENCES are the backbone of inductive reasoning and so much of the LR. Inferences lead us "to identify and secure elements needed to draw reasonable conclusions; to form conjectures and hypotheses; to consider relevant information and to reduce the consequences flowing from data, statements, principles, evidence, judgments, beliefs, opinions, concepts, descriptions, questions, or other forms of representation." If we are strong at inductive logic, our abilities to make inferences will include querying evidence, generating alternative conclusions and evidence sources, and drawing conclusions. Certainly, just as we saw above, we rely on the ability to reason critically about the relationships between questions and answers and this ability leads us to sufficient explanations of answers. Solidly-grounded inferences allow us to see the difference between a conclusion which might be true and one which must be true, or a conclusion that creates logical possibility without logical necessity.

Inferences Example:

Jones runs a center against domestic violence, and promotes the center through "art against violence" theatre and gallery galas. She believes that engaging the public through art—especially art that does not shy away from the realities of domestic abuse—will facilitate community dialogue about domestic violence and better prevention techniques as a whole. Youth, especially, enjoy participating in the galas and their parents often accompany them to Jones's events.

Which one of the following propositions is best illustrated by the passage?

A. The best way to educate the community about domestic violence prevention is through art.
B. Dialogue about difficult topics is necessary.
C. Youth benefit the most from using art to facilitate conversation about potential crime.
D. Using unconventional means to communicate truth about difficult topics can have a lasting impact that can prevent future harm.
E. Centers that have youth and parental support are much more likely to be effective in the community.

Answer Explanation:

This is an excellent example of the "inference" purpose for the LSAT. It takes a passage that makes an argument, provides you with five answer choices that are not directly stipulated by the text, and asks you to determine which of them is "best illustrated" by the passage—or, most strongly justified by the passage. Each of them reflects a type of logical leap—but the correct answer is a strongly-justified leap. Note that the correct answer for this question will be supported by the premises, and may be an inference of it. Strike (B) from consideration, because it is too broad, and is not about using art to prevent violence in the community. (A) might eventually be supported, if given other information, but the passage does not need to make the claim that art is the best way to educate the community—it is simply *Jones's* way. It is not clear from the text that youth are the most to benefit from Jones's efforts—their parents come too, so eliminate (C). (D) is an appropriate illustration of the passage's meaning. Art is typically not a venue for a community conversation, but Jones hopes it can have an impact on youth as they mature, and parents now. This makes (D) a better solution than (E), which is not factually supported by the passage.

EVALUATION is a logical process, "to assess the credibility of statements or other representations which are accounts or descriptions of a person's perception, experience, situation, judgment, belief, or opinion; and to assess the logical strength of the actual or intended inferential relationships among statements, descriptions, questions, or other forms of representation." A key part of your ability to do well on the LSAT is your ability to evaluate statements, arguments, disagreements, and inferences. Related to those skills are evaluative-type of skills that are needed to assess suppositions and arguments. You will be able to distinguish between what is asserted as fact (and what is actually fact), as well as distinguish fact claims from value claims. You can pinpoint logical flaws, including arguments from authority and from emotion, or arguments that are too poisoned by bias to be veridical. Finally, a significant component of evaluation is weighing the justification (i.e., evidence, proof, or reasons for a particular conclusion). The disagreement questions are an excellent example of how the LSAT will test your ability to evaluate processes, and these are growing in popularity. In these questions, you will read the perspectives of two interlocutors, and determine (and / or assess) the reasoning each uses to espouse their views. In short, you have to *evaluate* them for soundness!

Evaluation Example:

George: I can't believe you set me up with a woman who is bald!

Elaine: You are wearing a toupee. Do you see the irony here? You're rejecting someone because they are bald. YOU'RE BALD!

George: No... I *was* bald.

The dialogue between Elaine and George provides the most support for holding that they would disagree about the permissibility of which one of the following?

A. Gustavo purchased two blocks of land from Bernadette for the purpose of sheep farming. During negotiations, Bernadette said that if the place was worked properly, it would carry 2,000 sheep. (Bernadette had never carried on sheep-farming on the land.) Gustavo bought the place believing that it would carry 2,000 sheep.

B. Mac was forced into bankruptcy and put his hotel up for sale, stating that it was already let to a 'most desirable tenant'. The Millers agreed to buy the hotel but then discovered that the tenant was bankrupt.

C. Miles owns a popular low-carb bakery and wants to take over the space currently occupied by an Italian restaurant next door. When his neighbor will not sell to him, Miles creates fake social media profiles and posts negative online feedback for the Italian restaurant, which eventually leads to its closing.

D. Trantham owns two hair salons and agreed to sell one to Keegan, in part because Trantham told Keegan that he was moving abroad and did not intend to work in the second salon. But, Trantham continued to work at the second salon and most of his clients followed him, leaving Keegan without a customer base.

E. Prior to purchasing a parcel of land, Elisa asked the seller's lawyer if there were any restrictive covenants on the land and the lawyer said he did not know of any. Little did Elisa know that the lawyer had not bothered to read the documents.

Answer Explanation:

This disagreement question is an evaluation, as well as an inference. (It actually is quite a difficult question, because you have to figure out what the disagreement is about, think about the reasoning each has within the disagreement, and *apply* that principle of disagreement to other issues.) In this instance, you are required to infer some principle that serves as the basis for the disagreement between George and Elaine, and see if you can formalize it enough to be reflected in other scenarios that don't have anything substantively (just formally) to do with George and Elaine's disagreement. In this dispute, George and Elaine disagree about the content of personal integrity—whether George (who is bald and misrepresents himself by wearing a toupee) should be offended to date someone who is bald. The principle of disagreement is about whether you can consistently require something of someone that you do not require of yourself. (A) is not a good match, since Bernadette's misrepresentation is about something with which she does not have a background. (B) includes a misrepresentation about someone else. (C) is an excellent choice, since Miles misrepresents himself to provide further misrepresentation about the Italian restaurant—a restaurant that is in competition with his own, low-carb restaurant. (D) includes a misrepresentation based on events that come after the sale of a property, so is not an appropriate choice. (E) is not a misrepresentation, but an instance of poor legal counsel. (C) is the best choice.

Approaching the LR: Two Strategies

There is one common, fairly effective method for approaching the questions on the LR section, that is a modified RAG technique specifically for short passages like those on the LR: Read the *question* first, then read the passage (look for evidence that directly ties into the question you've just read), generate your own explanation for a correct answer, and then match your response to the listed questions. We can call the strategy where you read the passage after you read the question, and you read the answers after you think of your own answer an "ante hoc" ("before this") strategy.

(ante hoc Strategy on the LSAT)

Because each problem presents a short argument and a question, students taking the LSAT have two primary strategies they can choose from to ascertain the order in which they can choose to receive the information. In the ante hoc strategy, you will read the question for the passage *before* you read the argument. The following example presents a question which, when read before the argument, directs the student who is taking the LSAT to consider while reading the argument how it may be weakened.

Scientist: The essence of our efficacy as scientists is credibility, which comes through a commitment to the scientific method. Recently, some scientists, in a race to be the first to make a breathtaking discovery, have skipped important repeatability steps that are required to remain credible. We need to hold each other accountable to uphold the method to preserve truth. Our mission is not just a commitment to the method—it's a commitment to the public trust to preserve and communicate truth. We cannot be driven by a desire for fame or patents. Otherwise, we are mercenaries.

Which one of the following criticisms would most weaken the passage's contention that scientists' mission is to uphold the public trust?

A. There isn't just one truth for science to preserve, which allows specialization across fields in science, technology, engineering, and math.
B. The reason the scientific method requires repeatability is because scientific truths are defeasible.
C. The mission of academic scientists is to land research grants that allow continued research, rather than the preservation of truth.
D. A scientist only needs to be responsible, rather than credible.
E. There is nothing illegal about being a mercenary, or about profiting off of scientific innovation.

In the question, you, as the test-taker, are asked to find a criticism of the scientist's argument, which claims that scientific work relies essentially on its public credibility which comes through a dedication to the scientific method. By reading the question beforehand, the student taking the LSAT is directed to read the passage to find a way to weaken that view (and the conclusion is clearly explicated in the question). Students taking the LSAT may benefit from knowing in advance how to approach the passage before they read it. The ante hoc strategy enables the student taking the LSAT to read the argument with an inserted question already in mind, perhaps suggesting a key premise or perspective worthy of attention. This question tells you which part of the passage will be contested by the correct solution—that scientists have a mission to uphold the public trust. Remove from consideration answer choices that are not critical of this as the mission of scientists. (E) is about whether scientists can consistently be mercenaries, so should be removed, and (A) does not contest whether science has a mission that relates to the public trust; rather, it expands what the public trust includes. (C) is an attractive choice, because it offers an alternative mission to preserving trust. (D) is not a good answer in comparison, because it would have to assume that scientific responsibility is somehow divorced from creditability. (B) is excellent, because it shows an internal inconsistency with the view that science's mission is about the public trust—how can its mission be about trust in scientific principles when the method is committed to truths that can be defeasible? When compared to (C), (B) is better, because (B) shows an internal inconsistency with the passage, and (C) demonstrates an alternate mission for science.

There is longitudinal evidence to suggest that using an ante hoc strategy (like that of semi-elimination, for example) as part of a comprehensive toolkit of LSAT skills, can positively correlate to success on the LSAT. For example, if you raise questions of the passage beforehand (to narrow the context for which questions could apply) you could be led to more efficiently find evidence within a passage that relates to the questions you raised. This suggests that by reading the question before the argument, the ante hoc strategy may facilitate comprehension and recall of the argument's premises, a necessary step to solving logical reasoning problems and to saving time when moving between passages and answer sets. The type of analysis in many logical reasoning problems explicitly requires the student taking the LSAT to comprehend and recall specific premises in an argument in order to recognize the appropriate answer response. If you are able to effectively use an ante hoc strategy for the LR questions, you may have found a more efficient method to solve them rather than the exhaustion method.

A potential difficulty with the ante hoc strategy for the LR is that there are a host of questions on the section for which spending time formulating potential answers of your own would be confusing, ineffective, and wasteful. For example, if the question asked you to identify which of the answers would most weaken a case, you could spend

time thinking of a multitude of various evidential claims that would weaken an argument provided, but none of them would be reflected in the set of answer choices available to you. It can also be very difficult for you, especially if you are on the last scored section of the exam, to generate your own answers or, more distressing, to come up with the correct response. Many questions ask you something to the effect of what "cannot" be true, for example, and there are many potential responses you could give that are inconsistent with the passage. And, when you're exhausted, you are unlikely to come up with your own. Regardless of whether you use ante hoc question strategies, you can be active in engaging with the problem sets so that, rather than being surprised by a correct answer, you anticipate finding it.

Post hoc Strategy on the LR

The other variation in the order in which the problem information is received is the post hoc strategy, in which students who take the LSAT simply receive the information in the same order as it is presented, i.e., by reading the question after the argument. In the post hoc strategy, the test taker assimilates the argument's information without any directions from the problem's question and remains open to all of the argument's possible inferences. The following example presents a question that requires the test taker to simply recognize one of the possible inferences that can be properly drawn from the argument's premises.

(post hoc example)

If Sofie does not study for her constitutional law class, she is likely to lose her spot as the top student in the course. In that case, either the professor will be unlikely to write her a letter of recommendation or she will have to grovel to do additional research for the professor to earn back her good graces. But if the professor declines to write her a letter of recommendation, Sofie will have a difficult time getting into law school. Moreover, Sofie can avoid losing a chance at getting into law school only if she grovels to do additional research.

Which one of the following statements follows logically from the statements above?

A. If Sofie has to grovel to do additional research, the amount of studying she will have to do for her constitutional law course will continue to increase.
B. If Sofie will not be able to get into law school, either it will because she did not get a letter of recommendation or because she did not grovel to do additional research.
C. Sofie's best chance at getting into law school is to study for constitutional law.
D. Sofie cannot study for constitutional law without sacrificing her spot at the top of the class.
E. Either Sofie will have to study for constitutional law or Sofie will lose her spot at the top of the class.

Now, if you used an ante hoc method, you would be in a pickle. Without referring to the answer choices, there are a number of sound conclusions that can be drawn from these premises; but out of necessity, only one of them can be recognized among the answer choices. As with other questions that require you to supply a logical inference, set up the argument in its logical form first to help you see which statement is consistent with the passage. The passage's argument says: "If A, then B; if B, then (C v D). If ~C, then E. (D, then ~E)."

The passage does not tell us if Sofie does or does not in fact study for constitutional law; rather, it sets up conditional options for consequences coming out of that decision. Since you cannot provide a conclusion to the argument, you can see which of the answer choices are consistent with—fulfill the logic of—the argument form provided above. (A) must be dismissed, since the only thing we can conclude from Sofie having to grovel for additional research is that she will avoid losing a chance to get into law school. (B) is also not a good choice. These disjuncts are true only if Sofie does not study for her con law class, but if she studies for con law, she will not need these disjuncts. (C) is an excellent choice—it avoids the disjunct (C v D), which either leads to Sofie having a tough time getting into law school or having to grovel for extra research—neither of which are good options for her compared to studying for con law. Of course, (D) is false, given the logic of the argument in which if she *doesn't* study she gives up her top spot. And, (E) does not follow, because all we know from the first premise is that if Sofie does not study, she will lose

her top spot. (C) is the correct answer. It seems that a thorough read of the answer choices will expedite a correct response. By not previewing the question, it may be that we are able to remain open to any of the argument's possible inferences and recognize the correct one from among the answer choices.

Research on the post hoc strategy suggests that it can be an effective tool to increase LSAT success when used judiciously on questions that you could not otherwise be answered correctly. This is especially true when the answer choices contain conditions or new information that leads to a better understanding of the passage. This suggests that by reading the question after the argument, the post hoc argument strategy may enhance the type of conceptual learning necessary to make a correct inference. The type of analysis in many logical reasoning problems requires the student who is taking the LSAT to consider the argument from a broad perspective. The research suggests that the post hoc strategy may be an appropriate method to solve the following problems, especially: drawing proper conclusions, identifying valid and invalid inferences, and recognizing unwarranted assumptions. These tasks may lead to many possible solutions and the reader may be better served by remaining open to any one of them in order to recognize it among the answer choices.

Comparing the Two Strategies:

Research on the success measures for students who use the two strategies suggest that the post hoc strategy may not demand the same level of organizational skills required than when using the ante hoc strategy, but may be more effective only for those who are already strong test-takers. The post hoc strategy helps direct the students' attention to general information in the paragraph that is likely to be discussed in subsequent paragraphs. The post hoc strategy's placement of the question after the argument may help student taking the LSAT relate the previous information from the argument to upcoming information in the answer choices and still keep the two sources of information separate. Reading the question after the argument may serve to place a buffer between the argument and the answer choices so that test takers do not mistakenly confuse given facts with incorrect inferences.

In terms of success rates between the two strategies, there is no reason to worry. No significant differences in the test scores of the two strategy groups have been noted. Therefore, initial problem-solving strategy preferences don't appear to have a significant effect on logical reasoning performance—but practicing with them does. Most students use one strategy exclusively, and you should use the one that feels most comfortable and helps you effectively and efficiently answer LR questions.

On to LR Problem Types!

There are many different types of logical reasoning questions, all of which are geared to test your acuity in handling various logical components of an argument and in identifying and eliminating various logical flaws that are found in the argument. In the remaining part of the chapter, each potential variation of LR problem types will be discussed, and you will be given a potential LR question that corresponds to that problem type.

LR Problem Type: Conclusions

You are already adept at identifying conclusions, and making sure that they follow from an argument's premises (if deductive) or are strongly tied to the argument's premises (if inductive). Although it might seem basic to you, the ability to identify an argument's conclusion is a fundamental skill that is tested by the LR section of the LSAT. Sometimes, you will be asked to choose the "main point" or conclusion from among the answer choices. Those

should be less challenging, and questions that you can identify as the first to be completed within the LR section. In other instances, you will be asked to supply a conclusion that is missing or ill-formed within the short passage. Any good argument will relate the conclusion to the justification for that conclusion. Those questions demand an evaluation of evidence, and so can be a bit richer to assess. You will typically have the conclusion at hand but will have to determine either whether evidence is missing or whether the evidence that is supplied by the author is successful to justify the argument.

Conclusion questions should be the most readily-identifiable for you. They will invariably be explicitly about the argument's components (premises, evidence or justification, and conclusion). You could see them worded like: Which of the following most logically completes the argument? Which of the following most accurately represents the author's main idea? Which one of the following most accurately expresses the conclusion drawn in the argument? Which of the following accurately expresses the main conclusion of the author's main idea?

There aren't any tricks or devices you need besides your ability to do the basic LSAT logic you've learned here to answer the question successfully. The only real worry you will have to concern yourself with is to be on the lookout for a plurality of plausible conclusions among the answer choices. Differently than the AR, on the LR there will be answers that could compete as the "best choice" among answer choices, particularly for inductive arguments. You have the ability to choose from among those answers to the correct one. You will avoid choosing an answer that simply restates evidence from within the passage (because you will avoid circularity). The correct answer will logically follow but not duplicate the logical function of premises within a passage.

Brief Practice: Conclusions on the AR!

Directions: *Read the short passage, then choose the best (most accurate and complete) answer.*

Tuition at the State University has quadrupled in the last 20 years. Tuition at the University is proportionately raised when the State cuts funding to the school and refuses to provide building, teaching, and laboratory space to the campus.

Which one of the following accurately reflects the conclusion for this paragraph?

A. The State should freeze tuition rates so that students can adapt to the already-demanding tuition increases.
B. The University has had to continually raise tuition to accommodate the funding cuts it has experienced from the State.
C. The University is in a funding crisis due to the gradual erosion of State funding for the University's essential services.
D. The tuition policies at the State University are no longer regulated by the State.
E. The University has egregiously raised tuition over the last two decades.

Answer Explanation:

The language in the question is an immediate tip-off that we are being asked a conclusion question. (I *really hope* you could identify a conclusion question when the question explicitly asks you for the conclusion!) You are not being asked to hunt down a conclusion within the passage, but to provide the passage's conclusion. The passage itself will help you. It is only two sentences, and so asking yourself what the logical upshot of those two statements together will give you a good idea of what the conclusion will be. (In this case, it should be something to the effect of, "When State funding is cut to the University, the University has to increase tuition.")

You can then look at the answer choices and which ones relate to your idea about what the conclusion is. While you are doing this, you can remove any given responses that either don't relate to your idea or are not in some way indicated by the premises. This lets you narrow down the choices considerably. Of the five here, (B) and (C) strongly correlate to the conclusion you identified prior to reading the answer choices. There is one completely irrelevant

answer choice (A), which takes a factual passage and changes it to a moral one. One answer choice, (D), is outside of the scope of the passage because there isn't enough factual information to demonstrate that the tuition policies at the State University are no longer regulated by the State. Another answer (E) contains emotional language ("egregiously") not contained in the passage, and so indicates it cannot be suitable as a correct choice. (B) and (C) deserve consideration, but reflection will show that (B) must be correct. It indicates a conclusion "the University has had to continually raise tuition" along with a reason, "to accommodate the funding cuts it has experienced from the State," that is clear and consistent with both statements in the passage. (C) would be too much of an extrapolation. It might be true that quadrupled tuition over two decades is in fact "a funding crisis" and the justification for that crisis is "the gradual erosion of State funding for the University's essential services". The justification for the crisis is indeed supported by the text, but the "crisis" aspect isn't. So, (B) is the best answer.

You might want to quibble about whether a "crisis" in fact isn't supported by the text. *As a conclusion question,* the "crisis" cannot be justified. It is, instead, an inference that extends beyond the passage, though is supported by it. If you were asked an *extension question*, which would look like, "The passage provides the most support for which one of the following statements?" you would be justified in answer (C). But, for conclusion questions, stick to the content that is given to you in the passage.

LR Problem Type: Extension

Extension questions aren't merely those that ask you to make inferences from within the argument, either to particular points of evidence or to a conclusion. Rather, extension questions in the LR will ask you to extend the argument's logical implications out to beyond the information given to you in the text. The correct answer will be consistent with the passage, supported by it, but you can think of the extension as the logical next step for the argument—*if the argument's position is true, what is the next, strongly supported point?* It could be that the question itself asks you to infer, but instead, you will probably be asked to identify an answer that is supported by the argument made by the author. Extension questions frequently look like: Which answer is most strongly supported by the narrator's argument? The evidence/premises/argument in the passage provide the most support for which one of the following statements? Extension questions *also* couple with disagreement questions, so that you are asked to make an inferential extension of the argument made in the passage and apply that to a disagreement that the interlocutors in the passage have. That sort of question might look like, "The statements above provide the most support for holding that Person A would disagree with Person B about which one of the following?" This is an extension question because we have not been told by the passage that Person A and Person B disagree about the correct answer choice, *but based on the content of the passage about what they do disagree about,* you will make the extension inference that they will disagree about the new thing, too.

Regardless of whether the extension is happening for a disagreement or the logical *next step* of the argument, the correct answer fundamentally will reflect a strong inferential tie to the argument in the passage (so is supported by evidence in the text), is relevant (even if expansive) to the topic at hand in the text) and, importantly, is *different from the conclusion.* Inferences are not a restatement of the conclusion. Inferences will be grounded in the soundness of an argument and will connect to the evidence within it. But, the best answers to extension questions will take the appropriate, logically-connected step from the argument. You can remove answers that are irrelevant, that are not directly tied to the text, or that require imagination rather than logic to make the inference.

Brief Practice: Extension Questions on the LR!

Directions: Read the short passage, then choose the best (most accurate and complete) answer.

Eight in 10 US adults watch cooking shows at least rarely. Half of Americans watch cooking shows at least occasionally and more. One-third (34%) of US adults do so occasionally and 15% watch cooking shows very often. This is great news for advertisers because data show that cooking shows inspire purchases. Besides trying to make the dishes shown on cooking channels, those who watch can be influenced to purchase food

they see being prepared, along with the gadgets the star-chefs use. More than half (57%) of those who watch these shows say they have purchased food and more than one-third (36%) say they have purchased small kitchen gadgets as a direct result of something they've seen on a cooking show.

Which one of the following is most strongly supported by these statements?

A. Advertisers have done little research into the typical consumer who isn't watching cooking shows, and continuing advertising investment is not prudent.

B. Cooking shows are viewed by a greater proportion of US adults than are other prime-time network programs.

C. Advertisers for cooking programs in the US are missing an opportunity if they do not market their culinary tools and food items used by star-chefs on US cooking programs.

D. Advertising executives see the value in advertising on cooking shows in the US market because there is a good chance they enjoy cooking programs as well.

E. Advertisers should compare whether teens and early adults tend to watch cooking shows so they can adjust their investments accordingly.

Answer Explanation:

The question reveals that you have an extension question because it is not asking you to go within the text for an argument evaluation, but to *use the text to support a claim*. Attempt to extract the argument that is being made as you read the passage, so that you can know what reasons support the conclusion and so can be used to support the extension inference. As you read the answer choices, you should remove from consideration any that are irrelevant to the passage, are not closely connected to it, or that require imagination instead of inference to justify the claim.

The passage (and its relationship to the answers) can be confusing because it clearly has been written as a result of research. It is data-driven, after all. But, the text does not actually say anything about the nature or scope of advertising research, and certainly any inferences about whether continuing advertisement investment in these programs is "prudent" would not be justified, so remove answer (A). Similarly, eliminate choice (D), because the text doesn't relate to what program preferences the advertisers have. Response (E) is completely irrelevant to this passage, which is not about the purchasing behavior of teens and young adults. The remaining two choices are (B) and (C). Clearly, (C) is the better choice. It might not be too far of a stretch, based on this data, that adults view cooking shows at a higher rate than other shows, but that isn't closely tied *to the main point* of the passage. Answer (C), however, is strongly justified in the passage (both the data that show consumers are purchasing food and equipment they watch on star-chef shows, and from the contention that the data are good news for advertisers). (C) does *extend beyond* the passage, but closely relates to it and is logically implicated by it.

LR Problem Type: Assumption Argument Completions

On the LR sections of the LSAT, you will be asked to provide assumptions that are required for the success of an argument within the passage. (Parenthetically, it is a crucial skill for you, as an aspiring attorney, to figure out assumptions made by people who are giving arguments, so think of Assumption Argument Completions as a good workout to prep you for your future profession!) Many people call assumptions that are needed to complete an argument "necessary assumptions." Necessary assumptions—if they were included in the actual passage—would function as evidence to justify the conclusion within the text. They are, instead, left out of the argument despite being required for the argument to succeed. Assumption Argument Completion questions, in essence, require you to find the missing premise within an argument so that the argument becomes *complete*. For these types of questions, you will typically encounter an argument that derives a conclusion from incomplete premises. (You can see the value of your logical training here, since applying a *modus ponens*, for example, to a passage can help you discover what premise is missing and needed for the conclusion to follow logically.) The challenge of Assumption Argument Completions is to determine what missing true statement could complete the conclusion towards its deductively valid end.

The type of assumptions we are talking about here is different than others that could be made within a passage (there are a range of assumptions that could be made, actually). You might have to identify erroneous or fallacious assumptions that are actually stated within the passage. You might have to identify assumptions that *justify* or provide more information for a particular argument, but are not required for it to succeed formally. The assumption questions that help complete an argument will function differently from these. They will be hidden premises that are either inferred by the author or completely left out, but they are needed for the validity and/ or soundness of the given argument. *The reason you are asked to identify these kinds of assumptions is to complete—rather than critique—the argument.* Other argument questions will ask you to identify assumptions as a way of critique. You will be able to identify Assumption Argument Completion questions by the question asked. There truly is a spate of ways in which you could see Assumption Argument Completion questions on the Logical Reasoning section: "The argument within the passage depends on assuming which one of the following?", "Which one of the following is an assumption required by the argument?" "Which one of the following is an assumption required by the argument above?" "The interlocutor's conclusion follows logically if which one of the following statements is assumed?' "Which one of the following is an assumption on which the author's reasoning depends?" "The narrator's argument depends on assuming which one of the following?" "On which one of the following assumptions does the argument depend?" "Which one of the following, if assumed, would allow the conclusion to be valid?" "Which one of the following, if assumed, enables the narrator's argument to be properly inferred?" "The passage's argument requires the assumption that . . . ."

> ## FUN FACT
>
> *Will you be a good lawyer? Studies have proven that to be a good lawyer, you need* **cognitive** *and* **noncognitive** *abilities that are desirable for the excellent practice of law, including analysis and reasoning, research and information-gathering skills, communications, planning and organizing, conflict resolution, client and business relations, working with others, and positive character traits.*

Imagine that my teenager says, "I need to get my license soon. The café said they would hire me if I had reliable transportation." There is something logically missing from her two statements. The first statement is a conclusion: she needs to get her license. She intends the second statement to provide support for that conclusion: she can get a job if she has reliable transportation. The missing assumption, then, will link the job to the license. She is assuming that if she has her license, she has access to reliable transportation, when that is neither explicitly true nor stated in the argument. To complete the argument, we would need to supply the missing premise, something like, "If I get my license, I can actually drive the car you guys bought me."

Insider Insight: Assumption Word Tip-offs

We have covered tip-off words for a range of syllogisms, propositions, premises, and conclusions, but it makes sense here to take a breather to identify words whose presence *frequently* (though not necessarily *always*) indicates that an assumption is being made. Just like when you identify tip-offs for other sections of the LSAT, if you circle these words in the passages, especially if they relate to Assumption Argument Completion questions, you will position yourself to more efficiently, effectively answer questions that relate to assumptions within a passage. Here they are:

> **Assumption Tip-offs:** *assume, assuming, rely, presume, presumption, presuppose, presupposition, depend on, assumption, suppose, supposition, supposal, conjecture, assuming, taking for granted, accepting, given that, suspicion, surmise, theorization, hypothecation. hypothesis, theory, postulate, stipulate, premise.*

Remember, the "Assumption Argument Completion" questions require you to supply, through the correct answer, the evidence that the author's argument relies upon but doesn't clarify. When you encounter Assumption Argument Completion questions, look for information that is necessary to the argument but also is not provided by the author. In these LR question types, the author always needs assistance to explain a premise that s/he was taking for granted. The successful answer will strongly tie the stated, existing premises to the author's conclusion. (This is why running a *modus ponens* or *modus tollens* first to see what is missing can be helpful. The correct answer will also be an assumption that directly relates and ties the premises corporately to the conclusion.) The result is that the strongest answer will often relate information from the premises to the conclusion.

Brief Practice: Assumption Argument Completions on the LR!

Directions: Read the short passage, then choose the best (most accurate and complete) answer.

> To be considered for a VP position in the company, a candidate must be related to a family member of President McCoy. Further, no candidate who is related to a Hatfield can be considered for a VP position. Thus, Carl McCoy, a cybersecurity expert with an MBA, cannot be a candidate for the head of the cybersecurity division, because he is married to Elizabeth Hatfield.

The argument's conclusion follows logically if which one of the following is assumed?

A. Anyone with an MBA who is not married to a Hatfield is eligible for the head of the cybersecurity division.
B. The head of the cybersecurity division is a VP position.
C. An MBA is not a sufficient condition for candidacy to the head of cybersecurity position.
D. If Carl was not married to a Hatfield, he would be hired as the head of the cybersecurity division.
E. The head of cybersecurity cannot be related to a Hatfield because it would present a conflict of interest for the person in that position.

Answer Explanation:

You can see immediately that this is an Assumption Argument Completion question. The conclusion of this passage (i.e., that Carl McCoy cannot be a candidate because he is married to Elizabeth) requires an assumption, and once that assumption is supplied by you, the argument's other premises will be securely tied to the conclusion made by the author. Your first step in this argument is to identify the two necessary conditions stipulated by the President for those who are hired at the VP position. They are 1) that only family members of President McCoy can be VPs and 2) that relations of Hatfields cannot be VPs. What position is Carl up for? The *head of the cybersecurity division*. In terms of concept only, a "head" does not seem to indicate "VP", at least not on its face. And, yet, we are faced with the conclusion that Carl cannot be a candidate for the position. So, there are two logical implications that can be made if he cannot be a candidate: although Carl is a McCoy, he is not a family member of President McCoy; and, that the head of cybersecurity is indeed a VP position. Only (B) is the answer that is a derived logical implication from the text, and can function as a way to logically secure the argument:

> Premise: To be considered for a VP position in the company, a candidate must be related to a family member of President McCoy.
> Premise: No candidate who is related to a Hatfield can be considered for a VP position.
> (Implied) The head of the cyber division is a VP position.
> Premise: Carl is a cybersecurity expert who is married to Elizabeth Hatfield.
> Therefore: Carl cannot be a candidate for the head of the cybersecurity division.

(B) makes the argument logically valid, and is suggested by the text. In contrast (to complete our own evaluation of the answer choices, neither (A) nor (C) are evidentially tied to the passage; (E) provides a possible explanation for why relations of Hatfields cannot be heads of the cyber division, but the answer is not strongly tied to the other evidence provided in the text. (D) might be a candidate for an extension question, but not for an Assumption Argument Completion question, because it is not an implication of the evidence here, which just says that Carl cannot be a candidate.

LR Question Type: Role Questions

It is not uncommon on the LR section to see questions about the roles played by a statement within the passage. Don't be intimidated by these—if you know how to find the premises, assumptions, and conclusions of an argument, you will be able to answer questions about the role the statements within a passage play. The passage is presenting reasons for a particular view. Those reasons are meant to provide evidence, or persuade, or to critique. They might draw an analogy or serve as an example to illustrate some point being made by the argument. An important part of evaluating arguments in the LR section of the LSAT is your ability to home in on the purpose or function of elements within an argument.

These will be easily-identifiable question types on the exam. Almost always they will include the words "role" or "function," such that ,"What role does Statement X play in the argument?" or "The reference to Y in the passage that relates to further information Z plays which one of the following roles in the argument?" or, even, "Which one of the following most accurately describes the role played in argument by the claim that [Y]?"

The *role* of information within a passage is completely determinate on the logical structure of the argument, and that information's participation in the argument. If the information provides support, it probably is a premise. If the statement makes a point, it probably is a conclusion. If the proposition gives a reason, it may be a premise or will provide evidence. The *process* of identifying the role relates to determining the logical function of the statements within the argument. To properly assign a role to a statement, you first will need to extract the argument (ideally, in its logical form) from the passage. You'll remember how to do this from our foray into logic. Once you have identified the conclusion, you'll be able to compare the statement that makes up the conclusion in the passage to the statement the question directly asks you about. If the question is about the conclusion, you'll know that the role of that statement is to provide a main point. If the question turns out to be about something other than the conclusion, then you may have to do more work to correctly match the role with those provided in the answer choices.

Popular answer choices for roles within passages that are not conclusion-based include: "to provide evidence supporting" "to illustrate" "to serve as an example of" "to function as evidence for X" "to provide possible evidence that is mentioned then dismissed," "premise offered in support," "provides a causal explanation," "is the conclusion," and "is a claim the argument shows is inconsistent". Regardless of the format of the question on your LR sections, the process to identify the role remains the same. You will identify the conclusion, find evidence for it, relate that to the LR question, and then match that role within the argument to the answer choices available to you.

Insider Insight: Process for Role Questions on LR

There is a word of advice as you prep for the "what role does this serve" questions on Logical Reasoning. Do not start with the statement being identified. You can identify what kind of question you are being asked first, of course, but make sure that you don't evaluate the statement the question is asking you to evaluate prior to reading the passage. For role questions, the most impactful activity you can do is to extract the argument in logical form. Once you do that, you will know which statements within the passage function as premises, assumptions, evidence, analogies, examples, criticisms, or support. Rather than emphasizing the single statement the question is asking you about, you should focus on understanding the argument itself (formally), then you will *easily* be able to answer the question. By that time, you will be ready to match the statement being asked about in the passage to its role in the argument that you have formalized. Going into the role example with a complete understanding of the formal structure of the argument will help you approach the statement in question knowing already how that statement functions in the argument. By following the process, you will have eliminated any chance for error! When you are ready to answer, you'll already be on the lookout for "sibling answers" (for more, see the chapter on Insider Insights) that mimic the correctness of the actually-correct answer choice but are similar enough to trip up the casual reader.

LOGICAL REASONING
CHAPTER 6

Brief Practice: Role Questions on the LR!

Directions: Read the short passage, then choose the best (most accurate and complete) answer.

The pace of game in baseball (from pitchers shaking off signals to batters dancing in and out of the batter's box) has led to a now-common complaint that the length of the game has eroded the number of true baseball fans. Purists of the sport contend that the game should be left alone, and that changes to the structure of the game will irrevocably harm the sport. But, a century ago, purists complained that changes should not be made to the number of batters in a line-up or a manager's ability to pinch-hit or run; yet those changes ensured baseball's success into a new century. So, contemporary baseball should integrate slight shifts to strengthen the sport and the fanbase.

The reference to the complaint of purists a century ago plays which of the following roles in the argument?

A. evidence to support the claim that the changes to the game of baseball will fundamentally destroy the sport

B. an illustration of the general hypothesis advanced, that the nature of the game of baseball is inseparable from the desires that purists of the sport have for it

C. an example of a cultural view that itself changed without a further detrimental effect on the game of baseball overall

D. evidence that it is unwarranted to claim that baseball's fanbase is eroding due to changes in the game's structure

E. possible evidence, mentioned and then dismissed, that might be cited by supporters of the purists' view that the passage criticizes

Answer Explanation:

This rich answer set requires careful reading, after walking through the process for the Role Questions you see on the LR. We want to extract the argument made within the passage. The conclusion of the argument is "contemporary baseball should integrate slight shifts to strengthen the sport and the fanbase." The reasons given include that baseball's pace is too slow and has led to a reduction in the fan base, and that past changes (such as the number of batters in a line-up or a manager's ability to pinch-hit or run) ensured baseball's success into a new century.

We can structure the content above in the following way:

1. If baseball wants to continue in popularity, it will need to make some changes to the pace of the game.

2. Some argue the pace shouldn't change, to remain pure.

3. The result is that baseball won't continue in popularity.

4. But the arguments in 2 are flawed because they mimic those of 100 years ago that were flawed.

5. Baseball does want to remain popular.

6. ∴ Contemporary baseball will need to make some changes to the pace of the game.

This is a complex hypothetical syllogism that has to defeat an opponent's argument (i.e., that of the purist) to demonstrate the main point. Now that we have each part of the argument set out, we are able to focus on the passage the question asks us about.

The question is specific to one portion of the text—that purists a century ago were found demonstrably wrong in their belief that changing baseball would hurt the sport. This is the second time "purist" is used in the passage. The author is comparing contemporary baseball purists to purists over a century ago. Armed with that knowledge and our statement to evaluate, we know that the author is using the purist statement as an example or an analogy to prove

the point that changes have in the past been good, despite the complaints of those purists. The argument strongly correlates the error of the purists a century ago with purists of the sport now, so your correct answer will reflect that correlation. (A) should immediately be removed, because it contradicts the conclusion. (B) is also wrong, although more deceptively so—although the passage talks at length about what the purists of baseball have and now want, it concludes that those desires are separate from the vitality of the game. (E) should also be removed after careful reading. Careful reading is required because (E) is intentionally complex: it suggests possible, not actual evidence; that evidence is mentioned but dismissed; that evidence could be cited by supporters of the purists; the evidence cited by supporters of the purists would be criticized by the passage. Although it is true the passage does deny the purists view, it does so by introducing the purists' view itself as evidence against purism- it does not criticize any evidence that purists accept because it does not provide evidence produced by purists. (C), however, is both clear and correct. The purists a century ago had a view that changed (purism about baseball today no longer refers to a view about the lineup or pinch runners), but baseball did not suffer as a result.

Flaw Questions on the LSAT

About 10% of the questions on the LR section of the LSAT will ask you to identify some flaw in the reasoning of a passage. This shouldn't be surprising, given that the LSAT is a logic test and a key part is to assess the validity and soundness of deductive arguments and the inferential strength of inductive arguments. The "finding flaws" questions provide the LSAC with a quantitative measurement of your ability to identify (and, potentially, critique) bad reasoning in other people's arguments. Differently than the arguments that we have covered thus far, however, there are several types of flaw questions. (*Note well*: although the flaw questions differ on the LR from those on other sections of the exam, all of the flaws on the LSAT relate to formal and informal fallacies. Make sure that you have reviewed Chapter 3 "Logical Flaws" really well, and are conversant in the main types of flaws that you might find on the LSAT.)

From the outset of the Flaw Questions, we will be keeping the provided argument at the forefront of our deliberation. After extracting whatever components are available to us for the argument (we know they probably will be woefully incomplete since they are "flaw" questions!), then we can determine what is missing from the argument or, indeed, what is present but should not be. With flaw questions, you sometimes will be aware that you are being asked a flaw question (for example, you might see: "Which one of the following most accurately describes a flaw in the argument provided by the passage?" or "The author's reasoning is flawed because it fails to recognize/take into account that X."). There are other times when the question is a bit more opaque. You might, for example, see, "The argument is questionable because it fails to consider [Y]", or, "Which one of the following, if true, casts the most doubt on the evidence offered in support of the conclusion?", or, "The argument is vulnerable to criticism on the basis of which of the following?" In any case, the question is asking you to find what is wrong in the argument.

> **EXPERT TIP**
>
> Writing on the essay is **scored higher in proportion** to the level of detail in the essay, how many arguments are assessed in it, whether a decision-making procedure is used, and the level of integration of evidence from the prompt into good justification.

One particularly pernicious, but rare, problem set on the LR will challenge you to identify a flaw that equivocates between necessary and sufficient conditions. Even if it isn't the case that the flaw in your particular question confuses necessary and sufficient conditions, the LSAT loves to provide answer choices in which attention is drawn to the fact that agents frequently confuse necessary and sufficient conditions! When you get these, they will frequently be in the answers, and will read, "X confuses a condition sufficient for bringing about a certain outcome for one that is required to bring about that outcome".

Some people struggle to understand the difference between necessary and sufficient conditions, but we were

introduced to the conditions in Chapter 1 and extensively worked with the conditions in Chapter 2. There are some conditions *the absence of which* would mean an event would not occur. These are necessary conditions. Necessary conditions are required in order to produce a consequence. Sufficient conditions are those that are enough for a consequent to occur. They might not be necessary for the event to occur, but they are enough for an event to happen. If you want to go to a law school that requires the LSAT, a necessary condition is that you take the LSAT. But, it isn't enough. Taking the LSAT is not a sufficient condition to being a lawyer. You need to do a lot of things to be a lawyer, and the exam, though a necessary condition, is not a sufficient one. We'll switch the example to reinforce the difference. I want to stay awake late working tonight, and drinking coffee is not necessary for me to meet my goal of staying up late to work, but it is sufficient to keep me awake. It isn't necessary, but it is sufficient. There could be other sufficient conditions. If I go for a run late at night, that will also be sufficient to keep me awake late into the night. There are a couple of takeaways here: there might not be a condition necessary for an event to occur, and there may be a number of conditions which are sufficient for an event to occur.

Brief Practice: Most Vulnerable LR Questions!

Directions: Read the short passage, then choose the best (most accurate and complete) answer.

Adult child: My mom constantly worries about me about becoming a diabetic because she thinks I eat too much sugar. But she has not done the research, which instead suggests that eating sugar before lunch and avoiding it after lunch has a negligible impact on diabetes rates in America. I do not eat sugar after lunch, so my risk for contracting diabetes is extremely low.

The reasoning in the adult child's argument is most vulnerable to criticism on the grounds that this argument:

A. infers a cause from a mere correlation
B. relies on a sample that is too narrow
C. misinterprets evidence, by thinking a result is likely as evidence that the result is certain
D. mistakes a condition sufficient for bringing about a result for a condition necessary for doing so
E. relies on a source that is probably not well-informed

Argument Explanation:

Questions that ask you to identify the susceptibility or vulnerability of a claim are LR criticism or weaken question types but, at root, are flawed reasoning questions. For these questions, recapitulate the argument and pinpoint where the weakness resides. Sometimes the argument will commit a formal fallacy, sometimes it will commit an informal fallacy, and at other times the argument might rely on a faulty assumption. This argument has an adult indicating that he disagrees with his mom, who believes he is susceptible to becoming diabetic, but his reason for rejecting that claim is that he only eats sugar before lunch and sugar before lunch hasn't been shown either to reduce or increase diabetes rates. As you scan your answer choices, you might be tempted to choose answer (E), because we really are not sure what that source for his data would be. But the passage does not provide the source of the adult child's research, so we can't cast suspicion on it. (B) and (D) should be removed as possibilities, because neither can be inferred from what is given as evidence. Both (A) and (C) are better choices. (A) is a strong answer, because the adult child correlates eating sugar after lunch with causing diabetes (and, of course, not eating sugar after lunch with preventing diabetes). (C) might be, if the author thinks that the likely result (that his own diabetes risk is low) is certain. But, the adult child does not say that he will not incur diabetes, but rather that the evidence suggests he is at a lower risk because he does not eat sugar after lunch. The best choice among (A) and (C), then, is indeed (A).

LR Question Type: Paradox

You won't see many paradox questions on the LSAT, but out of two LR sections, you are likely to see at least one. A "paradox" refers to two statements that seem, minimally, incongruent. We like to think of paradoxes as puzzles or

knots that we have to make consistent with each other in order to solve the puzzle or disentangle the paradox. There could be a number of reasons for the paradox. It could be that the facts don't yield a particular conclusion. (Health disparities research is very interested in paradoxes of health, for example, for populations which have the highest morbidity indices and yet live longer than populations without those indices.) It could be that there is a curious causal relationship that just cannot be adequately explained. So, these questions put you in a position to explain the paradox or, more frequently, resolve the paradox. (Which, let's face it, is pretty fun!)

The tip-off within the LR questions for paradoxes is usually straightforward. You will be asked which of the answer choices helps, or is most effective, to resolve a paradox. Or, the question may ask you to explain a discrepancy, paradox, or conflict. Don't be surprised if the "paradox" or "discrepancy" is qualified with "apparent" or "seeming," because the writer might not take a view on whether the paradox is a true paradox.

In actuality, paradox questions can be answered effectively if you pay close attention to the *justification* provided within the argument. The justification will give you the evidential information you need to be able to explain, resolve, solve, dissolve, or dissipate the seeming discrepancy within the passage. Generally, what generates the paradox within the passage are two views that are in conflict. You, the test-taker, buy into the idea that there is a paradox because we tend to think that two opposing views are incommensurate, on their face. That is true (of course! The LSAT depends on that logical truth.) But, in the LR passages, the two seemingly disparate informational pieces really are commensurate. You will need to think carefully about their relationship to answer correctly. Approaching the question with care will help you, first, to understand the paradox and why the author believes it is paradoxical, and then you will need to ensure there are no assumptions that are driving either position. Rather than formulating your own answer before approaching the possible solutions, instead start with understanding the paradox, identify the two views or statements that are in tension, and then think about one particular statement that could make the two positions commensurate with each other so that both points of view are true. Then evaluate the answer choices with the same motive—find the answer that makes both seemingly incommensurate views "fit" with each other and be true.

Brief Practice: Paradox Questions on the LR!

Directions: *Read the short passage, then choose the best (most accurate and complete) answer.*

It's pretty well-known that the most successful pitchers in baseball history have been ostensibly unathletic-looking. Many are overweight (even some current Major League pitchers today are almost morbidly-obese), and others have no defined muscles at all. Although there are some pitchers, of course, that take pitching seriously, it is a documented facet of baseball history that (even today) some of the best pitchers in baseball were either seriously out-of-shape or never athletically strong.

Which one of the following, if true, helps to dissolve the apparent paradox represented in the passage?

A. Pitchers only pitch on a several-day rotation so are not as physically taxed as everyday baseball players.
B. Other athletes in professional football, hockey, and (occasionally) in basketball are out of shape or unmuscular but are athletic superstars.
C. Even morbidly obese or strikingly unmuscular individuals can throw a ball hard.
D. Muscle memory and flexibility are the two leading contributors to any pitcher's success.
E. As we learn more about nutrition and fitness, there will be far fewer out of shape athletes in professional baseball.

Answer Explanation:

The paradox should be apparent: there are unfit people (whether very overweight or not strong) who have succeeded and continue to succeed at the highest levels in pitching, which, as a sport, seems to require being fit. To resolve the paradox, we need an answer that might not be tied closely with the text but is inferentially supported by it. The correct answer must be *consistent with the passage*, even if it uses the text as a launchpad for its success.

Then, we can work the answer choices. (A), does not untangle the paradox of how ostensibly out of shape, unathletic people can perform excellently at an unathletic task several days a week. (B) actually has the opposite effect of untangling the web, because it intensifies the paradox— not only is it true that pitchers in baseball demonstrate this phenomenon, stars in all of the major sports do, too. (C) mistakes a fact about the point of the case. The issue isn't whether any individuals can throw a ball hard (only one aspect of pitching) but is instead about how to account for their professional success at pitching. (D) is an excellent option. It suggests that, rather than physical acumen, two other components are the key indices for success in pitching—muscle memory for performing the task well, and physical flexibility (which individuals of all shapes, sizes, and athletic ability can attain). And, for due diligence, (E) is not the correct answer because it does not show now why we have this phenomenon in athletics.

LR Question Types: Most Strengthens and Most Weakens

You already know that you are supposed to be on the lookout for accessible questions to approach first on the LR section of the LSAT. You know that "main point" questions typically are the easiest to answer, and so the first to be approached. But, a close second are the "most strengthens" and (third) the "most weakens" arguments. When you are asked to strengthen an argument, you only need to provide support for it. You don't have to undermine the claim, you just have to choose the answer that most readily and deeply lends support to the claim made in the passage. Even for "weaken" questions, in which you need to undermine the main claim made, we tend to be pretty good at poking holes in everyday reasoning. And, you have the benefit of a logic-based LSAT prep, which has prepared you to best support or damage arguments and reasoning that is put before you. Given that you already have logic at hand, the "most strengthens" and "most weakens" questions on the LR should be quite accessible to you, and you won't need to work too terribly hard to apply that logical acumen to the structure of any given LSAT LR passage.

"Most Strengthen" passages very often will simply ask you which of the answer choices most strengthens the argument provided by the passage. But, it also may ask you which of the conditions *if true* would be most likely to improve, bolster, support, reinforce, or fortify a particular argument. The role of the strengthen questions is to test your ability to *demonstrate* how well the argument logically is tied together. You will show that the relationship between the conclusion and the premises is airtight from a logical perspective. "Most Weaken" passages also will ask which of the answer choices most weakens or "most seriously weakens" the argument. The point of the weaken questions in LR is to demonstrate that there is a faulty connection between the conclusion and the reasons that are meant to show that the conclusion is justified. Frequently, those passages also include the "if true" qualifier for their question, and may additionally ask you which answer would most damage, harm, impair, or worsen the argument, or the evidence provided by the argument.

In terms of format, there is one aspect in which the LR strengthen and the LR weaken questions are fairly far apart. Quite regularly within the LR strengthen questions, you will be the recipient of "EXCEPT" questions, in which four of the five answer choices on a particular question will strengthen the argument but one will not. The correct answer will undermine the main point (or, weaken it!). For LR weaken questions, you can see "EXCEPT" questions, though from a statistical standpoint, you are more likely to see them on

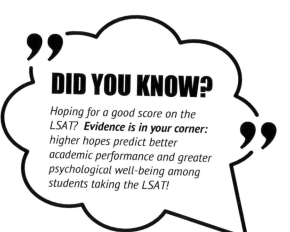

DID YOU KNOW?

Hoping for a good score on the LSAT? **Evidence is in your corner:** *higher hopes predict better academic performance and greater psychological well-being among students taking the LSAT!*

strengthen questions. Just remember on the "weaken" questions in which you are told that all of the answer choices but one will weaken the passage's argument, the correct answer will be the one that strengthens the argument. In both cases, you will find the outlier, and the correct answer will be the opposite of the strengthen/weaken operator.

Before we practice these questions, it is worthy to note two more commonalities between the question types. First, as briefly referenced above, almost all of the "strengthen" and "weaken" questions depend on a qualifier within the question of "if true." That is a formal technique that we learned in Chapter 1 with basic logic. To claim that an argument is sound is to say that *if the premises obtain in the real world,* the conclusion will happen. We assume that our correct answers are true *for the sake of argument* but this does not commit you to believing the in-the-real-world truth of any particular premise, conclusion, or answer on the LSAT. (It should also be noted that strengthen and weaken questions do not corner the market on qualifying "if true" of the questions. So, rather than relying on the qualifier to point you to what kind of question it is—rely on the question!) Second, it is very common that test-takers believe the strengthen questions are more accessible than their weaken-question countertypes. You may want to rely on that anecdotal testimony to navigate through which questions you will engage with first on the LR.

Brief Practice: Most Strengthens LR Questions!

Directions: Read the short passage, then choose the best (most accurate and complete) answer.

Criminologist: The majority of drugs purchased online are sent through the mail, which leads to the potential for the sale of fake drugs. Most of these shipments are subjected to standard border control mechanisms, including X-rays and drug-sniffing dogs. But neither the FDA nor U.S. Immigration and Customs Enforcement knows what percentage of fake drugs are actually checked or confiscated every year because officials seize drugs only if they are both suspicious and likely to affect a large number of people. Clearly, stopping the scourge of fake medications would, at a minimum, require a great deal of cooperation among more than a handful of nations.

Each of the following, if true, strengthens the criminologist's argument *EXCEPT:*

A. Countries are not under pressure to pass more formal legislation or to enforce preexisting statutes and often have incentives not to.

B. Since 2011, countries can sign informal treaties to criminalize pharmaceutical fraud within their borders.

C. Policy experts believe to raise the standards for pharmaceuticals worldwide, we need a similar system that penalizes countries that don't enforce medicinal quality controls.

D. The World Health Organization hosts conferences in which countries meet to discuss what they can do together to reduce the number of falsified pharmaceuticals reaching patients.

E. Some pharmaceutical companies have tried to expand the fight against falsified drugs solely to protect their intellectual properties.

Answer Explanation:

Typically, in "strengthens" questions, we want to find the answer that strengthens the given argument, in which case the correct answer will not only be relevant, consistent, and obviously tied to the argument in the passage, but also will add evidential weight that was not already in the passage. In this passage, however, all of the answer choices *already strengthen* the Criminologist's arguments. Except one. Your job is to find that one. The result is that all of the propositions should be true and provide support for the criminologist's view. The statement that is either not true, inconsistent, irrelevant, or not justified in the text is the correct answer. You do not have to wander long to find it—(A) is not supported by the criminologist, who is arguing that a number of nations need to participate against the "scourge" of fake drugs sold and shipped online, and across borders. For confirmation, (B) would explain how border officials can have the authority to limit pharmaceutical fraud. (C) would describe how nations could cooperate to raise the standard. (D) demonstrates what nations are now doing to protect their mutual interests against fake pharmaceuticals, and (E) shows that companies are aiding in efforts for a legitimate drug trade.

LOGICAL REASONING
CHAPTER 6

Brief Practice: Most Weakens LR Questions!

Directions: *Read the short passage, then choose the best (most accurate and complete) answer.*

Program Manager: We are very happy with our employee-written policy regarding sexual harassment in the workplace, and all of our employees are on-board with following those policies. Recently, all of our in-and-out of state employees were given a survey and everyone who took it agreed that it was a good policy and they would follow it, which demonstrates what a successful policy it really is. So, we won't need any additional oversight from administration nor punitive measures in place to ensure that our employees are protected from sexual harassment.

Which of the following, if true, most seriously casts doubt upon the program manager's conclusion?

A. Only companies that directly work with this particular program manager are required to comply with the policy.

B. The reason the sexual harassment policy was written by employees was that there were several administrators who had been found to have several sexual harassment charges against them.

C. Upon external review of the policy and its implementation, most of the employees and companies that contract with this employer are not practicing the policy's provisions.

D. The program manager lost clients when he instituted the employee-written policy.

E. Research on employee-generated sexual harassment policies demonstrates that a necessary condition for their success is that upper administration follows the policies.

Answer Explanation

As we saw with the flaw "vulnerable" questions, casting doubt on an argument is typically far easier if the argument is flawed! So, in this instance, you are given an argument for why the home-grown, in-house sexual harassment policy doesn't need administrative oversight or punitive consequences for not being followed. You can extract the argument out of the passage. The conclusion is that additional oversight from the administration and punitive measures are not needed to ensure that employees are protected from sexual harassment. The support given includes that (a) the company has a harassment policy that the employees came up with; (b) all employees who took the survey agree to comply and that the policy is effective; and (c) an effective harassment policy is one that all employees will agree is effective.

Your role is to cast aspersion on the argument by determining which piece of extra information would be most damaging to the argument. We do *not learn* in the passage whether the employees who took the survey actually are guided by the policy in their actions. The result is that in option (A), only companies that directly work with this particular program manager are required to comply with the policy, but that means that the policy is effective only for those companies that do comply. Similarly, answer (E) also is not tied enough to the question of whether the harassment policy is and will be effective. (E) would be more attractive if any part of the argument suggested that the administration of the company committed to following the guidelines of the policy as well as the employees who drafted it. And, option (D) should be eliminated as completely irrelevant, since whether the Manager lost clients at the policy's implementation does not indicate the program is at all successful or would be. (You could only weakly infer that the clients dropped because they didn't want to follow the policy but in fact, an even stronger inference would be that they dropped because they didn't want to be in contract with someone who didn't have a bona fide sexual harassment policy in place!) The rest of the answer choices do cast a bit of doubt on the Program Manager's conclusion. (B) provides evidence that harassment has historically been a problem at the company and so casts doubt by suggesting that serious problems of this nature have existed (and could persist). It wouldn't be a surprise if historical problems that aren't effectively dealt with remain a problem, even if the employees generate their own policy. Response (C) is far stronger as a correct answer choice. It indicates that the Program Manager's conclusion that no administrative oversight nor punitive measures are needed is simply false. External reviewers have determined that the new policy, for whatever it is worth, is not being followed, so it casts the most doubt on the Manager's claim.

LR Question Type: Pattern/Parallel Reasoning

A good critical thinker will be able to contrast and compare elements within disparate arguments to draw analogies, differences, patterns of reasoning, or parallel reasoning relationships between arguments. Within the LR section, there are Pattern or Parallel reasoning questions which measure your ability to identify similarly-structured arguments that may employ different concepts or focus on different topics to show that the arguments can have a logical relationship. In these questions, you identify the answer choice that exhibits reasoning that is *patterned after or parallel* to the reasoning in the argument. You may see the question invoke the terms "parallel reasoning," "closely parallels/resembles," "most similar," "shares the pattern of," or "is patterned after."

Unsurprisingly, your ability to extract the main passage's argument will be central to your success at finding the answer that exhibits a similar logical structure. Being able to evaluate the type of argument the passage is employing, any assumptions that are needed, and any logical flaws that could be made can determine whether and to what extent you are able to find patterns in the answer choice's reasoning. It isn't always true, of course, that you will be given a well-organized argument nor that you will be able to identify all of the flaws that are featured in answer choices for which there is an identifiable pattern. But, if you are engaged with a question that you can interact with logically, on the basis of its form, you will be in a solid position to structure the parallel argument to show what patterns emerge, even from imperfect arguments. The upshot? Your ability to use logic will help you understand the main passage's argument. Your ability to apply that logic to answer choices will help you see similarities in form. When you know the structure, the content is easier to assess.

> ## DID YOU KNOW?
>
> *Prior to 1979, the LSAT was shrouded in secrecy, and the LSAC refused to grant access to the tests to test takers, researchers, or state governments, so there was no independent way to analyze the appropriateness of questions, the correctness of answers, or even the accuracy of scoring of individual examinations. The State of New York was the first to pass a "**Truth in Testing**" law (1979) to require testing agencies to disclose test questions and answers to the state.*

Consonant with the questions being "pattern" questions, there are generally remarkable patterns that emerge from correct and incorrect answers on these sorts of questions on the LR section. Think about what the correct answer should do in resemblance/relationship questions. Correct answers will reflect a similar logical structure as the argument within the main passage. They almost invariably will *not* share content. The similarities between the argument and the correct answer will be formal, rather than substantive. The subjects involved, and their ordering, can differ as well as long as the basic logical structure is the same between them.

Correlatively, wrong answers also are patterned for these kinds of resemblance/parallel question types on the LSAT. In wrong answers, *content rather than formal structure* is usually similar—this is how the LSAC writers can trip you up for Parallel arguments. If two arguments are both talking about Icelandic snow, they must be using parallel reasoning, right? Well, as you know, that is incorrect. What matters is the *reasoning* rather than the topic, or substance, of what either the passage or the answers are about. Wrong answers get something about the structure wrong, whether it is a missing relationship between the premises and the conclusion, whether a logical flaw is introduced, or whether there is a consequent that is missing. Wrong answers will violate some logical rule of framing good arguments, whereas the correct answer will include all of the aspects of the original argument that made it a strong, compelling argument.

There is a word of caution as you extract and compare reasoning structures for Parallel Reasoning questions. It is frequently true that most students use too much time on these sorts of questions, for two reasons. First, Pattern/Parallel questions usually are longer to read (because each answer is giving an argument, which you have to weigh for whether it has the same pattern as the passage. Use Brake! and Shot Clock to keep track of your time during the LR. If you have time for the Pattern/Parallel, use the end time to work those questions. The second danger is that

you can give in to the temptation of extracting the logical form of every answer choice. You can do that, of course, but only if the Shot Clock is going your way. Much more expedient is to review the answer choices and choose the two which seem on their face to be similarly reasoned. If you find the correct answer, you will have saved yourself significant time. If you don't, you haven't spent any more time by going into your third choice than if you had pulled the structure for every answer in the first place.

Brief Practice: Pattern/Parallel Reasoning Questions

Directions: *Read the short passage, then choose the best (most accurate and complete) answer.*

Imagine a pediatrician has been told some confidential personal information by one of her minor patients, a teenager. The confidential information poses potential risks for the future health and well-being of the patient. She feels compelled to keep the confidence of her young patient, but also to let the teen's parent know that the teen is in trouble. Since the pediatrician has competing moral obligations, she is not morally obligated to either the teen or the parent.

Which one of the following arguments is most similar in its reasoning to the argument above?

A. Americans believe that we have the unencumbered right to say whatever we want. It is also claimed that we have the obligation to be civil to others. But civility requires that we respect the rights of others. So, if you are a civil American, you will respect the rights of others, even if they say something with which you disagree.

B. Parents can get their kids to be obedient by agreeing to give them gifts, even if they don't actually plan to. The only way parents can get their kids to be obedient is to be dishonest with them.

C. If the photographer puts significant effort into using filters for her customers, they might be so impressed with the filters but not the photos. Sofie decides not to use filters to save time for the customers, and so they were not impressed with the photos.

D. If a driver uses the electronic toll lane, she will be taxed for the use of the road. If the driver is taxed for the use of the road, the state will issue fines until she pays the tax off. But, in this case, the state has not issued fines to the driver, so either the driver doesn't have to pay off the tax, or the state didn't have the right to tax her.

E. If the professor gives a comprehensive final exam, she will either need a grad student to help her grade or will miss the grading deadline. The department does not have funds for a grad student, and she will lose her summer health insurance coverage if she does not submit final grades on time. She really depends on her health insurance, so she will have to find a way to fund a grad student to grade the exams.

Answer Explanation

Remember to think of "pattern" questions or "parallel reasoning" questions as analogies from the given argument's form or content to that represented in the answer choices. You are being asked to demonstrate a logical parallel between the argument and the reasoning in the correct answer. This passage requires you to draw an analogy in the argument's form. The first thing you should do is think of the form of the argument presented in the question. We can think of the argument as a basic modus ponens:

(1) If a doctor has competing moral obligations between a parent and a minor child, the doctor has moral obligations to neither. (If P, then Q)

(2) The doctor has an obligation to the teen that competes with her obligation to the parent. (P)

(3) The doctor does not have a moral obligation to either the teen or the parent. (Therefore, Q)

This is a valid argument, and your job is to see which answer choice also uses a *modus ponens* form. (B) does not

(it argues from one instance of a fact to a universal of it); (C) commits the logical fallacy of denying the antecedent (If P, then Q; ~P; so ~Q); (D) is valid, but is a *modus tollens* form (If P, then Q; ~Q, so ~P). Similarly, (E) is also valid, but is a disjunctive syllogism (Either P v Q, ~P, so P). The only answer that relies on a *modus ponens* is (A). Although there are added premises, it uses a *modus ponens*: If you are civil, you respect the rights of others; You are civil, so you respect the rights of others (even if you disagree with the person).

To Sum Up:

We have covered significant ground in this chapter. We began with obfuscation and intentional ways in which the LSAT writers will attempt to thwart you. We discussed ways of thwarting those attempts to thwart you! You were introduced to formal obfuscation in arguments, and at each step of the Logical Reasoning prep, you were given examples to work on and evaluate. Then, we moved to strategies for attacking the LR inductive and deductive arguments, and you were introduced to Venn Diagrams as a way of easily, effectively, and efficiently modeling syllogisms. We next discussed five potential strategies for approaching the LSAT LR multiple-choice questions to eliminate time-intensive and unnecessary deliberation. (You can use all of them throughout the exam, or really hone a handful to work well.) We looked at four main logical abilities that are tested within the Logical Reasoning section, and you worked through examples for each. Cutting-edge research on two main strategies for approaching the question itself (rather than the whole problem) was discussed. And, finally, we went through main types of questions you will see on the LR section, and we discussed how to approach them, strategies for working them, and success tips before giving examples of all of them for you to work through. Congratulations on finishing the LR prep!

CHAPTER VII

ARGOPREP
LSAT
INSIDER INSIGHTS

ARGOPREP LSAT INSIDER INSIGHTS
CHAPTER 7

You've processed a lot of information for this exam, and you might worry that there are so many insider, pro insights that you wouldn't be able to remember them all and it might get in the way of your success. Never fear! Here is a compendium of the Insider Insights for the LSAT you can only get through ArgoPrep.

The LSAT is one massive logic test, replete with games, comparisons, puzzles, and assumptions. It is given to you as a series of passages and multiple-choice options (except for the unscored writing essay.) Three awesome features of this multiple-choice exam for the LSAT should excite you: 1) there are no weighted questions (unlike, for example, on the GRE) so you shouldn't let any particular question suck your time; 2) you will only have one correct answer per question; and 3) wrong answers don't count against your score—only correct answers are scored, so you are at an advantage when you answer *all questions*, even if you aren't 100% sure you're right.

We've tackled specifics of the LSAT throughout this book, but there are insider-insight strategies for approaching the questions on the LSAT that will make your life easier on the exam, and lead you to better success on it. This chapter is a compendium of all of the unique-to-ArgoPrep Insider Insights as you get ready to approach the exam.

Insider Insights for Approaching the Exam

Insider Insight 1: Brake!

Most students open up a test book and work the problems from start-to-finish, left-to-right, top-to-bottom as they have done for their entire lives. This is a bad way to take a test! Why? You'll sap your energy working questions that you should really come back to, and your confidence might be shaken for questions you should easily know by questions that sucked up your time.

You already know how important time management is for this exam, and you know that all answers count equally. That means you should identify which questions are easy and work on those first. If you quickly answer as many easy questions—that count the exact amount as hard questions—you can dedicate your remaining time to questions that aren't obvious right away. So, before you answer any questions in any section of the test, scan the questions briefly and put a star next to the questions that jump out to you as ones you can easily answer. *Then, start with those questions!* You'll have finished a large part of the test... *correctly*...and then you can spend the rest of the solid amount of time you have left to questions that need a little bit more work.

In Chapter 1, we discussed "Brake!" as a strategy. Almost invariably, test prep companies will have you memorize charts for time management. But Brake! truly is the only time management tool you need. Rather than using every minute working every question, like the other test prep companies would have you do, the best advice for most test takers is to "BRAKE". Stop, evaluate which questions among a set need less time and go after getting those questions correct. Since all of the test questions count the same, it makes no sense to do the questions in order and to sap your energy from the outset with the most difficult questions. (You do not get any extra credit for solving the hardest questions, so brake. Skip questions that give you a hard time initially, mark them and come back to them.) Just make sure you come back and complete all of your questions—even if you have to use Letter of the Day (a reminder is below if you need it!).

> **EXPERT TIP**
> On the analytical reasoning section, students tend to begin to rapidly-guess beginning on question 12. Students who use **interpretive techniques** take longer to answer the remaining questions, but perform at much higher rates.

Insider Insight 2: Visualize the Answer!

Another mistake students tend to make is that they look at the five answer options for each question *before* they think about what the correct answer could be. But, your first thought is often right when you approach multiple-

choice questions and the same is true for the LSAT. Your intuitions—especially after learning the basic logical tools you need to win at this exam—are frequently compatible with the right answer. That doesn't mean your first guess is often right—instead, you should visualize the correct answer before you see which answers are available to you.

Most multiple-choice questions should be done by working the answers. But, working the answers *after* you already have a sense of what the answer should be will put you on the right track to eliminating answers that you know can't be correct, and then homing in the proper answer that is listed. So, visualize the correct answer first if you can, and then be smart about eliminating wrong answers.

Insider Insight 3: Wildly Wrong Answers! Sibling Answers!

Once you've answered the questions for each section that are obvious to you, you can go back to the ones that will require a little bit more time and work. Remember, the LSAT is essentially a *logic puzzle*, even more than it is a test about skill. So, know how the game is built. Here's an inside insight you need to know about people who are writing the LSAT: they will always give you an answer choice that is *wildly wrong*. For challenging questions, find the one answer that is wildly wrong, and cross it out!

That will leave you with four answers. Of those four, two of them will be *sibling answers*. Sibling answers are closely related, look a lot alike, and it can be confusing to tell them apart. When you get sibling answers, *ignore the answer that is not a sibling*. It won't be correct. That leaves you with a 50% chance of getting the answer correct, even if you aren't sure about which of the siblings is the right answer.

Insider Insight 4: Never, Always, All, None!

You know that you will be called upon to answer questions about all of a certain set, questions about logical necessity, and questions about logical impossibility. *Apart from questions about logical necessity,* guess which answer choices on the LSAT are *almost never* a correct option? The choices that include absolutes are *almost never* correct. (We can't use an absolute to absolutely deny the correctness of any absolute!)

If you see answer choices that include the words "Never, Always, All, or None" for questions that are not about logical necessity, put an asterisk by them, and be on the look-out. Typically, the only correct answer choices that include an absolute are questions for which *every answer* choice contains an absolute. If you know this ahead of time, it can save you time. You'll only need to carefully read answer choices with your asterisk only if the other answer choices just don't fit.

Insider Insight 5: LETTER OF THE DAY (LOTD)!

You remember this strategy from Chapter 1, right? LOTD is an absolute must on Exam Day. Before you take the test, pick out your favorite letter, A, B, C, D, or E. That single letter is your Letter of the Day. For any question that you have visualized the correct answer, eliminated obviously incorrect answers, can't find the siblings, and still can't come up with the right answer, you are going to answer with your Letter of the Day. It's the Letter of the Day because you are going to use the letter you have chosen every time you have visualized, eliminated, and are stuck.

Like any Insider Insight, LOTD is meant to give you an advantage when properly used but it cannot be a substitute for solid prudential reasoning. That means you need to be smart about LOTD. Let's imagine that your Letter of the Day is 'B,' and you are on a problem that you have visualized, worked, and eliminated an answer choice as obviously false. If the answer choice you've eliminated as incorrect is 'B'—guess what your answer choice *won't be*, even if it's the Letter of the Day? Use the LOTD in cases in which you are actually stuck, rather than on answers you know can't be true. Also, if you've been able to get down to the sibling answers on the exam, but neither of the siblings is your Letter of the Day, choose the sibling answer over the LOTD. Letter of the Day is for when you've used the other insights and you still aren't sure about the correct answer—as well as for when you have just about run out of time, have a few questions remaining in a section but don't have time to work them. Those are questions that require your LOTD.

Insider Insight #6: Sometimes, Often, Usually, Generally

Remember the "Never, Always, All, None" insight steered you away from answers that include absolutes? The "Sometimes, Often, Usually, Generally" insight is based on evidence from past exams-- answer choices that allow for some exceptions *tend* to be correct. (Just like with the insight about absolutes, this doesn't mean that the correct answer will always be general, it means instead that often the answer that contains more probabilistic descriptions is correct for questions that include logical possibility or which ask you for an inference to the best explanation.)

You'll use this insight after you've eliminated the *wildly wrong* answer and identified the *sibling answers*. Of the siblings, if an answer choice contains "sometimes, often, usually, generally", it probably is the correct response.

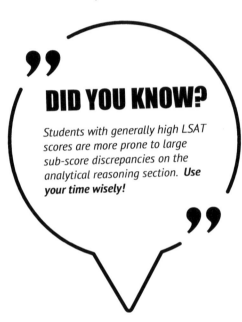

DID YOU KNOW?

*Students with generally high LSAT scores are more prone to large sub-score discrepancies on the analytical reasoning section. **Use your time wisely!***

Insider Insight 7: Twins, Not Siblings!

You're already on the lookout for *sibling answers* because you know that the LSAT writers are going to want to stump you with two answers that resemble each other and are hard to logically discern between. But, if you find out that sibling answers are actually *twins*—you've scored a big win! Since two identical answers—*twin answers*—can't be both correct, you know that neither one of them is right!

Sibling answers can be turned into twin answers through the use of negatives. Let's imagine that you have the following two answers listed, and you have not been able to eliminate either one as a logically possible answer:

A. Spencer was primarily interested in determining whether Hawk had access to the gun, which was not in the swimming pool area with Susan at the time of the shooting.

B. Susan was in the swimming pool at the time of the shooting, but couldn't have not been with the murder weapon, or so Spencer opined, which led to the issue of whether Hawk could have been.

The use of the double-negative makes the answer in B basically a twin of A. In both cases, Spencer is trying to determine where Hawk is in relation to the gun, because the gun was not in the pool area, since Susan was there but Hawk wasn't. Regardless of what the question is that corresponds to these answer choices, neither A nor B is going to be a correct answer because they are essentially the same.

Insider Insight 8: Grammar Matters!

Your question and your answer choices need to agree grammatically to function logically in the same way, so—grammar matters! You have already diligently practiced assigning new logical terms in translations to subjects which do not match other subjects already translated within a passage. The result is that if your answer choices--especially for LSAT passages in which you are identifying the main conclusion, supplying premises, or picking out assumptions of the argument—do not reflect pronoun, verb, or numerical agreement with the question—CROSS THEM OUT! You don't have to waste time trying to figure out if it is correct, because the grammar already has shown that it isn't.

There's one more application of the "Grammar Matters!" insight: if a question on your exam tells you that all of the answers are correct "except" one, read carefully! Occasionally, you'll be able to find the "except" answer by figuring out which answer doesn't grammatically make sense. If the grammar isn't right, CROSS IT OUT!

Insider Insight 9: Order Matters!

Just like Grammar Matters (!), so can order. Although you are going to go through a subsection and answer the questions that jump out to you as easy first, after that, answer questions in the groups that correspond to their main passages. (This is especially true in the Reading Comprehension and Analytical Reasoning sections, which provide groups of questions around a single passage.) Often, correctly-solved questions can give us clues about how other questions are answered. (Although you will remember not to allow your correct answers on one question to influence the answers in another—especially on Analytical Reasoning—if the conditions are different from each other.)

Insider 10: True or False! (T v F)

We already know that we have to read "except" questions carefully. But, there's another trick to solving "except" questions more effectively. You know that all answers are correct except one. So, go ahead and turn each answer into a True or False (T v F) statement. Every part of a true sentence has to be true, so for every answer choice that you discover is true in all of its components, write "T" for "True" to the left of it. When you find any part of an answer false, the whole statement is false, so mark an "F" to the left of the option, for "False." Long propositions, especially which include many logical pivots and notations, are more prone to have one part of the statement that is false. As soon as you have your false phrase in any of the answers, you have your "except" answer correctly identified!

Insider Insight #11: Shot Clock!

Although Brake! is the best time management reminder, it doesn't take the place of knowing when you started a section, how much time is left on a section, and how much time you are going to devote to harder questions on any given section. Keep your eye on the shot clock so you don't run out of time. Different passages will require you to manage the clock differently, but without doubt, the Reading Comprehension section is solely designed to test your Shot Clock management. It *is designed to exploit your perceived inability to manage too many texts*. There are between 4500 and 8000 words in an RC section total. College students on average read 400 words per minute, and the passages in the RC section typically are technical, and frequently draw from journal articles in top fields in academia. The result is that the average student will need a minimum of 20 minutes just to read the section. If you spend 20 minutes reading the passages, you only have 15 minutes remaining to answer the approximately 25 RC questions that will be on the exam. The LSAT isn't a math test, but...do the math! The LSAT folks are happy to see you try to read all of these passages, but it makes sense instead to use a technique that helps translate the RC section from a long trek through rich paragraphs which you will barely finish—if you're lucky—to a logic test that is easily digestible. The successful exam taker is able to make distinctions between questions that are completely finished and require more time to solve, and problems that cannot be completed in the available available time remaining, and so require LOTD. Use Brake! as an offensive strategy to solve as many direct, accessible problems as possible as quickly as you can. Use Shot Clock as a defensive strategy to avoid wasting time and expending effort on question sets in which there is a high degree of possibility that you either won't finish or won't succeed if you spent time working the problem. If you can use them both, you will have developed an advance skill that can set you apart from other test takers and maximize your success on the LSAT.

Insider Insight #12: Structure of the Exam

Keep the structure of the exam in mind when you are keeping the Shot Clock in view. The exam will have two LR sections, 1 AR section, and 1 RC section that are scored. It also will contain 1 *experimental* section that is unscored. *You won't know which section is experimental*. The experimental section could be an extra LR, AR, or RC section but regardless of what kind of section it is, the section will masquerade as a regular section so you will need to do as well as you can on all sections you attempt. Each section is 35 minutes, and they could come *in any possible order,* except the writing section will always be last. The final section is also unscored, and it is the writing section. Here's a useful graph:

LSAT test structure

Logical Reasoning (two sections), 35 minutes each	Number of Questions: 24-26
Analytical Reasoning (one section), 35 minutes	Number of Questions: 23-24
Reading Comprehension (one section), 35 minutes	Number of Questions: 26-28
Experimental (LR, AR, or RC), (one section), 35 minutes	Number of Questions: 23-28
Writing Sample (one section), 35 minutes	1 essay required (unscored)

Insider Insights into Translations

Insider Insight #1: *Translating Ideas in LSAT Passages.*

We want *all nouns* to be translated into our logical form. Why? Nouns are the building blocks for logic because they signal to the scholar that a new idea is being predicated. All new ideas are new logical terms! So, for any noun, translate it by giving it some completely arbitrary letter. *For our purposes, I am going to translate nouns into their first letter to avoid confusion. I strongly recommend that you do the same!* Now, any letter can be capitalized or put into small-case, which is helpful for us. Here are two Gensler rules rules we learned in Chapter Two you need to use when you are translating nouns: 1. Translate general ideas with lower case letters. A general idea is any category, including: car, philosophy, shoes, dancer, apron, charger, belt, deodorant, lawyer, child, ice cream, workbook, hazard, tootsie roll, etc. Hint: general ideas take an indefinite article, "a" or "an". 2. Translate specific ideas with uppercase letters. Specific ideas pick out a particular among the general category, including: Paris, Wollstonecraft, the birthplace of democracy, the book, this ice cream cone, her shoes, the fragrant deodorant. Hint: specific ideas take on the definite article, "the". Here are some examples of how to translate general ideas:

> ***General Ideas:***
>
> a softball team = S
>
> a simple plan = P
>
> a state of contentedness = C
>
> a belief in God = G
>
> an intelligent woman = W
>
> an automatic transmission = T

Here is how you take those general ideas, and translate their specific counterparts:

> ***Specific Ideas:***
>
> Jill's softball team = s
>
> the plan = p
>
> the contemplative life = c
>
> Mike's belief in God = m
>
> the most intelligent woman = w
>
> this car's transmission = t

Insider Insight #2: Logical Notation.

Make your life waaaaay easier! (Both in-and-out of the LSAT!) Use logical notation to simplify arguments and to shorten the amount of time you need to sketch and evaluate arguments. Here are basic logical notations that you should memorize COLD to make translations on the exam seamless:

> · "and", so "Gustavo and Jill" can be abbreviated, "G·J"
>
> ⊃ "if-then", so "If I want to rock the LSAT, then I will study," translates to "A ⊃ B"
>
> ≡ "if and only if", so, "I will prep for the LSAT if and only if I use ArgoPrep" translates to "P ≡ A"
>
> v "or", so "I will study for the LSAT, or I will watch the movie," translates to "A v B"
>
> ~ "not", so "I will not watch the movie," translates to ~B
>
> ∴ "therefore", so "Thus, I will study for the LSAT", translates to "∴A"
>
> • "necessary", or a necessary condition, so "I must study," translates to •A
>
> ◊ "possible", so "I could study," translates to ◊A

Insider Insight #3: Translating Sentences.

When you take the LSAT, your job is going to be to translate and evaluate the translations for validity so that you can make inferences required by the questions on the test. But it can be tricky to take a paragraph and translate each proposition into logical form. Make sure that you only assign letters in translation to main ideas, and that when you assign letters, you give a new letter to a new idea. Here's the key thought: if you move from a *general category* (let's say, "judges") to a *specific category* ("the best judge in Houston"), you need to assign different letters to them because they connote different ideas.

If I have a sentence such that, "Judges are concerned with human rights issues," I know that I can translate that, "J is C." But, this is different than, "Ravi is a judge who is concerned with human rights issues," which translates, "r is C." We can tweak this further to indicate that "All judges should care about human rights issues," to read, "All J is C." (Note that the "should" has moral, but not different

EXPERT TIP

You will get a 15-minute break after the 35-minute period for Section 3 has concluded. **Take the break!** *Stretch, do jumping jacks, get outside of the room and refocus for the remainder of the 4 hour period.*

logical, force in translation.) Or, how about, "No judge should forget to care about human rights issues," which translates, "No J is F." And, a further alteration would indicate, "Ravi is not a judge who has forgotten human rights issues," and would be translated, "r is not F."

Insider Insight #4: Translating Tip-Offs.

Tip-off words are in-sentence signposts that a logical function might be performed. Context will always be the determinate as to whether a tip-off is being used correctly. So, the following are tip-offs that you may be running into either a premise, conclusion, or an assumption within an argument:

Premise Tip-Offs in the LSAT: It's a given that, research shows, historically, evidence suggests, for, because, inasmuch as, notwithstanding, insofar as, although, assume, except, suppose, despite, despite the fact that, in spite of, assuming, after all, for these reasons, since, it follows from this....

Conclusion Tip-Offs in the LSAT: thus, therefore, hence, so, it follows that, in light of this, in view of this, suggests, indicates, proves, means, accordingly, shows, can be inferred, nevertheless, results, however, it must be that, it must be the case that, it cannot be that, it cannot be the case that, this demonstrates that....

Assumption Tip-Offs in the LSAT: assume, assuming, rely, presume, presumption, presuppose, presupposition, depend on, assumption, suppose, supposition, supposal, conjecture, assuming, taking for granted, accepting, given that, suspicion, surmise, theorization, hypothecation. hypothesis, theory, postulate, stipulate, premise.

The tip-offs can help. When you do not have a tip-off, you'll need to do some reflection about the passage to see what the main point is. If you can identify the main point in a short, succinct phrase or sentence (using your own words), then you can ask yourself what reasons given in the passage support or reject that particular conclusion.

Insider Insight #5: Connotation, Equivalence, and Translation.

When you are translating, it is imperative to know whether similar words that are used in a passage have equivalent meaning, and it is just as essential to determine whether two sentences assert the same meaning. If they have *equivalent meaning,* you do not need to use a new letter term when you translate them. This means that your ability to discern connotation is really important. When determining whether two sentences assert the same proposition apply the following technique: 1.) Try to classify and define the concepts first to identify what words the concepts designate. Translate each new, important logical idea with a new term. 2.) Ignore differences in connotation, when it simply isn't important. (Ex: sweat, perspire, and glisten have differences in connotation, but in essence mean the same thing, and you wouldn't use new terms for them because they logically are equivalent.) 3.) Find a literal interpretation of all metaphors, and use the same term as their literal ideas within the passage.

Insider Insight #6: Identifying the Form of an Argument.

What sets this prep series apart from any other is that it gives you the logical tools to work this exam for what it is—a logic exam! Central to your prep success, then, is your ability to identify the form of arguments. Here is the insider insight that will help you succeed:

ARGOPREP
ARGOPREP.COM/LSAT

How to find the form of an argument:
1.) Find the conclusion (the <u>main point</u>).
2.) Find reasons for the conclusion. (These are the <u>premises</u>.)
3.) Make sure the premises prove the conclusion.
4.) In your own words, list the premises first, followed by the conclusion.
5.) Find the *antecedent* (what sets the condition) for each premise, and then the consequent to each premise.
6.) Assign a letter (*p, q, a, b,* etc.) to each new predicate.
7.) Check for validity and soundness.

Insider Insight #7: *Automatically Valid Logical Forms.*

You have uncovered how important it is for you to know, identify, *and construct* logically valid arguments from the passages on the LSAT. All you have to do is memorize four automatically valid forms! All valid arguments on the LSAT will fit one of these four forms (there might be additional premises or reasons given, of course), and since the forms of these arguments automatically guarantee their conclusions, you should know these without struggle before the exam. These automatically logically valid forms follow *"rules of inference"* for their structures, which guarantees their conclusions:

Modus Ponens	*Modus Tollens*	*Hypothetical Syllogism*	*Disjunctive Syllogism*
If p ⊃ q	If p ⊃ q	If p ⊃ q	p ∨ q
p	~q	If q ⊃ r	~p
∴q	∴~p	p	∴q
	∴r		

Insider Insight #8: *Murky Translations.*

Most of the time, writers don't write in "all" or "some" language, and that can cause problems in translations. You need some practice in translating idiomatic terms that will come up, and I want to give you some insider insight into how these terms function logically on the LSAT!

"All". You know that "All" translates over into your logical form. But, how many ways are there to say "all"? It turns out...quite a few! Here are some examples, *all* of which translate into "All A is B":

   "All baseball players love to slide."

   "If you are a baseball player, you love to slide."

   "You're not a baseball player unless you love to slide!"

   "No one can be a baseball player unless they love to slide."

   "Every baseball player loves to slide."

   "Each baseball player loves to slide."

Every one of these sentences is logically equivalent to each other, and we would translate them all in the form, "All A is B," or for these particular letters, "All P is S."

"No." Just like "all," "no" is a universal term—it indicates an empty set. And, just like our positive universal, there are many common English propositions that all translate the same way. I'll use my baseball player example to show these:

"No baseball players love to slide."

"No one who is a baseball player loves to slide."

"There isn't a single baseball player that loves to slide."

"It's false that any baseball player loves to slide."

"It's false that some baseball player loves to slide."

"If you're a baseball player, then you do not love to slide."

"If someone is a baseball player, s/he cannot love to slide."

"Each baseball player doesn't love to slide."

"Every baseball player does not love to slide."

Just like with our *all* translations, *all of these sentences translate to,* "No P is S." All of them! They are all logically equivalent. You will just have to commit these to memory as crucial steps to translating LSAT passages correctly. Also, don't forget that if you have "No P is S." recognize that you can translate this to "All P is not S."

EXPERT TIP

*You can improve your analytical reasoning abilities by thinking about **counterfactuals**. (A counterfactual is a conditional whose antecedent is false and whose consequent describes how the world would have been if the antecedent had been true.)*

"Some". Translating "some" need not be difficult, but understanding non-universal terms can be. If I said, "Some baseball players love to slide", you know to translate that, "Some P is S." No problem. But what about, "It isn't the case that baseball players don't love to slide"? Could you translate, "Evidence shows that there are baseball players who love to slide"? What about, "I know at least one baseball player who loves to slide"? Or you could say, "At least once, a baseball player loved to slide," as well as, "One or more baseball players on this team love to slide." For all of these propositions, you translate, "Some P is S."

But, it can be difficult to translate "some" terms along with a "not" or a "no". If you have the sentence, "It isn't true that all baseball players love to slide", the proper translation is not "No P is S," but, "Some P is not S." But, if "it isn't true that some baseball players do not love to slide" means you need to follow the negatives and translate this universally, "All baseball players love to slide," or our original, "P is S."

Quantifiers. We call logic that works with "some" and "all", *quantificational logic.* In quantificational logic, the *existential quantifier,* "(∃x)" stands in for *at least one but not all.* These English words are usually "some", "someone" or "something". If *someone* sells paletas, we would translate this, "(∃x)Px" (For some x, x sells paletas.) Now, let's say that Ron sells paletas. "x" no longer serves us logically, because we know who it is that sells paletas. So, the (∃x)Px just becomes "Pr" ("Ron sells paletas"). But, for many instances in which you will be translating, you won't know the specific someone or someones being referred to. You will just use (∃x) to stand in for "some."

To logically learn more about the "someone" being talked about in a proposition, you can use other logical functions along with your existential quantifier. If I wanted to say that there is someone who sells paleta and is handsome, I would translate this, "(∃x)(Px · Hx)" which reads in English, "for some x, x sells paleta and is handsome."

"All" is also a quantificational term, which means "inclusive of a set." Instead of the existential quantifier (∃x), we use the universal quantifier (x) to mean "all/any". If I write (x)Px, then I mean "for any x, x sells paleta". Correlatively, (x)(Px · Hx) indicates that "for any x, x sells paleta and is handsome."

"*Any.*" You might be tempted to translate "any" into "all." But that isn't necessarily a sound translation. If you have a translation that includes the word "any", see if you can rephrase the sentence to *not include the term,* and then

translate the sentence. Here are some good guidelines. If you want to translate, "Not any lawyer is righteous," (that is weird English phrasing, but you could see it), you would write, "No lawyer is righteous," and translate it, "No L is R". Frequently, it will be the case that "not any" is universal for "none" or "no one in the group." And, sometimes "any" does stand for "all"—context will provide the clues.

"But." Any terms that we use to pivot away from a stated position, "however, nonetheless, despite, although, yet, both, etc.) are not *negations* logically, in most cases. Typically, they are *conjunctions.* They join two disparate ideas. If the sentence reads, "You are a baseball player but you love to slide," two ideas are being predicated of you, *both* that you are a baseball player *and* that you love to slide. So, you translate this sentence, "P · S."

"Assuming That...". So many assumptions will be tested on the LSAT! And you will have to know how to unearth, and translate, them! How do you translate propositions that include an assumption, or translate the injected assumption? If I say, "You are a college student, assuming that you're 18-24," I'm really setting a condition on whether you are a college student. I am saying, "You are a college student if you are 18-24." So, the sentence, "College student, assuming that 18-24," translates into "If A then C", or (A ⊃ C), for "Age, then College."

It's important to note that "assuming that" is equivalent logically to some other, ordinary English phrases, such as "given that" and "provided that". Here is how you would translate a series of different English phrases using these types of conditional phrases:

1. Provided that you're 18-24, then you're a college student.　(A ⊃ C)
2. You're a college student if you're a 18-24.　(A ⊃ C)
3. You're a college student, given that you're 18-24.　(A ⊃ C)

"Unless". "Unless" demonstrates a stipulation on an event. If you and I are studying for the LSAT, and I throw my laptop at you, and you (justifiably) get angry, I might tell you, that you can't be mad unless you were really working hard. The "unless" there functions as a type of necessary condition on the event of you being angry—you must have been studying hard. You will see "unless" frequently within your LSAT passages. They usually mean "do this... *or else!"* There are two ordinary English sentences in which you'll see unless:

1. You can't be mad at me unless you were studying hard. *or*
2. Unless you were studying hard, you can't be mad at me.

Translating "unless" isn't difficult, because it has the disjunctive "or else" flavor. Use your regular condition terms. Here's one way to do it, as a disjunction:

1a. Either you were studying hard, or you can't be mad at me. (H v ~M) *or*
2a. Study hard, or you cannot be mad at me. (H v ~M)

If you're uncomfortable using the disjunctive function (although it is fun!), you can also think of "unless" statements as a type of hypothetical, in which you say, "If you aren't studying hard, then you can't be mad at me." That makes the "unless" function as an "if not":

1b. If you aren't studying hard, then you can't be mad at me (If ~H ⊃ ~M) *or*
2b. If you are mad at me, you were studying hard. (If M ⊃ H)

"Necessary/Necessary Condition." An antecedent is a necessary condition for a consequent if the consequent can only occur if the antecedent occurs—it cannot occur if the antecedent also does not. But it can be difficult to know how to translate for these types of conditions. Imagine the following example, "A PhD. is required to teach at this university." The equivalent sentence we can work with is, "A Ph.D. is a necessary condition for someone to teach at this university." Let's say that the LSAT asks you to identify which of the answer choices is necessary for the conclusion to be true. How do you go about translating that sentence to be able to be formalized into logical form? Well, to say that something is necessary for another thing just means that if it does not occur, the other thing doesn't occur either. So, any proposition that has the form "A is necessary for B," or "A is a necessary condition for B" will be translated, "If ~A, then ~B", which for our example means, "If ~P, then ~T" (if you're not a PhD., you can't teach"). *One more way* you can translate a necessary condition is "If B, then A" (since an inference from this is that if A does not occur, ~A, then B cannot occur either, ~B).

Another reminder for necessary conditions: you can have more than one of them. If you have several conditions—both of which *must be true* for a consequent to occur—you'll need to rely on the conjunction "and" to help. Imagine, in our example, that it is necessary for a person to have a Ph.D. and publish in order to be a teacher at a university. To translate this, you know that it isn't enough to be a Ph.D. (although it is necessary), and it isn't enough to publish (although it is also necessary). *Both* are necessary conditions. So, the translation would look like, "(If (~P · ~B) ⊃ ~T)" which reads in common English, "If you don't have a Ph.D. and don't publish, then you can't teach."

"Sufficient/Sufficient Condition." Sufficient conditions are enough *to explain* that another thing will occur. A condition does not have to be necessary to be sufficient. Translating sufficient conditions is actually really easy! If A is a sufficient condition for B to occur, we translate this simply, "If A then B".

"Necessary and Sufficient Condition." Necessary and sufficient conditions are co-dependent conditions, or conditions that require each other for either of them to occur. The way we talk about these conditions is "A *if and only if* B." Those conditions *are definitionally true,* so if A occurs, B must and if B occurs, A must. (We also have a short-cut for abbreviating "if and only if" conditions which can save you time: either "iff" or "≡.") By the way, another way of saying "if and only if" in *regular English* is "Just if." If you tell me that you'll go to see the new superhero movie "just if Robert Downey, Jr is in it" you are telling me that it's true that you'll see the superhero movie with me, if and only if, Robert Downey, Jr is in the movie. We translate "just if" identically with "*iff,*" or with the "≡." Formally, we would say (S ≡ D), "superhero movie just if Downey", which is equal to (D ≡ S).

"Only if" is different logically. It might seem intuitively true that "only if" conditions are *if and only if* conditions, but they aren't! Let's imagine I now say that I'll go to the new superhero movie with *you only if* Robert Downey Jr. is in it, I am actually saying that *If Robert Downey Jr. is in the superhero movie, then I will see it with you.* That makes the "only if" a simple condition. The condition to see the movie is if this actor is in it. We would formalize that condition, "If D ⊃ S."

Here is a quick-reference table of how to translate conditions:

Type of Condition	Necessary Conditions	Sufficient Conditions	Necessary and Sufficient Conditions
How the Condition Appears	Being an A thing is a necessary condition for being a B thing.	Being an A thing is a sufficient condition for being a B thing.	Being an A thing is necessary and sufficient to being a B thing **and** being a B thing is necessary and sufficient to being an A thing.
What Does It Mean?	Every B thing is an A thing.	Every A thing is a B thing.	A is equivalent to B, so neither B nor A subsist without each other.
How Is it Translated?	"~A ⊃ ~B" *and* "B ⊃ A"	"A ⊃ B" *and for multiple* "(A · B · C) ⊃ D"	"A ≡ B" which is equivalent to "B ≡ A"

Insider Insight #9: *Identifying Modal Concepts*

It is quite easy to identify when the exam is asking you to choose logical possibility and when it is saying a consequence is logically required, or necessary.

Here are some terms you could frequently see to tip-off logical possibility:

some, might, could, perhaps, can, may, possibly, possibly will, only if

Here are some terms that indicate logical necessity:

all, no, must, cannot, needs, obliged, should, require/required, necessary and sufficient

Notes:

Insider Insights into Argument Refutation

Insider Insight #1: Reductio ad Absurdum

Don't forget reductios! The easiest way to refute an argument is to show that its conclusion "reduces to the absurd." So, start your refutation by assuming the conclusion of your opponent. If you run your argument that starts with your opponent's conclusion and you hit a contradiction, you have shown that your opponent's view is logically nonsensical—it reduces to the absurd.

Insider Insight #2: Automatically Invalid Arguments

I've set you up for LSAT success by providing Insider Insights into automatically valid arguments (see Insider Insights on Translation), but you can save yourself time and correct answers by watching out for these two automatically invalid forms. Even though these forms are easy, they mimic the structure of logically valid forms *(modus ponens and modus tollens)*, but there are important differences that happen in the second premise, so watch out! These structures are automatically INVALID—their form cannot guarantee the truth of the conclusion. These are automatically logical fallacies, and can never be good arguments. Avoid these arguments!

Denying the Antecedent	*Affirming the Consequent*
If p $\supset$ q	If p $\supset$ q
$\sim$p	q
$\therefore \sim$q	$\therefore$ p

Insider Insight #3: User Error and Disjunctive Syllogisms.

The easiest way to ensure that user error flaws do not occur on disjunctive syllogisms on the LSAT is to make sure that you translate the syllogisms correctly. Most of the user errors occur at the point of when a disjunct does not occur, or when it is unclear whether a disjunct occurs. But, what if the LSAT passage tells you something to the effect of "Neither A nor B"? In such a case, you have to negate the entire disjunction, so you would write "$\sim$(A v B)." But, what does "$\sim$(A v B)" mean? The user error tends to be to want either A or B to occur, to show that the other disjunct could not occur. But, denying that the disjunct is true means that *neither disjunct is true*. The result is that when you have a proposition, $\sim$(A v B), you then conclude: (($\sim$A) • ($\sim$B)). In everyday English, $\sim$(A v B) means, it is true *both* that A did not occur and that B did not occur. The insider insight takeaway is that if you negate an *entire disjunctive proposition*, you end up with a *conjunction*.

Insider Insight #4: Correlation vs. Cause Flaws

There are so many instances in which you could be called upon to identify flaws between correlations and causes on the LSAT that we can actually thematize the types of questions you could be asked. If you see questions of these particular forms, you can be confident that the correct answer will always relate to the issue of correlation:

Flaw Questions:

"Flaw" questions require you to pick out the logical flaw that undergirds a particular argument. You will probably see quite a few of these. Since 2007, questions that asked the test-taker to "identify the flaw in the reasoning" have comprised no less than 10% of all Logical Reasoning test questions—and have comprised up to 20% of them. You will want to be able to pick out logical flaws in arguments and to be able to know the difference between correlation and cause because most of the correct answers in flawed-reasoning questions will represent the difficulty of associating correlation and cause. Answer choices which indicate that the argument, "infers a cause from a mere correlation" will be the correct answer for arguments that are based on reasoning that depends on correlation.

Assumption Questions:

You'll see "assumptions" in two places on the LSAT: as a question, and as an answer choice. Answer choices will tell you that the argument, "assumes that a correlation between two ideas is evidence that one is the cause of the other." This just is the logical problem of correlations! So, if you know that the passage that you are working with sets up the problem of correlation, this will be your correct response. But, the most common place you will find assumptions on the exam is in the questions on the Logical Reasoning sections. They typically have the form, "The [interlocutor's] conclusion follows logically if which [answer choice] is assumed?" When you are asked this question of passages which rely upon correlation/causation reasoning, your correct response typically will present some substitute cause to the association provided by the text.

Strengthen Questions:

For questions that confuse correlation and causation, a simple way to correct the logical error is to *strengthen* or *improve* the evidential link between the antecedent and the consequent. You can think of strengthening questions as ways to help the author prove his or her point. You can provide better justification, bring in more data, or address a potential criticism of the view espoused in the test. As with assumption questions, eliminating an alternative cause is a way to strengthen a correlation and causation argument. Another possible correct answer involves other examples that corroborate the causal relationship.

Weaken Questions:

One way to weaken a correlation/causation question should be obvious: you show that the author confuses cause with correlation. And, you will be given this option frequently on the LSAT. The correct answer choice will provide you with an opportunity to evaluate the passage, rather than describe the passage. To weaken a correlation and causation argument, you want to show that you should look to do the opposite of what you would do in the strengthen context. So, you should look to establish, as opposed to eliminate, an alternative cause, or show that in another similar situation the correlation in the argument didn't hold up.

Insider Insight #5: *Refuting Inductive Arguments.*

There are many ways you will need to address flaws in inductive arguments, whether there are *rational tests* you can apply, such as problems of coherency, consistency, or definitional meaning or *empirical tests*, such as data inference problems, problems of witness testimony not matching a conclusion, or contrary testimony. But, here are three ways you can evaluate inductive inferences that you should have on hand as you approach inductive inferences on the LSAT:

-- **Comprehensiveness**. For inductive arguments, there must be a comprehensive quality of the sample that ensures an adequate representation of an entire group. Does the conclusion apply to everybody in a similar way?

-- **Sample Size.** The more instances a class of things has been observed, the more reliable is the generalization that the argument makes. Does the sample size reflect the same representative number of things made by the generalization?

-- **Randomness**. To yield the best representation, the samples should be somewhat unrelated if they are to represent a clear majority among a varied group. Is the sample group taken randomly?

Insider Insight #6: Proper vs. Improper Appeals to Authority

Proper appeals to authority are those in which the entirety of the justification for a claim is grounded in something *additional to* the authority of the testifier. The testifier will be an expert (specifically on the topic at hand), but other evidence can be given, such as data sets, experiential evidence, agreement with other experts in that field, or first-hand testimony. The logical difficulty with *improper* appeals to authority is that the sole justificatory force of the argument—the reason you believe it is true—is that it comes from an authority, and it is not always true that authorities are right on their subjects, or that they can speak authoritatively to a given subject. When you are attempting to differentiate between an appeal to authority that is proper or improper, try to figure out whether there is further justification given for the argument than simply the authoritative force of the expert. But, we also can use a logical test to see if the appeal to authority is proper:

Premise:	Expert A says X about topic Y.
Premise:	Expert A is an expert about topic Y.
Premise:	There is additional support for the conclusion about X.
Conclusion:	There is evidence that X is true.

Insider Insight #7: Ad Hominem Arguments

Many ad hominem arguments that you are going to find on the LSAT are bad arguments, but some may bait you into thinking that there is a logical fallacy when there isn't. We do have a logical tool at our disposal to properly weigh whether the argument you are reading employs a fallacious ad hominem. Arguments which use emotional content about the expert, or other non-rational features, to conclude that an argument must be rejected should be suspect. But, one argument form that helps us figure out whether an "against the man" argument could be inductively strong would have the following form:

Premise:	Person A believes X.
Premise:	But, to believe X, A would have to rely on incomplete, inaccurate, and/or biased information.
Conclusion:	It is improper for A to believe X.

Notes:

ARGOPREP LSAT INSIDER INSIGHTS
CHAPTER 7

Insider Insights into Passages

Insider Insight #1: *Pre-Screen Your Long Passages.*

"Pre-screening" means that you'll look at any questions in a Reading Comprehension or long Logical or Analytical Reasoning section before you actually read the passage itself. There are two reasons that support this practice. First, pre-screening will give you an idea of what sort of logic problems are being asked of you before you read the passage itself. Second, you will get clarification about what the long passage is actually about, and so will get a heads up when you actually RAG the passage about what content will be relevant for you to hone in on. The overall results are that you will actually spend less time reading and you will understand better what you are reading.

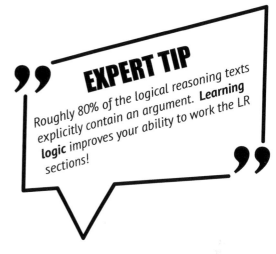

EXPERT TIP

Roughly 80% of the logical reasoning texts explicitly contain an argument. **Learning logic** improves your ability to work the LR sections!

Insider Insight #2: *RAG (Read for ArGumentation).*

Hopefully, you will have practiced the RAG technique so extensively that it is now simply part of how you approach long passages on the LSAT. But, in case you need a refresher, no problem. There are seven steps to the RAG technique. You'll "pre-screen" first (see above) by reading the passage question first, but not their answers. Then, you do each of the following:

1. Read the first and last sentence of the first paragraph.
2. Summarize in your own words (write down key phrase).
3. Read the first and last sentence of the final paragraph.
4. Summarize in your own words (write down key phrase).
5. Read the first sentence of every paragraph in-between the first and last paragraphs.
6. Summarize in your own words (write down key phrase).
7. Read the passage, if necessary.

Insider Insight #3: *Easiest Passages First.*

After doing a glance at all of the passages offered to you, you should work through the passages that you think are easiest first, and save the most difficult for last. Each scholar may have different standards for what constitutes the "easiest," but for many, those that are in fields furthest away from a student's major might be the most difficult. Of course, most scholars will also look at the length of a passage as an indication as to whether it is difficult—which is OK, but I find that the number of questions is more indicative of difficulty than simply length of the passage.

Insider Insight #4: *Most Passages are Badly Written.*

The passages are intended to drag you down by their use of jargon, their length, and the lack of structure in and between paragraphs. The passages themselves can run more than 600 words and include a significant amount of material that you will never use. The LSAT writers are counting on the fact that they can throw you off by not using headings, by condensing several paragraphs worth of material into one, or by including material that reflects competing viewpoints. Also, most of the passages are written as an editorial (even if they are science-based). Rather than reporting facts and data, the passages are often rife with opinions that are not strongly justified. (This helps the writers test your inference ability.) But, so much opinion-content can be off-putting.

Insider Insight #5: *Most Passages Make You Feel Unprepared for Their Vocabulary.*

The more time you spend stumbling over unfamiliar words, the less time you have to read the questions and solving the puzzles they present to you. If you use the RAG method of approaching, you are far better off than a student who has a better vocabulary but spends inordinate amounts of time reading every word of the exam. That *isn't* to say that vocabulary isn't important. Instead, you can place the proper value on vocabulary. It is a tool. If you have it as a tool and use it properly, it can benefit you. If you do not have it, it cannot benefit you. However, if you use it improperly, it will hurt you.

Insider Insight #6: *Description Questions vs. Expansion Questions*

The RC typically asks two types of questions: description questions and expansion questions. Description questions will direct you to identify the answer that best describes the principles, examples, or conditions that the passage stipulates. These are fairly easy questions because they usually direct you to the passage line (the lines are numbered) in which the ideas or concepts they are asking you about are found. You can relate description questions to keywords within the passage. Expansion questions are more difficult and have a different function than description questions. Expansion questions focus on what *could*, what *must*, and what cannot satisfy certain conditions – so they expand logically from what is given in the passage.

> ## EXPERT TIP
>
> *Even the best, perfect scores on the LSAT can include mistakes. What sets the 1% scores from the 99% scores is that the 1% spends time thinking about what questions they struggled with in prep.* **Focus on what you struggle with**, *and learn from your mistakes!*

Expansion questions demand that the reader go beyond the main point of the text and infer a further proposition from what is given in the text. If you employed the RAG technique to the passage that corresponds to the question, you will have pulled out the main premises and conclusion and would be able to see which RC answers are best suited as inferences that are tightly tied to the content of the passage but appropriately predictive based on that content. Expansion questions test your ability to make logical inferences, and your ability to do this is enhanced if you have enough time to think clearly about your options. Employing RAG will give you time and comprehension advantages over others who are taking the LSAT.

Insider Insight #7: *Wrong Answers in Disguise*

Especially in passages (whether in the RC or LR sections), make sure not to focus on picking out the right answers to the exclusion of identifying the wrong answers. There are some patterns of wrong answers that you should know and be on the look-out for. First, wrong answers often *repeat* the content of the passage. Exam-takers get lulled into the comfort of similarity, and yet very infrequently is it true that a correct answer mimics the content exactly of the passage. Second, wrong answers *misinterpret the conclusion* of the argument within the passage. They might use obscure language and seem authoritative but actually misrepresent the conclusion. Third, *overgeneralization* invariably indicates a wrong answer choice. The correct response will be specific enough to relate to the main argument within the passage. The main argument will never be general, so the correct response will never overgeneralize! Finally, wrong answers are often disguised as true content that does not meet the conditions placed by the argument or the question itself.

Insider Insight #8: *Tessellations.*

Remember tessellations are patterns of errors within answers (EWA) that can distract you from the right answer and so should be avoided. There are many Tessellations: *Tessellation #1:* Repeating Repeaters. You will be attracted to answer choices that quote the passage directly. *Tessellation #2:* Obscurity Attracts. When you are on the receiving

end of obscure, technical language and you see obscure, technical language within an answer choice, rather than working the logical form of the argument given, it can be much easier just to give into the obscurity and choose the technical answer. *Tessellation #3:* Condition Flipping. You've already worked a good amount of these arguments, and so you are already familiar with how easy it can be to "flip" a condition so that you create a valid argument out of an invalid argument by setting up an antecedent that really is a consequent, or vice versa. That leads to a conclusion that can't be guaranteed. *Tessellation #4:* Hyped Conclusions. Writers on the LSAT will include answer choices that overgeneralize and overstate, or underdetermine and understate part of the conclusion and so can't meet the conditions which are provided to you in the passage. *Tessellation #5:* Truthiness. That's right—included in your answer choices will be those that are true but aren't true enough. They have a "truthiness" about them that is attractive, they are compelling because they make good sense, but even true answers that do not fulfill all of the conditions from the passage and are not correct. Don't be fooled by this pretty tessellation! *Tessellation #6:* Fake News. Unfortunately, there will be some answer choices that use very similar language as the passage (like in Tessellation #1), but get a condition or a modal term wrong, or they might misconstrue or wrongly illustrate part of the passage. It seems like news, it rings true to your ears, but ultimately, it is wrong.

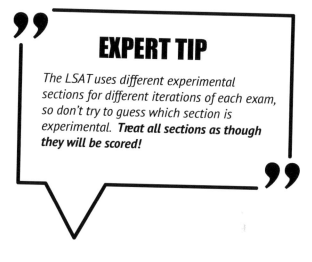

EXPERT TIP

The LSAT uses different experimental sections for different iterations of each exam, so don't try to guess which section is experimental. **Treat all sections as though they will be scored!**

Insider Insight #9: How the LSAT Writers Get You to Pick the Wrong Answer in LR

The LSAT writers love the LSAT and believe in its efficacy as a tool to measure your ability to apply logic in a myriad of ways. They want to deceive you, get you to waste your time, entrap you into small mistakes, and lead you to the wrong answer by a myriad of different means. The best way for the LSAT writers to do so on the LR sections is to get you to believe that the wrong answer is the correct answer. Sometimes that takes more work on their part than on others, sure. But, any time the LSAT writers convince you that a wrong answer is a right one is too many. There are some Insider Insights you can use to be on the look-out for overt (and sometimes subtle) tricks the LSAT writers rely upon to get you to buy in to the wrong answer. First, the LSAT writers know that almost all of the test-takers are students who have not been trained in the logic they need to take the LSAT, and so they rely on patterns that obfuscate improper logical inferences. A common way they do this is to confuse you with modal terms of logical possibility and necessity. You know that if something *could* be the case, then answer choices that *cannot* occur are eliminated. If something *must* occur, answer choices are eliminated that could not occur, but also that could occur, since "could" connotes logical possibility rather than logical necessity, like "must."

Another way they sucker the unsuspecting student to choose wrongly is by mirroring language in the answer choices with language in the passage. (This happens in the Reading Comprehension section, too, and we discussed an example in the RC of when this can be pernicious.) They can provide hyperbolic answers that seem outlandishly ("wildly wrong") attractive because they are not nuanced. Very rarely are outlandish answers correct. They will also provide you with a false disjunction (also discussed in our chapter on Logical Flaws), where they create a disjunct that isn't related to the argument at hand so that you don't actually focus on the argument at hand.

Insider Insight #10: New Conditions in Questions

For the Analytical Reasoning section questions, you will be given new conditions within certain questions, which will help you solve individual questions within a broader question set. It's incredibly important to remember that conditions that are introduced in the questions do not carry over into other questions. They are *question specific*

conditions. You will use them to help flesh out your condition map and solve that single question, and then you will forget it as a condition for your passage. One more crucial feature of new conditions in questions to remember is that the *correct answer will always relate to the new condition.* Since the passage contains conditions for all questions, the only reason to introduce a new condition is to produce an answer that cannot be generated from the passage alone. The new condition will always give rise to the correct answer. If you see an answer choice, for questions that introduce a new condition, that does not depend upon the new condition for you to determine the answer, eliminate it. It will not be correct.

Insider Insight #11: Complex, Complex Sets in Analytical Reasoning

This insider insight involves how to approach practicing logic games within the AR section. Although most will just say—"Diagram and Practice"—there are differences among sets that, if you can identify them, can help you approach them so that you can work them successfully. Rather than just running headlong into practicing complex exercise sets for Analytical Reasoning, first try to identify what sort of complex scenarios you are being given for any exercise set. One type of complex scenario that is additionally complex is whether there are other conditions that are placed on a certain smaller set of subjects within the group. This is a different complex, complex scenario than the kind that places additional conditions on the order of sub-groups within the question set. Of course, the Ultimate Complex, Complex Scenario will combine the features of each type, and place additional conditions on a smaller set of subjects as well as conditions on the ordering of the groups.

Insider Insight #12: The Texas Two-Step: a Method for "Which of the following, if true, would determine all groups?" questions on the Analytical Reasoning section.

All right, you are going to see time-suck questions on the AR that ask you something to the effect of, "If true, which of the following conditions would determine the position/organization/composition of every member of every group?" These should be a benefit to you—if you are given a condition that determines the membership of an entire group, or determines the order of all of the subjects, there is no ambiguity about what the correct answer could be. Rather than adding a condition for you, this question's *answers* are a set of conditions, and you will have to identify which of them, if true, could help you identify the constitution of all groups (or, the ordering of all subjects). The huge temptation for this kind of question is to waste too much time mapping out each wrong answer. Instead, use the Texas Two-Step to chop massive amounts of time and hone in quickly only on answer choices which have a high degree of probability of being true, even without running a logical test on them.

Step One is to, once you face one of these questions, ask yourself (without looking at the answers) what the conditions of the passage already tell you about the subjects within the passage that could provide you with a lot of information as long as you knew about them. Once you think about these, then go to Step Two.

Step Two is also easy: eliminate any answer choice that does not include a condition about the subjects you identified in Step One as those that would provide significant information if you had a condition about them. You should be able to eliminate *a minimum of two answer* choices just by applying the Texas Two Step. Then, once you have your (much smaller) handful of potentially correct answers, test the answer choice that, based on the amount of information that would be generated from having more knowledge about that subject, would give you the best chance at predicting group information about the other subjects. Remember, though, for any answer choice, *as soon as you hit an uncertainty in a group, move to the next answer choice.* The questions that ask you to identify a condition that sets up the correct set-up for all other groups means there cannot be indeterminacy with an answer. So, as soon as you find indeterminacy, move on to the next answer choice!

Insider Insight #13: Maximum/Minimum Questions on the AR section.

Although you never want to make the mistake of importing new conditions from old questions into the question you are working on, it isn't actually true that the work that you do in other AR questions does not help inform your work in subsequent questions. This is especially true when you are dealing with "minimum/maximum" questions. If you get a question that asks you "What is the maximum number of subjects that can be classified into Category X"

and you worked on a previous question within the question set that had more subjects in Category X than in other questions, you should start with the set up for the question that yielded the maximum (or, minimum, depending on the question) number of subjects.

Insider Insight #14: Process for "Role" Questions on LR

There is a word of advice as you prep for the "what role does this serve" questions on Logical Reasoning. Do not start with the statement being identified. You can identify what kind of question you are being asked first, of course, but make sure that you don't evaluate the statement the question is asking you to evaluate prior to reading the passage. For role questions, the most impactful activity you can do is to extract the argument in logical form. Once you do that, you will know which statements within the passage function as premises, assumptions, evidence, analogies, examples, criticisms, or support. Rather than emphasizing the single statement the question is asking you about, you should focus on understanding the argument itself (formally), then you will *easily* be able to answer the question. By that time, you will be ready to match the statement being asked about in the passage to its role in the argument that you have formalized. Going into the role example with a complete understanding of the formal structure of the argument will help you approach the statement in question knowing already how that statement functions in the argument. By following the process, you will have eliminated any chance for error!

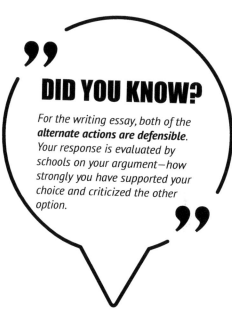

DID YOU KNOW?

*For the writing essay, both of the **alternate actions are defensible**. Your response is evaluated by schools on your argument—how strongly you have supported your choice and criticized the other option.*

Insider Insight #15: Use of Deductive or Inductive Arguments on the LR Section

As you know from our LSAT logic training, there are key differences between deductive and inductive arguments, and you are prepared to evaluate both kinds on the exam. The most relevant difference between the two types of arguments is that problems that draw valid conclusions frequently require that you rely on formal, deductive reasoning skills that can be governed by the rules of logic from Chapters 1 and 2. The LR problems that require you to engage with questions in which there are unwarranted, broken, or weak inferences typically require inductive reasoning skills. When you aren't taking the LSAT, it's frequently the case that you can be persuaded by inductive arguments and can find deductive arguments unpersuasive, for a host of reasons. The LR section of the LSAT, however, is mostly myopically focused on generating conclusions that are validly deduced by given premises within an argument. (In those questions, you will be asked to find the answer that supports the conclusion or that picks out the right-making feature of an argument.)

Almost invariably, the LSAT LR section will use inductive arguments for when you are required to find bad reasoning within a passage or to extract an informal fallacy that the author is trying to use to ground the provided argument. So, whereas the deductive components of the LR section frequently have you reaffirm the strength of the arguments, the inductive components are used to undermine the argument or to pick out some wrong-making feature of the argument.

Insider Insight #16: Strengthen and Weaken Questions on the LR

Concerning format, there is one aspect in which the LR strengthen and the LR weaken questions are fairly far apart. Quite regularly within the LR strengthen questions, you will be the recipient of "EXCEPT" questions, in which four of the five answer choices on a particular question will strengthen the argument but one will not. The correct answer will undermine the main point (or, weaken it!). For LR weaken questions, you can see "EXCEPT" questions, though from a statistical standpoint, you are more likely to see them on strengthen questions. Just remember on the "weaken" questions in which you are told that all of the answer choices but one will weaken the passage's argument, the correct answer will be the one that strengthens the argument. In both cases, you will find the outlier, and the correct answer will be the opposite of the strengthen/weaken operator.

NOTES
CHAPTER 7

WORKS CITED

Austin, K., Christopher, C., & Dickerson, D., "Will I pass the bar exam? Predicting student success using LSAT scores and Law School performance," Hofstra Law Review, 45(3), Spring 2017, 753-784.

Bailey, Andrew, "The Logic of Immortality: Plato's Phaedo and the Argument from Affinity," Minerva 9 (2005), http://www.minerva.mic.ul.ie/vol9/Immortality.html

Berkowitz, R., "One point on the LSAT: How much is it worth? Standardized tests as a determinant of earnings," American Economist, 42(2), 80–89.

DeGroff, E. A., & McKee, K. A., "Learning like lawyers: Addressing the differences in law student learning styles," BYU Educ. & LJ, (2006), 499-548.

Dempsey, K., & Armstrong, S., The impact of additional time on LSAT scores: Does time really matter? The efficacy of making decisions on a case-by-case basis. ProQuest Dissertations Publishing, 2004.

Espinoza, Leslie G. "LSAT: Narratives and Bias, The." Am. UJ Gender & L. 1 (1993): 121ff.

Gensler, Harry. *Introduction to Logic,* third edition. (London: Routledge), 2017.

Harrington, Michael, The Other America: Poverty in the United States, (Harmondsworth, Middlesex: Penguin), 1981.

Harris Poll Analytics, "8 in 10 US Adults Watch Cooking Shows," (August 2010), https://www.marketingcharts.com/television-13719

Henderson, W. D., "The LSAT, law school exams, and meritocracy: The surprising and undertheorized role of test-taking speed," Tex. L. Rev., 82, (2003), p 975ff.

Kahne, J. and Bowyer, B. "The Political Significance of Social Media Activity and Social Networks," *Political Communication,* 35:3 (July 2018), 470-493, doi: 10.1080/10584609.2018.1426662.

Kruikemeier, S. and Shehata, A. "News Media Use and Political Engagement Among Adolescents: An Analysis of Virtuous Circles Using Panel Data," *Political Communication,* 34:2 (Apr 2017), 221-242, doi: 10.1080/10584609.2016.1174760

Kuncel, Nathan R.; Klieger, David M, "Application patterns when applicants know the odds: Implications for selection research and practice," Journal of Applied Psychology 92:2, (Mar 2007): 586-593.

Lander Philosophy, "Venn Diagrams", online resource, accessed October 2018, https://philosophy.lander.edu/logic/syll_venn.html .

Maeder, D. W. *The effect of problem-solving strategies on LSAT logical reasoning performance.* ProQuest Dissertations & Theses Global, (1997).

Raloff, Janet. "Teen Vaping Soars Past Cigarette Use," Science News for Students, Apr 28, 2016, https://www.sciencenewsforstudents.org/article/teen-vaping-soars-past-cigarette-use

Rand, K. L., Martin, A. D., & Shea, A.M., "Hope, but not optimism, predicts academic performance of law students beyond previous academic achievement. Journal of Research in Personality, 45(6), 2011, 683-686.

Sanders, R., "Intense prep for law school admissions test alters brain structure," Berkeley News, August 22, 2012, http://news.berkeley.edu/2012/08/22/intense-prep-for-law-school-admissions-test-alters-brain-structure/

Shultz, M., & Zedeck, S., "Admission to Law School: New Measures," Educational Psychologist, 47(1), January 2012, 51-65.

Willging, T.E. & Dunn, T.G., "The moral development of the law student: theory and data on legal education," Journal of Legal Education, Vol. 31, No. 3/5 (1982), pp. 306-358.

PRACTICE TEST

LSAT®

Law School Admission Test

This exam has five sections (two Logical Reasoning, one Reading Comprehension, one Analytical Reasoning, and one unscored Writing Essay). Each section is 35 minutes long. Try to take this full exam in one sitting to simulate real test conditions.

While taking this exam, refrain from listening to music, talking to others, watching TV, or having access to a cellular device.

Fill in each answer bubble clearly. If you need to erase, do so without extraneous marks.

Take all of your notes on the exam itself. On the actual LSAT, the exam booklet includes notepaper that will be submitted along with your answers.

Concentrate and GOOD LUCK!

Visit us at: **www.argoprep.com/lsat**
for video explanations.

ARGOPREP
ARGOPREP.COM/LSAT

Fill in each answer bubble clearly. Mark only one answer to each question. If you need to erase, do so without extraneous marks.

SECTION 1

1. Ⓐ Ⓑ Ⓒ Ⓓ Ⓔ
2. Ⓐ Ⓑ Ⓒ Ⓓ Ⓔ
3. Ⓐ Ⓑ Ⓒ Ⓓ Ⓔ
4. Ⓐ Ⓑ Ⓒ Ⓓ Ⓔ
5. Ⓐ Ⓑ Ⓒ Ⓓ Ⓔ
6. Ⓐ Ⓑ Ⓒ Ⓓ Ⓔ
7. Ⓐ Ⓑ Ⓒ Ⓓ Ⓔ
8. Ⓐ Ⓑ Ⓒ Ⓓ Ⓔ
9. Ⓐ Ⓑ Ⓒ Ⓓ Ⓔ
10. Ⓐ Ⓑ Ⓒ Ⓓ Ⓔ
11. Ⓐ Ⓑ Ⓒ Ⓓ Ⓔ
12. Ⓐ Ⓑ Ⓒ Ⓓ Ⓔ
13. Ⓐ Ⓑ Ⓒ Ⓓ Ⓔ
14. Ⓐ Ⓑ Ⓒ Ⓓ Ⓔ
15. Ⓐ Ⓑ Ⓒ Ⓓ Ⓔ
16. Ⓐ Ⓑ Ⓒ Ⓓ Ⓔ
17. Ⓐ Ⓑ Ⓒ Ⓓ Ⓔ
18. Ⓐ Ⓑ Ⓒ Ⓓ Ⓔ
19. Ⓐ Ⓑ Ⓒ Ⓓ Ⓔ
20. Ⓐ Ⓑ Ⓒ Ⓓ Ⓔ
21. Ⓐ Ⓑ Ⓒ Ⓓ Ⓔ
22. Ⓐ Ⓑ Ⓒ Ⓓ Ⓔ
23. Ⓐ Ⓑ Ⓒ Ⓓ Ⓔ
24. Ⓐ Ⓑ Ⓒ Ⓓ Ⓔ
25. Ⓐ Ⓑ Ⓒ Ⓓ Ⓔ
26. Ⓐ Ⓑ Ⓒ Ⓓ Ⓔ
27. Ⓐ Ⓑ Ⓒ Ⓓ Ⓔ
28. Ⓐ Ⓑ Ⓒ Ⓓ Ⓔ
29. Ⓐ Ⓑ Ⓒ Ⓓ Ⓔ
30. Ⓐ Ⓑ Ⓒ Ⓓ Ⓔ

SECTION 2

1. Ⓐ Ⓑ Ⓒ Ⓓ Ⓔ
2. Ⓐ Ⓑ Ⓒ Ⓓ Ⓔ
3. Ⓐ Ⓑ Ⓒ Ⓓ Ⓔ
4. Ⓐ Ⓑ Ⓒ Ⓓ Ⓔ
5. Ⓐ Ⓑ Ⓒ Ⓓ Ⓔ
6. Ⓐ Ⓑ Ⓒ Ⓓ Ⓔ
7. Ⓐ Ⓑ Ⓒ Ⓓ Ⓔ
8. Ⓐ Ⓑ Ⓒ Ⓓ Ⓔ
9. Ⓐ Ⓑ Ⓒ Ⓓ Ⓔ
10. Ⓐ Ⓑ Ⓒ Ⓓ Ⓔ
11. Ⓐ Ⓑ Ⓒ Ⓓ Ⓔ
12. Ⓐ Ⓑ Ⓒ Ⓓ Ⓔ
13. Ⓐ Ⓑ Ⓒ Ⓓ Ⓔ
14. Ⓐ Ⓑ Ⓒ Ⓓ Ⓔ
15. Ⓐ Ⓑ Ⓒ Ⓓ Ⓔ
16. Ⓐ Ⓑ Ⓒ Ⓓ Ⓔ
17. Ⓐ Ⓑ Ⓒ Ⓓ Ⓔ
18. Ⓐ Ⓑ Ⓒ Ⓓ Ⓔ
19. Ⓐ Ⓑ Ⓒ Ⓓ Ⓔ
20. Ⓐ Ⓑ Ⓒ Ⓓ Ⓔ
21. Ⓐ Ⓑ Ⓒ Ⓓ Ⓔ
22. Ⓐ Ⓑ Ⓒ Ⓓ Ⓔ
23. Ⓐ Ⓑ Ⓒ Ⓓ Ⓔ
24. Ⓐ Ⓑ Ⓒ Ⓓ Ⓔ
25. Ⓐ Ⓑ Ⓒ Ⓓ Ⓔ
26. Ⓐ Ⓑ Ⓒ Ⓓ Ⓔ
27. Ⓐ Ⓑ Ⓒ Ⓓ Ⓔ
28. Ⓐ Ⓑ Ⓒ Ⓓ Ⓔ
29. Ⓐ Ⓑ Ⓒ Ⓓ Ⓔ
30. Ⓐ Ⓑ Ⓒ Ⓓ Ⓔ

SECTION 3

1. Ⓐ Ⓑ Ⓒ Ⓓ Ⓔ
2. Ⓐ Ⓑ Ⓒ Ⓓ Ⓔ
3. Ⓐ Ⓑ Ⓒ Ⓓ Ⓔ
4. Ⓐ Ⓑ Ⓒ Ⓓ Ⓔ
5. Ⓐ Ⓑ Ⓒ Ⓓ Ⓔ
6. Ⓐ Ⓑ Ⓒ Ⓓ Ⓔ
7. Ⓐ Ⓑ Ⓒ Ⓓ Ⓔ
8. Ⓐ Ⓑ Ⓒ Ⓓ Ⓔ
9. Ⓐ Ⓑ Ⓒ Ⓓ Ⓔ
10. Ⓐ Ⓑ Ⓒ Ⓓ Ⓔ
11. Ⓐ Ⓑ Ⓒ Ⓓ Ⓔ
12. Ⓐ Ⓑ Ⓒ Ⓓ Ⓔ
13. Ⓐ Ⓑ Ⓒ Ⓓ Ⓔ
14. Ⓐ Ⓑ Ⓒ Ⓓ Ⓔ
15. Ⓐ Ⓑ Ⓒ Ⓓ Ⓔ
16. Ⓐ Ⓑ Ⓒ Ⓓ Ⓔ
17. Ⓐ Ⓑ Ⓒ Ⓓ Ⓔ
18. Ⓐ Ⓑ Ⓒ Ⓓ Ⓔ
19. Ⓐ Ⓑ Ⓒ Ⓓ Ⓔ
20. Ⓐ Ⓑ Ⓒ Ⓓ Ⓔ
21. Ⓐ Ⓑ Ⓒ Ⓓ Ⓔ
22. Ⓐ Ⓑ Ⓒ Ⓓ Ⓔ
23. Ⓐ Ⓑ Ⓒ Ⓓ Ⓔ
24. Ⓐ Ⓑ Ⓒ Ⓓ Ⓔ
25. Ⓐ Ⓑ Ⓒ Ⓓ Ⓔ
26. Ⓐ Ⓑ Ⓒ Ⓓ Ⓔ
27. Ⓐ Ⓑ Ⓒ Ⓓ Ⓔ
28. Ⓐ Ⓑ Ⓒ Ⓓ Ⓔ
29. Ⓐ Ⓑ Ⓒ Ⓓ Ⓔ
30. Ⓐ Ⓑ Ⓒ Ⓓ Ⓔ

Fill in each answer bubble clearly. Mark only one answer to each question. If you need to erase, do so without extraneous marks.

SECTION 4

1. (A) (B) (C) (D) (E)
2. (A) (B) (C) (D) (E)
3. (A) (B) (C) (D) (E)
4. (A) (B) (C) (D) (E)
5. (A) (B) (C) (D) (E)
6. (A) (B) (C) (D) (E)
7. (A) (B) (C) (D) (E)
8. (A) (B) (C) (D) (E)
9. (A) (B) (C) (D) (E)
10. (A) (B) (C) (D) (E)
11. (A) (B) (C) (D) (E)
12. (A) (B) (C) (D) (E)
13. (A) (B) (C) (D) (E)
14. (A) (B) (C) (D) (E)
15. (A) (B) (C) (D) (E)
16. (A) (B) (C) (D) (E)
17. (A) (B) (C) (D) (E)
18. (A) (B) (C) (D) (E)
19. (A) (B) (C) (D) (E)
20. (A) (B) (C) (D) (E)
21. (A) (B) (C) (D) (E)
22. (A) (B) (C) (D) (E)
23. (A) (B) (C) (D) (E)
24. (A) (B) (C) (D) (E)
25. (A) (B) (C) (D) (E)
26. (A) (B) (C) (D) (E)
27. (A) (B) (C) (D) (E)
28. (A) (B) (C) (D) (E)
29. (A) (B) (C) (D) (E)
30. (A) (B) (C) (D) (E)

READING COMPREHENSION
SECTION 1
27 QUESTIONS
35 MINUTES

Directions: Each set of questions in this section is based on a single passage or a pair of passages. The questions are to be answered on the basis of what is **stated** or **implied** in the passage or pair of passages. For some of the questions, more than one of the choices could conceivably answer the question. However, you are to choose the **best** answer; that is, the response that most accurately and completely answers the question, and blacken the corresponding space on your answer sheet.

Passage for questions 1 through 8

Since the Copernican revolution, there has been a schism between analytic philosophy and Continental philosophy; graduate philosophy programs in universities, for example, tend to train philosophers in
(5) analytic methods, and some to train in the Continental tradition, but rarely are pluralist programs found. Both analytically trained scholars and Continentally-trained philosophers have tended to support this separation, in large part because the current conventional wisdom
(10) holds that analytic philosophy should be rooted in logical rigor and precision, with a commitment to modal reasoning, whereas Continental philosophy depends largely on description and sometimes narrative to communicate its truths.
(15) Certainly it is true that analytic and Continental philosophy are distinct philosophical methods, but why have the two become siloed apart from each other within the discipline of philosophy? Why aren't more pluralist programs found? The answer could
(20) reside in a deeper cultural chasm within the U.S., in which generalism is often viewed with suspicion. If a philosopher has the knowledge base and expertise in a single area, they are often vaunted as an intellectual leader; whereas someone with broad knowledge of
(25) various methods could be seen as an amateur in at least one of the areas of philosophy.
There have been some philosophers from both analytic and Continental traditions who speak out in favor of "crossing the divide". John Tienson, a
(30) metaphysician who is largely revered for his careful, succinct work on essences, regularly teaches graduate students a class on philosophical pluralism. Sara Bernstein, a Continental scholar who focuses on race and gender, organizes conferences about "Bridging the
(35) Traditions". Pluralists, of course, are keen to join the conversation, regardless of who is leading it. Kristie Dotson, an acclaimed African American epistemologist who was trained at one of the leading pluralist programs in the country, the University of Memphis,
(40) has challenged the view that analytic and Continental

traditions are fundamentally distinct methods. Given that she was trained in both Continental and analytic philosophy, she indicated she is not persuaded that the two have nothing to do with the other. In fact,
(45) understanding the history of philosophy means that one realizes that constraining philosophy to one method will silence unique and beautiful voices.
Dotson contends that to persist in the restrictive approach between analytic and Continental philosophy
(50) prevalent in the U.S. is detrimental to the future of philosophy, because each genre shares in the nature of the other. Indeed, her analytic philosophy offers example after example of integrating Continental methods, including those of DuBois and Audre
(55) Lorde. Her use of these scholars can only be properly regarded as narrative epistemology, because she speaks about the epistemology of testimony through narrative, without also requiring a systematic structure of argumentation. Yet her narrative epistemology also
(60) presents the elements of rigorous argumentation in such a way that potential interlocutors are led to take account of narrative details within a logical flow. Therefore, while the language is literary, it often comes to constitute, cumulatively, a work of narrative
(65) analytic philosophy. Similarly, many passages in her analytic philosophy, though undeniably dialectical, are persuasive because she is using narrative and literary expressions. Dotson bridges the gap between analytic philosophy and Continental philosophy not
(70) only by writing in both languages, but also by fusing the two methods within individual works.

GO TO THE NEXT PAGE

READING COMPREHENSION
SECTION 1

1. Which one of the following most accurately expresses the main point of the passage?

   (A) Working against a bias that has long been dominant in the U.S., recent philosophers like Kristie Dotson have shown that the use of narrative can effectively enhance analytic philosophy.

   (B) Kristie Dotson's successful blending of analytic philosophy and Continental philosophy exemplifies the recent trend away from the rigid separation of the two genres that has long been prevalent in U.S. philosophy.

   (C) Kristie Dotson's narratives present clusters of detail to create a cumulative narrative without requiring the reader to interpret it in a dialectical manner.

   (D) Unlike many of her U.S. contemporaries, Kristie Dotson writes without relying on the traditional techniques associated with analytic philosophy and Continental philosophy.

   (E) Kristie Dotson's work has been widely acclaimed primarily because of the narrative elements she has introduced into her analytic philosophy.

2. Which one of the following is most analogous to the philosophical achievements that the author attributes to Dotson?

   (A) A mechanic combines nontraditional synchronization methods and traditional calibrations from technology and old-school techniques to create a new engine.

   (B) A theologian becomes a pastor and does well, partly due to many years of university study of ancient texts.

   (C) An athlete who is also a coach partners with a Little League to stage practice adult/child baseball games to teach children about health and sports.

   (D) An artist sculpts a new monument by combining features of her last three pieces into the new piece.

   (E) A composer defies convention and directs an orchestra that combines aspects of opera and jazz.

3. According to the passage, in the U.S. there is a widely held view that

   (A) analytic philosophy should not involve narratives

   (B) unlike analytic philosophy, Continental philosophy is rarely an academically serious endeavor

   (C) graduate writing programs focus on analytic philosophy to the exclusion of Continental philosophy

   (D) Continental philosophy is most effective when it incorporates rigorous structure

   (E) American culture is suspicious of generalists

4. The author's attitude toward the deep rift between analytic philosophy and Continental philosophy in the U.S. can be most accurately described as one of

   (A) disapproval of presuppositions underlying the divide

   (B) perplexity as to what could have led to the development of such a divide

   (C) ambivalence toward the effect the divide has had on U.S. philosophy

   (D) pessimism regarding the possibility that the divide can be overcome

   (E) astonishment that academics have overlooked the existence of the divide

READING COMPREHENSION
SECTION 1

5. In the passage, the author speculates that a cause of the deep divide between Continental philosophy and analytic philosophy in the United States may be that

(A) training graduate students in analytic philosophy is different from training graduate students in Continental

(B) analytic and Continental philosophers each tend to see their method as superior to the other

(C) publishers often pressure philosophers to concentrate on what they do best

(D) a suspicion of generalism deters philosophers from dividing their energies between the two methods

(E) Continental philosophy is more widely read and respected than analytic philosophy

6. In the context of the passage, the author's primary purpose in mentioning Dotson's own justification in being a pluralist (<u>last sentence of the third paragraph</u>) is to

(A) indicate that Dotson's vision as a philosopher derives in large part from the international character of her academic background

(B) point to an experience that reinforced Dotson's conviction that analytic philosophy and Continental philosophy should not be rigidly separated

(C) suggest that the habit of treating analytic philosophy and Continental philosophy as nonoverlapping domains is characteristic of English-speaking societies but not others

(D) posit a further reason Dotson gives to ensure a diversity of perspectives are present in philosophy

(E) specify what Dotson believes is the origin of her opposition to the separation of Continental philosophy and analytic philosophy in the U.S.

7. It can be inferred from the passage that the author would be most likely to believe which one of the following?

(A) The value of narrative for analytic philosophy resides in its representation of a sequence of events or values, rather than in its ability to evoke feelings in the reader.

(B) The way in which Dotson blends methods in her argumentation is without precedent in U.S. philosophy.

(C) Dotson writes in both analytic philosophy and Continental philosophy, and her arguments frequently contain elements of both.

(D) Narrative that uses poetic language is generally superior to rigorous analytic philosophy.

(E) Philosophers who successfully cross the generic boundary between analytic philosophy and Continental philosophy often try their hand at genres such as art, theatre, and literature as well.

8. If this passage had been excerpted from a longer text, which one of the following predictions about the near future of philosophy in the U.S. would be most likely to appear in that text?

(A) Because of the increased interest in pluralist philosophy, the small market for pure, rigorous analytic philosophy will likely shrink even further.

(B) Narrative analytic philosophy will probably come to be regarded as a sub-genre of Continental philosophy.

(C) The number of philosophers who write in both analytic and Continental philosophical methods will probably continue to grow.

(D) There will probably be a rise in specialization among philosophers in university philosophy programs.

(E) Philosophers who continue to work exclusively in analytic philosophy or Continental philosophy will likely lose their audiences.

GO TO THE NEXT PAGE

READING COMPREHENSION
SECTION 1

Passage pair for questions 9 through 14

The two passages discuss recent legal analysis of the concept of "coercion" in the work of theorist John Rawls. They are adapted from two different papers collected in a recent edited volume on the topic.

Passage A

The thesis that coercion can only show due respect for persons as ends (or as sovereign interpreters of morality's requirements) when it can be reasonably justified to those subject to the coercion has a wide
(5) currency, and it is sometimes attributed to Rawls.

But this is not the best interpretation of Rawls, and we should reject the view that the main purpose of public reason is to legitimate or render permissible
(10) coercion or threats of coercion against individuals. Though some of Rawls's remarks do point in this direction, he never explicitly formulates or develops his view in this way, and he rarely mentions coercion in his discussion of public reason. In fact, the
(15) conception of respect for persons remains vulnerable to the same objection pressed against the appeal to autonomy. That is, the Kantian idea of respecting persons as ends-in-themselves will be the subject of reasonable disagreement among citizens in a well-
(20) ordered society, and so grounding a commitment to public reason in this way is unstable. And, there is no good reason to believe that coercive rules or actions always stand uniquely in need of justification when compared to non-coercive alternatives.

Passage B

(25) While Rawls certainly does confirm that he is trying to work out what the foreign policy of a liberal people should be in *Law of Peoples,* he also suggests that an alternative interpretation of his project is plausible when he constantly reiterates that his view offers a
(30) realistic utopia. The phrase suggests that he is trying to determine the conditions under which a utopian world order might be possible, although he constantly emphasizes that it must also be realistic. Here, Rawls aims to establish under what conditions we can secure
(35) a peaceful and stable world order, rather than one which is just. If securing a peaceful world order is our primary objective, we should sanction coercion only in the most essential cases. The notion of legitimacy plays a key role, since Rawls is concerned with the
(40) legitimacy of global coercive political power, rather than working out a more robust conception of justice as fairness. Legitimacy is a more permissive standard than justice and this is the relevant issue in working out core matters related to a peaceful and stable
(45) world order.

9. Both passages were written primarily to answer which one of the following questions?

(A) Can reasonable people agree that justice includes the state right to coerce, according to Rawls?

(B) Is it possible for the state's use of coercion to be consistent with a Rawlsian conception of utopia?

(C) What are the grounds of a well-ordered society, for Rawls?

(D) Does a peaceful and stable world order require a commitment to public reason, for Rawlsians?

(E) Why does Rawls distinguish between justified coercion and legitimate, non-coercive actions by the state?

10. Each of the two passages mentions the relation of coercion to

(A) fairness

(B) justice

(C) a well-ordered, stable society

(D) public reason

(E) utopia

GO TO THE NEXT PAGE

11. It can be inferred that the authors of the two passages would be most likely to disagree over whether

   (A) legitimate, coercive action by a state is better justified than illegitimate, non-coercive action by a non-state actor

   (B) fewer differences than similarities exist between Rawls's utopian society and today's democracies

   (C) public reason can justify coercive government action that can lead to a utopian state

   (D) coercive government action must be justified through legitimacy or justice

   (E) non-coercive action is always preferable than coercive action

12. The authors would be most likely to agree on the answer to which one of the following questions regarding the role of coercion and public goods?

   (A) Does Rawls believe utopia is realistic, given the misuse of coercion in some democratic states?

   (B) Do we have a human right not to be coerced?

   (C) Will a populace generally tend towards the good without governmental intervention?

   (D) Is a state-sponsored media a good that could be used coercively by the state?

   (E) Is a peaceful, well-ordered society always just?

13. Which of the following positions of the first passage might the author of the second passage establish as a condition for securing a peaceful, stable world order?

   (A) That the original position allows us to ground a commitment to public reason to respecting persons

   (B) That Rawls does not explicitly mention coercion in his discussion of public reason

   (C) That public reason legitimates threats of coercion against individuals

   (D) That coercion is respectful if it can be reasonably justified

   (E) That reasonable people can disagree about whether and how to respect persons as ends-in-themselves

14. Which one of the following is the most accurate characterization of a relationship between the two passages?

   (A) Passage A and passage B use different evidence to draw divergent conclusions.

   (B) Passage A poses the question that passage B attempts to answer.

   (C) Passage A proposes a hypothesis that passage B attempts to substantiate with new evidence.

   (D) Passage A expresses a stronger commitment to its hypothesis than does passage B.

   (E) Passage A and passage B use different evidence to support the same conclusion.

GO TO THE NEXT PAGE

READING COMPREHENSION
SECTION 1

Passage for questions 15 through 20

The following passage is modified from a recent article on intellectual property cases.

Both judicial opinions utilize the same three ethical frameworks: common good, utilitarianism, and rights/duties. Efficiency considerations concerning the firm, the legal system, and overall welfare maximization
(5) were expressed or implied in both cases as well. Further, not only is there an overlap among ethical frameworks, but also there is an overlap between ethical and efficiency criteria as well. Not surprisingly, some statements that consider costs and benefits
(10) can be interpreted as a utilitarian approach or wealth (welfare) maximization approach. Further, the efficiency goal of welfare maximization seems to be seen by the court as a component, perhaps a very important component, of the common good. It is
(25) safe to assume that the underlying ethical dilemma in intellectual property cases within the pharmaceutical industry revolves around incentivizing inventors, protecting inventors from theft of their labor, while at the same time enabling the distribution of life-saving
(30) and health enhancing drugs to benefit individuals and populations. As such, judges are placed in a position of taking into account the needs of all stakeholders. Then, judges must interpret the law considering the impact on current and future researchers and
(35) inventors, as well as the impact on individuals and patients. This is no easy task. Accordingly, a single lens is not sufficient to address the complexity of these judicial decisions because the possibility of harm to the current or future inventors and individuals as well
(40) as populations is too great.

15. Which one of the following most accurately expresses the main point of the passage?

(A) Since distribution of a pharmaceutical drug is controlled by the manufacturer rather than by the researcher who creates the original formula of the drug, sale of even generic drugs should not be considered theft of intellectual property.

(B) The ethical frameworks required to guide judicial decision-making for pharmaceutical intellectual property cases are diverse, complex, and integrated into the interests of all stakeholders.

(C) The main ethical problem with intellectual property of the pharmaceutical industry revolves around the tension between the developers who want to make money and the patients who might not be able to afford the drugs.

(D) It is short-sighted to see the ethical dilemmas of drug sales as pertaining only to current drug manufacturers; rather, judges need to take a longitudinal view of the ethical problems for those who will research in the future.

(E) The most important component of the common good, as it relates to the pharmaceutical industry, is the efficiency goal of welfare maximization.

16. Which one of the following is closest in meaning to the terms "efficiency considerations/efficiency criteria/efficiency goal" used in the first five sentences of the passage?

(A) best use of time and money in relation to patient need

(B) best use of lab space and research tools

(C) best use of judicial time

(D) best use of marketing plans and medical resources

(E) best application of ethical frameworks to legal issues

GO TO THE NEXT PAGE

17. With which one of the following claims about pharmaceutical intellectual property rights would the author be most likely to agree?

(A) Pharmaceutical companies cannot receive adequate protection unless current intellectual property laws are strengthened.

(B) Pharmaceutical formulas cannot be protected from unauthorized distribution without significantly diminishing the health rights of patients.

(C) The significant need for medical advancement means judges are unlikely to limit the pharmaceutical industry's growth.

(D) The complex legal issues surrounding pharmaceutical intellectual property means that it is a category mistake to use ethical frameworks to make judicial decisions about it.

(E) Judicial activists who would want to limit the amount of profit pharmaceutical companies make must be aware of the harm they can cause to researchers, companies, and to patients by stemming the flow of invention.

18. Based on the passage, the relationship between the efficiency goal of welfare maximization and the common good could be best characterized as analogous to the relationship between

(A) building a green space for community members to enjoy but restricting its use to those who pay an entrance fee

(B) a federal mandate against the sale and use of a drug and a state allowing the recreational sale and use of the same drug

(C) incentivizing the use of solar panels through tax deductions

(D) allowing campus carry by licensed gun holders on a college campus but restricting open carry

(E) giving tax breaks to car companies to build energy efficient vehicles but not providing tax breaks to citizens who purchase the vehicles designed through the tax-incentivized invention

19. The passage most strongly implies which one of the following?

(A) a multifaceted application of ethical theories to intellectual property cases still can come down to the simple question of "Who should benefit?".

(B) the judge, who controls who is the owner of intellectual property, should be considered a participant in research innovation as well.

(C) intellectual property rights do not extend to pharmaceutical companies.

(D) the primary role of the judge in the intellectual property debate is to protect inventors from intellectual theft.

(E) ethical frameworks compete with welfare maximization approaches.

20. Based on the passage, this author believes that judges in intellectual property cases would be likely to agree to each of the following statements EXCEPT:

(A) standardizing intellectual property law through congressional legislation will sometimes be unnecessary, given the complexity of the morally relevant considerations each case brings.

(B) whether competition in the pharmaceutical industry is legally appropriate and fair may depend on the patient base for any given drug on the market.

(C) a community ought to determine the most appropriate methods for evaluating the wealth efficiency maximization values for any given market.

(D) the production of generic drugs from competing vendors could constitute theft of intellectual property.

(E) determining the legal balance between an industry's right to earn a profit off of innovation and a community's public need requires judges to be thoroughly trained in ethics.

GO TO THE NEXT PAGE

READING COMPREHENSION
SECTION 1

Passage for questions 21 through 27

The following passage is modified from a recent academic article on the habitat selection of wintering lemmings.

Some small mammal populations are famous for their phenomenal cyclic fluctuations in abundance. Small mammal species with a wide geographic distribution tend to exhibit more pronounced population cycles
(5) at northern latitudes where seasonality is strongest. During the cold and dark Arctic winter, small mammals may spend up to 9 months of the year under the snow. Winter remains the least known period of their annual cycle, yet this period may play a key role
(10) in their population dynamics. At northern latitudes, snow cover dramatically changes the structure and functioning of ecosystems in winter. Temperature gradients within the snow result in the formation of a stratum of fragile and loosely arranged snow crystals
(15) near the ground, which creates a subnivean space, the primary wintering habitat of small mammals.

Their survival is dependent upon accessibility to food and the protection against harsh temperatures and predators offered by this particular environment.
(20) Freeze–thaw cycles induced by warm winter temperature disturb the subnivean space and may lead to the formation of ice at ground level, which prevents rodents from feeding on the vegetation. Small mammals require a high rate of food intake
(25) because of their low digestive efficiency and high metabolic rate increased by cold. Therefore, limited accessibility or depletion of winter food may induce a deterioration of their physiological condition and increase mortality. Winter reproduction under the
(30) snow occurs in some species of small mammals and is especially common in lemmings. In fact, successful reproduction under the snow is often considered a necessary condition for the occurrence of a peak in abundance in cyclic lemming populations. The early
(35) onset of a thick and dry snow cover combined with the absence of freezing rain and days with above zero temperatures should favor survival and reproduction.

Recent evidence suggests that population cycles of small mammals of the tundra may be fading out
(40) in some areas, especially in Fennoscandia. Increased frequencies of freeze–thaw cycles during the winter due to climate warming and their influence on snow conditions have been invoked as a possible cause for the dampening of these. Alterations in snow cover
(45) may also affect winter predator–prey interactions. Even if subnivean specialist predators, such as stoats and weasels, should continue to be efficient predators during winter, thick snow cover may reduce the success of other predators of small mammals, such as arctic
(50) foxes or snowy owls. There is increasing evidence that the winter dynamics of these populations may be dominated by the effect of stochastic climatic events on snow conditions.

Previous studies suggested that freezing rain and
(55) frost/thaw events should reduce small mammal winter survival both directly and indirectly. Directly, such climatic events reduce the thermal protection offered by snow cover, fragment the subnivean space through the formation of an ice crust, and can induce
(60) water flooding. These phenomena may greatly reduce the probability of individuals surviving the entire winter by increasing thermal stress and reducing food availability, and possibly by the drowning of animals during floods. Indirectly, mild weather during
(65) the winter may reduce the protection offered by snow cover against some generalist predators, such as arctic foxes and increase the competition among predators for lemmings during the winter. Therefore, alterations of winter climatic conditions brought
(70) by the current global warming could reduce small mammal winter survival and destabilize their cyclic population dynamics, which would affect the whole tundra ecosystem.

21. The primary purpose of the passage is to

(A) explain how the lemming reproduces given the conditions of a changing tundra ecosystem

(B) present some recent scientific research on why the population of Fennoscandian mammals is falling

(C) present the author's scientific contributions to research about the relationship of climate change to the population patterns of lemmings

(D) assess the value of previous studies on the relationship between cold weather events and small mammal winter populations

(E) describe two different views on subnivean space and predator/prey populations

GO TO THE NEXT PAGE

READING COMPREHENSION
SECTION 1

22. Which one of the following statements best expresses the main idea of the passage?

(A) Subnivean specialists have established that predator populations are unaffected by the depth of snow cover, but the populations of the lemmings are.

(B) Subnivean specialists have established that thermal protection offered by deep snow drifts will lead lemmings to leave relatively flat, wet tundra.

(C) Subnivean scientists have established that snow depth is fairly important in explaining the winter habitat selection of brown lemmings particularly.

(D) Subnivean scientists have concluded that climate change is the leading direct and indirect factor on small mammal winter populations in Arctic ecosystems.

(E) Subniviean scientists have concluded that the predation of lemmings is directly correlated to overwinter ground temperature.

23. Which of the following statements, if added to the passage, would bolster the author's claim that snow cover dramatically impacts the structure and functioning of ecosystems in winter?

(A) During the cold and dark Arctic winter, small mammals may spend up to 9 months of the year under the snow.

(B) Temperature gradients within the snow result in a subnivean space by forming a stratum of fragile and loosely arranged snow crystals near the ground.

(C) Small mammal species with a wide geographic distribution tend to exhibit more pronounced population cycles at northern latitudes where seasonality is strongest.

(D) The cold, wet Arctic habitat is characterized by polygon tundra, that forms wet meadows, fens, and a mesic habitat.

(E) The probability of encountering lemming nests increases with increasing heterogeneity of the microtopography, slope of the terrain, and non-linear landscape level.

24. Which of the following strategies is most similar to the author's research strategy as it is described in the passage?

(A) to determine the mating habits of lemmings, a biologist enters the ecosystem of the mammal to test temperature settings each day of winter

(B) to determine whether certain mammals reproduce under certain weather conditions, a biologist measures the weather conditions

(C) to determine whether the populations of predators and prey depend on ecosystem climate conditions, biologists manipulate the climate conditions and measure the mammal populations

(D) to determine the relationship between climate change and reproduction behavior of mammals, biologists sampled winter nesting sites and measured temperature and precipitation variability on those sites

(E) to determine the probability of encountering lemming nests in snow-covered areas, biologists identified subnivean spaces by a relatively low abundance of lichen cover

25. It can be inferred from the passage that Arctic stochastic climatic events of the sort that would impact lemming populations would include which of the following?

(A) Arctic drought, which limits the formation of subnivean spaces for lemmings to nest

(B) periods of heavy rain, which can flood subnivean spaces and reduce species diversity

(C) aboveground biomass erosion, which causes species-specific reproductive loss for mammals that nest in the Arctic tundra

(D) Arctic warming, which can fluctuate the freeze-thaw cycle of the Arctic biomes, and interrupt the ability of mammals to nest

(E) a subduction zone shift in the Atlantic Ocean, which causes the rare event of rising ocean levels in the Arctic and the destabilization of mammal subnivean habitats

GO TO THE NEXT PAGE

READING COMPREHENSION
SECTION 1

26. Which one of the following best describes the organization of the passage?

(A) A hypothesis is presented and defended with supporting examples.

(B) A conclusion is presented and the information supporting it is provided.

(C) A thesis is presented and defended with an argument.

(D) Opposing views are presented, discussed, and then reconciled.

(E) A theory is proposed, considered, and then amended on the basis of evidence.

27. Based on the passage, identify why successful reproduction under the snow is not a sufficient condition for a peak in cyclic lemming populations.

(A) the early onset of a thick and dry snow cover combined with the absence of freezing rain and days with above zero temperatures favors survival and reproduction

(B) at the landscape scale, the selection of the winter nest sites is generally affected by the same variables in both predators and prey

(C) stochastic climate events demonstrate that unpredictable causal chains can interfere with typical scientific predictions about lemming reproduction

(D) mean snow depth over subnivean sites does not differ between random sites and sites where lemming nests were depredated by predators

(E) elevation and slope aspect do not affect nest site selection, and plant variables have a relatively weak influence on nest site selection

END OF SECTION

IF YOU FINISH BEFORE THE TIME ENDS, YOU MAY CHECK YOUR WORK ONLY ON THIS SECTION. DO NOT GO TO ANY OTHER SECTION IN THE TEST.

Directions: Each group of questions in this section is based on a set of conditions. In answering some of the questions, it may be useful to draw a rough diagram. Choose the response that most accurately and completely answers each question and blacken the corresponding space on your answer sheet.

Passage for questions 1 through 6

Each of exactly six baseball pitchers—Jackson, Karns, La Russa, Napoli, Ohtani, and Pacheco—are either active or disabled for tonight's Cubs game. For Joe Madden to generate the line-up, he has to keep track on two lists by ensuring the following conditions are met for his players:

Karns is disabled if Jackson is active.
Ohtani is active if Jackson is disabled.
If La Russa is active, then both Napoli and Pacheco are disabled.
If Napoli is disabled, then so is Ohtani.
If Pacheco is disabled, then both Karns and Ohtani are active.

1. Which one of the following could be a complete and accurate list of the six players that are active for Joe Madden?

   (A) Jackson, Karns, Ohtani

   (B) Jackson, Napoli, Ohtani, Pacheco

   (C) Karns, La Russa, Ohtani

   (D) Napoli, Ohtani

   (E) Napoli, Pacheco

2. If Pacheco is disabled, then which of the following must be true?

   (A) Jackson is disabled.

   (B) Karns is disabled.

   (C) La Russa is active.

   (D) Napoli is disabled.

   (E) Ohtani is disabled.

3. If Karns is active, then which one of the following must be true?

   (A) Jackson is active.

   (B) Napoli is active.

   (C) Ohtani is disabled.

   (D) Pacheco is active.

   (E) Pacheco is disabled.

4. Which one of the following CANNOT be a pair of disabled players on Madden's list?

   (A) Jackson and Karns

   (B) Jackson and Pacheco

   (C) Karns and Ohtani

   (D) Napoli and Ohtani

   (E) Napoli and Pacheco

5. If Napoli and Ohtani are on different lists, which one of the following must be true?

   (A) Jackson is active.

   (B) Karns is active.

   (C) Pacheco is disabled.

   (D) Four players are active.

   (E) Four players are disabled.

6. What is the minimum number of players that could be active, for Madden?

   (A) zero

   (B) one

   (C) two

   (D) three

   (E) four

GO TO THE NEXT PAGE

ANALYTICAL REASONING
SECTION 2

Passage for questions 7 through 11

The University hired a new President, and in her first day of office, she wanted to visit academic departments that needed to hire tenured faculty: History, Civil Engineering, Art, Theoretical Physics, Philosophy, and Architecture. She only had time to meet with the faculty of these departments once during her first day, and could not have other meetings scheduled that day. Due to the teaching schedules of the faculty in those departments, she had to schedule her meetings around the following considerations:

Civil Engineering must be the third meeting of the day.
History must meet with the President before she meets with Theoretical Physics.
The meeting with Philosophy must occur before both History and Architecture.

7. Which of the following could be the order in which the meetings are held?

(A) Philosophy, Architecture, History, Theoretical Physics, Civil Engineering, Art

(B) Theoretical Physics, History, Civil Engineering, Architecture, Art, Philosophy

(C) Civil Engineering, Architecture, Philosophy, History, Theoretical Physics, Art

(D) Civil Engineering, Art, Philosophy, Architecture, Theoretical Physics, History

(E) Philosophy, Art, Civil Engineering, History, Architecture, Theoretical Physics

8. If the President meets with the Art faculty first, which meeting must she hold second?

(A) Philosophy
(B) Civil Engineering
(C) History
(D) Architecture
(E) Theoretical Physics

9. Which of the following statements must be true?

(A) Civil Engineering meets with the President before Art.

(B) Theoretical Physics meets with the President before Architecture.

(C) Philosophy meets with the President before Theoretical Physics.

(D) History meets with the President before Architecture.

(E) Civil Engineering meets with the President before Philosophy.

10. Which of the following statements could be true?

(A) Civil Engineering could be the first meeting.
(B) Architecture is the last meeting.
(C) Theoretical Physics is the second meeting.
(D) Philosophy is the third meeting.
(E) History is the last meeting.

11. Which of the following meetings could not be held immediately after the faculty meeting with Civil Engineering?

(A) Theoretical Physics
(B) Philosophy
(C) Architecture
(D) Art
(E) History

ANALYTICAL REASONING
SECTION 2

Passage for questions 12 through 18

Jerry Smith, an air traffic control expert, has an extremely busy day ahead of him. Eight airplanes: one each from Quantas, Regent, Southwest, TAKA, Virgin Atlantic, WestJet, Yeti Air, and Zambezi Air are vying to land within minutes of each other, and only one runway is currently open to accommodate them. Jerry can land the airplanes safely only if the following conditions are met:

Virgin Atlantic must land before both Yeti and Quantas.

Quantas must land before Zambezi Air.

TAKA must land before Virgin Atlantic but after Regent.

Southwest must land after Virgin Atlantic.

Regent must land some time before WestJet.

12. Which of the following could be the order, from first to last, in which Jerry could safely land the airplanes?

   (A) TAKA, Zambezi, Virgin Atlantic, Regent, WestJet, Yeti, Southwest, Quantas

   (B) Zambezi, Regent, WestJet, Quantas, TAKA, Virgin Atlantic, Yeti, Southwest

   (C) Regent, WestJet, TAKA, Virgin Atlantic, Quantas, Zambezi, Southwest, Yeti

   (D) Zambezi, WestJet, Regent, TAKA, Virgin Atlantic, Yeti, Quantas, Southwest

   (E) Regent, WestJest, TAKA, Virgin Atlantic, Zambezi, Southwest, Yeti, Quantas

13. Which of the following statements could be true?

   (A) Yeti is the second airplane to land.

   (B) Regent is the third airplane to land.

   (C) Quantas is the fourth airplane to land.

   (D) Southwest is the fifth airplane to land.

   (E) Virgin Atlantic is the sixth airplane to land.

14. If Virgin Atlantic lands before Zambezi does, then which of the following could be true?

   (A) Regent is the second airplane to land.

   (B) TAKA is the fourth airplane to land.

   (C) Quantas is the third airplane to land.

   (D) Virgin Atlantic is the fifth airplane to land.

   (E) Zambezi is the sixth airplane to land.

15. If TAKA is the second airplane to land, which one of the following must be true?

   (A) Southwest lands before TAKA.

   (B) Virgin Atlantic lands before WestJet.

   (C) WestJet lands before Virgin Atlantic.

   (D) Yeti lands before Quantas.

   (E) Zambezi lands after WestJet.

16. If Quantas is the fifth airplane to land, then each of the following could be true EXCEPT:

   (A) Zambezi is the third airplane to land.

   (B) TAKA is the second airplane to land.

   (C) Virgin Atlantic is the third airplane to land.

   (D) WestJet is the fourth airplane to land.

   (E) Yeti is the sixth airplane to land.

17. If TAKA is the third airplane to land, then which of the following must be true?

   (A) Southwest is the seventh airplane to land.

   (B) WestJet is the second airplane to land.

   (C) Quantas is the fourth airplane to land.

   (D) Virgin Atlantic is the fifth airplane to land.

   (E) Yeti is the seventh airplane to land.

18. If Zambezi is the seventh airplane to land, then which of the following could be true?

   (A) Regent is the second airplane to land.

   (B) Southwest is the fourth airplane to land.

   (C) WestJet is the fifth airplane to land.

   (D) Virgin Atlantic is the sixth airplane to land.

   (E) Yeti is the eighth airplane to land.

GO TO THE NEXT PAGE

ANALYTICAL REASONING
SECTION 2

Passage for questions 19 through 23

The seven Graper teenagers are working diligently to earn money for their upcoming family vacation by trying to get their dad's old clunker up and running, and ready to sell. Over a three-day period, the siblings complete five tasks in this order: they remove the engine, recalibrate the engine cylinders, reassemble the head, reupholster the car, and repaint the car. Based on their age and abilities, they assign tasks each person can do:

Sofie: reassemble the head
Shannon: reupholster, paint
Elizabeth: remove the engine, paint
Allie: remove the engine, reupholster
Jessica: recalibrate the engine, reassemble the head
Jill: reupholster
Cory: recalibrate the engine, paint

The teens ensure that the work is completed in an orderly manner, and so they impose the following rules on their work:

A maximum of five workers can work at a time.
At least one task will be done each day.
Reassembling and painting will be done on different days.
Each teen does at least one task during the project, but no more than one task per day.
Each task is worked on by exactly one worker, completed the day it is started and before the next task begins.

19. Which of the following could be a complete and accurate list of the members of this crew?

(A) Sofie, Shannon, Elizabeth, Allie
(B) Sofie, Shannon, Allie, Jessica
(C) Shannon, Elizabeth, Allie, Cory
(D) Shannon, Elizabeth, Jill, Cory
(E) Sofie, Shannon, Jessica, Jill, Cory

20. If the installation takes three days, and if the same two teens work on the first and third days, then which one of the following could be the pair of siblings who work on those two days?

(A) Shannon and Elizabeth
(B) Elizabeth and Allie
(C) Elizabeth and Jessica
(D) Allie and Cory
(E) Jessica and Cory

21. Each of the following could be a complete and accurate list of the members of the crew EXCEPT:

(A) Shannon, Elizabeth, Allie, Jill
(B) Elizabeth, Allie, Jessica
(C) Sofie, Shannon, Elizabeth, Jessica
(D) Elizabeth, Jessica, Jill, Cory
(E) Allie, Jessica, Jill, Cory

22. If the installation takes three days, and if the upholstering is done on the third day, then which one of the following could be a list of all the crew members who work on the second day?

(A) Elizabeth
(B) Allie
(C) Cory
(D) Sofie and Shannon
(E) Jessica and Cory

23. Which one of the following could be a pair of siblings of the crew, both of whom work on the same days as each other and each of whom perform two tasks?

(A) Sofie and Jill
(B) Shannon and Allie
(C) Elizabeth and Jessica
(D) Allie and Jessica
(E) Jessica and Cory

END OF SECTION

IF YOU FINISH BEFORE THE TIME ENDS, YOU MAY CHECK YOUR WORK ONLY ON THIS SECTION.
DO NOT GO TO ANY OTHER SECTION IN THE TEST.

STOP

Directions: The questions in this section are based on the reasoning contained in brief statements or passages. For some questions, more than one of the choices could conceivably answer the question. However, you are to choose the **best** answer; that is, the response that most accurately and completely answers the question. You should not make assumptions that are by commonsense standards implausible, superfluous, or incompatible with the passage. After you have chosen the best answer, blacken the corresponding space on your answer sheet.

Questions 1 through 25

1. To be considered for a VP position in the company, a candidate must be related to a family member of President McCoy. Further, no candidate who is related to a Hatfield can be considered for a VP position. Thus, Carl McCoy, a cybersecurity expert with an MBA, cannot be a candidate for the head of the cybersecurity division, because he is married to Elizabeth Hatfield.

   The argument's conclusion follows logically if which one of the following is assumed?

   (A) Anyone with an MBA who is not married to a Hatfield is eligible for the head of the cybersecurity division.

   (B) The head of the cybersecurity division is a VP position.

   (C) An MBA is not a sufficient condition for candidacy to the head of cybersecurity position.

   (D) If Carl was not married to a Hatfield, he would be hired as the head of the cybersecurity division.

   (E) The head of cybersecurity cannot be related to a Hatfield because it would present a conflict of interest for the person in that position.

2. Imagine a pediatrician has been told some confidential personal information by one of her minor patients, a teenager. The confidential information poses potential risks for the future health and well-being of the patient. She feels compelled to keep the confidence of her young patient, but also to let the teen's parent know that the teen is in trouble. Since the pediatrician has competing moral obligations, she is not morally obligated to either the teen or the parent.

   Which one of the following arguments is most similar in its reasoning to the argument above?

   (A) Americans believe that we have the unencumbered right to say whatever we want. It is also claimed that we have the obligation to be civil to others. But civility requires that we respect the rights of others. So, if you are a civil American, you will respect the rights of others, even if they say something with which you disagree.

   (B) Parents can get their kids to be obedient by agreeing to give them later gifts, even if they don't expect to give them later gifts. The only way parents can get their kids to be obedient is to be dishonest with them.

   (C) If the photographer puts significant effort into using filters for her customers, they might be so impressed with the filters but not the photos. Sofie decides not to use filters to save time for the customers, and so they were not impressed with the photos.

   (D) If a driver uses the electronic toll lane, she will be taxed for the use of the road. If the driver is taxed for the use of the road, the state will issue fines until she pays the tax off. But, in this case, the state has not issued fines to the driver, so either the driver doesn't have to pay off the tax, or the state didn't have the right to tax her.

   (E) If the professor gives a comprehensive final exam, she will either need a grad student to help her grade or will miss the grading deadline. The department does not have funds for a grad student, and she will lose her summer health insurance coverage if she does not submit final grades on time. She really depends on her health insurance, so she will have to find a way to fund a grad student to grade.

GO TO THE NEXT PAGE

LOGICAL REASONING
SECTION 3

3. College graduation is a milestone for most people, and marks a move of independence for most graduates in the U.S. This can come with a period of grief, as well, as the graduate understands that s/he cannot return to the life of a child. A danger exists for the graduate—she or he can reminisce ....

Which one of the following most logically completes the argument?

(A) about his/her own childhood

(B) and worry that his/her own lives are about to end

(C) until s/he starts to plan goals for the next stage of her/his life

(D) and forget to make choices that will ensure their success in the future

(E) to reflect on how to change patterns of behavior in college

4. Comedian George Burns: You know, when I was breaking into show business, I figured out a little stunt, myself. I had a lot of cards printed to give out to booking agents and theater managers, and they were made out of fine linen with engraved lettering, and it said, "Be the first one to hire George Burns." My friends thought they were too expensive, but they weren't. Those cards lasted me seven years.

The success of the comedic line in Burns's commentary comes from which fundamental implication of the passage?

(A) Well-made business cards last a long time in a wallet, where they can stay for years without helping an actor gain exposure.

(B) Evidence suggests that the more business cards an actor hands out, the more exposure he or she will have.

(C) So many people wanted to be the first to hire George Burns that linen business cards became collector items of value when he became famous.

(D) Investing in your future is ironic because your future success largely depends on other people's view of you.

(E) Comedy requires finding humor in your own life experiences, so making business cards of out linen instead of paper generated humor for Burns.

5. Scientist: Volcanoes with low silica content can contribute to significant changes in the climate, if they emit chlorofluorocarbons, which deplete ozone and can cause global warming. But, basaltic (black rock) volcanoes don't actually emit significant amounts of chlorine or bromine. Instead, they often give off ozone. Ozone is also a greenhouse gas, so depleting it would cause global cooling, not warming.

Which one of the following, if true, would count as evidence against the scientist's explanation of basaltic volcanoes' impact on the environment?

(A) Chlorine and bromine are not emitted in a volcano's plume, but are expelled under the ocean through its vents.

(B) Global warming is also caused when naturally occurring ozone from basaltic volcanoes meets chlorofluorocarbons from man-made pollutants in the atmosphere.

(C) Volcanologists have not yet developed the technology for determining how much chlorine and bromine are expelled by basaltic volcanoes.

(D) Dust and other particles from volcanoes can trap the Sun's radiation back to the earth's surface, which then can cause global warming.

(E) There are far fewer basaltic volcanoes that have erupted this century than at any other time in recorded history.

GO TO THE NEXT PAGE

LOGICAL REASONING
SECTION 3

6. Aristotle: The highest good is an active life of contentedness and virtue, lived according to our best activity—the use of reason.

Which individual pursues the highest good, according to Aristotle?

(A) Farrah signed up for monthly payroll deduction to Oxfam during an employee charitable competition because she wanted to increase her chances of winning the raffle.

(B) Lakeisha gave peanut butter packets to a homeless woman at the corner because she worried the woman would steal if she was hungry.

(C) Jordan donated to a micro-lending site because he was guaranteed to get his money back.

(D) Jasmine never had extra money to donate, but noticed that new hires frequently could not afford to dress professionally. She worried they would not be promoted without proper dress, so organized a professional clothing drive for her company.

(E) Madison donated end-of-year excess of her department's F&O budget to a University charity, because if she did not expend it, upper administration would sweep the funds for the next year, and not allocate the funds in future years.

7. Advocates of wind energy are hailing a recent study on the health benefits of nearby wind turbines. The study found annual carbon dioxide emissions were reduced by 490,000 tons because of wind-generated power. Scientists working on the study estimate that is the equivalent of pollution from 94,000 automobiles. The study also determined wind power reduced sulfur oxide emissions, typically associated with fossil-fuel-fired energy plants, by 201 tons and nitrogen oxide emissions by 123 tons. But some have criticized the impact of wind farming on mountain communities, especially, and have argued that wind energy developers should be required to file a decommissioning plan for any grid-scale development and provide a performance bond to guarantee the funding for decommissioning when a project no longer produces power. Therefore, the future for wind energy....

Which one of the following most logically completes the argument?

(A) looks promising for growth but its efficacy remains contingent on community good will

(B) is questionable due to its potential for worse environmental consequences than its proponents advertise

(C) will probably remain less popular than other types of energy sources

(D) requires that purely technical problems be solved before it can succeed

(E) depends on whether wind energy produces a net reduction in environmental degradation

GO TO THE NEXT PAGE

8. The increase in sales of electric and hybrid vehicles in the US during the Great Recession was largely due to buyers who had never purchased a hybrid or electric vehicle taking advantage of the "Cash for Clunkers" program. In recent years, the shift towards owning hybrid and electric vehicles has reversed, and this trend should continue. The new oil boom has ensured that large gas and diesel vehicles are back on top of the market, and the US dependency on fossil fuels guarantees that new car owners will continue to gravitate towards gas vehicles over the next 10 years.

Which one of the following, if true, would most seriously weaken the argument?

(A) Adults aged 18-24 have experienced the steepest decline in vehicle ownership since the beginning of the Great Recession.

(B) Car ownership in general has declined over the past 3 years.

(C) New technology will undoubtedly make entirely new energy options available in the auto industry over the next 10 years.

(D) The Big Three US auto companies will be pushing hybrid technology more than ever in the near future.

(E) Gas prices will once again soar in the US to above $5/gallon in the next three years.

9. Body cameras are becoming an indispensable tool for law enforcement throughout the country, and communities ought to invest in them whenever they have the resources to do so. Body cameras help prevent misinterpretations about the work of police officers, clarify the events at chaotic crime scenes, and protect the public interest in maintaining integrity in the law enforcement sector. Municipalities have a vested interest in preventing misinterpretations, clarifying chaotic events, and protecting the public interest.

Which one of the following most accurately expresses the main conclusion of the argument?

(A) The obligations of law enforcement may be impeded if they attempt to pursue the public good without the use of body cameras.

(B) Evolving best practices for law enforcement agents include using body cameras in as many scenarios as possible.

(C) Law enforcement personnel sometimes neglect to adequately consider the risk of pursuing the public good without the use of body cameras.

(D) Whenever possible, municipalities should refrain from interpreting evidence from law enforcement when it is obtained without the use of body cameras.

(E) The use of body cameras can be an effective way of ensuring integrity in law enforcement.

LOGICAL REASONING
SECTION 3

10. The pace of game in baseball (from pitchers shaking off signals to batters dancing in and out of the batter's box) has led to a now-common complaint that the length of the game has eroded the number of true baseball fans. Purists of the sport contend that the game should be left alone, and that changes to the structure of the game will irrevocably harm the sport. But, a century ago, purists complained that changes should not be made to the number of batters in a line-up or a manager's ability to pinch hit or run; yet those changes ensured baseball's success into a new century. So, contemporary baseball should integrate slight shifts to strengthen the sport and the fanbase.

The reference to the complaint of purists a century ago plays which of the following roles in the argument?

(A) evidence to support the claim that the changes to the game of baseball will fundamentally destroy the sport

(B) an illustration of the general hypothesis advanced, that the nature of the game of baseball is inseparable from the desires that purists of the sport have for it

(C) an example of a cultural view that itself changed without a further detrimental effect on the game of baseball overall

(D) evidence that it is unwarranted to claim that baseball's fanbase is eroding due to changes in the game's structure

(E) possible evidence, mentioned and then dismissed, that might be cited by supporters of the purists' view that the passage criticizes

11. In 1995, when the Women's National Basketball Association (WNBA) was created, no one—not even its financial backers—believed the league would survive more than two decades. Each year of its existence, experts in sports media and sports marketing warned that there was not a fanbase sufficient enough to keep the WNBA alive in cities like Tulsa, Minnesota, and San Antonio. Yet, the WNBA persists in the US with two conferences, a loyal fanbase, and average league attendance per game of 7500 fans.

Which one of the following, if true, most helps to explain the difference between the predicted success of the WNBA, and the continued persistence of the WNBA today?

(A) Experts in marketing and the media are mostly familiar with male fanbases, but the WNBA has a higher female:male ratio than other major sports.

(B) Corporate sponsorship of major sports has decreased overall since 1995, except for sponsorship of basketball, which has slightly increased.

(C) The league has adapted to market factors by placing teams in cities with high participation of women in high school and college sports, moving to smaller stadiums to maximize the fan experience, and attracting male NBA talent to serve as coaches.

(D) Tulsa and San Antonio lost their WNBA teams in the last decade, but those teams relocated to popular tourist destinations, Dallas and Las Vegas.

(E) The WNBA was the first of the major sports leagues to adopt the practice of placing sponsor logos on the front and back of their jerseys.

GO TO THE NEXT PAGE

12. First generation college students do not have a parent who graduated from college. In our first generation student group on our campus (R), half of the group are transfer students (T) from a nearby community college (C). (That mirrors the student population of campus R as a whole, which is comprised of 50% of T students from C and other universities.) All the students from C end up becoming T students when they graduate, and the percentage of other, non-T student populations in the first generation student group are negligible compared to that of the T students, it follows that there are twice as many T students from C on campus R than T students from any other university.

The conclusion of the argument follows logically if which one of the following is assumed?

(A) T students from any campus only transfer once.

(B) T students are not as strong academically as traditional students.

(C) All of the C students become T students at R when they graduate.

(D) None of the students at C are first-generation college students.

(E) It is easier to transfer to R than to be admitted as a traditional college student because of articulation agreements between R and C.

13. If you've ever fried an egg on a hot sidewalk in Texas, you know that the albumen heats up, expands, and quickly is cooked to the firm whiteness you would expect of a restaurant-quality egg. The yolk, however, might or might not firm up to an over-medium state, even if the surface temperature is 180 degrees. But, frying an egg on a stovetop always cooks the yolk to an over-medium state at 180 degrees. The only conclusion that can be made is that the single most important aspect of cooking an egg is the type of cooking surface being used.

Which one of the following, if true, most seriously weakens the argument?

(A) Frying eggs on a hot Texas sidewalk almost always cooks the yolk as well as the albumen.

(B) The yolk on an egg cooked on a stovetop will not reach an over-medium state if air conditioning is being used in the kitchen.

(C) A pancake cooked on a stovetop will cook more slowly than a Texas sidewalk that is a hotter temperature than the stovetop.

(D) Eggs that are cooked on a Texas sidewalk taste even better than eggs cooked on a stovetop.

(E) Frying an egg on a Texas sidewalk allows cooler, condensed air from nearby landscaping to circulate around the top surface of the egg, which creates inconsistent temperature surrounding the egg.

GO TO THE NEXT PAGE

LOGICAL REASONING
SECTION 3

14. A new form has been developed for the upcoming census. The form requires that residents of a dwelling indicate their citizenship status—a policy not enacted since Eisenhower. The changes are justified because the new form will allow each state to better meet the social service needs of its citizens and residents by predicting population growth of various demographic groups.

Which one of the following is an assumption that would allow the conclusion above to be properly drawn?

(A) The percentage of people across demographic groups who participate in the census will remain mostly unchanged from the last census.

(B) The likelihood that significant policy changes will result from the census is minute.

(C) No census form can accurately help municipalities, states, and the federal government predict social service needs of their residents.

(D) Population groups that need social services will be motivated to indicate their citizenship status on the new census form.

(F) The majority of demographic groups trust that their participation in the census benefits them and leads to positive public policy changes.

15. Ethicist: Every moral action must maximize positive utility, which often increases well-being of the agent, as well as the chances for good relationships with others. But not all actions that strive for positive utility are personally beneficial to the agent. Rather, attempts to achieve overall positive utility can decrease the chances that an agent has to seek out actions that solely benefit her. If an agent is unable to seek out actions that benefit her, she is harmed, and those around her may suffer from a lack of a feeling of well-being.

Which one of the following most accurately expresses the main conclusion of the ethicist's argument?

(A) If an action taken to secure the overall positive utility fails to enhance the welfare of the agent herself, that action cannot be morally permissible as a whole.

(B) Some agential actions that seek to maximize utility fail to be beneficial to the individual herself

(C) The only actions that are morally acceptable for a utilitarian are those in which the public good is promoted as well as the private interests of the moral agent.

(D) All agents in fact seek positive utility and their own feeling of well-being.

(E) It may be morally permissible to minimize positive utility for the public good, if it maximizes individual utility and a sense of well-being for the agent's loved ones.

GO TO THE NEXT PAGE

16. Rupp: Almost all eyewitness testifiers of violent crime believe that they can provide expert testimony about what happened during the event, but Innocence Project researchers have demonstrated that 73% of 239 convictions for violent crime overturned through DNA testing were based on eyewitness testimony. Eyewitness testimony should only be taken as defeasible evidence.

Whatley: We use inductive reasoning, based on empirical evidence, every day. In fact, we would not be able to find our cars, do our jobs, navigate a strange city, or have this conversation without epistemic belief in our senses. Our senses tell us the truth about most of the most important aspects of lived experience.

Based on their above statements, which of the following statements below is one which Rupp and Whatley would disagree?

(A) Data would show that 73% of things we believe to be true based on the senses is not true.

(B) Scientists can determine whether 73% of information we learn through the senses comes through visual content.

(C) Science itself is based on empiricism, and so should only be taken as providing defeasible claims.

(D) Most eyewitness testimony in non-stressful situations leads to true belief about our everyday lives and so should not be met with skepticism.

(E) If defeasible evidence can be shown to be false, the majority of claims made by police officers involved in crime scenes can be shown to be false as well.

17. City Manager: The risk management consultants we hired indicated that we are particularly vulnerable to a potential terrorist attack of our water main. Although most big cities could face this risk, since our city provides water for the entirety of the southern region of the state, millions of people would be in danger. Based on their report, I move to make shoring up the main our top priority.

The City Manager's argument is most susceptible to which of the following criticisms?

(A) The argument confuses what leads to a problem with how to appropriately solve a problem.

(B) The argument relies on view of experts, who may not have broad enough expertise to support the conclusion of the argument.

(C) The argument assumes that a relationship between two events means that one event is the cause of the other.

(D) The argument makes a faulty inference based on too small of a sample size.

(E) The argument reasons that a characteristic of a large system is also a characteristic of a smaller institution.

GO TO THE NEXT PAGE

18. To achieve a synergic relationship between robots and human workers, it is important that robotic technologies can seamlessly interact, collaborate, and be efficiently operated by human workers. Besides, the uptick of information and communication technology (ICT) systems is growing rapidly, and automated and robotic technologies should be capable of harmoniously interconnecting with these ICT tools, such as Building Information Modelling (BIM). More than 200 prototypes of construction robots have been developed since the 1980s, but very few have been commercialized and widely used.

Which of the following statements is best supported by the above information?

(A) Most engineers who are hesitant to embrace robotic technology violate best practices of the field.

(B) Innovation in the ICT field is falling behind other technology fields it should be dominating, and the impact is felt most in manufacturing.

(C) Evidence suggests that the development of construction robots has been hampered by the fear that robots will take over American jobs.

(D) Engineers will need to innovate for decades to make up the gap between the needs of ICT and BIM.

(E) Expansion of robotic technologies is needed for technologically-intensive fields, such as space exploration.

19. Criminologist: The majority of drugs purchased online are sent through the mail, which leads to the potential for the sale of fake drugs. Most of these shipments are subjected to standard border control mechanism, including X-rays and drug-sniffing dogs. But neither the FDA nor U.S. Immigration and Customs Enforcement know what percentage of fake drugs are actually checked or confiscated every year, because officials seize drugs only if they are both suspicious and likely to affect a large number of people. Clearly, stopping the scourge of fake medications would, at a minimum, require a great deal of cooperation among more than a handful of nations.

Each of the following, if true, strengthens the criminologist's argument *EXCEPT:*

(A) Countries are not under pressure to pass more formal legislation or to enforce preexisting statutes and often have incentives not to.

(B) Since 2011, countries can sign informal treaties to criminalize pharmaceutical fraud within their borders.

(C) Policy experts believe to raise the standards for pharmaceuticals worldwide, we need a similar system that penalizes countries that don't enforce medicinal quality controls.

(D) The World Health Organization hosts conferences in which countries meet to discuss what they can do together to reduce the number of falsified pharmaceuticals reaching patients.

(E) Some pharmaceutical companies have tried to expand the fight against falsified drugs solely to protect their intellectual properties.

20. Faculty member: Each student in the sociology class could choose which final project they were going to pursue: a written exam, an oral exam, a service learning project, or a research paper. The class was clearly opposed to the research paper option. Out of the 200 students in the course, 20 chose the research paper. Almost 140 students chose to take the written exam. Of the remaining students, 90% were sociology majors. Clearly, the students who took the written final were not sociology majors.

Of the following, which one most accurately describes the faculty member's strategy of argumentation?

(A) casts doubt on the justification for the conclusion based on the claim that the statistical sample does not represent all of the students in class

(B) questions a claim supported by statistical data by arguing that statistical data can be manipulated to support whatever view the interpreter wants to support

(C) attempts to refute an argument by showing that whether students were majors or non-majors, the distribution results could not be guaranteed

(D) criticizes a view on the grounds that the view is based on evidence that is in principle impossible to disconfirm

(E) makes an inference based on the distribution of students to final projects, on the grounds that non-majors were more likely to take the written final

21. All Honda vehicles are extremely reliable. All Lego vehicles are rarely reliable. Each of Sunay's vehicles are built with some Honda parts and some Lego parts. Therefore, Sunay's vehicles are moderately reliable.

Which one of the following uses flawed reasoning that most closely resembles the flawed reasoning used in the argument above?

(A) All medical doctors worth their salt went to school for a long time. But some medical doctors who aren't worth their salt did not go to school for a long time. Justine sometimes participates in school activities with gusto. Therefore, Justine sometimes thinks she will go to school for a long time.

(B) All ocean water is non-potable. All fresh water is potable. This water bottle contains a mixture of ocean water and fresh water, and so is moderately potable.

(C) All Air Force brats eventually move to England. All Army brats eventually move to Germany. Some Hernandez family members were in the Air Force and in the Army, and so some Hernandez family members live in England and some live in Germany.

(D) All mechanics know how to change oil. All philosophers know how to be a gadfly. Almeida has worked as a mechanic and as a philosopher. Therefore, Almeida knows how to change oil and how to be a gadfly.

(E) Grade A beans are sold by Bee Grocers. Grade Z beans are sold by Gross Co Grocers. Half of the beans in this barrel are Grade A, and half of the beans in this barrel are Grade Z, so half of the beans in this barrel are from Bee Grocers and half of them are from Gross Co Grocers.

GO TO THE NEXT PAGE

22. Adult child: My mom constantly worries about me becoming a diabetic because she thinks I eat too much sugar. But she has not done the research, which instead suggests that eating sugar before lunch and avoiding it after lunch has a negligible impact on diabetes rates in America. I do not eat sugar after lunch, so my risk for contracting diabetes is extremely low.

The reasoning in the adult child's argument is most vulnerable to criticism on the grounds that this argument:

(A) infers a cause from a mere correlation

(B) relies on a sample that is too narrow

(C) misinterprets evidence, by thinking a result is likely as evidence that the result is certain

(D) mistakes a condition sufficient for bringing about a result for a condition necessary for doing so

(E) relies on a source that is probably not well-informed

23. Court filing: A funeral home suffered a fire loss and was denied an insurance claim. An investigator got video to the National Insurance Crime Bureau (NICB) by uploading security footage onto an internet-based file-sharing site; the site then emailed NICB a link to the online folder containing the file. Neither folder nor video file was password protected, which meant that anyone with the URL could access the video file or folder on the internet. What began as an arson liability court case became one that involved the sharing of confidential information.

Which one of the following questions is best supported as the key question generated by the court filing?

(A) Is the file-sharing site legally liable for being a repository for privileged information?

(B) Should the insurer's lawyers be disqualified for accessing information investigators placed on a public server?

(C) Does the State Bar have an obligation to report ethics violations from insurer lawyers?

(D) Were attorney-client privilege and work product protections for the claim file waived by the way the insurer shared the file online?

(E) Does the insurer owe on a fire loss based on arson and other grounds?

LOGICAL REASONING
SECTION 3

24. Virtue Ethicist: An action is virtuous if it is the mean disposition between two vices, and is morally valuable because it contributes to human flourishing. An action is vicious if it is exhibits a character trait that is too deficient or in excess of virtue. Vicious action tends not to be morally valuable because it diminishes human flourishing. Thus, an action is also virtuous if it is not too deficient nor too excessive of virtue.

The virtue ethicist's conclusion follows logically if which one of the following is assumed?

(A) Only vicious actions would reasonably be expected to reduce the aggregate flourishing of the people impacted by them.

(B) It is epistemically indeterminate whether any action could both be virtuous and vicious.

(C) Any action that is not morally vicious is morally virtuous.

(D) There are actions that would we could reasonably expect to neither be valued nor disvalued morally.

(E) Only actions which lead to human flourishing ought to be performed.

25. Editorial: Most fans today still get their sports through a TV screen. They focus on a team first and their favorite players second. Yet as data-intensified games and fantasy sports gambling catches fire, the interest of mass-market fans will increasingly become all about players' data. Teams will seem like a means to an end--a way for players to perform so they generate data. The next generation of fans will be glued to individual players-or, more precisely, to the mountains of data that will be generated by their performance. We will arrive at a sports world where we don't even care what uniform a player wears; we'll just want to ogle his or her data.

The reasoning above conforms most closely to which one of the following propositions?

(A) The next generation of sports fan will be more data-driven than today, and will see loyalty to a sports figure as increasing their own bottom line.

(B) Sports teams have already seen the monetary value of individualizing the fan experience, and are enthusiastic for fans to be loyal to individual players.

(C) Sports marketing executives aim to create experiences that will appeal to specific market niches.

(D) In the future, sports will be unappealing if fans are not consulted during its metamorphosis.

(E) Fans are consumers, whose input impacts external rather than internal design components of the sports fan experience.

END OF SECTION

IF YOU FINISH BEFORE THE TIME ENDS, YOU MAY CHECK YOUR WORK ONLY ON THIS SECTION.
DO NOT GO TO ANY OTHER SECTION IN THE TEST.

STOP

259

LOGICAL REASONING
SECTION 4

25 QUESTIONS
35 MINUTES

Directions: The questions in this section are based on the reasoning contained in brief statements or passages. For some questions, more than one of the choices could conceivably answer the question. However, you are to choose the **best** answer; that is, the response that most accurately and completely answers the question. You should not make assumptions that are by commonsense standards implausible, superfluous, or incompatible with the passage. After you have chosen the best answer, blacken the corresponding space on your answer sheet.

Questions 1 through 25

1. Heidegger believed in an "alethic" conception of truth for aesthetics—that art reveals true being. The Student Government president is using Heidegger's view to argue that the University mascot should attend final exams to motivate students to perform well, in keeping with their identity as students of this university.

   This passage raises which of the following questions?

   (A) Can a student accurately apply Heidegger's aesthetics?

   (B) What truth about student life does a mascot at final exams represent?

   (C) Would Heidegger have presaged a student movement to use aesthetics to self-identify with a university brand?

   (D) To what extent are mascots representative of an identity relation?

   (E) What aspect of true being does a mascot represent for students?

2. My mom insists that I gargle with lemon if I feel a sore throat coming on. She believes that the acid in the juice burns the germs, and the vitamins bolster the immune system by being absorbed by the throat lining.

   Which one of the following assumptions, if true, supports the mother's argument above?

   (A) Bacteria that cause the throat to swell cause inflammation in other areas of the body and need to be treated immediately.

   (B) Healthy bacteria that line the esophagus are killed off when they come in direct contact with citric acid.

   (C) Absorption of vitamin C by moist tissue, when accompanied by ascorbic acid, is essential to strengthening the lining of tissue against harmful bacteria.

   (D) A sore throat is typically the first sign of a significant infection, which will migrate to other parts of the body if immediate interventions are not taken.

   (E) Over time, gargling regularly with lemons builds up the body's immune system to become resistant to negative bacteria that can cause common colds.

GO TO THE NEXT PAGE

LOGICAL REASONING
SECTION 4

3. Anthropologist: The moral issue of human deception, lying and duplicity is invariably an embodied play between the surface and depth of the skin and flesh. As a symbolic medium, the body can be divided between an interior and an exterior, where the interior is mostly a space associated with privacy and secrets. The act of hiding a thought, a design, a speech, even in constituting the dimension of the unsaid, constitutes an 'interiority', an abstract mental region superadded to the image of the carnal inside. the act of hiding disjoins the said and unsaid, then buries the unsaid in the corporeal space, that secret place of intention, unavowed thought, the dark seat of designs gets hollowed out. Interiority is the result of a divorcing action.

Which of the following, if true, would most strengthen the anthropologist's view?

(A) Agents are often self-deceived about whether their own statements are true or false.

(B) The truth or falsity of a claim is less about agreement with reality outside of the mind, and more about the phenomenological, lived experiences of truth.

(C) Agents who are good at deceiving others use means of measuring truth that are consistently more reliable than agents who consistently tell the truth.

(D) Unavowed thought is epistemically unknowable, so is not a good representation for the truth.

(E) It is a category mistake to qualify the interior life of the mind with moral predicates.

4. What is the nature of children's trust in testimony? Is it based primarily on evidential correlations between statements and facts, or does it derive from an interest in the trustworthiness of particular speakers? Recent work shows that, from an early age, children monitor the reliability of particular informants, differentiate between those who make true and false claims and keep that differential accuracy in mind when evaluating new information from these people. This selective trust is likely to involve the mentalistic appraisal of speakers rather than surface generalizations of their behavior, that challenges a purely inductive account of trust.

Which one of the following, if true, would count as evidence against the scholar's explanation of children's mentalist appraisal of testifiers?

(A) Children learn from formative past experiences that testimony usually corresponds with the facts, which can, via induction, be trusted on those occasions when the relevant facts cannot be checked.

(B) Children are sensitive to whether informants have proved accurate in the past and this affects their subsequent trust in that informant.

(C) Children may not be filtering their general experience of language to arrive at an expectation that testimony is reliable in some general sense.

(D) Children's surprisingly careful attention to the individual source of a given claim highlights the importance of social cognition in early trust.

(E) Developmental evidence demonstrates that generalized credulity in testifiers is not true of young children, even infants.

261

GO TO THE NEXT PAGE

LOGICAL REASONING
SECTION 4

5. If you've been around a college softball team, you know all softball players love to play cards. But, their locker-mates, the track team, are so serious that they never play cards. Part of the issue might be that everyone who plays cards loves to joke around when they play.

Which one of the following most logically completes the argument?

(A) Everyone who runs track loves to play cards but they do not during track season.

(B) No one who really likes to joke around plays cards.

(C) Track team members do not like to joke around.

(D) Track team members love to joke around but not around the softball team.

(E) Softball players only joke around when they are playing cards because they are less serious than their locker-mates.

6. If you skydive for the first time, your instructor will be disinclined to let you jump alone, and will instead counsel you to try a tandem jump. Tandem jumps allow you to jump from a significantly higher distance, create a longer freefall, and let you have enough time to attempt somersaults, spins, and other tricks first-timers would not be allowed to attempt on a jump. It's also true that tandem jumpers outnumber straight-line jumpers by 68% over time, which suggests the enduring popularity, and intrinsic enjoyment, of tandem skydives.

Which one of the following, if true, would most seriously weaken the argument?

(A) Skydive instructors earn a commission off of tandem jumps but not off of straight-line jumps.

(B) When given the options, most novice jumpers believe that tandem dives sound more fun.

(C) The percentage of injuries from tandem jumps is significantly higher than those from straight-line jumps.

(D) Straight-line divers tend to be more athletic, take greater risks, and are more experienced divers than divers who jump tandem.

(E) 80% of people who skydive only jump once in their lives, and their decision is most heavily influenced by the experience promised to them by their jump instructor.

7. Jorge: "Why didn't you include Luciana's submission in the gallery opening?" Kyana: "Because the submission was not of sufficient quality to be in the opening."

Kyana's response to Jorge commits which type of logical fallacy?

(A) evidential absence, which concludes that an opinion is false because there hasn't been evidence provided to prove it

(B) straw man, in which the speaker argues against a view her interlocutor did not make

(C) conditional logic flaw, that mistakes necessary for sufficient conditions

(D) circular reasoning, that begs the question

(E) temporal flaw, which assumes certainty that the future will resemble the past

GO TO THE NEXT PAGE

LOGICAL REASONING
SECTION 4

8. "Do no harm" is a self-evident principle, but these terms aren't obvious. Is it an absolute statement or a general, all-things-being equal statement? If taken as an absolute statement this isn't self-evident at all, and is, in fact patently false: if I trip, punch, or tie up someone attempting to kill my family, I harm him, and few would think this is wrong. So the words, "do no harm" must mean *generally*, or, *all things being equal*. Self-evident principles are obvious, beyond doubt when the terms are properly understood and, like moral virtues, good in and off themselves. But, arguments that use moral principles are fallible, debatable, and less valuable than self-evident principles themselves.

    The reference to the use of moral principles by the author plays which of the following roles in the argument?

    (A) contrast for the value of self-evidence and virtues, such that moral principles are valuable only for what they bring about

    (B) proof to support the claim that the principle "do no harm" is a general principle

    (C) a demonstration that absolute moral principles are logically and pragmatically flawed

    (D) an illustration of the general hypothesis advanced, that the nature of morality is that it always guides real-world decision making

    (E) an example of a social practice that has evolved over time without having a negative impact on social interaction

9. Situation: When we meet cannibalistic hunters in zombie comics, there are two laws in conflict: "Preserve one's own life," and "Don't kill innocent people."

    Analysis: Cannibals always face competing obligations, since the only way to preserve their own life is through killing innocent people so they can eat them.

    The analysis provided for the situation above would be most appropriate in which one of the following situations?

    (A) Doctors without Borders requires American physicians in private practice who travel with them to contribute to the cost of their medical trips abroad, which suggests American medical practices get rich off of sick people's suffering.

    (B) Some defense attorneys switch to prosecution because they do not feel comfortable defending clients who admit to them that they committed heinous crimes.

    (C) Conscientious objectors believe the oath of military service could contradict itself, if the oath of allegiance to defend the Constitution conflicts with the oath to obey the orders of the President of the United States.

    (D) Some who believe the sanctity of life is the fundamental legal and ethical principle also believe that capital punishment is appropriate punishment for guilty people responsible for the worst sorts of crimes.

    (E) Friends who discover their friends are cheating typically feel compelled to tell their partners about the adultery even when they promise not to disclose the infidelity.

GO TO THE NEXT PAGE

LOGICAL REASONING
SECTION 4

10. When her parents financially cut her off, Kristie decided to try her hand at ultimate couponing to save money. When she left the store after her weekly shopping trip, she found out she spent more money than she did prior to using coupons.

Each of the following, if true, helps to explain why Kristie spent more money, mentioned above, *EXCEPT*:

(A) Kristie's coupons were for items she did not ordinarily buy.

(B) The store Kristie shops at raises the prices each week on items that are discounted by the coupons.

(C) The store was out of the brands that Kristie had coupons for, so she had to purchase the name brands of those items.

(D) Kristie splurged on items she ordinarily would not have because of the cost savings of the coupons

(E) The coupons Kristie used could not be combined with any other offer.

11. Joel: Tony Romo is one of the best quarterbacks of all time, and one of the top three Cowboys players ever. He's a 4-time Pro Bowler...I cannot wait until he is inducted into the Hall of Fame!

Jill: Keep dreaming. Romo only won two playoff games ever and never advanced past the divisional round. If he's one of the best Cowboys, what does that say about the Cowboys?

Which one of the following most accurately expresses the point at issue between Joel and Jill?

(A) whether Tony Romo meets the sufficient conditions to be inducted into the Hall of Fame as one of the best quarterbacks ever

(B) whether Tony Romo is one of the best quarterbacks of all time and one of the top three Cowboys ever

(C) whether playoff wins indicate success at the quarterback position

(D) whether being to the Pro Bowl multiple times is sufficient to induct a quarterback into the Hall of Fame

(E) whether the fact that Tony Romo is one of the best Cowboys players of all time is sufficient to induct him into the Hall of Fame

12. George: I can't believe you set me up with a woman who is bald!

Elaine: You are wearing a toupee. Do you see the irony here? You're rejecting someone because they are bald. YOU'RE BALD!

George: No... I was bald.

The dialogue between Elaine and George provides the most support for holding that they would disagree about the permissibility of which one of the following?

(A) Gustavo purchased two blocks of land from Bernadette for the purpose of sheep farming. During negotiations, Bernadette said that if the place was worked properly, it would carry 2,000 sheep. (Bernadette had never carried on sheep-farming on the land.) Gustavo bought the place believing that it would carry 2,000 sheep.

(B) Mac was forced into bankruptcy and put his hotel up for sale, stating that it was already let to a 'most desirable tenant'. The Millers agreed to buy the hotel, but then discovered that the tenant was bankrupt.

(C) Miles owns a popular low-carb bakery and wants to take over the space currently occupied by an Italian restaurant next door. When his neighbor will not sell to him, Miles creates fake social media profiles and posts negative online feedback for the Italian restaurant, which eventually leads to its closing.

(D) Trantham owns two hair salons and agreed to sell one to Keegan, in part because Trantham told Keegan that we was moving abroad and did not intend to work in the second salon. But, Trantham continued to work at the second salon and most of his clients followed him, leaving Keegan without a customer base.

(E) Prior to purchasing a parcel of land, Elisa asked the seller's lawyer if there were any restrictive covenants on the land and the lawyer said he did not know of any. Little did Elisa know that the lawyer had not bothered to read the documents.

GO TO THE NEXT PAGE

13. Scientist: The essence of our efficacy as scientists is credibility, which comes through a commitment to the scientific method. Recently, some scientists, in a race to be the first to make a breathtaking discovery, have skipped important repeatability steps that are required to remain credible. We need to hold each other accountable to uphold the method to preserve truth. Our mission is not just a commitment to the method—it's a commitment to the public trust to preserve and communicate truth. We cannot be driven by a desire for fame or patents. Otherwise, we are mercenaries.

Which one of the following criticisms would most weaken the passage's contention that scientists' mission is to uphold the public trust?

(A) There isn't just one truth for science to preserve, which allows specialization across fields in science, technology, engineering, and math.

(B) The reason the scientific method requires repeatability is because scientific truths are defeasible.

(C) The mission of academic scientists is to land research grants that allow continued research, rather than the preservation of truth.

(D) A scientist only needs to be responsible, rather than credible.

(E) There is nothing illegal about being a mercenary, or about profiting off of scientific innovation.

14. What if the early settlers of our country just said, "I quit."? They faced starvation, disease, death on a daily basis and still managed to carve a country out of the wilderness with zero government assistance, National Healthcare, MRE's, GPS, Bug Out vehicles, or smart phones. We come from those same people who braved the elements, sailed across seas for months and landed in a foreign land with not much more than the clothes on their backs.

Which one of the following uses flawed reasoning that most closely resembles the flawed reasoning used in the argument above?

(A) What can I tell you? She grew up in Detroit, so of course she would believe that Fords are the best vehicles in America.

(B) Ruth's father was a Lutheran minister, she was raised in the Lutheran church, and was confirmed as a Lutheran in the 8th grade. She is bound to be committed to some Lutheran causes and so isn't the best person to give you an objective opinion.

(C) Kara really drank the Kool-Aid when she went to her university. Whether we're talking about the school's crazy traditions, the residence life, the motto, or the fight song, she was a dedicated student and alum. Since you are an alumnus from a rival school, you shouldn't date her.

(D) Susan holds a meeting to discuss reducing discrimination against women at the company. Men are invited to the meeting but are not allowed to contribute to the discussion.

(E) Alenia often makes hasty decisions because she usually fails to stop and consider the consequences of her choices.

GO TO THE NEXT PAGE

15. If Sofie does not study for her constitutional law class, she is likely to lose her spot as the top student in the course. In that case, either the professor will be unlikely to write her a letter of recommendation or she will have to grovel to do additional research for the professor to earn back her good graces. But if the professor declines to write her a letter of recommendation, Sofie will have a difficult time getting into law school. Moreover, Sofie can avoid losing a chance at getting into law school only if she grovels to do additional research.

Which one of the following statements follows logically from the statements above?

(A) If Sofie has to grovel to do additional research, the amount of studying she will have to do for her constitutional law course will continue to increase.

(B) If Sofie will not be able to get into law school, either it will because she did not get a letter of recommendation or because she did not grovel to do additional research.

(C) Sofie's best chance at getting into law school is to study for constitutional law.

(D) Sofie cannot study for constitutional law without sacrificing her spot at the top of the class.

(E) Either Sofie will have to study for constitutional law or Sofie will lose her spot at the top of the class.

16. Jones runs a center against domestic violence, and promotes the center through "art against violence" theatre and gallery galas. She believes that engaging the public through art—especially art that does not shy away from the realities of domestic abuse—will facilitate community dialogue about domestic violence and better prevention techniques as a whole. Youth, especially, enjoy participating in the galas and their parents often accompany them to Jones's events.

Which one of the following propositions is best illustrated by the passage?

(A) The best way to educate the community about domestic violence prevention is through art.

(B) Dialogue about difficult topics is necessary.

(C) Youth benefit the most from using art to facilitate conversation about potential crime.

(D) Using unconventional means to communicate truth about difficult topics can have a lasting impact that can prevent future harm.

(E) Centers that have youth and parental support are much more likely to be effective in the community.

GO TO THE NEXT PAGE

LOGICAL REASONING
SECTION 4

17. Political Scientist: Proclamation 3447 signed by President Kennedy on Feb. 3, 1962, established the embargo against Cuba to reduce "the threat posed by its alignment with the communist powers." The embargo was strengthened by the Cuban Liberty and Democratic Solidarity (Libertad) Act of 1996 which specified conditions for terminating the embargo. According to US law, Cuba must legalize all political activity, release all political prisoners, commit to free and fair elections in the transition to representative democracy, grant freedom to the press, respect internationally recognized human rights, and allow labor unions. The US should maintain the Cuba embargo because Cuba has not met the conditions required to lift it.

Which one of the following most accurately expresses the main conclusion of the political scientist's argument?

(A) Ending the Cuba embargo before Cuba meets the conditions specified by US law would make the United States look weak.

(B) The US can terminate the Cuba embargo only when specified conditions specified by US law are met.

(C) The Cuba embargo enables the United States to apply pressure on Cuba to improve its human rights and political repression record.

(D) Given that Cuba persists in the behaviors that led to the embargo, the United States cannot consistently lift it.

(E) Cuba should continue to be subject to sanctions because it is known to have repeatedly supported acts of terrorism.

18. Egoist: A psychological fact about humans is that they always act in their own self-interest. Even individuals who give of themselves do so because they benefit in some way from it. The result is that all actions are motivated by self-interest and, so, are capricious.

Which one of the following most accurately describes a flaw in the egoist's argument above?

(A) The argument assumes, without providing justification, that if an act is not motivated out of self-interest, it is capricious.

(B) The argument overlooks the fact that an action need not be capricious simply because the agent benefits from performing the action.

(C) The argument begs the question that self-interested actions benefit the agent.

(D) The argument assumes, without providing justification, that actions made from self-interested motivations are always capricious.

(E) The argument overlooks the fact that an agent who acts from a motive of self-interest may nonetheless be dependable.

GO TO THE NEXT PAGE

LOGICAL REASONING
SECTION 4

19. Alejandra needed to hire a new director for Civic Engagement, a post that required a background in grant writing, strong communication skills, and the ability to connect public, private, and educational sectors towards a common goal of more impactful civic engagement for all stakeholders. Brian came from the private sector and was dedicated to creating new partnerships for caring in communities. Mel brought years of experience working for one of the largest cities in the country, and developing their "urban-serving" mission. Alejandra decided the position should go to the person who had the strongest background working in the corporate sector, so she hired Brian instead of Mel.

Alejandra's decision most closely conforms to which one of the following principles?

(A) A direct relationship exists between a candidate's work background and the quality of work you can expect him/her to provide.

(B) Candidates should apply to the position who are more likely to get the most community groups to participate in civic engagement.

(C) Working from the private sector prepares candidates for a position as the Director for Civic Engagement.

(D) The best way for employers to know which candidate is the best fit for them is by researching each candidate's background.

(E) Employers should hire candidates whose backgrounds align with the direction and goals for the organization.

20. Commentator: Eating meat is wreaking havoc on the environment. Cultured meat products from plants can be scaled and may offer something closer to real meat than any other invention in the works. By its nature, it would offer the complex flavors of meat. The problems are many: scientists must figure out how to build intramuscular fat, sinew, cartilage, and even bone, and a structure to mimic veins and blood vessels that will keep the cells fed so they don't become gangrenous. The work is so expensive that the steps forward are likely to come from trying to produce organs for transplant. Despite the challenges, because raising livestock is such an inefficient use of land and water, creating cultured meat alternatives from plants is the best way to improve our environment.

Which one of the following, if true, would most weaken the commentator's argument?

(A) "Clean meat" is grown in a lab from a small amount of animal stem cells, and requires far-fewer resources to develop than plant-based "meat" does.

(B) Even if we can establish that cultured meat can be healthy, many people prefer to eat meat and are willing to pay for it.

(C) Cultured meat products can provide the nutritional equivalent of meat without using land and water resources.

(D) A healthier, better approach is not to make plants that taste like meats, but plants that taste better than meats.

(E) The fractionation process required to culture plants into meat is highly energy intensive.

LOGICAL REASONING
SECTION 4

21. Socrates once said that "all evil is merely ignorance". What could he have meant? He believed that all people seek the good, but many are ignorant of how to pursue and achieve the good. Ignorance can lead people to do the wrong thing to achieve things they believe are good, or are desired. The result is that even the most hardened criminals pursue their evil acts out of ignorance—either ignorance that what they are doing is wrong, or ignorance about how to achieve the good in their lives.

Which one of the following principles, if valid, would most help to justify the passage's argument?

(A) Everything in nature acts according to its best function, so people act according to their best reason.

(B) God created teleologically, so all of human actions tend towards a purpose or goal.

(C) Humans are essentially animals and act to fulfill their base desires.

(D) People only seek the good to avoid punishment for doing the wrong things.

(E) Moral education helps all individuals learn what the good is, and to seek it in the right way.

22. The practical use of lithium-sulfur (LiS) batteries is largely hindered by their poor cycling stability because of the shuttling of soluble lithium polysulfides (LiPSs) in a slow redox reaction. Physical and chemical confinement by carbon or non-carbon hosts has been used to block LiPS shuttling, but this may only be a complete solution to the problem if it combines with LiPS fast conversion into an insoluble sulfide. Here we report a twinborn TiO_2 TiN heterostructure that combines the merits of highly adsorptive TiO_2 with conducting TiN and achieves smooth trapping/diffusion/conversion of LiPSs across the interface. Such an interlayer is expected to promote the practical use of LiS batteries because of the simple processing and the resulting outstanding capacity and cyclic performance. Such a heterostructure suggests a new way to produce multifunctional interlayers that improve the performance of energy storage devices. Therefore, the future for LiS batteries...

Which one of the following most logically completes the argument?

(A) is questionable because current technology results in slow reaction kinetics and low blocking efficiency

(B) looks promising as next-generation energy storage devices but their efficacy remains contingent on developing a more efficient way to restrain LiPS shuttling

(C) requires that LiS batteries diffuse surface carbon substrate away from its conductivity path

(D) is that they will probably remain less popular than other energy sources

(E) depends on whether the public can understand the twinborn heterostructure developed by scientists for better energy absorption rates

GO TO THE NEXT PAGE

23. Sartre: there are irrational values—beauty, charm, and so on. Or rational, if you like, since you can provide an interpretation, a rational explanation. But when you love a person's charm you love something that is irrational, even though ideas and concepts do explain charm at a more intense degree.

The reasoning in the argument is most vulnerable to criticism on the grounds that the argument

(A) confuses an interpretation that requires imagination with an explanation which requires reason

(B) takes for granted that if someone is loved on the basis of a particular characteristic, that love will be communicable through reason

(C) generalizes, from the fact some traits are ephemeral to the fact that they are experienced by most people in the same way

(D) fails to consider the possibility that beauty and charm are rational concepts exactly because they can be explained through ideas

(E) assumes that values that are not concrete are irrational, and so inexplicable, when instead they are knowable through ideas and concepts

24. The research study evaluates the effectiveness of virtual-reality (VR) audio-visual distraction goggles on pain and behavior scores in 8-12 year old dental patients receiving routine dental care. The virtual-reality goggles have a small screen inside of them along with headphones, and plays a movie or cartoon to immerse the patient during treatment. We anticipate a reduction of pain and anxiety levels of up to 80% in pediatric patients, which (though initially pricey) should motivate most pediatric dentistry clinics to use VR devices.

Which one of the following assumptions underlies the argument in the passage above?

(A) The benefits of anxiety-free dental care for pediatric patients are numerous and should be pursued.

(B) The best way for children to overcome their anxiety about dental care is to be distracted from it.

(C) VR technology provides an anxiety-free environment for children receiving dental care.

(D) The possibility of overcoming pain and anxiety for children undergoing dental care outweighs potential risks and costs associated with VR.

(E) VR technology will help lessen the costs associated with children who exhibit anxious behavior in the dentist office.

GO TO THE NEXT PAGE

LOGICAL REASONING
SECTION 4

25. In response to allegations that he knew for years that some of his players were committing sexual assault, the football coach said, "One needs to consider the source of these accusations of my players and the fact that it makes these accusers instant celebrities. Whatever the source, this has nothing to do with football and so nothing to do with me. I do not recollect ever being told about these events prior to them landing on the front page, and whatever trash is in the reports you think I have read—I haven't read them! Why would I read trash, when I have a job to do? It is the athletic director's responsibility to take out the trash, and it is my job to get the boys ready to play on Saturday."

The coach's argument is vulnerable to each of the following criticisms *EXCEPT* which of the following?

(A) He does not consider his own bias in protecting his players.

(B) He takes for granted that the report is the only source of information necessary to make an educated decision about how to respond to assault .

(C) He does not recollect being told about events that he should have a recollection about.

(D) He admits he did not study the report and does not think it is his job to do so.

(E) He takes a side in the dispute—against the purported victims—while claiming he does not have a knowledge base from which to act on the claim.

END OF SECTION

IF YOU FINISH BEFORE THE TIME ENDS, YOU MAY CHECK YOUR WORK ONLY ON THIS SECTION.
DO NOT GO TO ANY OTHER SECTION IN THE TEST.

271

ESSAY WRITING PROMPT | 35 MINUTES

Directions: The scenario presented below describes two choices, either one of which can be supported on the basis of the information given. Your essay should consider both choices and argue for one over the other, based on the two specified criteria and the facts provided. There is no "right" or "wrong" choice: a reasonable argument can be made for either.

The Davis Smith Jones Energy Company wants to take over a large conglomeration of energy-producing power projects in the territory of a Native American tribe, but can only do so if a mediator finds that it can operate the project more effectively than the tribe's current provider, Evans Thud Karns Power. A mediator, Hilborn LLC, is brought in and faces two options in setting up outside environmental studies and negotiating offers between DSJ, ETK, and the tribe: either accept offers from both companies and recommend the decision that best benefits the community; or tell the two companies that the environmental study—rather than community impact-- will determine the mediation recommendation. Using the facts below, write an essay in which you argue for one option over the other based on the following two criteria:

- Hilborn's fundamental loyalty is to the tribal community.

- Hilborn must go to a non-tribal research firm, with a strong anti-energy plant political platform, for the environmental impact study.

Evans Thud Karns currently runs a massive, connected Western Power Company and operates an energy-producing project, composed of a sequence of plants, generators, and reservoirs on tribal land. An environmental study is required for recertification of their work. Hilborn is sure ETK will have the lowest bid. The tribe has an acrimonious relationship with ETK, however, in part because they do not believe that the promised economic benefits have been generated from the original contract. ETK refuses to incorporate findings from prior ethnographic studies into its best practices, it frequently fails to respect the tribe's sacred spaces, and the tribe's water has turned an odd color. More people than ever are employed in the community, however, which has improved the lives of some families.

DSJ has faced its own issues. Although it has been lauded by other communities that have used its services for its clean energy initiatives, it is frequently in court with local governments over its refusal to pay for road damage caused by their equipment. They do not counsel their itinerant workers on off-the-job behavior, which has led to multiple arrests of their workers across several states, and they house their workers in cramped, dirty conditions that would be in violation of non-tribal housing codes. DSJ notoriously has butted heads with Hilborn over its political leanings and DSJ is unsure that Hilborn can provide a fair recommendation to the tribe for its bit. For its part, Hilborn has good reason to suspect DSJ will perform better on the study but is also certain it risks alienating the tribe by not considering community impact into its recommendation.

ANSWER KEY AND EXPLANATIONS

Visit us at: **www.argoprep.com/lsat** for video explanations.

ANSWER KEY FOR THE PRACTICE TEST

SECTION 1 (READING COMPREHENSION)

1.	B	8.	C	15.	B	22.	D
2.	E	9.	B	16.	A	23.	B
3.	E	10.	C	17.	E	24.	D
4.	A	11.	D	18.	E	25.	D
5.	D	12.	E	19.	A	26.	E
6.	D	13.	E	20.	C	27.	C
7.	A	14.	A	21.	C		

SECTION 2 (ANALYTICAL REASONING)

1.	B	8.	A	15.	E	22.	E
2.	A	9.	C	16.	A	23.	B
3.	B	10.	B	17.	B		
4.	E	11.	B	18.	E		
5.	A	12.	C	19.	B		
6.	C	13.	D	20.	D		
7.	E	14.	E	21.	A		

SECTION 3 (LOGICAL REASONING)

1.	B	8.	E	15.	B	22.	A
2.	A	9.	B	16.	E	23.	D
3.	D	10.	C	17.	B	24.	C
4.	A	11.	C	18.	B	25.	A
5.	B	12.	C	19.	A		
6.	D	13.	E	20.	E		
7.	A	14.	D	21.	B		

SECTION 4 (LOGICAL REASONING)

1.	E	8.	A	15.	C	22.	B
2.	C	9.	C	16.	D	23.	E
3.	B	10.	E	17.	D	24.	D
4.	A	11.	A	18.	B	25.	C
5.	C	12.	C	19.	E		
6.	A	13.	B	20.	A		
7.	D	14.	B	21.	A		

READING COMPREHENSION
SECTION 1 ANSWER EXPLANATIONS:

1. **(B).** First, eliminate answers you know are not the main point of the passage. Doing so allows you to eliminate (E) straightaway, since the main point of the passage is not about Kristie Dotson's philosophy. (C) is eliminated because the passage is less interested in Dotson's presentation of literary tropes and more about the methods of philosophy being at odds, or compatible with, each other through her work. That leaves us with (A), (B), and (D). (D) is factually incorrect. Dotson does rely on traditional techniques and can speak both "languages" of the traditions. (A) is not a strong answer, because the main point isn't about whether the use of narrative can effectively enhance analytic philosophy, although the relationship between narrative and analytic philosophy is a component of the main point. The remaining answer, (B) is correct, because the main point of the passage is to use Dotson's philosophy to demonstrate that the two traditions in philosophy do not need to be so divided.

2. **(E).** Analogies rely on the similarity of the two persons, things, or ideas being compared. In this question, the comparison point is with Kristie Dotson's philosophical achievements, so what is most relevant is the uniqueness of her achievements. We know from question #1 that her achievements are distinct because they bridge a divide in philosophical methods that otherwise are rarely brought together. The correct analogy will do the same thing. We can eliminate answers that do not bridge two disparate items that are rarely brought together. (C) and (D) are not correct for this reason. (C) introduces two items that are frequently together (sports and health), and (D) brings together aspects that are not extraordinary when put together (since we know artists frequently reuse designs from past successes). (B) should be eliminated for a different reason—the theologian doesn't bring together two or more different things. You are left with (A) and (E). (A) seems possible; a contemporary mechanic could use old and new school techniques to build a new engine, but those techniques are not as different as the divide that Dotson's work bridges—two methodologies that seem fundamentally different. The best analogy is (E), that of the composer who combines two things rarely heard together in an orchestral piece—opera and jazz.

3. **(E).** This is a straightforward, factual question which only requires a careful attention to the text. The question asks about a widely held view in the United States. The only place in the passage that discusses the deep cultural chasm in the US is in paragraph two. In that paragraph, it isn't true (B) that Continental philosophy is rarely seen as academically serious, and it isn't true (C) that graduate programs exclude training in Continental philosophy. (D) is substantively false, since the dichotomy presented by the text is between the narrative, descriptive methodology of Continental and the rigorous, modal structure of analytic philosophy. And, although (A) is a factually true inference from the text, that analytic philosophy shouldn't involve narratives is not a facet of a belief in the US, but a result of the analytic method itself. (E), then, is the best choice, since the deep chasm is attributable to the idea that pluralist philosophers do not specialize enough in either analytic or Continental philosophy.

4. **(A).** Attitude questions are difficult on the LSAT. Remember to exclude answer choices that are neutral, since attitudes about topics on the LSAT are not neutral. That allows you to exclude (C), since 'ambivalence' means a mixture of feelings that might not be determinate, either positively or negatively. You also can strike extreme answer choices, since the passage does not give off a vibe that is outright positive or negative. That means that (E) is not correct, since astonishment is an extreme feeling of shock or surprise. Now, you are able to see if the remaining answer choices are consistent with the facts of the case. (B) must be avoided, because we know from the text that the divide is largely one of methodological difference, and we are not perplexed that they are seen as so different among philosophers. (D) does not hold up under factual scrutiny, since Kristie Dotson's work is evidence that the divide has been overcome, and she is put up as a model for how to continue to do so. The correct answer, then, is (A), that the author disapproves of the presuppositions that perpetuate the divide in philosophy.

5. **(D).** This question requires an inference to be made about the best cause of the rift between analytic and Continental philosophy in the US. You first can find any answers that are inconsistent with the details within the passage, eliminate them, and then find the best answer remaining. (E) is false, based on the textual evidence, so should be the first answer to be removed from consideration. (C) is clearly ad hoc. The passage does not discuss publishing in philosophy, but even it if did, the fact that publishers want the best from their authors does not

weigh in on the differences between the two philosophical methodologies. (A), similarly, should be eliminated. You know from the passage that the analytic and Continental traditions are different in philosophy, but the text does not reveal clues as to whether the graduate training is different, and if it is, why that could be a source of the tension. (B) is a true inference from the passage, so you must determine whether it sufficiently answers the question. Although philosophers on one side view their work as superior, does that serve as the cause of the divide? Clearly, the feeling of superiority would result from a divide; if the rift was not present, there would not be feelings of superiority. That leaves (D) as the correct choice. A suspicion that a philosopher could not be both an expert and a generalist serves as a cause of the tension between philosophers who only focus on one method and those who borrow from both to build their arguments.

6. **(D).** This question requires you to look at the justification, or reasons that ground, Dotson's conviction that pluralist philosophy is both rigorous and persuasive. First identify answer choices that are not those that Dotson gives towards this conclusion. (A) can immediately be removed as a choice, since nothing in the passage demonstrates that Dotson's academic background is international in character. (C), also, is not supported by the text, despite the fact that the passage focuses on philosophy in the United States. Even if (C) was true, it would not serve as a reason for Dotson to be a pluralist. (E) must also be ignored, because the author never actually provides Dotson's own origin story with regards to opposing strict silos between philosophical methods. That leaves you with (B) and (D), both of which are internally consistent with the passage. Now you need to see which of those three provides the best justification for Dotson to be a pluralist. (B) would be excellent justification if it actually pointed to an experience Dotson had, but since the question specifically points you to the last sentence in the third paragraph, which is solely about the inclusion of philosophy for a diverse range of perspectives, (B) is not a strong candidate. (D), on the other hand, fits the bill. It specifically addresses the voices Dotson would like to have included in philosophy.

7. **(A).** This question requires you to make a logical inference to the best conclusion that is not directly given in the text. You need to use the evidence that is given to you in the text to make a strong inference. The inference should be true, and strongly supported by what is given to you in the passage. To start, you can eliminate inferences that are blatantly false, or that cannot at all be supported by the text. (B) cannot be correct, because you are told that there are pluralist programs in philosophy, and that pluralists are happy when philosophers in either tradition attempt to bridge the gap. (D) is also a false inference, because the passage delineates strengths of both analytic and Continental philosophy, and does not support an inference that either is superior to the other. (E) is an inference that could—but should not—be made. The author simply does not give any evidence to make a conclusion that philosophical pluralists could be aesthetic pluralists. Both (A) and (C) are supportable inferences, and your job is to see which one is the most strongly supported. (C) is not as good of an answer, here, because it sits more squarely on the factual side of the passage, and is less of an inference. You are told that Dotson is a pluralist and uses both methods in her writing. The best answer, then, is (A). Narrative is not typically used in analytic philosophy, but when it is, it communicates truth more effectively (than, for example, a logical proof) to the reader. You would not expect an analytic philosopher to be moved by a feeling invoked by a narrative, but by a sequence of events and truths offered by it.

8. **(C).** Questions that ask you to make predictions are really questions about inferences that can be made based on the evidential clues supplied by the reading. Start by eliminating answers that are not supported by the text, and then identify the most strongly-supported answer choice. From this list, (A), (C), and (E) emerge as the best contenders. (B) is removed because the text is clear that analytic philosophy, even when it integrates narrative, is still analytic philosophy (and Continental philosophy remains Continental even if it integrates more logical rigor than is typical). (D) is not supported by the passage—even if pluralists increase in philosophy, there is no evidence provided that more specialists in either method will emerge. From the three remaining, (C) is the best choice because the text offers evidence from a pluralist that philosophy should give voice to diverse scholars. The implication is that pluralism is itself one way philosophy can be diverse, and that a preeminent philosopher's commitment to diversifying the field will increase the numbers of pluralist philosophers. (A) is not as strong, because although it might be true that, if the number of philosophers remains the same and the number of

READING COMPREHENSION
SECTION 1 ANSWER EXPLANATIONS:

pluralists increases, by volume, the number of those doing analytic philosophy will shrink, you cannot give a prediction as to whether the market need (i.e., the number of jobs in philosophy) will follow suit. Similarly, even if there are more opportunities given to be able to pursue pluralist philosophy, the text does not provide evidence to support the view that the audiences for either analytic or Continental philosophy will diminish.

9. **(B).** In parallel passage texts, careful reading—with an eye towards finding points of contact and points of differences between the texts—is essential. This question requires a main theme for both passages, so remove answer choices that are not true for one of the passages, are not supported by one of them, or are not a main theme of either text. You can eliminate (C), because it is too general of a question. You already know that the main idea of the parallel passages is the role of coercion in Rawls, and this answer choice does not mention coercion. Similarly, although (D) is a question many Rawlsians can debate, it is not about the main idea (and, the main idea is about Rawls's view, and not about Rawlsians). That leaves (A), (B), and (E) as potential choices, from which you need to identify the best solution. (A) seems like a good candidate, but careful reading of the second passage shows that its author believes that Rawls's conception of coercion is juxtaposed against his view of justice as fairness. It is not, then, the best choice. The distinction that (E) makes is implicit in the second passage, but a careful reading will show both that the distinction it makes is not the actual one made in the passage, and that the first passage does not inquire whether legitimacy or justice are more permissive of coercion. The best answer, then, is (B). Although the first passage does not explicitly talk about utopia, like the second passage, you can easily infer it from its emphasis on whether a state (on Rawls's view) could use coercion and still respect autonomy or personhood.

10. **(C).** This question does not ask you to make a big inference, but to use the text as a sole guide for the correctness of the response. The passages should contain an explicit reference to the relationship between coercion and the correct answer choice. This allows you to eliminate (A), since Passage A does not discuss fairness; (B), because Passage A does not relate coercion to justice; (D), given that Passage B does not take up the concept of public reason; and (E), which offers a "utopia" that is only present in Passage B. (C), however, is a solid choice because Passage A relates the question of coercion to the well-ordered society, and Passage B relates it to a peaceful, (so, stable) world order.

11. **(D).** By reviewing these answer choices in relationship to the text, you will be able to identify (D) as the best solution to this inference. Passage B indicates that either the questions of legitimacy or justice can help Rawls address whether coercive action is justified by the state, but Passage A strongly implies that there may be instances in which justification for coercive action is not even required by the state. The two authors would disagree, then, about whether such action must be justified. In contrast, we do not have enough evidence from the text to know what the author of Passage A would say about (B). Answer (E) is simply false, since the authors agree that coercion is possible within a Rawlsian state. The authors would also agree with (C), even though the author of Passage A does not explicitly talk about a utopia, s/he does discuss the fact that coercion is a part of the government's options, under Rawls's view. (A) should be dismissed after careful reflection. Although inferences have to be made for this question, both passages give us enough information to suspect that the authors of both passages would probably agree with (A), and in the very least, we do not have enough information to infer that one of the authors would disagree with the claim made by (A). The best choice, then, is (D).

12. **(E).** This question is difficult because it asks you to predict the answer to a question that itself is based on inferences from the two passages. Take into account whether the potential answer choices are true, whether the predicted answer is supported by the text, and whether the authors of both passages would agree. From these bases, you can eliminate (C), which is too far outside of the scope of the evidence provided in the text (since the passages do not take up the question of whether people generally tend towards the good) and (D), which most clearly is out of the context of the passage, and for which you could not make a reasonable inference. You might think that (B) is a question that the authors could engage with, but neither passage actually takes up the issue of whether human (or civil, or moral) rights counteract with governmental coercion, and so you would have to speculate too far to correctly posit (B) as the answer. (A) could be correct, even though Passage A does

not explicitly name a utopia. But, the authors would have to agree on the likely answer to the question, and the author of Passage A is unlikely to agree that there could be misuse of coercion, although the author of Passage B seems to suggest that not all instances of governmental coercion is appropriate. The best answer is (E), because evidence from both passages indicates the authors would agree that the concepts of peace and a well-ordered society are not always compatible with justice, on Rawls account, which sets up their dual accounts of coercion and the state.

13. **(E).** This question requires an understanding, first, of what the second passage thinks is the relationship between a peaceful, stable world order and coercion. The author of the second text is saying that there could be conditions required for stability, and you can identify which condition from the first passage is a good candidate. The correct response will be true, and consistent with the evidence provided by the second passage. You can remove (A) immediately, because the first passage does not talk about the original position, nor its relationship to public reason. Although (B) states an aspect that is explicitly stated in Passage A, it conflicts with the view of coercion and the state in Passage B, and so must be rejected. Choice (C) is patently false, since the author of Passage A claims that we should reject the view that reason legitimates coercion. (D) must also be eliminated, because it is internally inconsistent and is also rejected as possible on Rawls's view by the author of Passage A. Option (E) is the best answer. It is consistent with the text of Passage A and establishes a condition that the author of Passage B would accept for a stable society: that respecting persons is an idea that is open for debate and can be placed as collateral for stability.

14. **(A).** The best approach to answering this question is to identify the main thesis of the two passages about coercion. You know that they conclude differently about the role of, and justification for, coercion in a democratic state, so you can remove answer choices that depend on the two passages making a similar claim. From this, you can remove (C), since the second passage cannot be read as a continuation of Passage A with new evidence, and (E), which claims the two have the same conclusion. Option (D) can be eliminated because the passages share a strength of commitment to their hypotheses. Answer (A) does the best job at showing the proper relationship, given that the passages say different things about coercion and the state and use different evidence to do so. Your choice is confirmed when you see that (B) cannot be true if Passage A ends up discussing a deontological respect for persons and Passage B does not take up that issue at all.

15. **(B).** The main point needs to be clear, correct, and essential to the passage. The fundamental point of this passage relates to the requirement of judges to interpret the law surrounding the intellectual property rights of the pharmaceutical industry through a complex system of moral and legal points of departure. This allows you to eliminate (A), because this passage does not discuss the issue of whether generic drugs are legally and morally permissible. (D) has an element of truth, because the passage does indicate that judges consider future stakeholders as well, but (D) does not encapsulate the main point concerning the ethical frameworks that govern judicial decision-making. (E) is factually correct, but is not tied to the judiciary or intellectual property so must be removed from consideration. (C) correctly identifies the tension identified in the passage, but does not integrate the need for judges to apply complex, multivaried normative lenses to the issue. (B), however, correctly underscores both the ethical issue involved in these cases, as well as the need for judges to think about a range of interests when making their decisions about pharmaceutical intellectual property.

16. **(A).** Although the three terms are different, the author of the passage means the same thing by them and relates them to the incentivization of pharmaceutical intellectual property. The incentive is, of course, money, which is tied as an efficiency quotient to how effective the drugs are to solve a medical problem. This makes (A) the stand-alone choice for the correct answer. If you are tempted to choose (B), note that the main issue of efficiency is not about physical space; judicial time (C) could be a consideration, but is not one named by the author as ethically relevant; and (D) is an echo of the considerations of (A), but (A) is more specific than (D) and tied to the other ethical issue of the patient, so is the correct answer.

17. **(E).** You need to make an inference, here, from the evidence given in the passage. Eliminate answers that are not justified by the text. (A) for example, is not grounded in evidence, because the passage does not discuss whether current intellectual property laws are sufficient. (B) is removed from consideration because the text does not at all delve into the formulas used, and the distribution involved, in pharmaceutical drugs. (D) runs counter to the main conclusion of the passage, which is that a number of ethical frameworks are required in these intellectual property cases, rather than just one or none. You are left with (C) and (E). (C) is correct that judges are unlikely to limit the pharmaceutical industry's growth, but the implication that the reason is because of the need for medical advancement is only thinly implied in the passage, when the author discusses future inventors. But, (E) is a strong inference from the evidence—harm can be caused to patients and to the industry by unjustified limits, and so judges need the guidance of a diversity of solid normative frameworks to guide their decisions.

18. **(E).** This very difficult question requires you to understand two rich terms in the passage-- the efficiency goal of welfare maximization and "the common good"- and their relationship before thinking about five other, non-related relationships. The "efficiency goal of welfare maximization" refers to getting the most (and best kinds) of benefits with the least amount of risk and cost to the public. "The common good" refers, of course, to goods of the public, who are not fiscally invested in intellectual property but benefit nonetheless through the research products of pharmaceutical companies. They are related in the passage in that the public health (a common good) depends upon research innovation in the pharmaceutical industry, but also cost-effective health care that is generated through competition in the industry. Whatever analogy is correct will show that there is a common good that has a gate surrounding it (i.e,. the gate of research competitiveness that allows companies to own their intellectual products and market them appropriately). First, eliminate analogies that do not reflect a relationship of a restricted-access good. (B) can be removed from consideration, because it inverts the relationship described in the passage, since the federal government sets up the restriction, and the state government makes the restricted item available. (C) should also be deleted from the list of possible answers, because there is not a restriction to be navigated. (D) does present a symmetrical restriction/access relationship as the original passage, but is not the right analogy because there is not a financial incentive that maps onto the restrictions that judges in the passage have to navigate. (A) and (E) are your two finalists and require deeper analysis. (A) has the right relationship—a community good is forwarded by a principality (i.e., the green space), but the common good is restricted by the principality by those who can pay whatever entrance fee is required. You can compare that relationship to (E), in which companies are given a fiscal incentive to create new products, those products are sold at a profit to people who can afford them, but the people who purchase them receive no fiscal incentive to purchase the new product. (E) is the best analogy for this question. The auto industry, similar to the pharmaceutical company, provides a beneficial product that the public needs. The government subsidizes the innovation of both industries. The public, which benefits from the innovative advances in both industries, still must pay the companies' asking prices for their products and do not receive a fiscal benefit for those purchases.

19. **(A).** For implication questions, the correct response will be justified by premises within the passage and supported inferentially by claims directly made within the text. Remove choices for which there is too great a logical leap to be made, and which run counter to what is said in the passage. (C), for example, is simply not grounded in the text. If anything, the text could be used to justify the view that the intellectual property rights of pharmaceutical companies could never be violated by a public need of their drugs. (D) is not an implication. The author claims that judges must consider the impact of "protecting inventors from the theft of their labor" and that the judge must interpret the law by considering the impact on all stakeholders (including inventors). (E) is stipulated in the text (in the "overlap" between ethical and efficiency criteria), although a small inference might be that the two "compete". Better inferences are made in (A) and (B). You could imagine the author making the claim, at least, that the judge in intellectual property cases is an agent in the research innovation chain with at least as much efficacy as the pharmaceutical company, since s/he writes that the judge has to be the final arbiter on a richly-valenced set of considerations for all stakeholders. But, the leap to whether the judge is a participant in research innovation is not strongly supported in the text as the inference made in (A). Answer (A)'s claim to the multifaceted application is a main theme in the passage, and the "no easy task" of addressing the question of who should benefit is suggested by the overlap between ethics and efficiency, as well as the fiscal impact of innovators and the impact on patients.

20. **(C).** You will expect that each of the listed answer choices will be true, consistent with the evidence in the text, and strongly implied by the passage. Remember that the question is not asking you what is in fact true about judges, but what the author would be likely to believe about judges based on what s/he has written in the text. The best approach is to evaluate each statement, since all but one of them will be correct and consistent with the reading. (A) should be included; the author believes that judges are a crucial part of the legal framework for intellectual property laws, and the "complex" considerations discussed in the passage suggest that there cannot be a one-sized-fits all approach to the law. (B), similarly, is consistent with the text. If the judge must weigh each case's audience, then it might be that in one case, for example, children who suffer from anaphylaxis, may need protection from exorbitant price increases to their drug, while those who suffer from a very rare strand of cancer may not require the same level of protection. (C), however, is not implied by the text. The author does not stipulate a type of cultural relativism in the text, in which each community decides the balance between patient care and industry market need. Even if a judge weighs each intellectual property case separately (and in relation to patient need), the conclusion does not follow that the decision for intellectual property cases ultimately resides with the community. (C) is the answer that does not fit. You can conclusively go with (C) after reviewing (D), which is strongly implied in the passage, and (E), which is justified in the last sentences of the passage.

21. **(C).** The correct answer will be the response that best captures the reason the author presents within the reading selection, so even choices that are factually true or strongly implied by the text may not be the best answer. (A), for example, certainly is one purpose of the text, but is not the best answer because it emphasizes how lemmings reproduce given climate change in their environment, and the passage is more about the impact of climate change on reproduction patterns in lemmings. (B) is, on one hand, too general—the passage is not just about presenting some scientific research—and on the other, too specific (although the population of Fennoscandian mammals is one topic of the article, it is not the sole focus). (D) is not correct, because although the passage mentions previous studies, it does not assess their value. (E) is not correct. Rather, (C) is the strongest answer. The purpose of the passage is to present this author's research on the changing winter habitat selection of nesting lemmings.

22. **(D).** Begin by eliminating answer choices that are factually false or inconsistent with the findings of the passage, and then remove answer choices that are tangential to the main thesis of the passage. (A) is false, since the reading indicates that the populations of foxes and stoats also correlate to the conditions of the snow in the Arctic. (C) is false, because it specifies that the brown lemming is particularly susceptible to snow depth. (B) and (E) are both true, but do not strongly represent the main thesis, since (B) does not point out the ecosystem's relationship to population numbers in lemmings and (E) does not serve to tie in the changing temperatures of the Arctic ecosystem to populations numbers in lemmings. (D), however, does a good job of integrating the concept of climate change to the population dimensions of both prey (lemmings) and predators (foxes, for example).

23. **(B).** The correct statement will strengthen a claim already made in the reading selection, so needs to be consistent with it, and the best answer will not bolster an ancillary or accidental point. You will need to read each response to ensure the correct response is the best of all of those provided to you. (A) is ad hoc; even if you learned (A), it does not relate importantly to the central claim the author makes about the relationship between snow cover and changing Arctic ecosystems. (C) is interesting, but introduces a new variable (mammals with a wide geographic distribution) that is not tied closely enough to the mammals discussed in this reading selection. (D) explains what the cold, wet Arctic habitat consists in, but does not itself bolster the author's claim about the relationship between snow cover for each of those Arctic terrains and the population of those small mammals. (E) is a good contender, because it maps onto the relationship the author makes between winter habitats and populations of lemmings, but introduces new conditions of those habitats that exceed that of the snow cover claim asked by this question. That makes (E) an inferior choice to (B), which specifically discusses the temperature of snow conditions to the creation of subnivean spaces in which lemmings reproduce.

24. **(D).** Prior to comparing the strength of each of these responses, you can first identify whether each choice relates to the main thesis of the passage, which you already identified in question 22. Doing so allows you to eliminate

(A) and (C), neither of which have textual support. (B), a simple measurement of weather conditions, is too banal and unspecific to adequately represent the scientific methodology provided by the passage. (E) is suggestive of the scientific rigor used by the author, but does not relate enough to the main point of the passage (since encountering lemming nests is insufficient to show the relationship the author draws between changing climates and reduced lemming populations). (D), however, best reflects the scientific methodology for the main thesis proven by the author.

25. **(D).** The answers to this inference question will go beyond what is given in the passage, and also be justified closely by it. The question centers around the meaning of stochastic, and you'll be at an advantage to know (although you can also infer it from the text) that stochastic means an event that can be analyzed but is itself unpredictable or stems from an unpredictable causal chain. You can eliminate answer choices that either are not stochastic, or are not stochastic events that the text suggests would impact lemming populations. (A), for example, is not typically a stochastic event, but one that is predictable given certain precursors. Heavy rain (B) could be stochastic, although the passage does not indicate that heavy rains as a stochastic event flood the spaces that lemmings populate. (C) could be a good contender, except that the author evaluates a range of lemming nesting sites that are not impacted by aboveground biomass erosion. (D) is a fantastic choice, especially since the author implies throughout the passage that global warming, specifically, is a major problem facing lemming reproduction. (E), if there was any evidence of it in the text, would be a good choice, but there is no relationship whatsoever given by the author between subduction zone shifts and a changing habitat for lemmings in the Arctic. (D) is the correct choice.

26. **(E).** This question is solely about how the evidence structurally relates to the thesis of the passage. This reading starts off with some facts about lemmings and what scientists know about their reproductive patterns, and it posits an inference that should be true: that the early onset of thick, dry snow, combined with the absence of freezing rain and days with above zero temperatures should favor survival and reproduction. But, the inference isn't true. Rather, "increased frequencies of freeze-thaw cycles during the winter due to climate warming and their influence on snow conditions have... dampen[ed] these." So, the organization of the passage is that a theory is proposed, considered, and then modified (here, the modification comes by elucidating the impact of shifting climate conditions on lemming populations). This organization structure should lead you to automatically eliminate (A) and (B). (D) should never be in consideration. (C) would be compelling to you, if you did not notice the shift in argumentation that occurs at the end of the second paragraph and the beginning of the third paragraph. Careful reading reveals the shift in organization that leads to the author's conclusion at the end of the passage.

27. **(C).** The success of this question depends on the logical distinction between a necessary and sufficient condition. A necessary condition is one that is required for something else to occur. A sufficient condition is not required, but its presence would be enough to explain why something else would occur. The passage gives you the necessary condition for successful reproduction under the snow: (A). But (A) clearly is not a sufficient condition for successful reproduction of lemmings under the snow, because the entire passage is about why there is an interruption in the cycle of lemming reproduction. So, some additional condition must explain the reproduction of lemmings in the interrupted cycle. (B) is not a sufficient condition to explain the changing in the reproductive cycle of lemmings because the variables that similarly impact other animals impact lemmings. This question requires a sufficient condition for the change in lemming reproduction. (D) is ad hoc, and cannot explain the relationship of climate change and lemming populations. (E), also, is a good candidate if we needed a further explanation for contributors to successful reproduction in lemmings, but cannot suffice for this particular question. Only (C) does that for you—that unpredictable extreme weather events interfere with what could typically be predicted and evaluated by scientists.

ANALYTICAL REASONING
SECTION 2 ANSWER EXPLANATIONS:

Passage for questions 1-6

For questions 1-6, you'll set up the conditions under which the baseball players are active or disabled together. From your set of conditions, you know the following:

J(a) [Note, this does not imply a biconditional. If J is active, K might be too.)

J(d) ⊃ O(a)

L(a) ⊃ (N&P)(d)

N(d) ⊃ O(d)

P(d) ⊃ (K&O)(a)

You have a condition for every player except for Ohtani, whether active or disabled, so you'll be able to use the questions to set up further conditions based on information in the question.

1. **(B).** This question asks you which list could be complete and accurate. It does not give us any conditional information to help you know whether it is in fact the list. Here you can identify answer choices in which you know the relationships do not match the conditions provided above. (A) must be eliminated, because it contends that Pacheco is disabled, in which case both Karns and Ohtani must be active. (C) cannot be correct, because it has La Russa as active, in which case, Napoli and Pacheco are disabled. But, if Napoli is disabled, Ohtani is disabled. (D) and (E) cannot be complete lists either, because nothing from your conditions excludes the possibility of Jackson and Pacheco from the active list if Napoli and Ohtani are active.

2. **(A.)** Here, we are introduced to new condition that can help us determine an answer. If Pacheco is disabled, we know that both Karns and Ohtani are active. This allows us to eliminate (B) and (E) from consideration. We can remove (D) as a possible choice, because if Napoli is disabled, so is Ohtani. If (C) is true, then Napoli and Pacheco are disabled, but we know in this case Napoli cannot be disabled, because that would disable Ohtani as well. That leaves us with (A) as the only possible answer choice remaining.

3. **(B).** This question does not give us much of a conditional to work with immediately, except the knowledge that whatever occurs as the correct choice must be a logical necessity—it must be true. Knowing that Karns is active does not give us any new information immediately. Instead, you have to work the answer choices to see what is logically necessary based on the information given. (A) is not logically necessary. You already know based on the first condition of the passage that it is logically possible for both Jackson and Karns to be active for Madden, so knowing that Karns is active does not itself help you know if Jackson is as well, (C) is true only if Jackson is disabled, but you cannot know if Jackson is active. (D) would make it such that Jackson is disabled, and Karns would be disabled, given the first two conditions, but the question tells us Karns is active. (E) is logically possible, but not a logically necessary answer, because if Pacheco is disabled, both Ohtani and Karns are active, but Ohtani is active if Jackson is disabled (and you cannot know if he is). Napoli must be active (B), however, because if Napoli is disabled, Ohtani would be, and you already know that if Karns is active, Napoli must be.

4. **(E).** Look for pairs of players that must be active, if they are together. Jackson and Karns could be disabled together (as you established during the logical analysis of the last question), so (A) is not a possible answer choice. (B) is not correct, because nothing in the conditions prohibit Jackson and Pacheco from being disabled together (although if they were, then Karns and Ohtani are active, but if Jackson is disabled, Ohtani is active). So, it is permissible for Jackson and Pacheco to be on the disabled list together. (C) Karns and Ohtani, similarly, can be on the disabled list at the same time, since in that case, Jackson would be active (and the only limit to Ohtani's active status is Jackson or Pacheco on the disabled list). You will also eliminate (D) as a contender, since Napoli and Ohtani can be co-listed on the disabled list, and the fourth condition of the passage is fulfilled. The only option that is not logically possible is (E), If Napoli is on the disabled list, so is Ohtani, but if Pacheco is disabled, Ohtani is active. This contradiction means that Napoli and Pacheco cannot concurrently be on the disabled list.

ANALYTICAL REASONING
SECTION 2 ANSWER EXPLANATIONS:

5. **(A).** This question demands that you run two options: Napoli active, Ohtani disabled; and Napoli disabled, Ohtani active. See what you can learn under the new conditions. You know that if Napoli is disabled, Ohtani is disabled, so the second configuration demanded by the question is not logically possible. This means that the only configuration that is possible with the two players on different lists is for Napoli to be active, and Ohtani to be on the disabled list. Given that constraint, you are looking for the answer that is logically necessary, rather than merely logically possible. You know it is not logically required that four players are active (D) or disabled (E), since if Napoli is active, Pacheco could be active (but not La Russa). If Napoli and Pacheco are active, they would be joined by Jackson (otherwise Ohtani would be active. That leaves Karns, La Russa, and Ohtani on the disabled list—so, neither (D) or (E) are logically required. This also shows that it is not required for either Pacheco or Karnrs to be on the disabled list, so you can eliminate (C) and (B). The only answer remaining is (A), which makes sense because if Jackson is disabled, Ohtani must be active, but you know from the beginning of the explanation that you can only consider Napoli to be active and Ohtani to be on the disabled list.

6. **(C).** You aren't given more conditions here, but you are given a new modal consideration: the least possible active players for Madden. You know from #5 that you could at have three players active together: Napoli, Pacheco, and Jackson. So eliminate (E). But, you also know that you cannot have everyone on the disabled list, since if Pacheco, Jackson, or Karns are disabled, another player is active, so (A) is not a possible number. You know (D) is a possible number but you aren't sure if it is a minimum number, so see if you can get (C) or (B) to work and eliminate (D). If La Russa is active, Napoli and Pacheco are disabled, but if Pacheco is disabled, Karns and Ohtani are active—which leaves us three. So, put La Russa on the disabled list.

Active List	Disabled Listw
	(1) La Russa
(2) Pacheco	(3) Karns (J to a); (4)

Next, put Pacheco on the active list (you don't want him on the disabled list, because he sends two guys to the active list), and see what follows. You might put Karns on the disabled list, but that puts Jackson on active—so the active list must at least have two players on it (either Karns and/or Jackson)—so you can eliminate (B) and see if two is the minimum.

Active List	Disabled List
	(1) La Russa
(2) Pacheco	(3) Napoli
	(4) Ohtani

This time, try Napoli next, which puts Ohtani on the disabled list. Perfect! You are left with Jackson and Karns. If we put Jackson the disabled list, that kicks Ohtani to active, and keeps us with two players on the active list, with Karns left.

Active List	Disabled List
	(1) La Russa
(2) Pacheco	(3) Napoli
(5) Ohtani	(4) Jackson
	(6) Karns

Shoot! If Karns is disabled, Jackson has to be bumped to active, which means that we cannot have a scenario in which there are two players minimum for Joe Madden to play as active players. We're back to three.

But instead of subbing Karns with Napoli on the disabled list, let's bump Jackson to the active list and see what happens.

Active List	Disabled List
	(1) La Russa
(2) Pacheco	(3) Karns
(4) Jackson	

ANALYTICAL REASONING
SECTION 2 ANSWER EXPLANATIONS:

You have Ohtani and Napoli left. What happens if you put them on the Disabled list?

Active List

(2) Pacheco
(4) Jackson

Disabled List
(1) La Russa
(3) Karns
(5) Ohtani
(6) Napoli

This is a consistent list: if Napoli is disabled, so is Ohtani, but putting Ohtani on the disabled list does not bump anyone else back to the active list. You have done it! You've shown that the correct answer is (C), two players at a minimum must be active for Joe Madden.

Passage for questions 7-12

You can set up the conditions fairly easily for this passage:

12[CE]456
{H}[TP]
{P}[H/A]

   Some deductions can be made from here. Since Civil Engineering is meeting #3, and Philosophy must come before History and Architecture, and History must meet before Theoretical Physics, you know Philosophy will be meeting #1 or #2, History will be either #2 or #4, and Theoretical Physics or Architecture will be either 4, 5, or 6 (depending on where History sits). You can use the rest of the clues from each of the questions to fill in what else is needed.

7. **(E).** Setting out clear conditions will help you with this fairly-straightforward question. The first condition is important—it helps you rule out (A), (C), and (D), since Civil Engineering is not the third meeting of the day in any of those answer choices, but must be the third meeting of the day given the conditions of the passage. The third condition (that Philosophy must meet with the President prior to History or Architecture) will help you remove (B) from consideration, since in it, Philosophy is the last meeting of the day. The only remaining, logically possible answer is (E), in which Civil Engineering is the third meeting, Philosophy meets before History and Architecture, and History also meets with the President prior to her meeting with the Theoretical Physics faculty.

8. **(A).** Establishing Art as the first meeting, with Civil Engineering as the third, eliminates (B). History (C) and Architecture (D) cannot meet before Philosophy, and so must be removed from consideration. Theoretical Physics, of course, must meet after History, so cannot be the second meeting of the day, which excludes the possibility of (E). Philosophy (A) is the correct answer, and allows for the other conditions to be met.

9. **(C).** This question is asking about logical necessity, rather than logical possibility, so whatever solution you choose, make sure that it is not merely included as possible by the conditions but instead is an answer that could not be otherwise, given what the passage tells us about the conditions. You know that Art could be the first meeting (see question 8), so it is not logically necessary that the third meeting with Civil Engineering must be before the meeting with Art, so cross out (A). (B) and (D) are both possible, since History must meet before Theoretical Physics but after Philosophy (which must meet before Architecture). But, since Philosophy must meet before History, which must meet before Theoretical Physics, answer (C) is logically required—by the principle of transitivity, Philosophy must meet before Theoretical Physics.

10. **(B).** Following the passage's clear conditions is an easy way to eliminate answer choices for this question. Answer choices (A) and (D) violate the first condition, since Civil Engineering must be the third meeting. Option (C) is logically impossible, because philosophy must precede the meeting with history, which itself must precede the meeting with Theoretical Physics. Similarly, you can eliminate answer (E), because you know the meeting with History comes before the meeting with Theoretical Physics. That leaves choice (B) as the correct choice, and it is indeed logically possible: Philosophy, History, Civil Engineering, Art, Theoretical Physics, Architecture.

ANALYTICAL REASONING
SECTION 2 ANSWER EXPLANATIONS:

11. (B). This is an example of when putting the logical implications of the conditions directly prior to answering all of the questions can really help set you up for success. You already stipulated that Philosophy cannot be later than second in the order of meetings, because Philosophy must meet before History, Architecture, and Theoretical Physics, and because Civil Engineering must be the third meeting of the day. The necessary conclusion that must be made in relation to this question is that Philosophy (B) cannot be the fourth meeting of the day.

Passage for questions 7-18

This is a difficult passage because of the number of variables present. You'll want a clear idea of the what the conditions entail prior to engaging with any of the questions. Here is what you have (listed as abbreviations in order):

V[Y/Q]   **Cannot be first**
Q [Z] {V[Z]}   Quantas (Virgin Atlantic is before it)
T [V] {Y/Q/Z}   Southwest (Virgin Atlantic is before it)
R[T] {R[V/Y/Q/Z]}   TAKA (Regent is before it)
V[S] {R[S/T/V/Y/Q/Z]}   Virgin Atlantic (TAKA is before it)
R[W] {R[T/V/S/Y/Q/Z]}   WestJet (Regent is before it)
                                        Yeti (Virgin Atlantic is before it)
                                        Zambezi (Quantas is before it)

Regent must, then, be the first airplane to land, because it must land before WestJet and before TAKA, and TAKA lands before Virgin Atlantic, which lands before Yeti and Quantas (and Quantas lands before Zambezi).

12. (C). Knowing that Regent will be the first to land is invaluable to navigate through this question. The only answer choices in which Regent precedes WestJet (which fulfills the last condition of the passage) are (C) and (E), which allows you to eliminate (A), (B), and (D). The first difference between (C) and (E) comes with the fifth landing, in which (C) has Quantas landing before Zambezi, Southwest, and Yeti (and (E) has Zambezi in the fifth spot). But, having Quantas land after Zambezi in (E) violates the second condition of the passage, and so the answer must be (C).

13. (D). This question requires that you think about logical possibility, rather than necessity. Your job is to find which of the answer choices is outside of the realm of logical possibility, given the conditions placed by the passage. Glancing at the answer choices will give you some easy ways to eliminate answers. You know that (B) cannot be correct, since Regent must be first. Virgin Atlantic cannot be sixth (E), because it must land before Yeti and Quantas, and Quantas must land before Zambezi. Yeti, of course, cannot be the second airplane to land, since Regent and Virgin Atlantic must land before it, so you can remove (A) as possible. That leaves (C) and (D). Quantas must land before Zambezi, and Virgin Atlantic and Regent must precede it as well. TAKA, however, must land before Virgin Atlantic, so Quantas could not be the fourth airplane to land. That leaves (D), which is a logically possible order of landing: Regent, WestJet, TAKA, Virgin Atlantic, Southwest, Yeti, Quantas, Zambezi

14. (E). This question also asks you to identify a claim that is logically possible, rather than necessary, based on an extra condition. You can eliminate answer choices that you know are false, based on the conditions already given. This allows you to get rid of (B), but also (A), since Yeti must follow Virgin Atlantic and Regent is the first to land. (D) is not possible since Virgin Atlantic must land before Yeti, Quantas, Zambezi, and Southwest. And, (C) cannot be correct because Virgin Atlantic, TAKA, and Regent must be before Quantas. Zambezi could be the sixth airplane to land, however, if the following order held: Regent, WestJet, TAKA, Virgin Atlantic, Quantas, Zambezi, Southwest, and Yeti. (E), then, is logically possible given the conditions of the passage.

15. (E). Landing TAKA second solidifies the logical possibility of most of the other landings, and that the correct answer will be logically required, given the conditions. You know (A) cannot be true because TAKA lands after Regent. After that, you have to test each of the statements to see if there are counterexamples which fulfill all of the conditions but undermine the possibility of the potential answer. (B), for example, is not

logically necessary, if the following landing order is followed: Regent, TAKA, WestJet, Virgin Atlantic, Quantas, Southwest, Yeti, Zambezi. Similarly, (C) is not logically required: Regents, TAKA, Virgin Atlantic, WestJet, Quantas, Southwest, Yeti, Zambezi. Of course, in none of these scenarios does Yeti land before Quantas, so (D) is not logically necessary. It is, however, necessary that Zambezi land after WestJet, since WestJet must follow Regent and TAKA, and TAKA must come before Virgin Atlantic (which lands before Yeti and Quantas—and Quantas must land before Zambezi). Given these conditions, the only logically necessary answer is (E).

16. **(A).** You can set up what you know about the order the flights must land if Quantas has the fifth landing spot. All of your statements could be logically possible except for one, so just need to find the single statement that does not fit with the conditions stipulated in the passage. Regents must be first, TAKA, WestJet, and Virgin Atlantic will compete for spots two-four (although TAKA must come before Virgin Atlantic). Quantas will be fifth. From these conditions, you know that (B), (C), and (D) are all logically possible—if TAKA is second, either WestJet or Virgin Atlantic will be third with the other taking the fourth spot. (E), of course, is possible under almost all configurations. That leaves (A) as the odd solution out, which is confirmed by the necessity of landings by TAKA, WestJet, and Virgin Atlantic.

17. **(B).** Our conditions require that Regent will be first, and if TAKA is third, WestJet will be in the second landing place. This allows you to choose (B) straightaway. To double-check your response, you know you can eliminate (D), since Virgin Atlantic must land before Yeti, Quantas, and Southwest, and Quantas must land before Zambezi, so Virgin Atlantic cannot be after the fourth spot. That makes (C) also false, given that the first four spots are taken. That leaves (A) and (E) as possible choices, both of which have an equal probability of being true, because neither Yeti nor Southwest must be followed by any other airline.

18. **(E).** The first four spots are fairly certain, and allow you to strike from consideration (A), since Regent must be first, (C), since WestJet is in the first four landing positions, and (D), because Virgin Atlantic must precede Yeti, Quantas, and Zambezi. (B) cannot be true, in consideration of the fact it must land after Virgin Atlantic, which precedes Yeti, Quantas, and Zambezi. The only viable answer that remains is (E), and, indeed, having Yeti follow Zambezi fulfills the various conditions of the passage.

Passage for questions 19-23

There are a number of conditionals at play in this thought experiment. Rather than being daunting, they can help you determine the answers with better specificity. There are 3 days, 5 tasks, and 7 teens. Two of the teens (Sofie and Jill) can only perform one of the tasks, and only one task can be worked on by any person at a single time.

19. **(B).** Think of the crew based on the tasks the teens can perform on any given day. There are five tasks that could be done at any one time, but they can only be worked on by a single person at a time. (A) cannot be correct, because Shannon and Elizabeth have duplicative painting talents, but no one would be able to recalibrate the engine. (C) also does not work, because of Shannon and Elizabeth's painting overlap, and the fact that there would be no one to reassemble the engine head. (D) similarly does not work, because replacing Allie with Jill does not give the team the ability to reassemble the engine head. (E) is not a live option for you, because it does not give you a teen who can remove the engine. (B), however, ensures that you can remove the engine, recalibrate it, reassemble the head, reupholster the car, and repaint it.

20. **(D).** If you have the same two teens work on the first and third days of assembly, you need to ensure that they have disparate enough skills to cover enough tasks to complete the project by the end of day 3. Strike the answers in which the teens together only perform three tasks. You will not want Elizabeth and Allie to work together, for this reason (so, eliminate (B)). You also do not want Jessica and Cory together, because they can only perform three tasks, so remove (E) from consideration. Shannon and Elizabeth (A's option) only perform three tasks. That leaves you with (C), Elizabeth and Jessica together have four different tasks and (D) Allie and Cory would bring four different tasks. Next, you need to see how the other teens could work on the second day to get

the tasks completed. If Elizabeth and Jessica (C) were the duplicated pair, you could have Elizabeth remove the engine and Jessica recalibrate the engine on Day One, but there would be nothing left within Jessica's talents to be able to have her work on Day Three:

Day One
Elizabeth (remove)
Jessica (recalibrate)
Sofie (reassemble)

Day Two
Jill (reupholster)

Day Three
Jessica (x)
Elizabeth (paint)

But, if (D) is correct, you could run the 3-day schedule like so:

Day One
Allie (remove)
Cory (recalibrate)

Day Two
Sofie (reassemble)

Day Three
Allie (reupholster)
Cory (repaint)

21. **(A).** This question is an except question, so all of the answer choices are correct, save one. To find that solution, you need to remember the order in which the tasks need to be completed (remove the engine, recalibrate the engine, reassemble the engine, reupholster the car, and repaint it) and map those onto the abilities of the teens before using the process of elimination to find which list does not contain a teen who can complete a necessary task. The only teens who can remove the engine are Elizabeth and Allie, so one of them needs to be on any complete list. Either one of them is on all of these options, so you move to recalibration, which can be done by Jessica or Cory. (A) contains neither, so must be the one choice that cannot be an accurate list.

22. **(E).** The framing of the question indicates that three tasks will be done on Day Three, since upholstering will be done that day. Set out the tasks that need to be completed each day so that you can visualize which teens could perform each task on any given day.

Day One
Remove
(Recalibrate)

Day Two
(Recalibrate)
Reassemble

Day Three
Reupholster
Repaint

The potential days a given task are delineated by these options—recalibration could occur on Day One or Day Two, but since reassembly and repainting cannot occur on the same day, and each day must have a task, there will either be one or two tasks on Day One, and one or two tasks on Day Two (but not both will have two tasks). Day Three's tasks are non-negotiable, under the conditions of this question. So, we match the potential Day Two tasks with the teens who could accomplish the tasks. Jessica can recalibrate and reassemble, but not on the same day. If Jessica recalibrates, Sofie could reassemble. If Cory recalibrates, either Sofie or Jessica could reassemble the head. Out of these, the latter is represented by (E). The others are incomplete, or, in D's case, do not cover the tasks that could need to be accomplished on Day Two.

23. **(D).** The easy way to start removing potential answers is to remove answers that contain Sofie and Jill, since neither teen can perform two tasks. (A) is immediately eliminated, since both Sofie and Jill are listed. Now, you can remove sibling pairs that share a task, since both are needed to perform two tasks each day, and tasks cannot be duplicated. This allows you to remove (E), since Jessica and Cory both recalibrate the engine, and (B), given that Shannon and Allie both reupholster. Now, remember the order in which the tasks need to be completed (**remove the engine, recalibrate the engine, reassemble the engine, reupholster the car, and repaint it**) and from (C), and (D), you can see which pairs produce the tasks that they need to complete in the proper order. (C) would require Elizabeth to remove the engine and Jessica to recalibrate it on Day One. Jessica would need to reassemble the head on Day Two (because one worker cannot do both of her assigned tasks on the same day). But, that leaves reupholstering and repainting as tasks. Elizabeth cannot reupholster, and since she would need to do her task on the same day as Jessica, both reupholstering and painting would have be done on Day Two, requiring an extra sibling. Option (D), however, fits the bill. Allie could remove the engine on Day One, and Jessica can recalibrate it. On Day Two, Jessica can reassemble the head and Allie can reupholster it, leaving Day Three and another sibling to repaint the car.

LOGICAL REASONING 1
SECTION 3 ANSWER EXPLANATIONS:

1. **(B).** The conclusion of this passage (i.e., that Carl McCoy cannot be a candidate because he is married to Elizabeth) requires an assumption, when tied to the other premises in the passage. There are two necessary conditions of the argument: that only family members of President McCoy can be VPs and that relations of Hatfields cannot be VPs. What position is Carl up for? *The head of the cybersecurity division.* So, there are two logical implications that can be made if he cannot be a candidate: although Carl is a McCoy, he is not a family member of President McCoy; and, that the head of cybersecurity is indeed a VP position. Only (B) is included in your answers as an implication of our evidence. Neither (A) nor (C) are evidentially tied to the passage; (E) provides a possible explanation for why relations of Hatfields cannot be heads of cyber, but is not strongly tied to what we know in the text. (D) is not an implication of the evidence here, which just says that Carl cannot be a candidate.

2. **(A).** This passage requires you to draw an analogy in the argument's form. The first thing you should do is think of the form of the argument presented in the question. We can think of the argument as a basic modus ponens:

    (1) If a doctor has competing moral obligations between a parent and a minor child, the doctor has moral obligations to neither. (If P, then Q)

    (2) The doctor has an obligation to the teen that competes with her obligation to the parent. (P)

    (3) The doctor does not have a moral obligation to either the teen or the parent. (Therefore, Q)

    This is a valid argument, and your job is to see which answer choice also uses a *modus ponens* form. (B) does not (it argues from one instance of a fact to a universal of it); (C) commits the logical fallacy of denying the antecedent (If P, then Q; ~P; so ~Q); (D) is valid, but is a *modus tollens* form (If P, then Q; ~Q, so ~P). Similarly, (E) is also valid, but is a disjunctive syllogism (Either P v Q, ~P, so P). The only answer that relies on a *modus ponens* is (A). Although there are added premises, it uses a *modus ponens*: If you are civil, you respect the rights of others; You are civil, so you respect the rights of others (even if you disagree with the person).

3. **(D).** This passage asks you to fill in the answer that is logically implicated by the passage. This text sets up a danger for the graduate that is in keeping with a feeling of grief, tied to reminiscence. You will be looking for an answer that is tied carefully to the content of the passage, but also has a danger. (A) does not have a danger for the graduate—in fact, it is pragmatically consistent for graduates and their families to reminisce about their childhoods during that time. (B) would represent a potential danger, but it is unlikely that college graduates are thinking about their own death. (C) is a potential response, since if the graduate only reminisces and does not plan for his or her future, they will not be ready to move onto the next stage. But, careful reading shows that (C) cannot be correct, because the answer is qualified by "until". It is not in itself dangerous for the graduate to reminisce *until* he or she is ready to plan—in fact, many might reminisce until they start planning. (The danger would be if they only reminisce and do not plan, but that is not included in this answer here.) Of course that exact danger is represented in (D), in which the graduate does not make choices to ensure his/her future success and so is a good choice. (D) becomes the best choice when we see that (E) only works for graduates who need to change patterns of behavior developed in college, and this passage gives us no indication that is something that any particular college graduate would need to do.

4. **(A).** This tricky text measures your ability to think about the logical implications of spoken text, in this instance one drawn from comedy. The success of Burns's monologue resides on the sentence, "Those cards lasted me seven years," and its relation to the cards being made of linen and the fact that George Burns was brand-new to show business. Think about those facts, even without looking at the answer choices, since the question asks you what makes this passage funny. It's funny because the cards were made out of permanent material but went unused because Burns was an unknown comedian. Now, you can turn to your answer choices and see that (A) is an excellent fit. (B) has nothing to do with the linen material of the cards; (C), if true, would not be funny and so cannot be correct. Similarly (D) is not funny, although it might be true generally or even particularly to the text. (E) is about comedy, and it is true that making the cards out of linen turned into a joke for Burns. But, (E) is not an implication of the passage—it may or not be a consequence of a fact, and so (A) is the best choice.

5. **(B).** This question asks you to undermine the position of the text's claim about the relationship between basaltic volcanoes and the environment, specifically. So you can eliminate answers that do not have to do with that relationship, like (D), which is not about basaltic volcanoes specifically, and (A), which is not about basaltic volcanoes and if it was, would not be enough to explain the amount of chlorine or bromine expended in the atmosphere (since it relates to what is happening below the surface). (C) is not supported in the text, given that the first sentence is a claim a scientist makes about the levels of the gases in the atmosphere as a result of volcanoes. That leaves you with an easy choice between (B), which provides an alternate explanation for why global warming is caused from basaltic volcanoes and (E), which tries to relate the number of volcanic eruptions (instead of the total amount of gases expended) to global warming.

6. **(D).** This question is an application question, which gives you a moral formula and asks you to apply it to the examples provided to see which character fulfills the equation for a moral agent (i.e., an agent who pursues the highest good, according to Aristotle). Each of your characters performs a permissible act, so you can't eliminate characters who performed badly. You then look for characters who pursue active, contented virtue that is also rational. On this basis, you can eliminate (E), since Madison is using good prudential reasoning, but her action is neither moral or immoral because it was not performed for the sake of virtue. Jordan, similarly, only risks giving because it is not a risk at all, so (C) is off the table. Farrah (A) gives to a charitable donation but only because she thinks she might personally benefit. Lakeisha (B) and Jasmine (D) both perform a right action from (if we're giving the benefit of the doubt) a virtuous motive. Aristotle might say, for example, that moral agents do not want other people to be put in a position to commit crimes to eat, so when Lakeisha gives the peanut butter she might do it for a good reason. But, being worried that someone would steal if she is hungry stands in contrast as a reason to (D), in which Jasmine does something at cost to herself to create a condition under which other, needy, people would benefit. In that light (D) is a better answer here than (B).

7. **(A).** This is another response in which you provide the conclusion to the argument. It can help to summarize the argument simply: Advocates show wind energy has significant health and green house benefits. Critics think mountain communities will bear a disproportionate economic burden if wind farms are unsuccessful and companies should take out bonds to economically protect those communities. The conclusion you have to supply marries those two views to project the future of wind power—based on those two competing views, there is good health evidence and financial worries for communities, so your answer should reflect those. You can start by eliminating choices that do not reflect those two opposing perspectives, including (B), which goes against the evidence here and only advocates against wind and (C), since it does not represent either view. You might be tempted by (E), but (E) does not represent the critics and essentially demands that we cannot predict. The question asks us to predict based on the stated opinions, so (E) must be crossed off as a possibility. (D) does present both views generally—since "technical problems" could refer both to the mechanics of farms that lead to good benefits and would need to be solved and to the economic and security issues that might need to be addressed before more wind farms are built. But, (A) is the best answer because it represents the promise of growth suggested by the proponents of wind power as well as the need to keep mountain communities (and so, detractors) content in order for the proposal to work.

8. **(E).** This question masquerades as a critique but is actually asking you to undermine the argument with additional, competing information. You are looking for an answer that if true would stand in contrast to the main point of the passage—which is that gas vehicles will be the primary purchase of new car owners for the next decade. Of the choices only one can be automatically eliminated for not being relevant, (B), since the passage is about a ratio of gas:hybrid/electric vehicles instead of the number of cars purchased total. (C) is the next answer choice to go; even if there are new energy options, those stand outside of the gas:hybrid/electric vehicle ration explored here. The remaining three choices are all relevant, and you have to uncover which one would impair the main contention of the argument. (A) can safely be removed; the imperative information we would need to make (A) correct would be that adults aged 18-24 are the largest group of new car buyers (as well as a further assumption that they are largely responsible for buying hybrid or electric cars). We cannot make those assumptions with any care. (D) is interesting; if the Big Three auto companies market hybrid technology more than ever, we

293

would expect a boost in the number of people buying hybrid vehicles. (E) is also a strong contender; if gas prices double or triple to Great Recession levels, we know that people will rush to purchase cars that do not use gasoline, or that use gasoline sparingly. Which most strongly weakens the claim? (E). Marketing campaigns are not always successful, so that even if—independent of gas prices—car companies more enthusiastically pushed hybrid technology, as long as gas remains cheap, people tend to stick with what they know. When prices soar, however, consumer demand changes. (E) is the best answer.

9. **(B).** The answer you choose should be another way of stating what is obvious in the passage as the main idea—the first sentence (the latter sentences provide justification for the conclusion). The only answer that repackages the first sentence of the passage is (B). (A) does not logically follow (police might be obligated to wear the cameras, but their obligation to the public is not impeded by whether they wear the camera—those are different). (C) might be true, but there is not a hint in the passage that law enforcement personnel have neglected to consider the risk, so it cannot be the main idea. (D) could be an implication of the passage; indeed, it might be the next sentence that is written, but is not the main idea of the given text. And (E) is certainly stated explicitly in the text, but as one of three benefits of body cameras. (B), however, accurately summarizes this passage's main idea.

10. **(C).** This rich answer set requires careful reading. The question is specific to one portion of the text—that purists a century ago were found demonstrably wrong in their belief that changing baseball would hurt the sport. You need to determine the role in the argument (an argument that concludes that baseball needs to make slight changes now to strengthen itself). The argument strongly correlates the error of the purists a century ago with purists of the sport now, so your correct answer will reflect that correlation. (A) should immediately be removed, because it contradicts the conclusion. (B) is also wrong, although more deceptively so—although the passage talks at length about what the purists of baseball have and now want, it concludes that those desires are separate from the vitality of the game. (E) should also be removed after careful reading. Careful reading is required because (E) is intentionally complex: it suggests possible, not actual evidence; that evidence is mentioned but dismissed; that evidence could be cited by supporters of the purists; the evidence cited by supporters of the purists would be criticized by the passage. Although it is true the passage does deny the purists view, it does so by introducing the purists view itself as evidence against purism- it does not criticize any evidence that purists accept because it does not provide evidence produced by purists. (C), however, is both clear and correct. The purists a century ago had a view that changed (purism no longer refers to the lineup or pinch runners), but baseball did not suffer as a result.

11. **(C).** To succeed here, you need to identify what the prognosticators suggested about the WNBA, and then use the correct answer choice to provide the best justification for the persistence of the WNBA. Unfortunately, there are no answer choices that are immediately removable from consideration, so each one will have to be compared to the text and each other to find the most plausible, strongest reason. Out of the five options (A) is the weakest, because it requires the most inference from answer to conclusion. If true, (A) would only explain the success of the league if the only factor in the continuation of the WNBA was a higher female fanbase (and that those experts would not have factored in a higher ratio of female fans in their predictions). (B) might be appropriate, since if we discover that corporate sponsorship for basketball generally has increased since 1995, we might expect that corporate sponsorship (so, market reach and consequent fan interest) might have particularly benefitted the WNBA sector of professional basketball. In comparison, (C) is a better answer. It explains the actual fiscal success of the league and the recruitment tools for fans, players, and staff. A reason (C) is such a good answer compared to the others is that it does not require you to make inferences beyond its facts. But, to further compare, (D) only thinly explains an inference—that Tulsa and San Antonio would not be popular tourist destinations (and, of course, San Antonio is one of the most popular tourist destinations in the U.S.). So, (D) is inferior to (C). As for (E), it does a good job of explaining an initial marketing move that could have contributed to fiscal sustenance, but is still insufficient to explain the length of time that the WNBA has survived—especially compared to (C).

12. **(C).** A missing premise is required for the argument provided in the text to be complete. Remove irrelevant premises, or those that are not supported in the text, in your first step. (B), for example, even if true, does not

lead to the conclusion that there are twice as many T students on R from C. (D) also can be removed—although it would be more difficult to explain the composition of the first generation student group if none of C's students are first gen, the question is actually about there being twice as many T students on R from C than T students from other universities—rather than the student group. (A) is insufficient to explain why there would be twice as many T students from C at R—students from another campus might transfer to R as well, or maybe all T students from non-C schools would end up transferring to R. As for (E), even if true, it would provide some explanation for why there are twice as many T students from C on R than other T students. The question now is whether (E) provides a *better* explanation than (C). (C) indicates that all students from C transfer to R, which provides an excellent reason for why C students would be the biggest T group on campus. (C), still is not an indefeasible claim, of course, since if C is smaller than any other university, it wouldn't make sense that C students would make up the biggest % of T students. But, from (C) and (E), (C) provides the best explanation without making large inferences.

13. **(E).** In contrast to question 12, here you are looking for the proposition that undermines the claims made in the passage. So, begin by removing answers that are consistent with the text, or that are irrelevant to it. (D) should be the first to go, because the taste of eggs is completely irrelevant to whether a cooking surface is the most important aspect of cooking an egg. From here, you need strong analysis of the possible solutions. (A) contrasts with what is in the text (that the yolk may or may not cook to over-medium), but whether they almost always do does not give enough information to support or undermine the conclusion. (B) is interesting, because it suggests that the air surrounding the cooking surface is as important as the temperature of the cooking surface. (C), however, does not help here, because it raises the issue of the surface *temperature* being the single important factor rather than the *surface,* so remove it from consideration. (E) is an excellent option because it takes what is suggested by (C) and further explains why the temperature surrounding what is being cooked is more important by the surface itself. So, (C)—in the absence of other, better, answers would be ok, but (E) does the best job of undermining the conclusion.

14. **(D).** Your job for this question is to strengthen the conclusion made by the argument with the statement that provides further support for it, so eliminate answer choices that either contradict the conclusion or do not provide further support for it. (C) is an answer choice that contrasts with the passage, and (E) is irrelevant (since whether demographic groups believe they benefit from the census does not alter the justification for changes to the form). If (A) is true, the conclusion is neither further supported nor undermined, so (A) is not a strong answer choice. (B) could be a continuation of the text, but does not explain why changes are justified (since the justification for the changes are that there will indeed be policy changes to better meet the needs of the demographics of the group). Of course, the policy changes the reader might have in mind might be those that would negatively impact groups that do not want to indicate their citizenship status, but we cannot know from the text. That makes (D) the best choice. If changes to the form are justified, it can only be because the groups that need services would want to be served by their municipalities, and so would need to be reflected by the census.

15. **(B).** If you follow the argument's logical form, you will be more easily able to identify the conclusion. The form is as follows: "All As are Bs. Some As are Cs and Ds. All As are not Es. (By implication, some As are not Es.) If not E, not C. That means that the conclusion will be If (A and not E), then it is possible not C." The form of the argument requires one possible conclusion—(B). If you are double-checking, (A) and (C) not supported by the text (and (C) includes a new distinction not made in the passage). (D) describes psychological but not ethical utilitarianism, and (E) would be possible if the "individual" and "public" utility swapped positions in the explanation.

16. **(E).** Here, compare each statement to the text, and decide whether they reflect a disagreement from a rationalist and empiricist based on eyewitness testimony for violent crime cases. (B) is irrelevant, so remove it. Rupp and Whatley might actually agree on (C) and (D)—you cannot infer otherwise based on the passage. That leaves (A) and (E), the best of which is (E). Rupp and Whatley might disagree on (A), but they also might agree that the 73% only applies to the types of experiences eyewitnesses have in stressful scenarios like those of violent crimes. But, (E) is strongly supported as a claim Rupp and Whatley will disagree about; it is specific to stressful situations, and is tied to the evidence that law enforcement personnel deal with, and are themselves witnesses to.

17. (B). The question is not asking which of the answer choices is a good criticism, but which of them would best serve to weaken the City Manager's argument. The argument relies on an argument from authority, based on the view of the consultants. That isn't enough to support (B), but it is enough to include (B) as a candidate. Compare the rest of the choices to it. (A) is not a strong candidate, because the City Manager does not explain how to solve the problem of "shoring up the main". For different reasons, (D) should be removed. There is not evidence that the manager bases the inference to protect the main on too small a sample, since the consultants apparently looked at "big cities", which is a relevant sample. (E) should also be eliminated, since nothing in the text indicates that the comparison of this region (which includes millions of people) would be a small institution compared to the sample large systems. (C), however, is a logical possibility, since the Manager could view that the terrorist attack could cause the risk to the region (and justifiably so). The task, then, is to compare (B) and (C) as options. (B) indicates that the experience of the consultants—who are used to big cities—might be insufficient to account for this unique region, in which this city (population unknown) provides water to subsequent millions. The distribution system for water might be completely different in this city's case. (C), however, may not indicate a logical fault in this case, since the relationship being looked at by the consultants is exactly one of cause. (B) is a better choice.

18. (B). Propositions that run counter to the passage should first be eliminated, as well as those that are irrelevant to the main point. (A) is not implied at all by the passage (since the text has not argued that embracing robotics is a best practice). Similarly, while (C) could be an imagined reason to explain the dearth of commercialized construction robots, it is not strongly supported by the passage. It is probable that tech intensive fields need robotics (E), but such a view—while consistent with the passage—really is ad hoc to it. (D) is possible, but ICT and BIM tech advances suggest that there is not a gap in innovation, but in commercialization, in which case (B) is the best answer.

19. (A). All of the propositions should be true and provide support for the criminologist's view. The statement that is either not true or not justified in the text is the correct answer. You do not have to wander long to find it—(A) is not supported by the criminologist, who is arguing that a number of nations need to participate against the "scourge" of fake drugs sold and shipped online, and across borders. For confirmation, (B) would explain how border officials can have the authority to limit pharmaceutical fraud. (C) would describe how nations could cooperate to raise the standard. (D) demonstrates what nations are now doing to protect their mutual interests against fake pharmaceuticals, and (E) shows that companies are aiding in efforts for a legitimate drug trade.

20. (E). Here, think about how the conclusion functions for the faculty member, and compare it to the verbs offered by the answer choices. The conclusion is that the written exam (taken by 140 students) was not taken by sociology majors. (We know that 36 students are sociology majors and 4 are not sociology majors but the other major breakdown is indeterminate.) Does the conclusion, then, function to "cast doubt/question/refute/criticize/ or infer"? Clearly, the author is inferring (E) on the basis of the distribution of some final projects to others who are more likely to take a written final (a faulty inference, of course, but an inference nonetheless). If you were assessing the faculty member, you would respond with (A), (C), or (D). (B) is not within the scope of the text, but (E) is the faculty member's approach.

21. (B). Rely on logical form to understand the passage and how other answer choices compare to it: "All As are Bs. Most Cs are ~Bs. All Ds are Es. So, All Ds are Bs." (Note that Sunay's vehicles, Ds, cannot be predicated as As or Cs but need a new logical term, since being made with some Honda parts is not logically identical to a "Honda vehicle".) (A) has the following form: All As are Bs; Some ~As are ~Bs. C is D, so C is B." Remove (A) from consideration. (B) is similar in construction to the argument: All As are Bs. All Cs are ~As. D is E, so D is (.5)B." The form of (C) is different: "All As are B. All Cs are Ds. Some Es are As and Cs, so some Es are Bs and Ds." A Venn Diagram will show this argument is different than that in question. Answer (D) has the following structure: "All As are Bs. All Cs are Ds. E is A and C. So, E is B and D." As you can see, (D) shares a form with (C), but not with the argument here. Solution (E) has the following framework: "As are Bs. Cs are Ds. (.5)Es are As. (.5)Fs are Cs. (.5)Gs are Bs and Ds." This is not close to the argument here, so (B) is the correct answer choice.

LOGICAL REASONING 1
SECTION 3 ANSWER EXPLANATIONS:

22. (A). You might be tempted to choose (E), but the passage does not provide the source of the adult child's research, so should be avoided. (B) and (D) should be removed as possibilities, because neither can be inferred from what is given as evidence. Both (A) and (C) are better choices. (A) is a strong answer, because the adult child correlates eating sugar after lunch with causing diabetes (and, of course, not eating sugar after lunch with preventing diabetes). (C) might be, if the author thinks that the likely result (that his own diabetes risk is low) is certain. But, the adult child does not say that he will not incur diabetes, but rather that the evidence suggests he is at a lower risk because he does not eat sugar after lunch. The best choice among (A) and (C), then, is indeed (A).

23. (D). Your job is to ascertain the main question prompted by the passage. All of the answer selections *could* be prompted by the text, so the correct one will be best supported by it. (A) would not be prompted by the court filing, since it is a lawyer's obligation, and not a file-sharing site, to ensure privileged information is not shared publicly. (B) is a possible question, if the insurer's lawyers knew confidential information was inadvertently shared on a public site, a conceivable question could arise as to whether they ought to have used that information. (C) seems unlikely, as it outside the main scope of the passage. (D) is also a good choice, since if information was shared on a publicly-accessible link, it would be a question as to whether the information is still privileged. (Is something a secret that is posted on social media, as an analogy?) (E) seems likely as an *original* legal complaint—that was the legal question at hand prior to the sharing of confidential information on the publicly accessible site. But, once the information was shared, it became secondary to the new question raised here. Between (B) and (D), (D) is most closely tied to the morally relevant considerations of this case. Whether the insurer's lawyers should be disqualified is an interesting question (in B), but a question that relates the passage to the answer solutions is best found in (D).

24. (C). You cannot accept (A) as an answer choice, because it is explicit in the text that vicious actions are those that diminish human flourishing. (It is not explicit that *only* vicious actions do this, but vicious action is stated as diminishing human flourishing, so the inference is not a large one.) It is possible that it would be hard to determine whether an action is virtuous or vicious, but based on the text, an action could not be *both* virtuous and vicious (B). (C) supports the text and makes the conclusion true. If actions that do not diminish human flourishing contribute positively to it, non-vicious actions would be virtuous. To perform due diligence, (D) is incorrect because we are not given a middle category in the text between virtues and vices (instead, virtues are the middle disposition between two vices). (E) is also not a good response because it is not an assumption. Although implied by "virtue", the truth of the passage's conclusion does not depend on this assumption.

25. (A). This question asks you to reframe the conclusion by way of the correct answer. (A) is an excellent choice to begin with, and you can compare the rest of the possibilities to it. (B) is also a good choice—except for the part that sports teams have bought into the individualization of the fan experience. Rather, fantasy sports has seen this value, according to the passage. (C) is correct, but is too general to be a reframing of the specific conclusion that fans in the future will only focus on individuals' data. (D) may be true, if we had more information, but is not supported by the text that is given here. (E) is correct for the passage, in that fans are consumers, but there is not enough in the evidence to say whether they impact external or internal design components, and what those might be. (A), then, is the best proposition.

LOGICAL REASONING 2
SECTION 4 ANSWER EXPLANATIONS:

1. **(E).** The correct question will be relevant to the main point (the relationship between theory—that art reveals true being—and the concrete, the mascot and exams). This allows you to eliminate (A), since the issue isn't whether students can apply Heidegger, and (D), given that the question isn't about identity relations. (B) is a possibility, except for the qualifier "student life"; alethic conceptions reveal true being, so the correct answer will relate to that. (C) is too far afield of the main point, and tangential to it. The best answer is (E), which raises the question relevant to establishing the mascot as aesthetic for this context, in Heideggerian terms.

2. **(C).** The conclusion of this passage is that my mother believes I should gargle with lemon when I feel a sore throat coming, and the rest of the text—and the correct answer—should help justify that conclusion. (A) is relevant, but too far of an expansion on the main idea since this passage is not about other parts of the body. (B) is a good answer inferentially because it explains why lemons might be the sort of thing to gargle with when sick—the acid kills the good cells so it might kills the bad ones too. But, it is only inferentially a good answer (perhaps citric acid only kills good cells) and you can compare to other choices for the best answer. (C), for example, is excellent. It explains how acid and vitamins (both mentioned by the author) could work to battle a sore throat. (D) is not as good an answer, because it does not explain why I need to gargle with lemon. (E) might suffice in the absence of other better answers, but it only builds a case for why a person would have good reason to gargle *regularly* instead of when s/he feels a sore throat coming on. (C) is the best answer.

3. **(B).** This passage is difficult in part because of its rich language. First, identify the conclusion the anthropologist is making: that deception is internalized in the body and manifests itself through internal separation within the self. The correct solution will add strength to this claim. Second, eliminate answer choices that are irrelevant or not closely tied to the conclusion. (E) should be the first to go, since the only moral issue in the text is that deception is a moral issue. (D), too, is removed since it does not relate to the main point. (A) relates to the issue of self-deception, which is too far from the main idea to provide justification for it. (C) is interesting because it indicates who agents are who are good at deception, but (B) provides further support for the anthropologist because it ties in the phenomenal (bodily) experiences of truth to the external truth of a proposition.

4. **(A).** To find the statement that undermines the argument here, have its main point in mind: that inductive views of testimonial inference for the development of trust for knowers in children needs to be supplanted with a mentalistic approach. Answer choices which *support* that view should be removed, including (B), which is a mentalistic view of epistemic development; (C), which supports the passage's claim of selective trust; and (D), which also supports the selective trust/mentalistic picture developed by the author. (E) is eliminated because it answers *who* has generalized credulity of testifiers, which leaves (A). (A) is an excellent choice because it defends the inductive account in a new way that is not presented in the text.

5. **(C).** Work this argument based on logical form. It requires you to find the conclusion, so set up your premises. This is a disjunctive syllogism: A v B (softball or track); If A, then C; if B then ~C. If C, then D. The conclusion must be that if C, then ~D (since you know that A, then C and D; and B, then ~C). Translating this back into English, If you run track, then you do not play cards. But, if you do not play cards, you do not like to joke around. Which answer choice indicates track members do not joke around? (C). (Note that you cannot include (D) because it introduces a new logical term.)

6. **(A).** This question requires you to undermine the main point, which is implied here—tandem jumps are more popular and enjoyable because they allow new jumpers to take bigger risks that new jumpers cannot take. (A) should be considered; if instructors earn more money off tandem jumps, the jumps might be "popular" only because they are the ones that are marketed heavily. (B) would explain the fun of the jump, so would not be a criticism of the passage. (C) does not undermine the main point of the passage, although it does call into question whether so many people *should be* making tandem jumps. (D) is a good response because it puts pressure on whether tandem jumping per se is more enjoyable—but the conclusion is about new jumpers, and straight-line jumpers are more experienced, so eliminate (D). (E) is an excellent support for the main point because it explains the enduring popularity of the sport. (A), then, is the best choice to undermine the argument.

LOGICAL REASONING 2
SECTION 4 ANSWER EXPLANATIONS:

7. **(D).** Kyana's response presupposes what it attempts to establish—that the submission was not of gallery-opening quality. That is circular reasoning (D), and is erroneous because it is logically void to form an argument from a premise that is the same as the conclusion.

8. **(A).** Isolate the "moral principles" part of the passage—you can see it sets up a contrast with self-evident principles. The correct answer will do the same. (A), of course does this the best. You know that moral principles are contrasted with self-evident principles, so (B) is eliminated as well as (D). (C) might tempt you, but the author does not reject moral principles logically and pragmatically, but rather questions their value compared to what is generally self-evident (a "basic" belief). (E) is irrelevant, so (A) is confirmed as the best choice.

9. **(C).** For situation/analysis questions, apply the analysis in the text to a new situation listed in the answer choices that is similarly logically framed. The *principle* the analysis uses is that individuals can face competing moral obligations that seemingly contradict. (A) does not act on the same principle, but shows a potential irony for American doctors who work with this group. (B) does not show a competing obligation, given that defense attorneys are able to get out of a difficult moral situation by joining the prosecution. (D) observes a seeming contradiction for those who believe in the sanctity of life and are proponents of the death penalty, but the contradiction is observed, instead of felt by the individuals who hold those beliefs. (E) is a potential choice, if friends have promised not to reveal a confidence but feel compelled (obligated) to tell their partner, but (C) is the best choice, because it reveals a competing obligation for the individual to uphold the Constitution but also to obey orders that might not uphold the Constitution.

10. **(E).** The solution will be the one response that does not explain the disparity between Kristie's new method for saving money and the fact that she spent more money. (A) explains that she spent money on items she ordinarily wouldn't (which would lead her to spend more); (B) and (C) both suggest why she would spend more, and (D) provides a description of a behavior—a "splurge"—that could lead her to spend more. (E), however, is not sufficient to explain why she spent more money, since she could still use the coupons to save money on the items she is purchasing.

11. **(A).** Disagreement questions require you to identify the fundamental point of contention between the interlocutors. Even though Joel is clearly a Tony Romo fan and Jill isn't, their disagreement is isolated here to Romo's potential for induction into the Hall of Fame, which is discernible by Jill's exclamation "Keep dreaming!". This allows you to eliminate (B) and (C), which aren't about the Hall of Fame. (D) is about Romo's Pro Bowl appearances, which Jill does not disagree about, so strike it. Jill, also, doesn't contest whether Romo is one of the best Cowboys (E), although she questions what that means for the Cowboys. So, (A) is the best response.

12. **(C).** This disagreement question requires you to infer some principle that serves as the basis for the disagreement in the dialogue, and apply that principle to other scenarios to see which answer choice the two interlocutors would also disagree about. In this dispute, George and Elaine disagree about the content of personal integrity—whether George (who is bald and misrepresents himself by wearing a toupee) should be offended to date someone who is bald. The principle of disagreement is about whether you can consistently require something of someone that you do not require of yourself. (A) is not a good match, since Bernadette's misrepresentation is about something with which she does not have a background. (B) includes a misrepresentation about someone else. (C) is an excellent choice, since Miles misrepresents himself to provide further misrepresentation about the Italian restaurant—a restaurant that is in competition with his own, low-carb restaurant. (D) includes a misrepresentation based on events that come after the sale of a property, so is not an appropriate choice. (E) is not a misrepresentation, but an instance of poor legal counsel. (C) is the best choice.

13. **(B).** This question tells you which part of the passage will be contested by the correct solution—that scientists have a mission to uphold the public trust. Remove from consideration answer choices that are not critical of this as the mission of scientists. (E) is about whether scientists can consistently be mercenaries, so should be removed, and (A) does not contest whether science has a mission that relates to the public trust; rather, it expands what the public trust includes. (C) is an attractive choice, because it offers an alternative mission to preserving

trust. (D) is not a good answer in comparison, because it would have to assume that scientific responsibility is somehow divorced from creditability. (B) is excellent, because it shows an internal inconsistency with the view that science's mission is about the public trust—how can its mission be about trust in scientific principles when the method is committed to truths that can be defeasible? When compared to (C), (B) is better, because (B) shows an internal inconsistency with the passage, and (C) demonstrates an alternate mission for science.

14. **(B).** This passage includes a logical fallacy, "flawed reasoning", and you need to determine which logical fallacy best fits the reasoning before going to the answer choices. The author uses a *genetic fallacy* in the text. There are two main types of genetic fallacies. One is found in (C), which faults Kara for associations she chose—here, within a particular university. The author of the passage is saying because the people we came from exhibited certain behaviors of survival, we can too. That type of genetic fallacy suggests certain behaviors are to be expected because of genetic factors beyond an agent's control. So, you can eliminate (A), which features a geographical factor. Remove (E) for being irrelevant. This leaves you with (B) and (D). (B) is a better choice, because it focuses on behavior ("Lutheran causes") that comes directly out of the background and choices of her father and family. (D) faults men generally for being men, rather than from the background men come from. The logical fallacy employed by the author's reasoning is grounded in faulting behavior based on what stock someone is genetically related to, so although (D) might be a solid option if other, better choices were not available, (B) is a better option.

15. **(C).** As with other questions that require you to supply a logical inference, set up the argument in its logical form first to help you see which statement is consistent with the passage. The passage's argument says: "If A, then B; if B, then (C v D). If ~C, then E. (D, then ~E)."

The passage does not tell us if Sofie does or does not in fact study for constitutional law; rather, it sets up conditional options for consequences coming out of that decision. Since you cannot provide a conclusion to the argument, you can see which of the answer choices are consistent with—fulfill the logic of—the argument form provided above. (A) must be dismissed, since the only thing we can conclude from Sofie having to grovel for additional research is that she will avoid losing a chance to get into law school. (B) is also not a good choice. These disjuncts are true only if Sofie does not study for her con law class, but if she studies for con law, she will not need these disjuncts. (C) is an excellent choice—it avoids the disjunct (C v D), which either leads to Sofie having a tough time getting into law school or having to grovel for extra research—neither of which are good options for her compared to studying for con law. Of course, (D) is false, given the logic of the argument in which if she *doesn't* study she gives up her top spot. And, (E) does not follow, because all we know from the first premise is that if Sofie does not study, she will lose her top spot. (C) is the correct answer.

16. **(D).** The correct answer for this question will be supported by the premises, and may be an inference of it. Strike (B) from consideration, because it is too broad, and is not about using art to prevent violence in the community. (A) might eventually be supported, if given other information, but the passage does not need to make the claim that art is the *best* way to educate the community—it is simply *Jones's* way. It is not clear from the text that youth benefit most from Jones's efforts—their parents come too, so eliminate (C). (D) is an appropriate illustration of the passage's meaning. Art is typically not a venue for a community conversation, but Jones hopes it can have an impact on youth as they mature, and parents now. This is a better solution than (E), which is not factually supported by the passage.

17. **(D).** This passage argues that the United States should not lift the embargo on Cuba because Cuba continues to exhibit behavior that threatens its people. (A) suggests that the United States would look weak if it lifted the Cuba embargo, which extends beyond the evidence of the text. (B) is factually true, and a good possibility. (C), however, goes farther than the text does. (And (E) suggests terrorism, which is not indicated in the passage at all.) This leaves (B) and (D). (D) specifies that there are behaviors Cuba exhibits that make it difficult for the US to *consistently* lift the embargo. This answer is in keeping with the list of conditions specified in the passage that would be required to be fulfilled for the US to lift the embargo with integrity. Although (B) and (D) are quite similar, (B) is general, and (D) focuses on the fact that Cuba "persists in the behaviors that led to the embargo", which is a solid expression of the main idea of this passage, and so is a better choice than (B)

18. (B). Whether you disagree with the fact the egoist posits, the logical flaw resides in the inference the egoist makes that self-interested actions are capricious. There is not logical justification for this inference given in the text, so the correct response will at least include that aspect of the flawed reasoning. You can remove (E), which equivocates between the agent and the action, and (C), which is not about the capriciousness of self-interested acts. (A) contradicts the text, which says all actions are motivated out of self-interest. (B) is an excellent choice because it describes the logical flaw behind claiming that self-interested acts are capricious. (D), in comparison, blames the author for not providing justification (an evidential, rather than a logical flaw). (B) is the most accurate answer choice.

19. (E). Break down Alejandra's decision process. The statement leading to Alejandra's conclusion regards her need to hire someone with a corporate background, so she most likely based her decision on a determinate of which candidate provides a better preparation to bridge the private sector with public and education—so that is the principle she is working from for this hire. (A) regards candidate quality but makes a faulty inference that is not supported in the text, so it can't be the right answer. (B) can't be the underlying principle, because it concerns community connections rather than candidate background related to the corporate sector. (C) may seem applicable at first, but it actually regards what the sector provides, rather than what candidates Alejandra should be looking for as potential hires. So the principle in (C) doesn't specifically relate to Alejandra's decision-making process. (D) seems like a solid choice. It acknowledges the importance of candidates' backgrounds to the position. However, the principle supports Alejandra's research activity rather than her decision to hire a candidate based on her research. So (E) is a better answer than (D). (E) best expresses the principle upon which Alejandra based her decision to hire Brian. It verifies that matching candidates' backgrounds to the mission and vision of an organization is the best way to hire someone.

20. (A). To weaken the argument, you need to first identify what it is saying. The argument's main claim is that cultured meat provides complex, but environmentally sound alternatives to raising cattle, which is environmentally destructive. It does not focus on benefits of cultured meat (so, eliminate (D)). (C) just is a reframing of the main point, and so does not weaken the argument. (B) would weaken an argument that cultured meat could replace meat in the market, but does not weaken the commentator's claim, which is about the environmental impact of cultured vs. regular meat. (E) is a contender—it suggests a threat to the environmental benefit claimed by proponents of cultured meat. (A), however, sets two processes (one involving meat, one involving plants) in comparison, and says that the meat option is less resource-intensive which, if true, is a real blow to the cultured meat claim. (A) is the best answer of the two.

21. (A). The argument presented by the author requires bolstering by one of the answer choices, so choose the one that is directly tied to the text, adds support to it, and does not fall outside its scope. (B) is outside the scope and not supported by it, so should be eliminated. (C) contradicts the text, which really centers around the reasons for which people act. There is not evidence in the text for (D). (E) would be an excellent extension of the passage, but (A) is both suggested by, and provides support for, the text. People act according to their best reason, so will seek good things, but if they do not have knowledge, their best reason will be limited and so will their choices.

22. (B). You need to complete the conclusion of the passage, which is technical in nature but still follows a structure that can lead you to the right response. The author indicates that there are technological advances that are "expected to promote the practice use of LiS batteries", so you know that the author suggests there is a strong future ahead for them. This allows you to eliminate (A), and (D), which is not logically implied by the text. The author does not suggest that the public needs to understand the technology to use it (E), so you can eliminate (E) as a possibility. Even if (C) is true from a technological standpoint, the *future* of LiS batteries is not dependent on that minute technological point. Rather, (B) is better—the future is contingent on further tech advances but is nonetheless promising.

23. **(E).** This is a difficult text because Sartre is not giving us a systematic argument, and is at one point trying to argue for irrationality. Each answer choice will have to be evaluated. (A) should be eliminated because imagination is not a component of Sartre's argument. (B) is inconsistent with Sartre's testimony, since he does not indicate that love is communicable through reason, but the opposite. (C) is a possibility, but it is unclear whether Sartre is making a generalization or is specifying someone particular with the "you" pronoun. (D) initially sounds possible, but recognize that Sartre does not fail to consider it as an option—rather, he rejects it as true, so (D) cannot be correct. (E) is a good selection. Sartre seems to conflate ideas and concepts with reason that is outside the scope of values that ground love, and sets them in contraposition to the inexplicable charms that ground love. But, if the concepts are knowable through ideas and concepts, they could be communicated through them too. (E), then, serves as a better choice than (C), which is unclear.

24. **(D).** Think of assumptions as missing premises that, if included in the passage, strengthen it. On that basis, (A) could be a possible option, though it is general and not tied too closely to the details of the text. (B) is an ad hoc observation, since the author does not claim that the study needs to find the *best* way to reduce anxiety in patients, but rather the study tests the effectiveness of this method to do so. (C) is not supported by the text, given that there was a reduction of anxiety by 80%, rather than an elimination of it by using VR. (D) is an appropriate assumption of the argument, since the conclusion is that there is a cost with VR that should be borne by offices to reduce pediatric anxiety for routine care. (E) is outside the scope of the study, and would require much more justification, given the "pricey" cost of VR to practices. (D), then, is the best option for this question.

25. **(C).** You need to find the solution which is *not* an appropriate criticism of the coach's statement. (A) is a solid criticism, since he does not consider that he has a conflict of interest to protect his program by not paying attention to the allegations. (B) makes his conclusion vulnerable to criticism. (C) is actually not a criticism of his argument, although he — as a coach and a person — might be blameworthy for not having a recollection. (D), of course, is critical of the fact that he states he did not read it and doesn't think he needs to, and (E) is a strong criticism against the coach's statement. (C) is the correct response.

11|19 -0

Made in the
USA
Middletown, DE